The Civil Law Of The Madras Presidency: As Contained In The Existing Regulations And Acts

Charles Robert Baynes

THE

CIVIL LAW

OF THE

MADRAS PRESIDENCY,

AS CONTAINED IN THE EXISTING REGULATIONS
AND ACTS,

WITH

INDICES, NOTES, &c.

COMPILED AND ARRANGED IN ACCORDANCE WITH RECENT
MODIFICATIONS.

BY

C. R. BAYNES, ESQ.

Civil and Session Judge of Madura.

MADRAS:

PRINTED BY PHAROAH AND CO.—ATHENÆUM PRESS, MOUNT ROAD.

1852.

PREFACE.

I HAVE endeavoured in the following pages, to arrange under proper and convenient heads, the laws appertaining to them respectively, so as to facilitate a separate study of each subject. No alterations have been introduced into the original text, save such as have been made by subsequent enactment: and they are marked by Italics.

The arrangement of the work, though the same principles have been kept in view, differs in some measure from that adopted in the "CRIMINAL LAW"—but not so much so as to take from it the character of an "Edition of the Civil Regulations in force." To have given merely their purport, in the way of commentary,—as has lately been done in a somewhat similar work published in Calcutta,—would have had this effect, and though it might have rendered *Study* more pleasant, would have left it incumbent on parties, having to make practical use of the Regulations, to refer to the original; which I imagine is the only safe, or authorized course. Every Student of Madras Law will of course possess himself of Mr. Clarke's excellent Edition of the Regulations in their original order, and shape; and I venture to hope that they will find my compilations of the Criminal and Civil Law useful auxiliaries in their pursuit.

Many circumstances and difficulties, which it is needless to mention here, and which perhaps only those who have attempted a similar task could understand, have prevented these first attempts being all I could wish, but if the plan and nature of the

771931

Work generally should meet approbation and encouragement, I will gladly undertake to spare no labour or trouble in their improvement—so soon as the gradual changes which are going on in our system of Law, may render a second Edition necessary and desirable.

MADURA, *March* 1852.

CONTENTS.

BOOK I.

CIVIL TRIBUNALS.

Constitution—Jurisdiction—Peculiar Procedure in, &c.

BOOK II.

REGULAR SUITS.

Trial and Decision of, &c.

BOOK III.

SPECIAL SUITS.

BOOK IV.

APPEALS.

BOOK V.

MISCELLANEOUS SUBJECTS.

GENERAL INDEX.

ABBREVIATIONS USED.

S. U. Sudder Udalut.

C. J. Civil Judge.

C. C. Civil Court.

S. J. Sub. Judge.

S. C. Sub. Court.

S. A. Sudder Ameen.

P. S. A. Principal Sudder Ameen.

V. M. Village Moonsiff.

D. M. District Moonsiff.

V. P. Village Punchayet.

D. P. District Punchayet.

Ct. Court.

BOOK I.

CIVIL TRIBUNALS.

Constitution—Jurisdiction—Peculiar procedure in, &c.

CHAPTER I.

VILLAGE MOONSIFF, REG. IV. OF 1816, &c.

II. Heads of villages shall, by virtue of their office, be moonsiffs within their respective villages.

III. First. In villages, whether permanently settled, rented, or in the hands of Government, where there may be more than one head man coming under the denomination of potail, reddy, peddacapoo, yajemaun, renter, or any other designation, the person who collects the revenue, and under whose authority the village servants act, shall be considered as the head of the village; no person shall act as head of the village, who does not generally reside in it; where there is but one resident renter of a village, he shall be considered as the head of the village; when the renter is not a resident, the person who rents, or manages, the village under him, shall be considered as the head of the village.

Second. Where from the names of two or more persons being introduced in the same pottah, as heads or renters of the village, or from any other cause, doubts may arise, as to whom the office of head of the village belongs, the collector shall select one person, and give him a pottah to act as the head of the village.

IV. First. Village moonsiffs shall not be required to take any official oath.

Second. Village moonsiffs shall not be liable to be called before the district moonsiff, to answer for their conduct as village moonsiff in any case.

Third. Village moonsiffs shall not be liable to be called before the zillah judge, to answer for their conduct as village moonsiff, except on charges of corruption, or of having exceeded the powers of fine, or imprisonment, granted to them by this Regulation.

V. First.   Village moonsiffs are empowered to hear, try, and determine, of their own authority and without appeal, such suits as may be preferred to them for sums of money or other personal property, the amount or value of which shall not exceed ten rupees.

Second.   Provided that, in the suits specified in the preceding clause of this Section, the cause of action have arisen within twelve years previous to the institution of the suit, or that the plaintiff do shew by clear and positive proof, either that he had demanded the money, or matter in question, and that the defendant had admitted the justice of the demand, or that he had directly preferred his claim within the period abovementioned to a competent authority, and in such case, that he assign satisfactory reasons to the moonsiff why he did not proceed in the suit, or prove that, from minority or other good and sufficient cause, he was precluded from obtaining redress.

VI.   Village moonsiffs are hereby prohibited from receiving, or trying, any suit for damages on account of personal injuries, or for personal damages of any nature.

VII.   Village moonsiffs are hereby prohibited from trying any suit in which they, or any of their immediate servants, are personally interested.

VIII.   Village moonsiffs are prohibited from trying and determining suits against any person, or persons, who may not be found to be actually resident within their jurisdiction at the time when such suits shall be preferred.

IX.   First.   Plaintiffs and defendants shall be allowed to employ a relative, a servant, or a dependant, to plead before the village moonsiff, on furnishing the person to be so employed with a vakalutnamah, describing his relation to his employer and the matter in which he is empowered to act.

Second.   Village moonsiffs shall not in any case permit any person to act as the vakeel of another, until such person shall have exhibited a vakalutnamah containing the information required by the preceding clause.

X.   First.   In hearing, trying, and determining civil suits, the village moonsiffs shall be assisted by the village curnums, or persons holding the office of curnum for the time being, a part of whose duty it shall be to attend as assessors to write the proceedings of the moonsiffs, and when required, to afford them their advice.   But the village moonsiff shall decide by his own opinion, whether it agree or not with that of the curnum.

Second.   The curnum shall keep registers of the suits preferred to the village moonsiffs, entering each complaint in the order in which it may be received.

XI.   The plaint shall state precisely the grounds of complaint, the time when the cause of action arose, the name and residence of the person or persons complained against, the total amount or value of the property claimed, and all material circumstances which may elucidate the transaction. .

XII.   First.   Upon a complaint being preferred in writing to the village moonsiff, he shall, by a verbal summons, require the defendant to appear before him in person or by vakeel, immediately, or within two days from the delivery of the summons.

Second.   The summons shall be served by the village servant, usually employed in carrying messages, who shall be accompanied by the plaintiff, or his vakeel, to point out the defendant and to explain to him the demand against him.

Third.   If a defendant, having been served with a summons in the mode above prescribed, shall neglect or refuse to attend within the time limited, the village servant shall be called upon to make solemn affirmation to the service of the summons; after which, the village moonsiff shall proceed to give judgment on the plaintiff's vouchers and the evidence of his witnesses.

XIII.   If the defendant shall attend in obedience to the summons, the plaint shall be read over to him, and if he shall acknowledge that the plaintiff has a claim upon him, the village moonsiff shall advise the parties to settle the matter amicably.   If the plaintiff be satisfied by the defendant, the village moonsiff shall cause him to execute a razeenamah, stating in what manner the defendant has satisfied him, which razeenamah shall be certified by the village moonsiff as having been executed in his presence, and he shall then deliver it to the defendant.   , .   • ..

XIV.   First.   If the defendant on the plaint being read over to him, shall object to the demand, and the parties shall be unable to adjust the dispute amicably, the village moonsiff shall deliver to the defendant a copy of the plaint and shall require him to deliver his answer immediately, or on a certain day, not more than five days, after the day on which the plaint was read.

Second.   The answer shall contain all that the defendant has to state regarding the case, and no further pleading shall be admitted.

Third.   When the answer has been filed, the village moonsiff, either immediately, or on a fixed day as soon after as the business before him will permit, shall examine the truth of the complaint or claim; If the parties are willing to dispense with the examination of witnesses, the village moonsiff shall give his decision on due consideration of the plaint and answer, and any vouchers which may be produced; or if either party is willing to let the cause be settled by the oath of the other, the village moonsiff shall give his decision according to such oath.

XV. First. Village moonsiffs are authorized to require the attendance of any person in their respective villages, who may be named as a witness by any party in a suit, by a verbal summons, fixing a day for the attendance of such witness.

Second. The summons shall be served by the village servant usually charged with carrying messages, attended by the parties or their respective vakeels to point out the witnesses.

Third. The village moonsiffs are authorized to cause a solemn affirmation to be administered to witnesses, in cases where they may deem it necessary.

Fourth. The village moonsiff shall, previously to the examination of a witness, inform him that he has authority to cause a solemn affirmation to be administered to him when he may think he is not giving his evidence correctly, which authority the village moonsiff shall exercise at his discretion.

Fifth. It shall not, in any case, be necessary to take the depositions of the witnesses in writing.

Sixth. If a witness, duly summoned, shall refuse to attend, or attending shall refuse to answer, such witness shall be liable to be fined for every such offence, at the discretion of the village moonsiff, in a sum not exceeding half a rupee.

XVI. First. If any person, whose testimony is necessary in a suit, shall be temporarily absent from the village, the trial of the suit shall be postponed until his return.

Second. If in any case the evidence of a person residing in a different village shall be required, provided that the village be

Sec. XV.—Witnesses, &c. appearing should be treated with respect due to their rank and station in life. C. O. S. U. 25th August 1823.

Sec. XVI.—Cl. 4. This is actually repealed by Section I. Act VII. 1841. It has been doubted however whether such repeal was intended, and whether Village Moonsiffs and Punchayets can conveniently employ the provisions of that Act. I have retained it in the text because it is at all events a good direction for proceeding under VII. of 1841— Call the prescribed "letter" a "Commission," and the "other Moonsiff," a "Court out of the jurisdiction," and the mode of proceeding will be very similar.

not farther distant than two coss, the moonsiff requiring his attendance shall address a summons to such person, containing the names of the parties in the suit and fixing a day for his attendance, and shall forward it to the moonsiff of the village in which such person shall reside, who shall cause the summons to be served by his own village servants, and shall return the summons, with a certificate that it has been duly served, to the moonsiff who issued it.

Third. Any person refusing or neglecting to attend on such summons, shall be liable to be fined in a sum not exceeding one half of a rupee, which shall be levied by the village moonsiff in whose jurisdiction such person may reside, on a communication of the order imposing the fine being made to such moonsiff, by the moonsiff by whom such order may be passed.

Fourth. If the person whose evidence is required shall reside at a greater distance from the village than two coss, the village moonsiff is authorized to request, by a letter bearing his signature, the moonsiff of the village in which the person whose testimony is required may reside, to examine such witness on written interrogatories prepared by one or both parties, or by their vakeels. The village moonsiff shall examine the witness or witnesses named in the letter, according to the requisition of it, and shall return the deposition of each witness duly subscribed by him, to the moonsiff of the village where the cause may be depending, by the time required in the letter, and every deposition so taken, shall be received as good evidence in the cause.

Fifth. Village moonsiffs shall not summon any woman to appear before them, whose rank or caste may render it improper to require her attendance; but when the evidence of such person is necessary, the village moonsiff shall require her to furnish her deposition in writing, duly attested. The deponent shall state in her deposition, that she is prepared to make solemn affirmation to the truth of her deposition if required.

XVII. The village moonsiffs, in suits depending before them, are hereby strictly prohibited from requiring securities of any kind from defendants.

XVIII. First. If a plaintiff shall not attend on the day fixed for the trial, and the defendant shall be in attendance before the moonsiff, the suit shall be dismissed, and shall not be revived, unless the plaintiff shall shew good and sufficient cause for his absence.

Second. If the defendant shall refuse to answer the plaint, or shall not attend on the day fixed for the trial, the village moonsiff shall proceed to try the cause ex parte, as prescribed in clause third, Section XII of this Regulation.

XIX.   Parties, or their vakeels, and witnesses, guilty of disrespect to a village moonsiff, shall be liable to be fined by him, in a sum not exceeding half a rupee.

XX.   When the parties have been heard, the exhibits received and considered, and the witnesses on both sides examined, the village moonsiff shall give judgment according to justice and right.

XXI.   The decree shall specify the names of the parties and the names of the witnesses examined, and the titles of the exhibits read.   It shall also contain an abstract statement of the principal grounds and reasons on which the decision may be passed.   It shall specify the sum of money or the value of the personal property adjudged.   The decree shall bear the signature or mark and seal of the village moonsiff and curnum, and shall be dated on the day on which it is passed.

XXII.   Village moonsiffs are hereby prohibited from allowing in their decrees a greater rate of interest in any case, than the courts of adawlut are permitted to allow by Regulation XXXIV of 1802.

XXIII.   Village moonsiffs shall have authority to allow in their decrees such reasonable periods for their execution as may appear just in particular cases, not however in any case exceeding three months.

XXIV.   First.   Village moonsiffs shall within three days after passing a decree, cause two copies of it to be prepared by the village curnum, and shall deliver one copy to each party ; the date of such delivery being certified by the signature of the moonsiff and of the curnum.

Second.   If the plaintiff or defendant shall not attend in person or by vakeel, to receive a copy of the decree, or shall refuse to receive it when tendered, the village moonsiff shall cause such omission or refusal to be noted on the back of the copy of the decree so omitted to be taken, or refused, and shall deposit it with the curnum for the purpose of delivering it to the party, if he shall afterwards claim it.

XXV.   No village moonsiff shall punish any party, vakeel, or

---

Sec. XXII.—That is 12 per cent, or less if stipulated : accumulation not to exceed Principal : no compound interest on intermediate adjustment, unless fresh bonds be executed for aggregate.

witness, in any suit before him, excepting under the provisions specified in clause sixth, Section XV, clause third, Section XVI and Section XIX of this Regulation; provided however, that if the party, vakeel, or witness, shall refuse, or be unable, to pay the fine, the village moonsiff may, at his discretion, commute such fine for twelve hours confinement in the village choultry.

XXVI.   Suits in which the village moonsiff is a party, shall be tried by the moonsiff of another village, or by any competent authority.

XXVII.   The village moonsiff is authorized to hear, try, and determine as arbitrator, suits for sums of money or other personal property, the amount or value of which shall not exceed one hundred rupees; provided both the parties interested in such suits, shall voluntarily agree in writing to refer them to his decision as arbitrator, and shall voluntarily subscribe bonds, in the presence of two or more credible witnesses who shall attest the same, binding themselves to abide by the decision of the moonsiff to whom they may refer the suit, whether he be the moonsiff of their own village, or of any other village.

XXVIII.   In trying the suits described in the foregoing Section, the village moonsiff shall be guided by the rules prescribed for his conduct in trying suits preferred to him under the provisions of Section V of this Regulation, so far as those rules may be applicable.

XXIX.   The decisions of village moonsiffs, either as moonsiff, or arbitrator, shall not be carried into execution by them in less than thirty days after the date on which copies of the decrees may have been furnished or tendered to the parties or to their vakeels; should either party present a petition to the zillah judge within that period, charging the village moonsiff with corruption or gross partiality, the zillah judge shall order execution of the decree to be stayed, and if the charge of corruption or partiality be proved to the full satisfaction of the zillah judge, by the oaths of two credible witnesses at the least, he shall annul the decision.

XXX.   First.   If the defendant shall not discharge the sum decreed against him within thirty days after the date on which copies of the decrees may have been furnished or tendered to the parties, or to their vakeels, or within the period limited in the decree, the village moonsiff shall, on the written application of the

---

Sec. XXX.—Execution of Decree cannot be delayed beyond three months, nor can personal arrest take place under V. Moonsiff's decree, C. O. 24th December 1829 C.

party in whose favour the decree may be given, attach the property of the party cast to the value of the sum decreed, and shall give immediate notice of such attachment and of the day fixed for the sale, to the district moonsiff, who shall send a peon to sell the attached property by public auction, in presence of the village moonsiff, at the expiration of the time fixed in the notice of sale.

Second. The peon deputed by the district moonsiff shall not have any charge of the property under attachment. His duty shall be to sell the property and receive the purchase money, from which he shall pay to the party in whose favour judgment may be given, the amount decreed, taking his receipt attested by the village moonsiff and curnum.

Third. The peon deputed by the district moonsiff shall be entitled to receive batta at the rate of two annas of a rupee per diem during his deputation, and the amount of such batta, together with every expense that may attend the sale, shall be defrayed by the party cast, or deducted from the proceeds of the sale, on the certificate of the moonsiff and curnum that such amount of batta and such expenses are correctly charged.

Fourth. If any surplus shall remain of the proceeds of the property sold, after satisfying the decree and defraying the expenses incurred, including the batta of the peon, it shall be paid to the party cast, and his receipt for the same attested by the village moonsiff and curnum shall be taken by the peon, and produced to the district moonsiff, along with the receipt of the party in whose favour the decree may have been passed, and the certificate of the village moonsiff of the amount of batta and expenses attending the sale, as the vouchers of his having correctly discharged his duty.

Fifth. Provided however, that in every instance of property being attached in execution of a decree, the village moonsiff shall cause public notice of the intended sale of such property to be given by beat of drum through the village, five days previous to the sale ; Provided further, that it shall be at the option of the party cast to satisfy the judgment at any time previous to the period fixed for the sale, and that on his satisfying the judgment by paying the amount to the village moonsiff, or to the peon if he should have arrived, together with the batta of the peon and all other attending expenses, according to a certificate to be furnished by the village moonsiff, the village moonsiff shall withdraw the attachment and restore the property to the possession of the owner.

Sixth. Resistance to a sale ordered by a village moonsiff shall be considered to be a breach of the peace, and shall be punished as such.

XXXI. The village curnum shall keep a register of all sales by auction in his village in satisfaction of decrees, noting therein the day of sale, the particulars of property sold, its amount, the name of the purchaser, and his residence.

XXXII. Suits tried by village moonsiffs shall be exempt from fees, stamp duties, batta and charges of every description, excepting those specified in Section XXX of this Regulation.

XXXIII. All fines levied by the village moonsiffs shall be sent at the end of each month to the district moonsiff, with a list stating the names and situations of the parties from whom such fines have been levied and the reasons for which the fines were imposed.

XXXIV. First. The village moonsiffs are prohibited from admitting as an exhibit, or from receiving in evidence, any obligation, bond, deed, or document, whether it be the original or a copy, of a description which is or may be required to be written on stampt paper or stampt cadjan, unless it shall have been duly executed on stampt paper or stampt cadjan of the description and value prescribed by the Regulations.

Second. A list of the prescribed rates of duties on stampt paper, and stampt cadjan, specifying the dates on which it was enacted that the collection of those duties respectively should commence, shall be furnished by the collectors to every village curnum in their respective zillahs, for the guidance of the village moonsiffs.

XXXV. First. Village moonsiffs shall be liable to prosecution in the *subordinate* zillah court for corruption in the discharge of their trust, by either party in the suit, and for any oppressive and unwarranted act of authority by the party injured, and upon proof of the charge to the satisfaction of the *subordinate judge, or Principal suddder ameen* he shall in the first mentioned case, adjudge the offender to pay the prosecutor three times the amount, or value of the money or property corruptly received, with all costs of suit; and in the second, award such damages and costs to the party injured as may appear to him equitable; But no village moonsiff shall be liable to be prosecuted for want of form, or for error in his proceedings or judgment; nor shall any process whatever be issued against a village moonsiff, who may be charged with corruption, or any oppressive and unwarranted act of authority, unless the judge shall be previously satisfied by sufficient evidence,

---

Sec. XXXIV.—Unstamped exhibits are admissible on payment of penalties under Sec. III Reg. II of 1825. Such penalties the V. Moonsiff remits to District Moonsiff with sums mentioned in previous Section.

that there is probable cause to believe that the charge is well founded, and unless the charge shall be preferred within three months from the date of the act complained of.

Second.   The subordinate judge, or principal sudr ameen shall, on charges of corruption, fine the party by whom or for whom the corruption may have been practised in the suit, provided he shall have assented to such corruption, in a sum equal to the value of the thing or sum of money which the village moonsiff may be proved to have so corruptly received.

Third.   If the corruption charged against any village moonsiff shall not be proved to the satisfaction of the judge, he shall award full costs and such damages to the village moonsiff as may appear to him equitable, and he shall levy a fine from the party making such groundless charge, not exceeding the value of the thing or sum of money charged to have been corruptly received.

XXXIX.   A copy of this Regulation shall be lodged with and preserved by each village curnum, for the information of the village moonsiffs.

Sec. XXXIX.—V. Moonsiffs are also required by Reg. XII, 1816—which see under "Collector"—to assemble punchayets for the trial of such cases as may be referred to them by the Collectors of Zillahs under that regulation: a copy of which is directed, by its 13th Section to be deposited with each village Curnum for the information of the Village Moonsiffs.

CHAPTER II.

II. First. Village moonsiffs are authorized to summon punchayets within their respective villages for the decision of suits for sums of money or other personal property, without limitation as to amount or value, in the two following cases.

Second. In suits where both plaintiff and defendant may jointly agree that the matter at issue shall be determined by a village punchayet without appeal, and may prefer a request in writing to the village moonsiff to summon a punchayet, whether he be the moonsiff of the village in which the parties reside, or of any other village ; or where one party having preferred a request in writing to the village moonsiff to summon a punchayet, the other party being an inhabitant of the same village on being summoned by the village moonsiff shall attend and voluntarily give his assent in writing to the village moonsiff agreeing to that mode of trial.

Third. *Proviso of limitation as in Cl. 2 Sec. V, Reg. IV.* 1816, *which see at p.* 2.

III. First. The village punchayet shall always consist of an odd number, never less than five nor more than eleven, and the majority shall decide.

Second. The village punchayet shall be composed of the most respectable inhabitants of the village, who shall be called upon to serve in rotation whenever their number is sufficient for this purpose ; and any inhabitant of the village refusing to serve on a village punchayet, shall be liable to be fined at the discretion of the village moonsiff in a sum not exceeding five rupees, which shall be levied if necessary, by the village moonsiff, under the provisions for the execution of decrees in Section XXX, Regulation IV, 1816.

Third. Any respectable inhabitant of a neighbouring village may be placed on a village punchayet, if he be willing to undertake the duty.

Fourth. When the parties in suits are of different castes, or professions, the village moonsiff shall in all practicable cases, name an equal number of persons of the caste or profession to which each party may belong, to compose a part of the village punchayet, and shall complete the punchayet by the selection of a person or persons belonging to a caste or profession different from that of both the parties.

Fifth.   If either party shall object to any one or more of the members nominated to compose the village punchayet, and the village moonsiff shall consider such objection to be well grounded, he shall withdraw the members objected to and appoint others to serve in their stead.

Sixth.   When the parties may desire it, they shall each name two members, and the village moonsiff shall name another person who may be unobjected to by the parties, to form the punchayet ; But on all other occasions, the whole shall be nominated by the village moonsiff; the practice of the parties naming two members each, shall never be allowed when it can be avoided

IV.   First.   The village punchayet being formed as prescribed in the foregoing Section, shall proceed to investigate the matter referred to them, in conformity to the following rules.

Second.   The village punchayet shall commence their proceedings, by requiring from the parties an agreement in writing to abide by the decision of such punchayet, whose names shall be inserted in the agreement, which shall be witnessed by the village moonsiff and curnum, and dated on the same day.

Third.   Vakeels for plaintiffs and defendants shall be admitted to plead before village punchayets, provided that every person so appearing as a vakeel, be a relative, servant, or dependant of the person by whom he may be employed ; and provided he be furnished with a vakalutnamah, describing his relation to his employer and the matter in which he is empowered to act: such vakalutnamah shall be exhibited by the vakeel, before he be permitted to do any act in the suit.

Fourth.   The parties being present in person or by vakeel, the village punchayet shall receive the written plaint of the complainant, which shall state precisely the grounds of complaint, the time when the cause of action arose, the name and residence of the person or persons complained against, the total amount or value of the property claimed, and all material circumstances which may elucidate the transaction.

Fifth.   The plaint shall be read to the defendant or his vakeel, and the defendant or his vakeel shall be required by the punchayet to give in his answer, either immediately, if he shall be prepared to deliver it, or on a day to be fixed, which shall not be later than one week from the reading of the plaint.

Sixth.   The defendant shall state in his answer all that he has to say regarding the case, and no further pleadings shall be admitted.

Seventh.   The village punchayet, after the answer has been given in, shall receive from the plaintiff and defendant their exhibits and lists of their witnesses, and shall fix an early day for the trial, with reference to the convenience of the parties and witnesses respectively.

Eighth.   The village punchayet shall immediately communicate the lists of witnesses and the day fixed for the trial, to the village moonsiff, who shall require the witnesses to be in attendance on that day.

Ninth.   The parties and witnesses being in attendance on the prescribed day, the village punchayet shall proceed to take the depositions of the witnesses, in the manner usual in the caste to which they may respectively belong, on separate papers or cadjan leaves in all cases in which the matter at issue may exceed the value or amount of twenty rupees ; the deposition shall be read over to the witness, who shall then subscribe the deposition with his, or her, name or mark.

Tenth.   In cases in which the matter at issue may be of smaller amount or value than twenty rupees, it shall be discretionary with the village punchayet to take the depositions of the witnesses in writing or not.

Eleventh.   The village punchayets are authorized to cause a solemn affirmation to be administered to witnesses in cases where they may deem it necessary.

Twelfth.   The village punchayets shall not put a question to any witness suggesting a particular answer, and shall previous to the examination of a witness inform him, that they have authority to cause a solemn affirmation to be administered to him when they may think he is not giving his evidence correctly, which authority the village punchayets shall exercise at their discretion.

Thirteenth.   If the parties or either of them, shall fail to appear in person or by vakeel, at the time fixed for the trial, the village punchayet shall suspend the trial and report it to the village moonsiff, who shall cause to be affixed in some conspicuous place of the village a notice, specifying that the suit will be tried on a given day, which shall not be less than five days from the date of the notice.

Fourteenth.   If the plaintiff shall not appear at the time fixed in the notice, the village punchayet shall dismiss his suit; which shall not be revived, unless the plaintiff shall shew good and sufficient cause for his absence.

Fifteenth.   If the defendant shall refuse to answer the plaint or shall not attend at the time fixed in the notice, the village punchayet shall proceed to give judgment on the plaintiff's vouchers and the evidence of his witnesses.

V.   In cases where a witness shall neglect to attend, or attending, shall refuse to give his testimony, or shall be otherwise guilty of disrespect to the village punchayet, as also where the evidence of a person is required who resides beyond the jurisdiction of the village moonsiff, as also in the cases of persons whose testimony may be required, but whose rank or caste may render it improper to require their attendance, as also when the parties or their vakeels may be guilty of disrespect to the village punchayet, the punchayet shall report the circumstances to the village moonsiff, who is hereby authorized and directed, on receiving such reports to take the same measures for procuring the attendance, or testimony of the witnesses, or for punishing the contempts, as he would have taken under Sections XV, XVI and XIX, Regulation IV, 1816, if the circumstances represented had occurred before himself.

VI.   When both parties have been heard and the whole of the evidence has been gone through, the village punchayet shall order the parties and witnesses to withdraw, and shall write their decree according to justice and right.

VII.   The decree of the village punchayet shall contain the names of the parties, and the names of the witnesses examined, and the titles of the exhibits read ; it shall also contain an abstract statement of the principal grounds and reasons on which the decision may be passed ; it shall specify the sum of money or the value of the personal property adjudged ; the decree shall bear the signature or mark of the members of the punchayet, and shall be dated on the day on which it is passed.

In cases where the minority of the members of the punchayet, may decline to sign the award of the punchayet, the signature or mark of the majority shall be sufficient to give legal validity to the award ; provided always, that in such case, it shall be incumbent on such majority to admit the minority to record and attest by their mark or signature their reasons for declining to sign or mark the award passed by the majority.—Act VIII, 1840.   •

VIII.   Two copies of the decree shall be prepared by the village punchayet, and shall be put under a sealed cover and delivered to the village moonsiff, who shall require the parties, together with the punchayet, to assemble immediately, or at a convenient day, not being later than three days from his receipt of the decree; the village moonsiff shall open the seal in presence of the parties and shall cause the curnum to endorse on each copy of the decree, the date of the delivery thereof, which shall be attested by the signature of the village moonsiff, the curnum, and any member of the punchayet; the village moonsiff shall then cause the punchayet to deliver to each party, in his presence, a copy of the decree; but no communication shall be made to the village moonsiff, or to either party, of the nature of the decree, previously to its delivery.

IX.   If either the plaintiff or defendant shall fail to appear in person or by vakeel, to receive a copy of the decree, or having attended shall refuse to receive a copy, the village moonsiff shall cause the curnum to endorse on the copy intended for such party, such omission or refusal, and the date; the village moonsiff shall attest the same with his signature, which shall be witnessed by the curnum and any member of the punchayet; the copy so endorsed shall be deposited with the village curnum, to be delivered to the party afterwards claiming it.

X.   The proceedings of the village punchayet shall be written, either by one of the members or by the village curnum, and no stamp paper need be used in plaint, answer, or any process.

XI.   First.   No appeal shall be permitted from decisions passed by village punchayets under this Regulation; but if the village punchayet shall be guilty of gross partiality, it shall be at the option of either party to bring the matter by petition, upon stamp paper of the prescribed rate according to the amount of the suit, before the *Subordinate judge of the zillah, or Principal sudder ameen (S. U. 4th March* 1844, *para* 6.)

Second.   The petition shall not be received unless it be presented, with the decree complained of, within thirty days after the date on which copies of the decree may have been furnished or tendered to the parties or to their vakeels.

Third.   If the petition be received, the judge or Principal sudder ameen shall order the execution of the decree to be stayed pending the enquiry.

Fourth.   If the partiality charged against the punchayet shall be established to the satisfaction of the judge, or Principal sudder ameen by the solemn affirmations of two credible witnesses at the least, he shall, in every case, whatever the amount or value of the suit may be, submit his proceedings with his opinion on the case of the *Civil judge of the zillah (S. U. March 4th* 1844, *para* 6 *)* who, provided the charge be proved by *such* proceedings to his satisfaction shall annul the decision, and the parties shall be at liberty to have recourse to another punchayet, or to any other competent jurisdiction.

Fifth.   Provided however, that where the decision of a second punchayet shall agree with the decision of a former punchayet in the same suit, it shall be final.

Sixth.   Petitions to the Subordinate judge or Principal sudder ameen of the zillah under this Section, shall be presented by the parties in person or by an authorized vakeel of the court, to whom a fee of four annas of a rupee shall be allowed and no more, and the parties shall not be subjected to any other charge whatever.

XII.   Village moonsiffs shall not receive or refer to a punchayet for trial, any suit for damages on account of personal injuries, or for personal damages of whatever nature.

XIII.   Suits tried by village punchayets shall be exempt from fees, stamp duties, batta and all charges of every description, except the cost of the paper or cadjan leaves on which the proceedings and decree may be written, the amount of which shall be inserted in the decree and be levied from the party cast.

XIV.   Village punchayets shall not allow in their decrees, a larger rate of interest than village moonsiffs are authorized to allow under Section XXII, Regulation IV, 1816.

XV.   In respect to the admission of obligations, deeds, and documents, the village punchayets shall be guided by the rules prescribed in Section XXXIV, Regulation IV, 1816.

XVI.   First.   Decrees of village punchayets in cases referred to them under this Regulation, shall be carried into execution by the village moonsiff under the rules prescribed in Section XXX, Regulation IV, 1816, provided the amount or value of the sum

---

Sec. XIV.—See note on Sec XXII, Reg. IV of 1816.

Sec. XV.—See note on Sec XXXIV, Reg. IV of 1816 explaining their admissibility on payment of penalty under Reg. II of 1825. Cl. 4. Sec. III of which Reg. directs that such penalties when levied by District or Village Punchayets shall be remitted to District Moonsiff.

Sec. XVI.—Cl. 3. The S. U. on 13th September 1837, on the question whether the limitations of this Section were extended by Sec. V, Reg. III 1833, i. e. whether District Moonsiffs could execute Decrees of Village and District Punchayets to the extent of the increased jurisdiction therein given to *themselves* ruled in the negative, stating that they could not sanction such proceeding—the law not having authorised it C. R. 855 p. 435.

of money or other personal property adjudged shall not exceed one hundred rupees.

Second.   In suits for sums of money or other personal property, the amount or value of which shall exceed one hundred, but not exceed two hundred rupees, the decrees of village punchayets shall be carried into execution by the district moonsiffs, on the written application of the party praying execution of the judgment.

Third.   In all other cases, the decisions of village punchayets shall be carried into execution by the subordinate judge or Principal sudder ameen in the mode prescribed by the Regulations.

XVII.   Petitions to the subordinate judge or Principal sudder ameen praying execution of the decisions of village punchayets, shall be written on stampt paper of the prescribed rate, according to the amount decreed, and shall be presented by the parties in person or by an authorized vakeel of the court, to whom a fee of four annas of a rupee shall be allowed and no more, and such application shall not be subjected to any other charge whatever.

XVIII.   First.   Any member, or members of village punchayets, shall be liable to prosecution in the subordinate zillah court for corruption in the discharge of their trust, by either party in a suit, which may have been referred to such punchayet; and upon proof of the charge to the satisfaction of the subordinate judge, or Principal sudder ameen, he shall adjudge the offender, or offenders, to pay the prosecutor three times the amount or value of the money or property corruptly received, with all costs of suit; but members of village punchayets shall not be liable to be prosecuted for want of form, or for error in their proceedings or judgment; nor shall any process whatever be issued against a member or members of a village punchayet who may be charged with corruption, unless the judge shall be previously satisfied by sufficient evidence, that there is probable cause to believe that the charge is well founded, and unless the charge shall be preferred within three months from the date of the act of corruption complained of.

Second.   The subordinate judge or Principal sudder ameen shall further fine the party by whom, or for whom, the corruption may have been practised in the suit, provided he shall have assented to such corruption, in a sum equal to the value of the thing or sum of money which any member or members of such village punchayet may be proved to have so corruptly received.

Third.   If the corruption charged against any member or members of such village punchayet shall not be proved to the satisfaction of the subordinate judge or Principal sudder ameen, he shall award full costs and such damages to the member or members complained against, as may appear to him to be equitable, and he shall levy a fine from the party making such groundless charge, not exceeding the value of the thing or sum of money charged to have been corruptly received.

XX. A copy of this Regulation shall be lodged with and preserved by each village curnum, for the information of the village moonsiffs and members of village punchayets.

Sec. XX.—Village punchayets are authorized by Sec. II, Reg. XII. of 1816 to hear and determine such suits as may be referred to them by the collectors of zillahs under that regulation, which see under "collector"—as also such as may be referred to them by that functionary under Sec. XV, Reg: V. of 1822.

CHAPTER III.

V. First. The number of district moonsiffs for each zillah, shall be fixed by government.

VI. The zillah civil judges shall recommend to the sudder udalut the persons whom they may deem fit for the office of district moonsiff, but no person shall be authorized to officiate as a district moonsiff without the previous sanction of the sudder udalut.

District moonsiffs shall receive such monthly allowances only, as may hereafter be fixed for their personal salary and the expence of their establishments.—*Sec. III, Reg. II,* 1834.

District moonsiffs shall not be entitled to receive any emolument whatever beyond their fixed monthly allowances.—*Act. V,* 1835.

No person whatever shall by reason of place of birth, or by reason of descent, be incapable of being a moonsiff.—*Sec. III, Act. XXIV,* 1836.

Every British born subject of the Queen, or descendant of such British born subject, who shall be appointed a moonsiff, shall in respect of all acts done by him as such, be liable to the same proceedings as well criminal as civil, and shall be amenable to the jurisdiction of the same tribunals, as if he were not of British birth or descent.—*Sec. IV.—Ibid.*

VII. First. Whenever a zillah civil judge shall see cause for

---

* There are three classes of these functionaries who receive different rates of Salary as laid down in C. O. S. U. 3rd May 1833, viz. 1st Class 140—2nd, 115—3rd, 100—besides an allowance for Office expences.
The rules relative to their eligibility, examination, qualifications, &c. will be found at the end of this Chapter—for their greater convenience most of the Circular Orders affecting them have been given or referred to in the notes—though they will appear again in the body of the Circular Orders, and for the same reason the following are here noted.
As to their possession of landed property, and trading.................No. 116.
Absence for five days ....No. 98.
Their travelling allowances...No. 99.

Sec. VII.—District Moonsiff cannot be suspended or fined by Principal Sudder Ameen—Section XI. Regulation VII. 1827—but Principal Sudder Ameen is to report misconduct or neglect to Civil Judge—Section XII.—*Ibid.*
The Civil Judge may visit the Moonsiff's Court for purposes of enquiry—See C. O. S. U. 23rd March 1828 and 15th May 1847.
A Moonsiff is liable to dismissal for borrowing money from suitors in his Court—C. O. S. U. 26th December 1836, No. 41, A—nor may he lend money to any person within his jurisdiction—C. O. 4th December 1845, No. 101.

removal of a district moonsiff, the judge shall report the circumstances of the case with his opinion to the sudder udalut, who will pass such order on the report as may appear to be proper.

Second.   Whenever a district moonsiff may be guilty of exaction or of any other gross act of misconduct, the civil judge is authorized to suspend him from his office ; but he shall report the circumstances of the case, without delay to the sudder udalut.

Third.   In other cases of misconduct and neglect of duty, which may not be of a nature to require either the suspension or dismissal of a district moonsiff from his office, the civil judge is authorized to impose on the moonsiff a fine, not exceeding twenty rupees in amount, and the order of the judge in such cases shall be final.

Fourth.   No district moonsiff shall be removed from his office unless the sudder udalut shall be satisfied that there is sufficient cause for his removal.

Whenever a collector or a subordinate or assistant collector shall receive information of any acts of extortion, undue exaction, or other gross misconduct alleged to have been committed by a district moonsiff, he shall make such enquiries as the nature of the case may suggest, for the purpose of ascertaining whether any grounds exist for a more full and formal investigation of the charge ; and if he shall find such grounds to exist he shall forward a statement of the case, together with the list of witnesses to the facts and circumstances thereof, to the zillah civil judge in order that he may proceed in regard to the accused in the mode prescribed by Section VII, Regulation VI, of 1816.—*Sec. VI, Reg. II, of* 1821.

VIII.   First.   District moonsiffs shall be liable to an action in the zillah *civil courts, Sec. XXIII, Act VII,* 1843, for corruption in the discharge of their trust, or for extortion, or for any oppressive or unwarranted act of authority, and upon proof of the charge to the satisfaction of the judge, he shall cause the offender to pay such damages and costs to the party injured, as may appear to be equitable.

Sec. VIII.—Moonsiffs are liable to be prosecuted for enforcing illegal decision of village moonsiff—C. O. 4th March 1817, and see also C. O. 1st December 1817, as to precautions which should be taken by district moonsiff to avoid such error.

Act III, of 1850.—All persons were previously so liable in cases connected with the arrears or exaction of rent under Sec. III, Act III, of 1839, which is superseded by this enactment.

Sec. XI, Cl. 1.—Inhabitant—either fixed resident, or resident at the time cause of action arises—See C. O. 30th March 1840.

Cls. 2 to 5.—These amounts, less originally, were increased by Sec. V, Reg. III, of 1833.

Cl. 6.—Suits on mortgages of more than twelve years standing, cognizable by moonsiffs —C. O. 14th October 1846, No. 107.

Second. District moonsiffs shall also be liable to a criminal prosecution for extortion or other acts of oppression committed by them in the discharge of their duty ; and on conviction before the session court shall be subject to fine and imprisonment proportionate to the nature and circumstances of the case ; but no moonsiff shall be liable to be prosecuted for want of form or for error in his proceedings or judgments : nor shall any process be issued against a moonsiff, who may be charged with extortion or any oppressive or unwarranted act of authority, unless the civil judge shall be previously satisfied by sufficient evidence, that there is reason to believe the charge to be well founded.

IX. Every person who may, in future, be appointed to the office of district moonsiff shall be furnished by the judge, with a sunnud drawn up according to the form No. 1 of the appendix to this Regulation ; and previously to entering upon the duties of his office, he shall *make and subscribe a solemn declaration in writing.* Act XXI, 1837, according to the form prescribed in No. 2 of the appendix.

X. Whenever a sunnud may be granted to a district moonsiff, under the preceding Section, a copy of it, under the official seal and signature of the judge, shall also be delivered to him, in order that it may remain permanently affixed in some conspicuous place in his court.

No person whatever by reason of place of birth, or by reason of descent, shall be in any civil proceeding whatever, exempt from the jurisdiction of the courts of the district moonsiffs in the territories subject to the Presidency of Fort St. George—*Sec. I, Act III, 1850.*

XI.—First. The persons who may be invested with the powers of district moonsiff under this Regulation, are empowered to receive, try and determine all suits preferred to them against any inhabitant of their respective jurisdictions, under the following limitations.

Second. For land exempt from the payment of rent in money or in kind, either to Government, or to any person representing Government and receiving its dues, the annual produce of which land shall not exceed *one hundred* rupees.

Third. For land subject to the payment of rent in money or in kind, either to Government, or to any person representing Government and receiving its dues, the annual produce of which land shall not exceed *one thousand* rupees.

Sec. IX, X.—Forms 1 and 2 omitted as being always at hand in the office when required.

Fourth. For houses, gardens, or any real property not of the descriptions before mentioned, the value of which shall not exceed *one thousand* rupees.

Fifth. For sums of money or other personal property, the amount of value of which shall not exceed *one thousand* rupees.

Sixth. Provided that in the cases specified in the preceding clauses of this Section, the cause of action have arisen within twelve years previous to the institution of the suit, or that the plaintiff do shew by clear and positive proof, either that he had demanded the money or matter in question, and that the defendant had admitted the justice of the demand, or that he had directly preferred his claim within the period abovementioned to a competent authority, and in such case, that he assign satisfactory reasons to the moonsiff why he did not proceed in the suit, or prove that, from minority or other good and sufficient cause, he was precluded from obtaining redress.

XII. First. District moonsiffs shall not receive or try any suit for damages on account of personal injuries, or for personal damages of any nature, without an order of reference to them from the zillah civil court.

Second. District moonsiffs are prohibited from hearing, trying or determining any suits in which they themselves, or their relatives or dependants, or other persons employed in their courts may be parties.

Third. District moonsiffs are farther prohibited from allowing any party in a suit to plead before them in forma pauperis *unless the suit be referred to them by the zillah civil courts.—(Cl. 2 Sec. III, IV, 1825.)*

A District moonsiff whenever a suit in which he may be directly or indirectly a party, or may be otherwise personally interested, shall be instituted before him, or depending in his court when he takes charge thereof, he shall forward the whole record thereof to the civil judge of the zillah—*(Cl. 2 Sec. III Reg. I, 1829.)* on his doing so the judge may refer it for trial either to a Sudder ameen, or another district moonsiff.—*Sec. XIX, Act VII, 1843.*

XIII. District moonsiffs are themselves to investigate the suits cognizable by them, in a public cutcherry or court room, and are not to allow their officers, servants or dependants, or any other

---

Sec. XIII.—For allowing such interference are liable to dismissal—C. O. 24th September 1840, No. 68.

The moonsiff's courts are not closed during the adjournment of the civil courts—C. O. 7th December 1829.

person to interfere therein. In receiving, trying and determining suits, they shall be guided by the rules prescribed in this Regulation ; and in points not expressly provided for in this Regulation, they shall observe as nearly as may be practicable, the rules prescribed in the Regulations for the guidance of the zillah courts in the trial and decision of civil suits.

The rules applicable to pleaders in the courts of the zillah judges shall henceforth be applicable as far as they are capable of application to pleaders in the moonsiff's courts—*Sec. XI, Act I, 1846.*

Whenever a pleader has conducted himself in such a manner in the court of a moonsiff, as would have rendered him liable to a fine if he had so conducted himself in the court of a zillah judge, it shall be competent to such moonsiff to impose such fine : provided that an appeal from all orders imposing such fine shall lie to the zillah judge whose decision thereon shall be final— *Sec. XII.—Ibid.*

XV. District moonsiffs are hereby prohibited from allowing in their decrees a greater rate of interest in any case than the courts of udalut are permitted to allow by Regulation XXXIV of 1802.

XVII. The plaint shall state precisely the grounds of complaint, the time when the cause of action arose, the name and residence of the person or persons complained against, the total amount or value of the property claimed, and all material circumstances which may elucidate the transaction.

XVIII. It shall be the duty of the district moonsiff to prevent the insertion in the plaint of any irrelevant matter. The plaint shall be signed and numbered, and dated in the order in which it may be received by the moonsiff; and the number of the suit, the names of the parties, the date on which the petition is received, the amount claimed, and the subject matter of the suit, the date and abstract of the decree, and the date on which copies of the decree were furnished or tendered to the parties, shall be entered in a book to be kept by the moonsiff, according to the form No. 3 of the appendix. The zillah civil judge shall inspect these register books at least once a year, with a view to ascertain that depending suits are brought to a hearing according to their order on the file, and shall require the district moonsiff to transmit them to the court for this purpose.

Sec. XV.—On the subject of interest see C. O. 28th September 1846, 26th April and 25th May 1847.

XIX. First. When the complaint shall have been thus received and entered in the book, the district moonsiff shall cause to be served on the defendant a written notice under his seal and signature, containing only the number of the suit, the names of the parties and a short statement of the demand, and requiring the defendant to attend in person or by vakeel, and to deliver an answer to the plaint on or before a certain day, which must be specified in the notice.

Second. The district moonsiff shall deliver the notice to the plaintiff or to his vakeel, and the plaintiff may either himself serve the notice on the defendant, or through any other person whom he may choose to employ for that purpose ; provided however, that the name of the person intended to be employed in this duty be, in all cases, endorsed on the notice by the district moonsiff, previously to its being delivered to the plaintiff or his vakeel for execution.

Third. The person through whom this notice may be served, shall require from the defendant a written acknowledgment, to be endorsed on the back of the notice, signifying that it has been duly served upon him ; and he shall further cause some of the defendant's neighbours, or other inhabitant, to witness the due execution of the service, and he shall at all times state in his report the name or names of such witness or witnesses.

XX. If a defendant, who may have been served with a notice, shall not appear in person or by vakeel within the time specified, and the moonsiff shall be satisfied by sufficient evidence, that the notice was duly served, or if the defendant having appeared shall refuse to answer the plaint, the district moonsiff shall proceed to try the cause exparte, and after examining the plaintiff's evidence in support of his claim, the district moonsiff shall give judgment in the same manner as if the defendant had appeared and answered to the plaint.

XXI. First. In cases in which a defendant to whom a notice may have been issued, may abscond or conceal himself, or cannot after diligent search be found, or shall refuse to give the required written acknowledgment, the person entrusted with the execution of the process shall certify the same on the back of the notice, and shall require some person or persons, being neighbours of the defendant, to attest the same.

Sec. XIX, Cl. 2.—Batta peons are now employed, and their remuneration is regulated by, C. O. 13th November 1843, No. 84.

Second. When a return to this effect is made, the district moonsiff shall cause a proclamation, written in the current language and character of the country, to be affixed in a conspicuous part of his own court house, and a copy of the same on the outer door of the defendant's usual place of residence, or some other conspicuous place near it; the proclamation shall contain a copy of the original notice, and shall state that, if the defendant do not appear in person or by vakeel within the period of fifteen days from the date of the proclamation, the suit will be brought to a hearing and determined without the appearance or answer of the defendant.

Third. If the defendant shall still not appear in person or by vakeel, the district moonsiff, on the expiration of the period limited in the proclamation, shall proceed to try and determine the suit exparte, as is prescribed in Section XIX of this Regulation.

XXII. In suits depending before them, the district moonsiffs are hereby strictly prohibited from requiring security of any kind from the defendants; if the moonsiff shall be satisfied by sufficient proof, that the defendant intends to abscond and to withdraw himself from the jurisdiction of the court, or that he means to dispose of the property in his possession for the purpose of avoiding the execution of an eventual judgment against him, the district moonsiff is hereby empowered to attach the defendant's property to the amount of the claim, and to hold it in attachment till the decree is satisfied.

XXIII. When the defendant shall attend, either in person or by vakeel, within the period limited in the notice or proclamation, or at any subsequent period before the plaintiff's evidence or proofs shall have been received in the case, he shall be allowed to take a copy of the plaintiff's petition and to file his answer to the complaint.

XXIV. It shall be the duty of the district moonsiffs to restrain and discourage, as much as possible, the insertion in the answer of any matter evidently irrelevant to the suit; but the defendant shall state in his answer all that he has to say regarding the case, and no further pleadings shall be admitted.

XXV. The district moonsiffs shall try all suits depending be-

---

Sec. XXIII.—An answer may be received at any time previous to the commencement of the examination of witnesses.—S. U. 16th March 1837.

Sec. XXV.—See Sec. II, Reg. VIII, of 1817, for exceptions to this general rule in the cases of " Soldier's Suits" which are to be brought to hearing, and decided, as speedily as may be consistent with the due administration of justice, without regard to their order on the file. See also on this subject, C. O. 20th September 1824. B. para 6, and C. O. 4th April 1825.

fore them, in the order in which they have been filed or numbered; provided however, that the zillah civil judge be at all times
authorized, either upon a report from the moonsiff, or upon other
grounds of information, to direct the moonsiff to bring any particular suit or suits to a hearing and determination, without attending to the regular order of the file.

XXVI. First. In cases in which the answer shall have been
filed, and the parties or either of them shall fail to appear in person or by vakeel, at the time when the suit is first called over for
trial, the district moonsiff shall suspend the trial, and shall affix in
some conspicuous place in his court house a notice, that the suit
will be again called over for trial after the expiration of a fixed
period, not being less than ten days. If the plaintiff shall not
appear before the district moonsiff in person, or by a vakeel duly
authorized, within the limited time, the district moonsiff shall dismiss his claim; if the defendant shall not so appear by the prescribed time, the district moonsiff shall proceed to try the cause
exparte.

XXVII. The district moonsiffs are to try the suits depending
before them, by hearing the pleadings of the parties, by examining their documents, and by taking the deposition of their witnesses,
in the presence of the parties or of their vakeels duly constituted; or if either party agrees in writing, to let the cause be settled
by the oath of the other without appeal, the district moonsiff shall
give his decision according to such oath.

XXVIII. First. If the plaintiff or defendant shall be desirous
of summoning any witnesses to appear before the moonsiff, and
such witnesses shall not attend at the requisition of the parties,
the district moonsiff is authorized to summon as witnesses any persons subject to his jurisdiction, excepting women whose rank or
caste may be such, as to render it improper to require their appearance in public; when the evidence of such women is necessary,
it is to be taken in the mode prescribed in clause fifth, Section
XVI, Regulation IV, 1816, (which see at page 4.)

Second. The summons shall specify the number of the suit on
the file, the name of the party at whose request it may be issued,

---

Section XXVI.—See C. O. 7th March 1842 and No. 32.
　Section XXVIII.—Cl. 3, Batta Peons to be employed, See C. O. 13th November 1843,
No. 84.
　All persons appearing, to be treated with respect due to their rank and station in society
and for attendance of Revenue Servants Moonsiff should apply through Zillah Judge.—C.
O. 25th August 1828.
　And of Village Officers through Tahsildar.—S. U. 16th October 1823 and 14th Nov. 1844.

and the names and residence of the witnesses ; and shall require them to appear at the court house of the district moonsiff on a specific day, and there to depose concerning the matter in dispute between the parties.

Third. The district moonsiff shall deliver the summons to the party applying for it or to his authorized vakeel, and such party or vakeel may either serve the summons himself or through any other person whom he may choose to employ for that purpose ; provided however, that the name of the person intended to be employed in this duty be, in all cases, notified to the moonsiff and endorsed on the summons, previously to its being delivered to the party or his vakeel for execution.

XXIX. First. If any person upon whom a summons may have been duly served, shall not attend on the day appointed, the moonsiff is authorized to attach any property belonging to such person, which may be found within his own jurisdiction. If after a reasonable time subsequent to such attachment, the person summoned shall still omit or refuse to attend, and it shall satisfactorily appear by the oath, *or solemn affirmation* of the party requiring his evidence, that the testimony of such person is material to the cause, the moonsiff shall report the circumstances of the case to the zillah civil judge, who will exercise his discretion in issuing such further process, in order to compel the appearance of the witness before the moonsiff, as might be issued under the Regulations if the suit were depending before the judge.

Second. If notwithstanding this further process, the attendance of the witness cannot be obtained, the civil judge shall, at his discretion, impose on such witness a fine, not exceeding in any case the value or amount of the property in dispute ; such fine shall be realized by the moonsiff under the provisions made for the execution of decrees by this Regulation.

Third. In cases in which a witness duly summoned may attend before the moonsiff, but shall refuse to give his evidence, or to subscribe his deposition, the moonsiff shall impose such fine upon him as may appear proper; the district moonsiff is, however, strictly prohibited from realizing such fine, if it exceed ten rupees, by his own authority, without first reporting the circumstances of the case to the zillah civil judge, who will either remit, or modify, or confirm the fine imposed by the moonsiff, who will proceed to realize it, if confirmed or modified, as is prescribed in the preceding clause.

XXX. First. If any district moonsiff shall require the evi-

Section XXX.—For Form of Commission for examination of absent witnesses under Act VII. of 1841,—See C. O. S. U. 13th Nov. 1843, No. 85.

dence of a person, not subject to his jurisdiction but who may reside in the same zillah, and such person shall not attend at the requisition of the parties, the moonsiff shall make a written application to the moonsiff within whose jurisdiction such person may reside, who will issue the necessary process for procuring his attendance.

Second.   If the residence of a witness shall be in another zillah, the moonsiff *shall proceed as directed in Act VII. of* 1841.

Third.   The moonsiffs are enjoined to take the depositions of witnesses attending before them, with all due expedition, so that they may not be exposed to any vexatious delay or unnecessary detention from their respective homes and employments.

XXXI.   The district moonsiffs shall administer to witnesses *the solemn affirmation prescribed by Act V. of* 1840.

XXXII.   The district moonsiffs are at all times authorized to cause the examination of a witness to be taken *without such solemn affirmation*, whenever the parties in the suit, or their respective vakeels, may agree to such witness being so examined.

XXXIII.   First.   It shall be necessary to take the depositions of the witnesses in writing only where the claim shall exceed twenty rupees.

Second.   In the examination of witnesses, the moonsiffs· are enjoined to prevent the parties and their vakeels from putting to them questions suggesting a particular answer, or on points evidently irrelevant to the matter in dispute.

XXXIV.   The deposition of every witness shall commence by specifying the name, the father's name (or if the deponent be a married woman, the name of her husband), the religion, caste, profession, age and place of residence of the deponent, and shall be subscribed by the witness, with his or her name or mark.

XXXV.   First.   No fees shall be levied on exhibits filed before the district moonsiffs, and exhibits shall be received in suits depending before them without any· written application for that purpose.   The moonsiffs are prohibited from admitting or filing as an exhibit, or from receiving in evidence, any obligation, instrument, bond, deed, or document, whether it be the original or a copy, of a description which is or may be required to be written

---

Section XXXV.—Moonsiff cannot make and give authenticated ' copies'.—See C. O. 30th May 1829.

on stampt paper or stampt cadjan, unless it shall have been duly executed on stampt paper or stampt cadjan, of the description and value prescribed by the Regulations, or *until the party presenting the same shall have paid a penalty equal to ten times the amount of the stamp duty which would have been payable on such bond or other instrument in the first instance if it had been prepared on paper or other material bearing the prescribed stamp.*—Cl. 1, Sec. III, Reg. II, 1825.

Second. Copies of all Regulations in force regarding stampt paper and stampt cadjans, shall be furnished by the zillah civil judges to every district moonsiff in their respective zillahs, for their guidance.

Third. When an exhibit is filed in a suit before the district moonsiff, it shall be dated, and signed or sealed by him, and shall be marked with some letter or number, to identify it, and such letter or number shall be distinctly referred to in those parts of the depositions of the witnesses, or of the proceedings, or of the decree, which may allude to such exhibit.

In cases where the penalty prescribed in Cl. 1 of this section may be levied by a village or district punchayet, the amount shall be remitted to the district moonsiff, with a memorandum of the date and place of payment, and the name of the party by whom it may be made.—*Cl. 4, Sec. III, Reg. II, 1825.*

District moonsiffs shall remit the sums received by them under the provisions of the above clause and also the amount of penalties levied by themselves under Cl. 1 to the zillah judge accompanied by a memorandum of the date and place of payment, the name of the party by whom it shall be made.—*Cl. 5.—Ibid.*

XXXVI. When the parties have been heard and the exhibits, received and considered, and the witnesses on both sides examined, the district moonsiffs shall give judgment according to justice and right.

XXXVII. The decree shall specify the names of the parties, and the names of the witnesses examined, and the titles of the exhibits read; it shall also contain an abstract statement of the material facts alleged in the pleadings of both parties, and the

---

Section XXXVI.—Must pass 20 decrees monthly, on the merits.—C. O. 20th Sept. 1824.
Two decrees, withdrawn or adjusted on Razeenamah after points given count as one.
Must sign in full and always in same character.—C. O. 13th Nov. 1843, No. 83.
The points and ground of judgment must be in writing of Moonsiff.—C. O. 18th Oct. 1844, No. 90.
Moonsiff may review his judgment, on obtaining permission, as other Courts.—C. O. 7th March 1842, No. 78.

reasons on which the decision may be passed. It shall state specifically the amount or value of the matter adjudged, and the amount of the costs or damages payable by the parties respectively. If any claim shall appear to the district moonsiff to be litigious and vexatious, he shall adjudge suitable costs and damages against the plaintiff, and insert the same in the mode above directed in the decree.

XXXVIII. First. When the decision shall have been thus passed, the district moonsiff shall cause two copies of it to be prepared, and after attesting them with his seal and signature, shall within one week after the date of the decree, tender the said copies in open court, both to the plaintiff and defendant, or to their vakeels respectively; he shall endorse on the said copies the date on which they may be tendered to the parties in open court, and if either or both of the parties shall fail to attend, or shall refuse to receive the copies so tendered, he shall certify the same on the back of the copies.

Second. Any district moonsiff who may be guilty of wilfully mistating or falsifying, or of causing to be mistated or falsified, the date and purport of the endorsement above directed to be written on the copies of the decrees, or of keeping back such copies of decrees from either of the parties, with the view of opposing a bar to their right of appeal, shall, on proof thereof to the satisfaction of the *sudder udalut, Sec.* XVII, *Act* VII, 1843, be liable to dismission from office, and to such discretionary fine to Government as may be deemed proper by that court.

XXXIX. The copies of decrees above directed to be tendered to the parties by the district moonsiffs, shall not be written on stampt paper, nor is the answer, or any part of the proceedings of any suit before the district moonsiff, required to be written on stampt paper *except the plaint under Act* XVII, 1848.

So much of Reg. XIII, 1816, and Sec. VII Reg. VII, of 1818 as relates to the levying of stamp duties instead of fees on the institution of civil actions, shall be applicable to the courts of the district moonsiffs in the presidency of Madras.—*Sec.* II, *Act* XVII, 1848.

XL. If a party, vakeel, or witness, in any depending suit,

Section XL.—It has been ruled that failure of witnesses or Parties to attend, or default of Vakeels or Parties in filing pleadings, &c. cannot be punished under this Section as a contempt " the disrespect referred to is the commission of some Act in open Court—not one of omission." It may be remarked however that more ample powers of punishment in such cases are now given to Moonsiffs in common with other tribunals by Act XXX, of 1841, while under Sec. XII, Act I, of 1846, they can fine pleaders for misconduct—to the same extent as the Zillah Judge.

shall be guilty of disrespect to the district moonsiff in open court, the moonsiff is empowered to impose a fine not exceeding one rupee, on the party, vakeel, or witness so offending ; and if the offender shall refuse or be unable to pay the fine, to commute such fine, at his discretion, for twenty-four hours confinement in the village choultry.

XLI. Third. The required monthly and half-yearly reports shall be enclosed in a cover addressed to the zillah civil judge, and sealed with the seal of the district moonsiff; the packet shall be forwarded to the judge either by the public dawk (the officers of which are hereby required to receive and convey such packets free of postage) or by a servant of the moonsiff, or the moonsiff may deliver it to the nearest police officer, who shall give a receipt for it and convey it to the judge.

XLII. The district moonsiff shall have authority to carry his decrees into execution.

XLIII. In suits for real property, not of the description mentioned in clauses 2 and 3 Sec. XI of this Regulation, and for sums of money or other personal property, the amount or value of which shall not exceed twenty rupees, the decision of a district moonsiff shall be final.

XLIV. If the suit shall have been regularly appealed, the execution of the district moonsiff's decree shall be suspended or otherwise, according to the orders he may receive from the zillah civil judge.

XLV. Whenever a party who may have obtained a decree in the court of a district moonsiff, shall be desirous of having it enforced, he shall present a petition to the moonsiff, either in person or through his vakeel; it shall state the number of the suit, the names of the parties, the date of the decision, and the total amount or value of the matter which may have been adjudged to the petitioner, either on account of the original claim or of costs of suit; the petition shall further state, whether an appeal has or has not been admitted from the moonsiff's decision.

Section XLII.—Execution of Decrees under following Sections and same general rules as other Courts. See title 'Execution of Decree'—a fictitious claim to property attached in execution is punishable by Moonsiff under Regulation I, of 1832.—See Interpretation, Fort Saint George Gazette, May 1846, Page 505.

Section XLV.—Under Sections XXX, and XVI, of Regulation IV, and V, of 1816 respectively—the District Moonsiff is required to co-operate in the execution of Decrees by Village Moonsiffs and Village Punchayets ; by enforcing an illegal Decree he renders himself liable to the penalties prescribed in Section VII, Reg. VI, of 1816 and is further amenable to prosecution by the parties.—C. O. 4th March and 1st December 1817.

XLVI.   In cases not appealable, and in cases appealable but which have not been appealed, if the defendant shall not discharge the sum decreed against him within thirty days after the date on which copies of the decrees may have been furnished or tendered to the parties or their vakeels, the district moonsiff shall, on the petition of the party in whose favor the decree has been passed, cause his decree to be executed; if it be for real property, by causing possession of the property to be delivered to the person to whom it may be decreed; if it be for personal property or a sum of money, by causing the specific thing to be delivered, or the value of it or the sum of money decreed to be levied by the public sale by auction of a sufficient portion, or, if requisite for the satisfaction of the decree, the whole of the lands, houses, and all effects either real or personal belonging to the party against whom the judgment may have been given, or by the attachment of his person, or, when it may be necessary, both by the sale of his property and effects and the attachment of his person.

XLVII.   On the attachment of the person of any party in satisfaction of a decree, the district moonsiff shall send him within twenty-four hours from the time of such attachment, under proper charge, to the zillah civil judge, to be confined in the zillah jail; he shall as soon after as possible, send to the judge a statement of the amount levied by the sale of his effects and of the balance still due by him.

XLVIII.   First.   In cases where a district moonsiff shall attach property in satisfaction of a decree, he shall notify the day fixed for the sale by auction of such property, by a written notice to be affixed fifteen days previously to the day of sale at his court house, and at some conspicuous place in the village where the property under attachment may be situated.

Second.   The district moonsiffs shall keep registers of all sales by auction in satisfaction of decrees ; the registers shall specify the day of sale, the particulars of property sold, its amount, and the name and residence of the purchaser.

XLIX.   Resistance to the sale or transfer of property attached in execution of a decree passed by a district moonsiff, shall be considered a breach of the peace, and shall be liable to be punished as such.

LI.   The district moonsiffs shall be authorized to realize the amount of fines which may be imposed by them, by the attachment and sale, if necessary, of the property of the offending party.

LII.　The district moonsiff, on or before the fifth of each month, shall transmit to the zillah civil judge all fines which he may have levied, or which he may have received from the village moonsiffs during the preceding month, accompanied by separate lists, stating the names and situations of the parties from whom such fines have been levied, and the reasons for which the fines were imposed.

LIII.　First.　In appealable suits, any person dissatisfied with the decision of a district moonsiff, shall be at liberty to appeal from it to the zillah civil judge, provided the petition of appeal be on the prescribed stamped paper and presented within thirty days after the date on which copies of the decrees may have been furnished or tendered to the parties or to their vakeels, in conformity with Section XXXVIII of this Regulation ; a discretionary power, however, is vested in the civil judge, of admitting appeals from decisions of the district moonsiffs, although the petitions may not be presented within the prescribed period, if the appellant shall shew satisfactory cause for not having before presented the petition.

Second.　All petitions of appeal from decisions of the district moonsiffs, are to be presented to the civil judge of the zillah in which the moonsiffs may officiate, and the moonsiffs are prohibited from receiving any petitions of appeal from their own decisions.

Third.　All petitions of appeal from decisions of district moonsiffs, are to be presented by the appellant in person, or by one of the authorized vakeels of the zillah civil court, and if the appeal shall be admitted and the appellant and the respondent shall not plead their cause in person, their respective vakeels are to be allowed the same fees as in other suits tried before the judge.

Fourth.　Decisions of the district moonsiffs are not to be set aside for want of form or for irregularity in their proceedings, but on the merits only.

Fifth.　When an appeal may be received from the decision of a district moonsiff, the zillah civil judge is empowered to suspend the execution of the decree, provided the party appealing against

---

Section LIII.—Cl. 1. Prescribed Stamp—The original plaint must now also be on the same stamp as is required on plaints in other Courts.—Sec. II, Act XVII, of 1848—i. e.

		Rs.
Under 16 Rupees	....	1
Above 16 not exceeding 32	....	2
„ 32 do. 64	....	4
„ 64 do. 150	....	8
„ 150 do. 300	....	16
„ 300 do. 800	....	32
„ 800	....	50

it shall give good and sufficient security within a reasonable period, to be fixed by the judge, to perform the decree of the court.

It shall be competent to *the zillah civil judges* to receive a summary appeal from the orders or decrees of the district moonsiffs, in cases in which such district moonsiffs may have refused to admit any suit regularly cognizable by them, or may have dismissed, on the ground of delay, informality or other default, without an investigation of the merits of the case, any such suit which they may have admitted, or any suit regularly referred to them by superior authority.—*Sec.* I. *Act* XVII, 1838.

The provisions contained in the 5th, and following clauses of Sec. V, Reg. XV, of 1816, of the Madras code regarding summary appeals, shall apply to the summary appeals preferred under the authority of this act.—*Sec.* II.—*Ibid.*

LIV. The zillah civil judges may for any reason that may appear to them sufficient, call up any causes that may be depending before the district moonsiffs.

When a zillah judge sees reasons for calling up under Section LIV, Regulation VI, of 1816, any cause that may be depending before a district moonsiff, he may refer it for trial to the subordinate judge, or Principal sudder ameen, of the zillah, or to a sudder ameen, or another district moonsiff.—*Sec.* XVIII, *Act* VII, 1843.

LV. Upon the death, removal or resignation of any district moonsiff, the zillah civil judge shall, if necessary, immediately nominate another person in his room, for the approbation of the sudder udalut, and shall cause all papers in the causes depending before the late moonsiff, to be delivered over to his successor, or otherwise to be disposed of, as circumstances may require.

LVI. First. *Subordinate judges and Principal sudder ameens,* — *Clause* I, *Sec.* XVII, *Act* VII, 1843, may refer any plaint received by them for trial and decision to any district moonsiff within their respective zillahs, whether for real or personal property, of the value or amount specified in Section XI of this Regulation.

Second. In the trial of such suits, the district moonsiffs shall

---

Act XVII 1838, Sec. I. This Act authorized reception of such appeals by Assistant Judges and Principal Sudder Ameens. The power was restricted to Civil Judges by Cl. 1, Sec. VIII, Act VII, of 1843—save under special circumstances provided for in the 2nd Clause of that Section.

Section II.—For these rules—see "Summary appeals."

be guided by the rules prescribed in this Regulation for their conduct in original suits cognizable by them as district moonsiffs.

LVII. First. The district moonsiff is authorized to hear and determine as arbitrator, all suits which may be voluntarily referred to him by both parties, whether for real or personal property, of the value or amount specified in Section XI of this Regulation.

Third. The district moonsiff, in cases so referred to him, shall take from the parties a bond, agreeing to abide by his decision ; such bond shall be executed in his presence and be attested by two credible witnesses.

Fourth. The district moonsiff in hearing and determining the suits above specified, shall be guided by the same rules as have been prescribed for his conduct in trying suits preferred to him under Section XI of this Regulation, so far as those rules may be found applicable.

LVIII. No appeal shall be permitted from decisions passed by district moonsiffs under the preceding section, but if a district moonsiff shall be guilty of corruption or gross partiality, it shall be at the option of either party to bring the matter by petition on the prescribed stamped paper, under the notice of the civil judge of the zillah, who, provided the petition be.presented within thirty days after the date on which copies of the decrees may have been furnished or tendered to the parties or to their respective vakeels, and provided the partiality or corruption charged against the moonsiff be established to his satisfaction by the oaths *or solemn affirmations* of two credible witnesses, shall annul the decree, and the parties shall be at liberty to have recourse to another moonsiff, or to any competent jurisdiction.

LX. First. The zillah *civil and subordinate* judges and *Principal sudder ameen—Cl. 2, Sec.* XVII, *Act* VII, 1843, are authorized to employ the district moonsiffs in delivering over formal possession of lands, houses, or other real property, in conformity with decrees regular or summary.

LXI. The district moonsiffs may be employed at the discretion of the zillah civil and subordinate judges, and Principal sudder ameens—*Cl.* 2, *Sec.* XVII, *Act* VII, 1843, in the attachment and sale of personal or real property for the purpose of realizing the amount of fines imposed by them, or by the sudder ameens, or of decrees regular or summary, passed by them or by the sudder ameens, or by village and district punchayets.

LXII. First. In all cases of inheritance of or succession to landed property, the mahomedan laws with respect to Mahomedans and the hindoo laws with regard to Hindoos, are to regulate the decisions of the district moonsiffs, and the district moonsiffs in all such cases are to obtain an exposition of the law from the law officers of the zillah civil court, to the judge of which they are to transmit a written abstract of the case for the purpose; such exposition however, is not to preclude a further reference to the law officers of the zillah courts upon such points of law as may arise upon the cause, in the event of its being tried in appeal.

Second. In all suits relative to the inheritance of or succession to landed property, the district moonsiffs are to affix in some conspicuous part of their court house a written notification of the claim preferred, with a requisition to all persons who may have any claim to the property sued for, to prefer the same within a limited period, and their decisions are to include all claimants to the property in question, who according to the law of the parties, whether Musselmans or Hindoos, have a just and legal title to share therein.

NOTE.—District moonsiffs are required by Sec. II, Reg. XII, 1816, which see under " Collector" to assemble punchayets for the trial of such suits as may be referred for that purpose by collectors of zillahs under the same general rules as laid down in Reg. VII, 1816, with the qualifications specified in Sec. VI, Reg. XII, of 1816.

APPENDIX.

NOTIFICATION.

FORT ST. GEORGE, *28th July* 1843.

The following Rules for the examination of Candidates for District Moonsiffships, are published for general information.

First. That at the four Stations named in the margin, there be appointed a Divisional Committee of Examination, consisting ordinarily, beside such person or persons as the Government may from time to time think fit, of.

Masulipatam. Chittoor. Calicut. Trichinopoly.

    1. The Zillah Judge.
    2. The Collector and Magistrate.
    3. The Sub Collector and Joint Magistrate.

Section LXII.—This reference was directed by Sec. IV, Reg. II, of 1828, to be made through the Register, to the Zillah Judge, in virtue of which, and under Act VII of 1843, it is now made direct through the Civil Judge of the Zillah.

Secondly.   That all Candidates for District Moonsiffships be required to send in their applications *prepared according to the Form A.* for examination to a *Civil* Judge of the Division within which they desire to be examined · at least two months before the examination to be held ; but that no such applications shall be presented to the Judge who is a Member of the Examining Committee. *The date of receipt of each application, shall be entered in it by the Judge to whom it is presented.*

Thirdly.   That the *Civil* Judge receiving the Candidate's application, after making such enquiries as he may deem proper, in order to ascertain that nothing exists against the character of the applicant to render him unfit to enjoy the privilege of examination, shall certify on the face of the application, that the Candidate may be examined.

Fourthly.   That the Divisional Committee shall meet *once in each year at its commencement,* for the purpose of examining Candidates certified to them for examination during the preceding *twelve* months, by *Civil* Judges within their Divisions.

Fifthly.   That the examination shall be conducted by the Committee in such manner as shall from time to time be prescribed to them by the Sudder Udalut.

Sixthly.   That at the conclusion of the examination, the Committee shall grant to such Candidates as they may deem proper, diplomas of fitness for employment as Moonsiffs, after such form as the Sudder Court may prescribe—and at the same time forward duly certified lists of such Candidates to the Sudder Udalut.

Seventhly.   That the possession of such diplomas shall entitle Candidates an application to be recommended by *Civil* Judges for vacant Moonsiffships, and to be appointed to such vacant Moonsiffships by the Sudder Udalut, before any Candidates not possessing such diplomas.

Eighthly.   That in case any *Civil* Judge shall, by reason of having received no application from a Candidate with a Diploma, recommend for nomination to the Sudder Udalut, to fill an existing vacancy, a Candidate without a diploma, the Sudder Udalut shall appoint to the vacancy any one from among the lists of passed Candidates, who may be willing to accept the vacant appointment, but the Sudder Court shall not delay the appointment for the purpose of making enquiry as to the willingness of any individual on the lists—on the contrary, if no application should be before them from any such person when the Judges nomination may be taken into consideration by the Court, they shall, unless they be aware of other objections, appoint provisionally the Candidate recommended by the *Civil* Judge, subject to his obtaining a diploma in due course under the following rule.

In cases of individuals, whose names are at the head of the list of Candidates who have received diplomas, refusing to proceed to any District to which they may be appointed, it shall be discretionary with the Sudder Udalut to admit or reject the grounds of unwillingness, and it will then be for the consideration of the Court, whether they shall again be nominated to a District Moonsiffship on the occurrence of a vacancy.

Ninthly.   That in case any person not possessing a diploma, be hereafter appointed a District Moonsiff under the last rule, he be required to present himself for examination to the Divisional Committee at the first examination held after the date of his appointment; and that if he then fail in obtaining a diploma of fitness, his appointment be deemed vacant.

Secondly—" *prepared according to Form A,*" &c.—These Rules were modified and amplified by G. O. G. 9th March 1844, published in the Fort Saint George Gazette of that year at p. 214.   The alterations thereby made in the former Rules are inserted in italics— Cl. 12 to 16 were then newly added.

Eighthly—For Form of Nomination Roll, see C. O. S. U. 4th Nov. 1844—No. 92.

Tenthly. That after effect has been given to these rules, if a Zillah Judge have good and sufficient grounds to believe from any proceeding or other information officially before him, that any Moonsiff under his control not previously examined, is not sufficiently qualified to discharge in a proper manner, the duties of his situation, he may with the concurrence of the Sudder Udalut require such Moonsiff to present himself for examination before the Divisional Committee at their next meeting: any Moonsiff who being so required may refuse to submit to examination, or being examined may fail to obtain a diploma, shall forfeit his appointment, and shall not be re-appointed to a Moonsiffship until he obtain a diploma of fitness.

Eleventhly. That in future no Sudder Ameen be appointed except he be one of three Moonsiffs recommended to Government for promotion to an appointment of that class by the Sudder Court; and unless he have served as a District-Moonsiff for at least twelve months previous to the date of recommendation.

Twelfthly. In addition to the usual remarks in the last column, all Certificates granted to Candidates shall bear on them, the result of the Judges enquiries into the character and respectability of the Candidates, together with any particulars relative to their family and connections which may seem worthy of notice.

Thirteenthly. Certificates are to be granted only to persons who may be inhabitants of, or employed within the jurisdiction of the Officer granting them, unless the applicant be precluded by the operation of Clause Second from presenting his application to the Judge of his own District, by reason of that functionary being a Member of the Examining Committee.

Fourteenthly. Persons under the age of 28 are not eligible to examination.

Fifteenthly. In renewing the Certificates of those who have already undergone examination the Judges are to mention in such Certificates, the number of times the Candidates have been examined, with reference to which the Court of Sudder Udalut will decide whether they will admit the Candidate to re-examination.

Sixteenthly. No Certificates are to be granted as at present later than two months before the yearly examinations: one month previous to which the several Zillah Judges will report to the Court of Sudder Udalut the number of Candidates whose names are registered for examination.

FORM A.

The application of ———— ———— an Inhabitant of ———— ———— ————

Whereas I am desirous of becoming a Candidate for the situation of Moonsiff, I request that, after making the necessary inquiries, you will grant me a Certificate prescribed by the 3rd Clause of the Rules for the examination of Candidates, dated the 28th July 1843 and published in the Gazette of the following 8th August.

Date of presentation of application to the Zillah Judge of ———— ———— ————

1	2	3	4	5	6	7	8	9
Name of the applicant and that of his father.	Age.	Religion and Caste.	Family residence, viz., Town or Village and Zillah.	Statement of previous employment.	Statement of landed property belonging to the Nominee and where situated.	Statement whether the applicant is a debtor or creditor of other parties, and if so, the place of residence of his debtor or creditor.	Statement whether the applicant is or is not engaged or concerned directly or indirectly in trading or in trade speculations; and if so of what kind.	Certificate of the Judge.

NOTIFICATION.

The following Rules for granting diplomas to Candidates who may on examination be found fit for the office of District Moonsiff, are published for general information.

1. Diplomas shall be granted by the Divisional Committee only to those Candidates, who may answer correctly the whole of the questions forwarded by the Sudder Udalut. Should a Divisional Committee be of opinion, that a Candidate who may not have answered all the questions, is otherwise eligible to the office of District Moonsiff on any special grounds, they shall forward the written replies of such Candidate, with a statement of the grounds on which they consider him entitled to a diploma, for the consideration of the Sudder Udalut, who will decide whether the Candidate shall receive a diploma or otherwise.

2. When the Members of any Committee are equally divided in opinion as to the propriety of granting or withholding a diploma, such equality of votes shall be held to render the Candidate ineligible.

3. No Member of any Committee shall vote regarding any Candidate to whom he may be in any way related.

4. Candidates who may be rejected at one sitting of a Committee, shall be entitled at the expiration of any period which the Committee may fix upon, with reference to the degree of knowledge evinced by such Candidates, when examined the first time, to appear a second time before them for examination : provided, however, that such Candidates shall renew their Certificates from the Zillah Judge previously to the second examination.

5. The Zillah Judge, to whom application may be made for a Certificate, shall after making such enquiries as he may deem proper, to ascertain, that the applicant is a person of respectable connexions, good character, and suitable attainments, certify on the face of the application, that the applicant may be examined. If, however, the enquiries made on these points prove unsatisfactory, or if the applicant be unable to produce credentials to his respectability, past conduct, and general qualifications, the Judge shall decline compliance with the application.

6. The Certificate to be granted by the Judge, shall be in the following terms :

" I do hereby certify, that I have satisfied myself that the bearer of this certificate, A. B., is a man fully fitted by respectability and good character, to fill the office of Moonsiff, and from the enquiries I have made, I have every reason to believe that he is qualified, from his past conduct, and general information, to enjoy the privilege of examination for the Office of Moonsiff." This Certificate shall then be transmitted to the Sudder Udalut who, if they be aware of no objection, shall certify as follows :

" The Sudder Udalut having inspected this Certificate, are aware of no objection to the examination of the Candidate.

(Signed) A. B.

Register.

7. When a Candidate appears before a Committee, if they shall be aware of objections to his Examination on the score of character, they shall refuse to proceed with his Examination and shall declare their objection in writing on the face of the Certificate, and transmit it to the Sudder Udalut for such orders or for such further enquiry as the Sudder Udalut may think proper.

RULES *for the guidance of the Divisional Committees in Examining Candidates for the Office of Moonsiff.*

1. The examination to be partly viva voce, and partly written answers to prepared questions.

2. The questions will be framed by the Court of Sudder Udalut from the Regulations and Rules of Practice for the guidance of the Courts of Civil Justice, and will be forwarded by them to the Examination Committees on the receipt of the prescribed reports—informing them that Examinations are about to be held.

3. The questions to be answered by the Candidates, without reference to books or other sources of information, in the presence of two Members (one of them being the Judge, or the Collector and Magistrate) of the Examining Committee. The several Members of the Committee, however, shall examine the replies, and report on the eligibility of the Candidates. Candidates will be at liberty to give their replies in whatever language they please; but it will be the duty of the Committee to satisfy themselves, that every Candidate, who may be considered qualified in other respects for the situation of District Moonsiff, possesses also a competent knowledge of at least one or more of the principal vernacular languages of the Madras Presidency.

4. After the Candidates shall have delivered their written replies to the questions, the papers of a District Moonsiff's case, which has been decided on its merits, shall be read by a Gomastah, seriatim, the final decree excepted, to the several Candidates, who shall then be required to record, in any language they may prefer, their opinions on the point at issue between the parties, and the manner in which the suit ought to be decided agreeably to the Regulations and the law of the parties. The opinions thus recorded, shall be examined by the whole of the Committee, to enable them to judge of the capacity and intelligence of the Candidates.

5. On the close of the Examination, the replies of the Candidates to the written questions, shall be forwarded to the Sudder Udalut.

6. The oral examination shall be conducted by a full meeting of the Examining Committee, who shall examine each Candidate separately, by questions from the Regulations relating to the constitution, extent of jurisdiction, powers, and course of procedure of the Courts of the Native Judges.

7. At the conclusion of the Examination, the Committee shall, as directed in the 6th of the Government Rules, grant to such Candidates as they may deem proper, diplomas of fitness for employment as Moonsiffs, according to the form furnished to them by the Sudder Court, and at the same time forward duly certified lists of such Candidates to the Sudder Udalut.

*   *   *   *   *

NOTE.—Paras 8 to 14, originally published with these rules, are identical with paras 1 to 7 of the preceding notification, and are therefore omitted here.

CHAPTER IV.

DISTRICT PUNCHAYETS, REGULATION VII. of 1816, &c.

II. First. District moonsiffs are authorized to summon punchayets within their respective jurisdictions, for the decision of suits for real and personal property, without limitation as to amount or value, in the two following cases.

Second. In suits where both plaintiff and defendant may jointly agree that the matter at issue shall be determined by a district punchayet without appeal, and may prefer a request in writing to the district moonsiff to summon a punchayet, whether he be the moonsiff of the district in which the parties reside, or of any other district; or where one party having preferred a request in writing to the district moonsiff to summon a punchayet, the other party being an inhabitant of the same district on being summoned by the district moonsiff shall attend and voluntarily give his assent in writing to the district moonsiff, agreeing to that mode of trial.

Third. Provided however, that in the cases specified in the preceding clause of this Section, the cause of action have arisen within twelve years previous to the institution of the suit, or that the plaintiff do show by clear and positive proof, either that he had demanded the money or matter in question and that the defendant had admitted the justice of the demand, or that he had directly preferred his claim within the period abovementioned to a competent authority, and in such case, that he assign satisfactory reasons to the punchayet why he did not proceed in the suit, or prove that from minority, or other good and sufficient cause he was precluded from obtaining redress.

III. First. The district punchayet shall always consist of an odd number, never less than five, nor more than eleven, and the majority shall decide; the district punchayet shall sit at the station where the district moonsiff's court is held.

Second. The district punchayet shall be composed of the most respectable inhabitants of the district, who shall be called upon to serve in rotation, and any native inhabitant refusing to serve on a district punchayet shall be liable to be fined at the discretion of the district moonsiff in a sum not exceeding ten rupees, which shall be levied if necessary by the district moonsiff under the provisions of Section LI, Regulation VI, 1816.

Third.   Any respectable inhabitant of a neighbouring district may be placed on a district punchayet, if he be willing to undertake the duty.

Fourth.   When the parties in suits are of different castes or professions, the district moonsiff shall in all practicable cases, name an equal number of persons of the caste or profession to which each party may belong, to compose a part of the district punchayet, and shall complete the punchayet by the selection of a person or persons belonging to a caste or profession different from that of both the parties.

Fifth.   If either party shall object to any one or more of the members nominated to compose the district punchayet, and the district moonsiff shall consider such objections to be well grounded, he shall withdraw the members objected to and appoint others to serve in their stead.

Sixth.   When the parties may desire it, they shall each name two members, and the district moonsiff shall name another person who may be unobjected to by the parties, to form the punchayet; but on all other occasions, the whole shall be nominated by the district moonsiff: the practice of the parties naming two members each, shall never be allowed when it can be avoided.

IV.   First.   The district punchayet being formed as prescribed in the foregoing Section, shall be assembled by the written summons of the district moonsiff, and shall proceed to investigate the matter referred to them in conformity to the following rules.

Second.   The district punchayet shall commence their proceedings by requiring from the parties an agreement in writing to abide by the decision of such punchayet, whose names shall be inserted in the agreement, which shall be witnessed by the district moonsiff and any two respectable inhabitants, and dated on the same day.

Third.   Vakeels for plaintiffs and defendants shall be admitted to plead before district punchayets, provided that every person so appearing as a vakeel be a relative, servant, or dependant of the person by whom he may be employed, and provided he be furnished with a vakalutnamah describing his relation to his employer and the matter in which he is empowered to act; and such vakalutnamah shall be exhibited by the vakeel, before he be permitted to do any act in the suit.

Fourth. The parties being present in person or by vakeel, the district punchayet shall receive the written plaint of the complainant, which shall state precisely the grounds of complaint, the time when the cause of action arose, the name and residence of the person or persons complained against, the value or amount of real or personal property claimed, and all material circumstances which may elucidate the transaction.

Fifth. The plaint shall be read to the defendant or his vakeel, and the defendant or his vakeel shall be required by the punchayet to give in his answer, either immediately, if he shall be prepared to deliver it, or on a day to be fixed, which shall not be later than one week from the reading of the plaint.

Sixth. The defendant shall state in his answer all that he has to say regarding the case, and no further pleadings shall be admitted.

Seventh. The district punchayet, after the answer has been given in, shall receive from the plaintiff and defendant their exhibits and lists of their witnesses, and shall fix an early day for the trial, with reference to the convenience of the parties and witnesses respectively.

Eighth. The district punchayet shall immediately communicate the lists of witnesses and the day fixed for the trial to the district moonsiff, who shall require the witnesses to be in attendance on that day.

Ninth. The parties and witnesses being in attendance on the prescribed day, the district punchayet shall proceed to take the depositions of the witnesses in the manner usual in the caste to which they may respectively belong, on separate papers or cadjan leaves in all cases in which the matter at issue may exceed the value or amount of one hundred rupees; the deposition shall be read over to the witness, who shall then subscribe the deposition with his or her name or mark.

Tenth. In cases in which the matter at issue may be of smaller amount or value than one hundred rupees, it shall be discretionary with the district punchayet to take the depositions of the witnesses in writing or not.

Eleventh. The district punchayets are authorized to cause a *solemn affirmation* to be administered to witnesses in cases where they may deem it necessary.

Twelfth. The district punchayets shall not put a question to any witness suggesting a particular answer, and shall previous to the examination of a witness inform him that they have authority to cause a *solemn affirmation* to be administered to him when they may think he is not giving his evidence correctly, which authority the district punchayets shall exercise at their discretion.

Thirteenth.   If the parties or either of them shall fail to appear in person or by vakeel at the time fixed for the trial, the district punchayet shall suspend the trial and report it to the district moonsiff, who shall cause to be affixed in some conspicuous place of the village wherein the defaulting party may reside, a notice, specifying that the suit will be tried on a given day, which shall not be less than five days from the date of the notice.

Fourteenth.   If the plaintiff shall not appear at the time fixed in the notice, the district punchayet shall dismiss his suit, and award him to pay all the expenses which may have been incurred by the defendant and by the witnesses of both parties in their attendance on the punchayet, and the sum so awarded shall be recovered from the property of the defaulting plaintiff in the mode prescribed in Section XLVI, Regulation VI, 1816, unless he shall immediately pay the amount.

Fifteenth.   If the defendant shall refuse to answer the plaint, or shall not attend at the time fixed in the notice, the district punchayet shall proceed to give judgment on the plaintiff's vouchers and the evidence of his witnesses.

V.   In cases where a witness shall neglect to attend, or attending shall refuse to give his testimony, or shall be otherwise guilty of disrespect to the district punchayet, as also when the evidence of a person is required who resides beyond the jurisdiction of the district moonsiff, as also in the cases of persons whose testimony may be required, but whose rank or caste may render it improper to require their attendance, as also when the parties or their vakeels may be guilty of disrespect to the district punchayet, the punchayet shall report the circumstances to the district moonsiff, who is hereby authorized and directed on receiving such reports, to take the same measures for procuring the attendance or testimony of the witnesses, or for punishing the contempts, as he would have taken under Sections XXVIII, XXIX, XXX and XL, Regulation VI, 1816, if the circumstances represented had occurred before himself.

VI.   When both parties have been heard and the whole of the evidence has been gone through, the district punchayet shall order the parties and witnesses to withdraw, and shall write their decree according to justice and right.

VII. The decree of the district punchayet shall contain the names of the parties, and the names of the witness examined, and the titles of the exhibits read; it shall also contain an abstract statement of the principal grounds and reasons on which the decision may be passed, it shall specify the value or amount of the personal property, and the value or the annual produce of the real property adjudged; the decree shall bear the signature or mark of the members of the punchayet and shall be dated on the day on which it is passed. If any claim shall appear to the district punchayet to be evidently litigious and vexatious, they shall' adjudge suitable costs and damages against the plaintiff, payable to the defendant, and insert the same in their decree.

VIII. Two copies of the decree shall be prepared by the district punchayet, and shall be put under a sealed cover and delivered to the district moonsiff, who shall require the parties together with the punchayet to assemble immediately, or at a convenient day not being later than three days from his receipt of the decree; the district moonsiff shall open the seal in presence of the parties, and shall endorse on each copy of the decree, the date of the delivery thereof, which shall be attested by his signature and the signatures of any two members of the punchayet; the district moonsiff shall then cause the punchayet to deliver to each party in his presence, a copy of the decree; but no communication shall be made to the district moonsiff or to either party, of the nature of the decree, previously to its delivery.

IX. If either the plaintiff or defendant shall fail to appear in person or by vakeel to receive a copy of the decree, or having attended shall refuse to receive a copy, the district moonsiff shall endorse on the copy intended for such party, such omission or refusal, and noting the date, shall attest the same with his signature, which shall be witnessed by any two members of the punchayet; the copy so endorsed shall be deposited with the district moonsiff, to be delivered to the party afterwards claiming it.

X. The proceedings of the district punchayet, shall be written by one or more of the members, and no stamped paper need be used in the plaint, answer, or any process.

XI. First. No appeal shall be permitted from decisions passed by district punchayets under this Regulation; but if the district punchayet shall be guilty of gross partiality, it shall be at the option of either party to bring the matter by petition, upon

---

Sec. VII.—Signature of the majority of the members is sufficient under Act VIII of 1840—which see under village punchayet at p. 14.

stamped paper of the prescribed rate according to the amount of the suit, before the *civil judge of the zillah.*—S. U. *March* 4, 1844, *paras* 8, 9.

Second. The petition shall not be received, unless it be presented with the decree complained of, within thirty days after the date on which copies of the decree may have been furnished or tendered to the parties or to their vakeels.

Third. If the petition be received, the *civil* judge shall order the execution of the decree to be stayed pending the enquiry.

Fourth. If the partiality charged against the punchayet shall be established to the satisfaction of the judge by the oaths *or solemn affirmation* of two credible witnesses at the least, he shall in every case, whatever the amount or value of the suit may be—*of his own authority—Sec.* XXI, *Act* VII, 1843—annul the decision; and the parties shall be at liberty to have recourse to another punchayet or to any other competent jurisdiction.

Fifth. Provided however, that where the decision of a second punchayet shall agree with the decision of a former punchayet in the same suit, it shall be final.

Sixth. Petitions to the *civil* judge of the zillah under this Section, shall be presented by the parties in person, or by an authorized vakeel of the court.

XII. The district moonsiffs shall not receive or refer to a punchayet for trial, any suit for damages on account of personal injuries, or for personal damages of whatever nature, without an order of reference to him from the *civil* judge.

XIII. District punchayets shall not allow in their decrees a larger rate of interest than district moonsiffs are authorized to allow under Section XV, Regulation VI, 1816.

XIV. In all cases of inheritance or of succession to landed property, district punchayets shall be guided by the rules prescribed in Section LXII, Regulation VI, 1816.

XV. In respect to the admission of obligations, deeds and documents, the district punchayets shall be guided by the rules prescribed in Section XXXV, Regulation VI, 1816.

XVI. First. Decrees of district punchayets in cases referred to them under this Regulation, shall be carried into execution by the

---

Sec. XIII.—See note on Sec. XXII, Regulation IV of 1846 at p. 6.

Sec. XV.—They are admissible on payment of prescribed penalties under Sec. III, Regulation IV of 1825.

district moonsiff under the rules prescribed in Sections XLVI, XLVII, XLVIII, XLIX and L, Regulation VI, 1816 : provided first, that if the suit be for land of the description specified in clause second, Section XI, Regulation VI, 1816, the annual produce of such land shall not exceed the sum of twenty rupees ; secondly, that if the suit be for land of the description specified in clause third, Section XI, Regulation VI, 1816, the annual produce of such land shall not exceed two hundred rupees ; and thirdly, that if the suit be for real property, not of the description abovementioned, or for sums of money or other personal property, the value or amount of such property shall not exceed two hundred rupees.

Second. In all other cases the decisions of district punchayets shall be carried into execution by the *civil* judge, in the mode prescribed by the Regulations.

XVII. Petitions to the *civil* judge of the zillah praying execution of the decisions of district punchayets, shall be written upon stamped paper of the prescribed rate, according to the amount decreed, and shall be presented by the parties in person or by an authorized vakeel of the court.

Judges of zillah courts may refer to subordinate judges, and Principal sudder ameens applications for the execution of decisions of district punchayets preferred under Section XVII, Reg. VII, 1816.—*Sec.* XX, *Act* VII, 1843.

XVIII. First. Any member or members of district punchayets, shall be liable to prosecution in the zillah court for corruption in the discharge of their trust, by either party in a suit, which may have been referred to such punchayet, and upon proof of the charge to the satisfaction of the zillah civil judge, he shall adjudge the offender or offenders, to pay the prosecutor three times the amount or value of the money or property corruptly received, with all costs of suit ; but members of district punchayets shall not be liable to be prosecuted for want of form, or for error in their proceedings or judgment ; nor shall any process whatever be issued against a member or members of a district punchayet, unless the judge shall be previously satisfied by sufficient evidence, that there is probable cause to believe that the charge is well founded, and unless the charge shall be preferred within three months from the date of the act of corruption complained of.

Second. The zillah *civil* judge shall further fine the party by whom, or for whom, the corruption may have been practised in the suit, provided he shall have assented to such corruption, in a sum equal to the value of the thing or sum of money, which any member or members of such district punchayet may be proved to have so corruptly received.

Third. If the corruption charged against any member or members of such district punchayet, shall not be proved to the satisfaction of the zillah *civil* judge, he shall award full costs and such damages, to the member or members complained against, as may appear to him to be equitable, and he shall levy a fine from the party making such groundless charge, not exceeding the value of the thing or sum of money charged to have been corruptly received.

XX. First. Every witness attending to give evidence before a district punchayet shall be entitled to receive batta at a rate not less than one, nor more than four annas of a rupee per diem, from the date of his departure from his village to the day of his return ; the rate of such batta to be determined by the district moonsiff with reference to his situation in life.

Second. The batta to witnesses shall be paid daily under the orders of the district moonsiff, by the party on whose behalf they may respectively be summoned.

Third. The district moonsiff shall levy from the party cast, and pay to the party in whose favour the decree may be given, the amount of batta which under this Section he may have paid to the witnesses summoned on his behalf.

Fourth. The amount of batta to witnesses, shall be specified by the district moonsiff on the back of the decree.

CHAPTER V.

COLLECTORS, JUDICIAL POWERS OF.

Collectors are hereby authorized to take primary cognizance, by summary process, of all cases which, under the provisions of Regulations XXVIII and XXX of 1802, were summarily cognizable by the zillah courts, with the exception of the cases referred to in Sections XXXV and XL, Regulation XXVIII of 1802; and they shall have power to assess such damages, penalties and costs as may appear to them proper, but not exceeding in any case the amount limited in the particular provision of the Regulation under which each case was respectively cognizable in the zillah courts.—*Cl.* 1, *Sec.* II. *Reg.* V, 1822.

Second. Provided however, that no damages, penalties or costs which a collector may award under this Section, shall be levied until after the expiration of the period hereinafter limited, during which an appeal may be preferred against the said collector's decision.—*Cl.* 2.—*Ibid.*

Plaintiffs and defendants shall be allowed to employ a relative, a servant, or a dependant, to act in their behalf in suits which may be brought before the collectors of zillahs under this regulation.—*Sec.* XIX.—*Ibid.*

Suits instituted before the collectors under this Regulation shall be exempt from all stamp duties and fees of every description,

Cl. 1, Sec. II, Reg. V of 1822.—The S. U. in their letter to Government 20th December 1824, pointed out that this authority to take primary cognizance of all cases which under the provisions of Regs. XXVIII and XXX of 1802, were summarily cognizable by the zillah courts, with exception of those referred to in Sections XXXV and XL, of the former, would be apparently inoperative and nugatory : as it was held that no suits were summarily cognizable by the zillah courts under those regulations save those referred to in Sec. XXXIV, Reg. XXVIII of 1802, which by Sec. VI, of this very Regulation (V of 1822,) are virtually still left and reserved to the Courts—for it directs that the petition prescribed by Sec. XXXIV, shall be presented to the District Moonsiff or Tahsildar who "shall proceed thereon as the native Commissioner was directed to proceed"—*i. e.* send the defaulter to the Judge—it is however manifest, as the Court observed, that cognizance of a variety of suits other than those last mentioned was *intended* to be given to Collectors by this enactment ; and as in consequence of the indeterminate expressions of the law, and the doubts and difficulties suggested and raised by the above quoted letter, great uncertainty still prevails as to the powers of the Collector under this Section, I have thought it best to insert Regs. XXVIII, and XXX of 1802, under this head ; entering in the text such alterations as are plainly and indubitably made by Reg. V of 1822—and noting the points on which doubts exist, or contrary opinions may be held.

whether decided by themselves, or under their orders by village
or district punchayets.—*Sec.* XX. *Reg.* V, 1822.

Proceedings before collectors under this Regulation shall be
summary, and summonses to parties and witnesses may be either
verbal or in writing, at the discretion of the collector : it shall
only be necessary for the collector to keep an abstract diary in the
language of the district, in the following form.

Names of Parties.	Abstract of Plaint.	Abstract of Decision.	Date of Delivery.

Sec. XXI.—*Ibid.*

Whenever any persons who may lay claim to lands or crops in
the possession of others, shall forcibly take possession of the disputed lands or crops, the party dispossessed shall be at liberty to
bring the case before the collector of the district, who, upon proof
of such forcible ejection, and of the actual previous possession by
such ejected party, shall cause the disputed lands or crops to be
restored to the complainant, or the value of the crops to be paid
to him if they shall be damaged, destroyed, or not forthcoming ;
and shall further award against the offender such costs and
damages as may be equitable.—*Sec.* XI.—*Ibid.*

An appeal shall be open to *the subordinate judge of the zillah*
by regular suit, from all decisions passed by the collector under
this regulation : provided the petition of appeal shall be presented
to the judge within thirty days from the date of the collector's
decision.—*Cl.* 1, *Sec.* XVI.—*Ibid.*

Decisions of the collectors are not to be set aside for want of
form, or for irregularity in their proceedings, but on the merits
only.—*Cl.* 2.—*Ibid.*

No property attached under regulation XXVIII of 1802, for
the discharge of arrears of rent or revenue, shall be sold, unless
pottahs shall have been granted, or tendered and refused ; nor
until previous notice shall have been given to the collector of the

Sec. XX, Reg. V of 1822.—There may be other " costs of suit" as expences of witnesses, &c.
Sec. XI, Reg. V of 1822.—Pending appeal, execution of judgment may be stayed as
to costs and damages only.—C. O. 10th December 1838.
Sec. XVI, Reg. V of 1822.—Or if no Subordinate Judge, then to Civil Judge—in
either case only special appeal, and that to S. U.—S. U. 4th March 1844, Para. 7.

district, and leave shall have been obtained from him for the sale.
—*Cl.* 1, *See.* III, *Reg.* V, 1822.

Second. Where property may be sold contrary to this rule, the defaulter shall be discharged of the arrear for which such attachment has been made, the property attached shall be restored to him, or the value thereof made good by the distrainer where it may have been damaged or injured, or may not be forthcoming : and distrainers shall further pay damages not exceeding the loss sustained in consequence of such attachment, with costs of suit.— *Cl.* 2.—*Ibid.*

Proprietors of land, and farmers of land, holding farms immediately from Government, shall have power to distrain without sending previous notice to any court of judicature, or to any public officer, the crops and products of the land, with the cattle and other personal property wherever found (as hereafter excepted) belonging to their under-renters, tenants, and ryots, for arrears of rent or revenue ; and to cause the said property to be sold for the discharge of such arrears. Under-farmers farming lands from proprietors of land shall have the same power to distrain the property of their under-farmers, tenants, or ryots, to enable them to enforce payment of arrears of rents and revenue. Land-holders and farmers of land shall exercise the powers hereby vested in them under the following rules and restrictions.—*Sec.* II, *Reg.* XXVIII, 1802.

When property may be attached for arrears of rent or revenue under regulation XXVIII of 1802, the distrainer shall without delay give notice thereof to the collector, either direct or through the tahsildar, or the principal revenue officer of the district.—*Cl.* 1, *Sec.* IV, *Reg.* V, 1822.

Property so distrained shall not be sold until the expiration of thirty days from the day on which the notice of attachment referred to in the preceding clause was given ; and until the expiration of that time, the defaulter shall be at liberty to appeal to the collector against the distraint of his property.—*Cl.* 2.—*Ibid.*

Cl. 1, Sec. III, Reg. V of 1822.—This is a modification of Sec. II, Reg. XXVIII of 1802, which allowed unconditional sale.

Cl. 2, do. —The Collector is clearly the authority before whom suits for *these* penalties are to be instituted—it would be inconsistent with the avowed objects of the Regulation to suppose that a regular suit in the Court is *here* meant—and this fact may fairly lead to a conclusion that the powers given by Sec. III, Reg. XXVIII of 1802—the language of which is precisely the same—were intended to be also exercised by the Collector.

Sec. II, Reg. XXVIII of 1802.—Sold, &c. not without leave of Collector.—Cl. 1, Sec. III, Reg. V of 1822.

If no appeal be made, the distrainer shall have authority, at
the expiration of the thirty days after notice given as above provided, to cause the distrained property to be sold in conformity
with the regulations.—*Cl.* 3, *Sec.* IV, *Reg.* V, 1822.

If an appeal be made, the collector shall without delay institute
a summary inquiry into the correctness of the demand for which
the property has been attached ; and if it shall appear that the
amount claimed is justly due, he shall issue his order for the sale
of the property to the district moonsiff, or other authorized person.
If a sum less than the amount demanded shall appear on enquiry
to be due, the collector shall order so much property only to be
sold as may be sufficient to discharge the debt.—*Cl.* 4.—*Ibid.*

When notice shall not have been given of property attached
for arrears of rent or revenue, as provided for in clause first of
this section, within thirty days after the attachment, the defaulter
shall be discharged from the arrear for which the distraint was
made ; and the distrainer shall be subject to the penalties prescribed in Clause second, Section III, of this regulation.—*Cl.* 5.
—*Ibid.*

Proprietors and farmers of land shall not distrain nor sell the
lands, houses, or other real property of their under-farmers, tenants, and ryots, or goods or money belonging to Government in
the hands of weavers, or manufacturers, or the loom thread, or un-
wrought silk, or materials of manufacture of weavers or manufacturers, or the tools of tradesmen or labourers, being under-farmers,
tenants, or ryots. Where distress may be levied contrary to this
rule, the defaulters shall be discharged of the arrear for which
such distress may have been levied ; the distrained property shall
be restored to them ; or the value thereof made good by the distrainers, where it may have been damaged or injured, or may not
be forthcoming. And distrainers shall further pay damages, adequate to the loss sustained in consequence of such attachment, or
sale, with costs of suit.—*Sec.* III, *Reg.* XXVIII, 1802.

The ploughs and implements of husbandry, the cattle actually
trained to the plough, and the seed-grain of under-farmers, ten-

---

Sec. III, Reg. XXVIII of 1802.—See note above on Cl. 2, Sec. III, Reg. V of 1822—
upon this and all other penal enactments of this Regulation, viz. Secs. IV and VI, Cl. 6,
Sec. VIII—Secs. IX, XIII, XIV and XV—Cl. 3, Sec. XIX—Secs. XXI, XXV, XXVI and
XXIX—the latter part of Cl. 3, Sec. XXXIV—Secs. XXXV, XXXIX and XL—the S.
U. observed in their letter of the 20th December 1844 above quoted, that they had
always been enforced by *regular* suits in the Courts, and consequently were not under
Sec. II, Reg. V of 1822, cognizable by Collectors. In reading each of these Sections
this doubt must be borne in mind, it is here brought to notice once for all.

ants, or ryots, shall not be distrained for arrears of rent or revenue, so long as other property may be forthcoming equal to the discharge of such arrear ; distrainers deviating from this rule shall be punished by an award to the party aggrieved, of damages adequate to the injury sustained, with costs of suit.—*Sec. IV, Reg.* XXVIII, 1802.

Where arrears of rent or revenue may be withheld beyond the day on which they fall due, according to the Kistbundy, or other engagement ; or (where no written agreement may exist) beyond the time when the rent or revenue became payable agreeably to local usage ; such under-farmers, tenants, or ryots, so withholding rents or revenues, shall be held to be defaulters.—*Cl. I, Sec. V. —Ibid.*

Where the arrears may not be paid on demand, the defaulters shall be liable to immediate distress ; notwithstanding the amount may, or may not, have been demanded of the surety.—*Cl. 2.—Ibid.*

Where distrainers may proceed to levy distress from an under-tenant (who has given security) without having previously demanded the arrear from the surety, the tenant shall give notice of the distress to his own surety, so as to enable him to discharge the arrear before the sale of the property attached ; it shall be further competent to the distrainer. to give notice to the surety, requiring him to make good the arrear.—*Cl. 3.—Ibid.*

It shall be at the option of distrainers either to distrain the property of the defaulter, or of the surety, or of both ; provided the whole distress do not exceed the amount of the arrear.—*Cl. 4.—Ibid.*

Distress shall not be levied on the property of the surety, until the arrear shall have been demanded from the defaulter ; unless the defaulter may have absconded, or be otherwise not forthcoming ; in which case, and in the event of the money not being paid by the surety on demand, his property shall be liable to distress, in the same manner as if the defaulter had been present, and served with the demand in the first instance.—*Cl. 5.—Ibid.*

Where property may be distrained, and sold for arrears of rent, and where it may be made to appear upon trial that no arrear was due ; the distrainer shall be made to return the property to the owner ; or to make good to him the value thereof, if it should have been sold, damaged, injured, or destroyed; or should not be forthcoming ; and shall moreover pay to the party injured, as damages, a sum of money equal to the value of such property, with costs of suit.—*Sec.* VI, *Reg.* XXVIII, 1802.

Where defaulters may tender the arrear demanded, in the presence of two credible witnesses, to the persons deputed to attach their property, such persons shall receive the arrear, and shall not proceed to the attachment.—*Sec.* VII.—*Ibid.*

Distrainers shall furnish to the persons employed to attach the property of defaulters, demands in writing, and signed with their names. specifying the amount of the arrear for which the attachment may be issued, and the date on which the arrear fell due. The persons so deputed shall produce the writing, as authority for making the attachment ; and, on the day on which the property may be attached, shall deliver a copy of such writing to the defaulter, endorsing thereon a list or inventory of the property attached, and the name of the place where it may be lodged or kept.—*Cl.* 1, *Sec.* VIII.—*Ibid.*

The writing shall further set forth the intention of the distrainer to bring the attached property to immediate public sale, unless the amount and expences of the attachment be previously discharged.—*Cl.* 2.—*Ibid.*

Where defaulters may be absent, a copy of the writing, with the endorsement, shall be fixed or left at his usual place of residence, before the expiration of the third day, calculating from the day of the attachment.—*Cl.* 3.—*Ibid.*

Where defaulters, on receiving notice, may neglect to pay the amount due, or to give satisfactory assurance or security to the distrainer for early payment; or where defaulters may have absconded, or may be otherwise not forthcoming, so that the notice cannot be served upon them ; the distrainer shall, in either case, transmit an inventory of such portion of the property attached, as can be brought to immediate sale, to the nearest *Tahsildar or public servant* expressly empowered to sell distrained property, *under Act* VII *of* 1839, with a written demand that the property may be publicly sold, for the discharge of the arrear due. —*Cl.* 4.—*Ibid.*

The amount of the property shall be specified in the application together with the place where the property may be in attachment, and (if it be the intention of the distrainer to remove it) the place to which the removal will be made.—*Cl.* 5.—*Ibid.*

Where persons vested with the powers of distraint may cause property to be attached, without furnishing the agents deputed for that purpose with the writing abovementioned ; or where such agents, having been furnished with the writing, may omit to deli-

---

Cl. 4, Sec. VIII, Reg. XXVIII of 1802.—" The distrainer shall, &c." *i. e.* after having given due notice, and obtained leave as prescribed in Secs. IV and V, Reg. V of 1822.

ver a copy of it, with the endorsement, to the defaulter ; or to leave, in the event of the defaulter's absence, such copy at his usual place of residence, within the limited time, the distrainer shall not be entitled to recover the arrear, for which the distress may have been levied ; but he shall restore the property to the defaulter ; or the value of it, if it shall have been sold, damaged, injured, or destroyed, or shall not be forthcoming ; and shall moreover pay costs of suit.—*Cl.* 6, *Sec.* VIII, *Reg.* XXVIII, 1802.

Where defaulters may tender payment of the arrear demanded, in the presence of two credible witnesses, after their property may have been attached, and prior to the day fixed for sale, together with payment of the necessary expences attending the attachment ; the distrainer shall receive the amount of such arrear and expences immediately upon the same being tendered, and shall forthwith release the property. In case of any dispute respecting the expences of the attachment, it shall be determined by the authorized persons of the district, or place, in which the distress may have been levied. The courts of udalut shall, on complaint, punish distrainers acting contrary to this regulation, by damages to be paid to the party injured, with costs of suit.—*Sec.* IX.—*Ibid.*

Distrainers shall not drive or convey distrained cattle or other property out of the limits of the estate, in which it may have been attached ; distrainers shall either leave the property upon the premises in the charge of proper persons, or drive or convey it, with due care, to a proper place, as near as possible to the premises within the limits of the estate.—*Sec.* X.—*Ibid.*

Distrainers attaching the crops or ungathered products of the land belonging to their under-farmers, ryots, or others, paying revenue through them, shall cause such crops or products to be reaped or gathered in due season, and shall store the same in proper houses or granaries upon the premises ; or (if no such place be on the premises) according to the usage of the country, as near thereto as possible within the limits of the estate. The expence of reaping, or gathering, and storing such crops or products, shall be defrayed by the owner upon his redeeming the property, or from the proceeds of the sale in the event of its being sold.—*Sec.* XI.—*Ibid.*

Distrainers shall not work the bullocks or cattle, or make use of the goods or effects, distrained ; they shall provide the necessary food for the cattle or live stock, the expence attending which

---

Secs. X. XI, XII, Reg. XXVIII, 1802.—Though no penalty is specified for the infringement of these rules by distrainers it is presumed that damages can be awarded if sustained by the breach of them.

shall be defrayed by the owner upon his redeeming the property, or from the proceeds of the sale in the event of its being sold.—*Sec.* XII, *Reg.* XXVIII, 1802.

Where property distrained may be stolen or lost, or damaged, or destroyed, while in the keeping of the distrainer, by reason of his not having taken the necessary precautions for the due preservation of it; the loss or damage shall be made good to the owner by the distrainer.—*Sec.* XIII.—*Ibid.*

The distress levied shall not be excessive; that is to say, the property distrained shall be as nearly as possible proportionate to the amount of the arrear. Where persons vested with the powers of distraint may attach property, the value of which may be disproportionate to the arrear, and where it may afterwards be proved that other property of less value for the liquidation of such arrear might have been distrained; the court of udalut shall award to the owner damages according to the circumstances of the case, with costs of suit.—*Sec.* XIV.—*Ibid.*

Attachments shall be made after sunrise and before sunset, and not otherwise. Where persons vested with the power of distraint may seize, or attempt to seize, the property of defaulters after sunset and before sunrise, for the discharge of arrears of rent or revenue, such distrainers shall not be entitled to recover the arrear; but (if the property should have been distrained) it shall be restored to the defaulter, or the value of it (if it should have been sold, damaged, or destroyed, or should not be forthcoming) with costs of suit.—*Sec.* XV.—*Ibid.*

Where under-farmers, or Ryots may make a fraudulent conveyance of property, to prevent the attachment of it for arrears, the court of udalut, upon proof thereof, shall cause the property to be delivered up to the distrainer, and compel the person to whom such transfer or conveyance may have been made to pay the distrainer damages, equal to the value of one half the property, with costs of suit.—*Sec.* XVI.—*Ibid.*

Where under-farmers, or Ryots may resist or cause to be resisted the attachment of property for arrears of rent or revenue in the mode prescribed by the regulations, so as to prevent the attachment from taking place; or may forcibly or clandestinely take away such property after it may have been attached; such persons' shall, on proof before the court of udalut, be made liable to damages to the distrainer, equal to twice the amount of the property rescued from attachment; and the property so taken away shall be liable to be attached again by the distrainer, wherever it may be found; such under-farmers, and Ryots, as well as all persons concerned in resisting the attachment, shall moreover be liable to be apprehended and prosecuted before the criminal courts, for any breach of the peace committed by them, in such resistance to the attachment; and the police officers, on information of such resistance, shall repair to the spot, and take measures as well to apprehend and send to the magistrate the persons who may appear to have broken the peace, as to support distrainers in the due exercise of the legal powers vested in them. Where persons not being defaulters, or responsible for defaulters, may claim a right to the property distrained, and the distrainer may, notwithstanding, cause the same to be sold; the claimants, on proof of such right in the Court of udalut, and in the event of the distrainer being unable to prove responsibility for the arrear of rent or revenue, on account of which the property may have been sold, shall recover from the distrainer the full value of such property, with costs and damages according to the circumstances of the case. But claims to crops upon the ground, or to gathered product of the ground, attached in the possession of the defaulter, whether founded upon a previous sale, mortgage, or otherwise, shall not bar the prior claim of rent or revenue due from the ground, upon which such crop or product may have been grown: it being the undoubted right of the owner of the land, or his representative, to consider the produce of it mortgaged to him for the rent of the land in the first instance, and in default of his rent being paid as engaged for (or determinable by local rates and usage, where there may be no specific engagement) to distrain and sell such part of the product as may be necessary to make good the arrear of rent or revenue due to him.—*Sec.* XVII, *Reg.* XXVIII, 1802.

Where persons not being owners may be convicted of forcibly or clandestinely taking away property once distrained; the Court of udalut, upon proof thereof, shall cause such persons to be imprisoned, until they restore the property or make good the value of it to the distrainer, and moreover to pay to him, as damages, a sum of money equal to the value of such property, with costs of suit.—*Sec.* XVIII.—*Ibid.*

Distrainers shall have power to force open any stable, cowhouse, golah, granary, or other building; to enter any dwelling-house, the outer door of which may be open, (excepting the apartments in such dwelling-house appropriated for the Zenana, or residence of women) and to break open the door of any room in such dwelling house, for the purpose of attaching property belonging to a defaulter and lodged therein. — *Cl.* 1, *Sec.* XIX.—*Ibid.*

Where distrainers may have reason to suppose that the property of a defaulter is lodged within a dwelling-house the outer door of which may be shut, or within any apartments appropriated to women, which by the usage of the country are considered private, such distrainers shall represent the same to the *head of police* (within whose jurisdiction the house may be situated) and on such representation, the *head of police* shall send a police officer to the spot, in the presence of whom distrainers may force open the outer door of such dwelling-house, in like manner as they may break open the door of any room within a house, except the Zenana. Distrainers may also, in the presence of the police officer, after due notice given for the removal of women within a Zenana, and after furnishing means for their removal in a suitable manner, (if they be women of rank, who according to the customs of the country cannot appear in public,) enter the Zenana apartments, for the purpose of attaching the defaulters property deposited therein. But such property, if found, shall be immediately removed from such apartments, after which they shall be left free to the former occupants; and nothing in this regulation shall be understood to authorize a distrainer or his agent to force open the door of a dwelling-house, or to enter the apartments of women which, by the usage of the country, are considered private, in any other mode than is herein prescribed.—*Cl. 2. Sec.* XIX, *Reg.* XXVIII, 1802.

Persons entering the apartments of women, or forcing open the outer door of dwelling-houses, contrary to the provisions of this regulation, shall be imprisoned for six months; the distrainer shall not recover the arrear for which the attachment may have been issued, but he shall restore to the defaulter any property which may have been attached; or pay the value of it, if it shall have been sold, damaged, or destroyed, or shall not be forthcoming; and the Court shall further award against such distrainer heavy damages, with costs of suit; and where persons may enter dwelling-houses or break open stables, cow-houses, golahs, granaries or other buildings not occupied by, or in the possession of, defaulters, to distrain property belonging to them, and no such property shall be found therein; the distrainer shall be liable to prosecution, by the occupant or possessor, for entering such house, or breaking open such stable or other building; and the Court shall award damages according to the circumstances of the case, with all costs of suit.—*Cl.* **3.**—*Ibid.*

Where persons authorized to distrain property for arrears of rent or revenue may apply to the *head of police*, to depute a police officer to be present at the time of making the attachment with a view to prevent resistance or other breach of the peace, the police shall (as far as may be in its power,) comply with such applications, and the police officers so deputed shall use every means in their power to prevent resistance or other breach of the peace ; in such cases, the police officers shall also give due attention to the whole conduct and proceedings of the distrainer, so as to be able to give evidence thereupon, if afterwards required.—*Sec.* XX, *Reg.* XXVIII, 1802.

At the expiration of the fifth day, and before the expiration of the eighth day, calculating from the day *on which the order of the Collector for the sale may reach the village where the property is under attachment—Sec. V, Reg. V,* 1822—distrainers shall apply to the *Tahsildar, or authorized public servant,* (*Act.* VII, 1839)—to have the same appraised and sold, who upon receipt of such application, shall proceed, in the following manner ; he shall fix up, on the outer door of his house, and at the place at which he may determine to dispose of the property, a list of the property attached, with a notice which shall specify ; First—The place at which the property is to be sold ; which shall be on the spot where it may be lodged by the distrainer, or at the nearest market, Bazaar, or Haut, or any place of public resort, where the officer may be of opinion that it is likely to sell to the best advantage. Secondly—The day on which the sale is to take place ; he shall fix as early a day for this purpose as may be compatible with the regular appraisement of the property and the publication of the intended sale of it, which is to be made by beat of drum, on one market day at the least before the market day on which the sale is to take place, as well as on the morning of the day of sale. The same rule shall be observed with respect to the sale of ungathered products, after the distrainer may have gathered and stored them, which products shall not be sold, until publication may have been made. Thirdly—The hour of the day when the sale is to be made, (which shall be during the hours of business, when the greatest number of people may be supposed to assemble.) The Tahsildar, or person authorized by Act VII, 1839, shall nominate two credible persons competent by their profession, trade, or occupation, to appraise the property ; the persons so appointed shall appraise the property, according to the current price which the several articles may then bear in the country, and shall deliver the particulars of the appraisement in writing, and attest the same with their signatures ; and shall certify, in writing, at the foot of the paper, that they have appraised the property according to the best of their knowledge and judgment. The *Tahsildar, or authorized person,* shall affix his seal to the paper of appraisement; and shall cause it to be stuck up on the outer door of his own house, and at the place where the property is to be sold. The property shall be brought to the place of sale on the morning of the day of sale, in order that it may be examined by the persons intending to purchase, unless it shall consist of grain or other products of the earth, the removal of which would be attended with considerable expence; in which case, samples only, indiscriminately taken from each article, shall be brought to the place of sale, and exposed for the purpose abovementioned. The property shall be put up to sale in one lot, or in two or more lots, as the *Tahsildar, or person authorized*, may think advisable. The property shall be disposed of for the highest price offered for it. Where the property may sell for more than the amount of the arrear, the overplus, after deducting the charges attending the attachment and sale of it, shall be paid to the defaulter. Where the proceeds of the sale may be insufficient for the discharge of the arrear and the expences attending the attachment and sale, the distrainer shall be at liberty to attach other property belonging to the defaulter, and to cause it to be sold to make good the deficiency. The *Tahsildar, or person authorized*, shall, in every case, examine the distrainer's statement of the expences attending the attachment, and sale of property; and shall reject any part appearing to him unreasonable. Where persons vested with the power of distraint may sell or dispose of property attached for arrears of rent or revenue, in any other mode than that prescribed by the Regulations, such persons shall forfeit the arrear for which the distress may be levied to the defaulter, and shall make good to him the value of the property sold or disposed of, with costs of suit. —*Sec.* XXI, *Reg.* XXVIII, 1802.

The property shall not be sold for other than ready money, to be paid at the time of sale; and the purchaser shall not be permitted to carry away any part of the property until paid for. Where the purchaser may fail in the payment of the whole or part of the purchase money within five days, calculating from the day following the sale; the whole of the property, or the part of it which may be unpaid for, shall be resold by the *Tahsildar, or person authorized*, on such day as he may fix, for the best price offered for it. The defaulting purchaser shall forfeit, to the distrainer, ten per cent of the amount of the price at which he may have purchased the property so resold, and shall make good to him any loss arising, as well as the expences incurred on the re-sale. If any profit accrue on the re-sale, it shall be accounted for to the defaulter.— *Sec.* XXII.—*Ibid.*

All Tahsildars within the territories subject to the presidency of Fort St. George shall be vested with the powers of commissioners for the sale of property distrained for arrears of rent or revenue, and shall be subject to all rules and provisions to which by any Law or Regulation such commissioners are subject.—*Sec.* II, *Act* VII *of* 1839.

Provided always, that in the exercise of these powers Tahsildars shall be subject to the control and superintendence of the Collector, and shall not be subject to the authority of the zillah judge, except in the case of any judicial proceedings.—*Sec.* III.—*Ibid.*

Provided also, that Tahsildars shall be subject to the same liabilities, in respect of the exercise of the said powers, to which they are subjected by Sec. X, Reg. IX of 1822, of the Madras Code, in cases in which they conduct sales under the provisions of that Regulation.—*Sec.* IV.—*Ibid.*

Provided also, that Tahsildars shall not be entitled to any fee or commission for selling such distrained property; but that all fees or commission which may be now lawfully taken by commissioners for the sale of such distrained property, shall be taken and carried to the account of Government.—*Sec.* V.—*Ibid.*

Tahsildars shall have authority, subject to the orders of the collector, to delegate the powers vested in them by the second section of this act to any public servants placed under their authority; and the provisions of the three last preceding sections of this act shall apply to all public servants to whom these powers shall have been so delegated, in the same manner as they apply to Tashildars.—*Sec.* VI.—*Ibid.*

Persons vested with the powers of selling distrained property shall not act in cases where they may be parties concerned for arrears due to themselves, or where they may be otherwise interested.—*Sec.* XXIV, *Reg.* XXVIII, 1802.

It shall be the duty of *persons authorized to sell* distrained property to prevent unfair practices, either in the appraisement, or sale of such property: and upon proof of their conniving at such practices, the Court of udalut shall cause them to make good any loss, or injury, which the party may have sustained thereby, with costs of suit.—*Sec.* XXV.—*Ibid.*

It shall not be competent to the distrainers, appraisers, or *persons authorized to sell under Act* VII, 1839, to purchase any part of property distrained, either directly or indirectly. Persons offending against this prohibition shall be made to restore the property to the defaulter, or shall pay the full value thereof in the event of its being damaged or destroyed, or not forthcoming; and shall moreover forfeit the purchase money, which shall be appropriated to the liquidation of the arrear; and shall pay all costs of suit. Distrainers acting contrary to this prohibition shall, in addition to the above penalties, likewise forfeit the arrear for which the property may have been attached.—*Sec.* XXVI, *Reg.* XXVIII, 1802.

It shall not be competent to the defaulters, nor for persons in their behalf, to bid for, or purchase, their property distrained. —*Sec.* XXVII.—*Ibid.*

Persons farming or under-farming lands, in the name of their children, dependants, or others, or in the names of fictitious persons, and giving themselves as the ostensible sureties for the performance of the agreements, but retaining the actual management of the lands, being in fact themselves the under-farmers, or Ryots of such lands, shall, to all intents and purposes, be considered as the under-farmers, and Ryots of such lands; and their property shall be liable to be distrained and sold for arrears, in the same manner as if the engagements of such lands had stood in their own names.—*Sec.* XXVIII.—*Ibid.*

Land-holders, and farmers of land, shall not confine or inflict corporal punishment on under-farmers, tenants, or Ryots, or their sureties, for the purpose of enforcing payment of arrears of rent or revenue. Where land-holders, or farmers, may offend against this rule, persons so punished or confined shall be at liberty, either to prosecute the offenders for assault or imprisonment in the criminal Court, or to institute a suit in the udalut of the zillah, which Court shall award damages against such offenders according to the circumstances of the case, with costs of suit.—*Sec.* XXIX.—*Ibid.*

Upon the death of persons vested with the power of distraint by this regulation, their heirs, or successors, entitled to the arrears due to them, shall have power to distrain the property of the defaulters, and their sureties, in the cases authorized, for the recovery of the same, agreeably to this regulation. Managers of the estates of disqualified land-holders, and managers of undivided estates belonging to two or more proprietors, (all of whom do not come within the description of disqualified land-holders) shall also have the same powers, for the recovery of arrears of rent or revenue, as the proprietors of the estates committed to their charge would be entitled to exercise under this regulation, if intrusted with the management of their own estates; subject however to the several rules, restrictions, and penalties, herein specified.—*Sec.* XXX.—*Ibid.*

Distrainers attaching the property of persons employed in the manufacture of salt, shall give notice (as early as possible after making the attachment) to the salt agent; In such cases, the property shall not be sold, until sufficient time may have been given to enable the Company's officer to satisfy the demand previously to the day of sale.—*Sec.* XXXI, *Reg.* XXVIII, 1802.

Tahsildars, or persons authorized to sell distrained property under Act VII, 1839, shall *levy* a commission of one anna in the rupee on the amount sales of the property sold by them, to be deducted from the proceeds and charged to the account of the defaulter, with the other expences attending the attachment; *and such commission shall be carried to the credit of Government, Section V, Act VII,* 1839. But no such commission shall be drawn, or any expence charged to the defaulter, beyond the expences actually and necessarily incurred, in the event of the sale being stopped by the discharge of the arrear, or otherwise.—*Sec.* XXXII—*Ibid.*

Zemindars, proprietors, or farmers of land, to whom an arrear of rent or revenue may be due from dependent Talookdars, or other under-tenants of whatever denomination, which cannot be realized by distraining the personal property of such under-tenant, or of the sureties, shall have power to cause the immediate arrest of such defaulters, and sureties, in the manner following.—*Cl.* 1, *Sec.* XXXIV.—*Ibid.*

The proprietor or farmer to whom the arrear may be due, or his authorized agent, shall present a petition to the *subordinate* Judge of the Zillah, or in cases wherein there may be reason to apprehend the immediate elopement of the defaulter or his surety to the district moonsiff or Tahsildar, Sec. VI, Reg V, 1822, setting forth the arrear due from the defaulter, and praying that he and his surety may be taken into custody, unless the amount be paid. On the receipt of a petition to this effect by a district moonsiff Tahsildar, he shall cause such party to be arrested : and, unless payment be made of the arrear demanded, shall, within twenty-four hours, cause him to be conveyed, to the *subordinate* Judge of the zillah ; the Judge shall proceed thereupon, in like manner as is hereafter provided in the event of the petition being presented to him, and of the party being arrested by his own order. But Tahsildars or district moonsiffs shall not detain defaulters or sureties in custody, without sending them to the Judge, above twenty-four hours ; under penalty of being dismissed from office, and made liable to prosecution for false imprisonment; unless the party in arrest may, by a written application, desire the same, for the purpose of adjusting the arrear with the party causing the

---

Sec. XXXIV, Reg. XXVIII. of 1802:—See note on Cl. 1, Sec. II, Reg. V of 1822, explaining that these duties, that Clause notwithstanding, remain to the Judge. ·

arrest ; and unless the latter may assent thereto ; in which case, the written acquiescence shall be superscribed or endorsed on the application, with the signature of the party acquiescing, and shall specify the time for which such assent to stay process may have been given.—*Cl. 2. Sec.* XXXIV, *Reg.* XXVIII, 1802.

Where petitions for arrest may be presented in the first instance to the *subordinate* Judge, he shall receive them, either in, or out of Court, from authorized agents ; the Judge shall issue a dustuck or order for the arrest of such party, and bring him before the Court, unless he pay the arrear demanded ; and if such payment be not made on the dustuck being served, or within twenty-four hours afterwards, the officer charged with the dustuck shall convey the party to the Zillah Court; provided however that where the party arrested may, by a written application, request a longer time than twenty-four hours to adjust the demand against him, and where the party causing the arrest may, by a written superscription or endorsement on such application, acquiesce therein, the officer charged with the dustuck shall delay the execution accordingly : and where the party at whose instance the dustuck may have been issued may, by a written application, declare himself satisfied and desire the arrest to be withdrawn, it shall be withdrawn accordingly ; the officers charged with the dustuck being paid batta, according to the established rate of allowance to persons deputed with revenue process.—*Cl.* 3.—*Ibid.*

Where defaulters, or their sureties, may be brought to the Zillah Court under either of the two preceding clauses, the Judge shall call upon them to answer the demand. Where the demand or any part of it may be denied, the Judge shall enter into a summary enquiry of the merits of the case, by examining the vouchers and accounts of the parties ; it shall be also competent for the Judge to refer the case to the Collector of the district for adjustment, in causes of this description which they may not be able to try without delay. Land-holders, and farmers shall be free to appoint and employ Vakeels, duly empowered, to attend such enquiries before Collectors, or summary enquiries before Judges of udalut.—*Cl.* 4.—*Ibid.*

Where such cases may be referred to Collectors for adjustment, the Collectors shall make report to the Judges. After receiving such reports, or after completing their own enquiries without reference to Collectors, Judges shall discharge the defendants with full costs and damages, where it may appear that arrears have not been due. But where it may appear that the arrear demanded, or a considerable portion thereof, is justly due from the defendant, he shall be kept in custody, until the amount of the arrear and interest thereon at the rate of one per cent per mensem, with costs of suit, may be discharged ; or until the plaintiff make application to the Court for the release of the defendant. Plaintiffs shall pay to such defendants, whilst in confinement, the same allowance, for their subsistence, as is fixed for other prisoners in the jail of the udalut, not exceeding four annas, nor less than one anna per diem.— *Cl.* 5, *Sec.* XXXIV, *Reg.* XXVIII, 1802.

Where under-farmers or other under-tenants, arrested as above described, may not discharge the arrear demanded, and may in consequence be taken in custody to the Judge of the Court of udalut, the proprietors or farmers of land to whom such arrear may be owing shall have power to attach the farm or other tenure of such defaulters, and to manage the same by their own agents, until the rent due, and the further rent which may become due after attachment, with interest upon the whole arrear at the rate of one per cent per mensem, may have been liquidated: but in such cases of attachment, proprietors, or farmers, shall not exact more from the cultivators of the soil, and other descriptions of inferior tenantry, whose rents for the current year may have been payable to the defaulters, than the defaulters would have been entitled to receive from them if the attachment had not taken place ; and in the event of the defaulters making good the arrear due from them, with interest at the rate of one per cent per mensem, at any time within the current year, the attachment shall be withdrawn ; and an account rendered to them of the receipts and disbursements, during the continuance of such attachment.— *Cl.* 6.— *Ibid.*

Where arrears may not be liquidated within the current revenue year, proprietors, or farmers of land in which the defaulter's tenure may be included (if such farmer's lease extend beyond the current year) shall have power to make, at the commencement of the ensuing year, such provision for the future receipt of the rents from the lands tenanted by the defaulters as they may judge proper, consistently with the rights of the other persons concerned. Where defaulters may be holders of other tenures, which, by the title deeds, or by the established usage of the country, are transferable by sale or otherwise, it shall be competent to proprietors. or farmers of land to bring such transferable tenure to sale, by application to the Court of udalut, in satisfaction of the arrear of rent or revenue ; and the purchaser shall become the tenant of such transferable tenure. Where defaulters may be lease-holders, or other tenants, having right of occupancy only during payment of certain rents, without right of property or possession, the proprietors of whom such tenures may be held, or the farmers, or other persons to whom such proprietors may have leased or committed their rights, shall have the right of ousting the defaulting tenants from the tenure. In the several cases enumerated in this clause (with the exception of that where a sale -of landed property may be desired) proprietors, and farmers of land shall be free to exercise the powers appertaining to them, without previous application to the Courts of Judicature; but they shall be responsible for all acts done by them, or by their agents, which may exceed those powers, and infringe the rights of under tenants. —*Cl.* 7, *Sec.* XXXIV, *Reg.* XXVIII, 1802.

Provided that no part of this regulation shall be construed to deprive Zemindars, and other land-holders, of the power of summoning, and if necessary, of compelling the attendance of their tenants for the adjustment of their rents, or of measuring lands within their respective estates which may be liable to measurement, under the conditions upon which such lands may have been leased or held, or for any other lawful purpose. For the regular exercise of such rights and powers, land-holders shall not be compellable to make previous application to the Courts of Judicature; and persons opposing them therein will, on proof in the Court of udalut, be liable to full damages and costs, besides being subject to penalty for breach of the peace in the Criminal Courts: but land-holders or their agents shall be answerable for abuse of the powers hereby vested in them; and on proof thereof, by the party aggrieved, in the Courts of udalut, shall be liable to full costs and damages, besides a fine to Government according to the circumstances of the case.—*Cl.* 8.—*Ibid.*

Persons confined under the fifth clause of the preceding section, and desirous of bringing the demand upon them to a regular judicial investigation and decision in the Court of udalut, shall be free to institute suits against the land-holders, or farmers, at whose instance they may have been so confined: for this purpose, in cases where the amount of arrear denied by such persons may be found upon trial not to have been due, judgment for full costs and damages against the party claiming such amount shall be given, with interest at the rate of one per cent per mensem, upon the amount of all monies paid in discharge of the demand.—*Sec.* XXXV.—*Ibid.*

Proprietors and farmers of land whose claims to arrears of rent or revenue may be rejected by the *subordinate* Judge of the zillah, on the summary enquiry provided by this regulation, shall also be free to institute regular suits in the Court of udalut for the recovery thereof; and where, on trial, the amount claimed by proprietors or farmers may be found to have been due, when judgment on the summary process was given against them in the first instance, they shall be entitled to recover the monies paid by them for costs, damages, or interest, under such judgment; and the Court shall further give a decree for the arrears of rent or revenue due to such proprietors or farmers, with interest at the rate of one per cent per mensem, and full costs incurred, as well on the summary enquiry, as on the regular suit.—*Sec.* XXXVI, *Reg.* XXVIII, 1802.

In respect that persons considering themselves aggrieved by the summary suits, as authorized under this regulation, can have remedy by a regular suit in the *subordinate* Zillah Court, no appeal shall lie to the *zillah civil* Court on such summary judgment.— *Sec.* XXXVII.—*Ibid.*

The rules laid down in the preceding sections for the recovery of arrears of rent or revenue due to proprietors, and farmers of land, shall be applicable to the managers of estates of disqualified land-holders, and of joint undivided estates; as well as to Collectors, or other public officers, holding lands in attachment, or making a khas collection on the part of Government, where no settlement may have been made with any proprietor, or farmer.—*Sec.* XXXVIII.—*Ibid.*

Where gomastahs, agents, servants, or officers, of persons vested with the power of distraint may attach, or cause to be sold, the property of under-farmers, or ryots, or of their sureties, or may do any act in the attachment or sale of such property contrary to this regulation, the parties aggrieved shall have remedy against the principals for such illegal attachment, sale, or act, whether the same may have taken place, or been done, by the orders, or with the knowledge of such principals, or not; provided that nothing contained in this section shall extend to subject distrainers to imprisonment, in the event of persons deputed by them to attach property entering the zenana or apartments of women, or breaking open a dwelling house, in any other manner than is provided in this regulation; unless it may be proved that such acts had been done by the order, or with the consent or knowledge, of such distrainer.—*Sec.* XXXIX.—*Ibid.*

Nothing contained in this Regulation shall be construed to prevent persons whose property may have been distrained or sold, from instituting suits in the Zillah Court of udalut against the distrainer, for injury sustained; nor to prevent land-holders, for farmers of land, or other persons vested with the power of distraint, from prosecuting, in the Zillah Court of udalut, for arrears due to them from under-farmers, or ryots, or their sureties. Where they may prefer the mode of procedure in the Zillah Court, to that of distraining personal property for the recovery of arrears, proprietors, or farmers of land shall be free to do so.—*Sec.* XL, *Reg.* XXVIII, 1802.

Suits instituted under this Regulation shall be heard, and determined, previously to any other suits which may be depending at the time of such institution.—*Sec.* XLI.—*Ibid.*

Zemindars, and other land-holders, and farmers of land, shall be free to delegate to their naibs, gomastahs, and other agents employed in the collection of their rents and revenues, the power of distraining, on their behalf, in the mode prescribed by this regulation; and the naibs, gomastahs, and other agents, to whom such power may be delegated by their principals, shall be free to proceed for the recovery of arrears of rent and revenue due to their constituents, in the same manner as the latter are authorized to proceed; subject however to their responsibility, in addition to that of their principals, for deviation from the regulations. But neither the land-holders, and farmers of land themselves, nor their agents, shall be liable to the penalties prescribed for a deviation from the regulations relative to the distraining for land-rents, unless such deviation may appear to have been wilful and intentional, or to have proceeded from gross neglect, and inattention to the rules prescribed. Where no such wilful deviation or neglect may appear, satisfaction shall be decreed to the party aggrieved for the actual damage only sustained, by reason of deviation from the prescribed process; and judgment shall not be given for such damages, where distrainers may shew that sufficient amends to the party injured had been tendered, as soon as the irregularity on the proceedings had been discovered, or at any time before the action for damages had been brought, and that such tender had been refused.—*Sec.* XLII.—*Ibid.*

Proprietors, and farmers of land, shall enter into agreements with the inhabitants and cultivators of land, on the terms on which they respectively occupy such lands; and the contracting parties shall be mutually bound to exchange their engagements in writing; the engagements of the proprietor being denominated, "Pottah," and the engagement of the Ryot being denominated "Mochulka."—*Sec.* II, *Reg.* XXX, 1802.

Sec. XLI, Reg. XXVIII of 1802.—From the wording of this Section the S. U. inferred in their letter to Government, 20th December 1824—that suits brought for recovery of penalties under this Regulation, had all been rightly treated as *regular* suits—but it might perhaps be argued that its provisions were intended to have reference only to the *regular* suits permitted and prescribed by Sections XXXV and XL, and not to the other cases, which the framers of the Regulation intended to be *summarily* conducted.

Pottahs and mochulkas shall be exchanged within six months, calculating from the time of the permanent assessment being fixed.—*Sec.* III, *Reg.* XXX, 1802.

Pottahs and mochulkas may be of four kinds, 1st, for the rent of villages in gross sums of money; 2dly, for a division of the produce of land; 3dly, for lands on which a money rent is assessed; 4thly, for lands charged with a grain rent.—*Cl.* 1, *Sec.* IV.—*Ibid.*

Pottahs and mochulkas shall contain the date of the month, and the year, on which they may be executed; the names and situation of the contracting parties.—*Cl.* 2.—*Ibid.*

Pottahs for village rents, shall contain the name of the village; the extent of the lands therein; the amount of the rent per annum; the period of the kists, which proprietors or farmers of land shall be compellable to adjust according to the time of reaping or of selling the produce of the land; and the coin in which the rent is to be paid.—*Cl.* 3.—*Ibid.*

Pottahs for the division of the produce of land shall be drawn according to the form prescribed in clause the third; but, in lieu of the money rent, such Pottahs shall specify the extent of the land, which the under-tenant, under-farmer, or Ryot, may engage to cultivate; and the rate of the cultivator's share of the different kinds of grain cultivated and produced.—*Cl.* 4.—*Ibid.*

Pottahs for lands on which a money rent is assessed shall, in addition to the items described in clause third, specify the rate of assessment on such lands, according to the land measure in use; and the rents on each description of land, or grain, as the usage may be.—*Cl.* 5.—*Ibid.*

Pottahs for lands charged with a grain rent, shall, in addition to the items prescribed by clause third, state the specific quantity of land occupied under this description of rent; the specific quantity of grain to be rendered; and the species of grain.—*Cl.* 6.—*Ibid.*

Pottahs, and mochulkas, shall be regularly signed and registered by the Curnum of the village, in which the lands engaged for are situated.—*Sec.* V.—*Ibid.*

Where the rents or revenues of land, payable either in money or kind to the proprietor, may have been collected under various denominations, in addition to that of the proprietor's share, such as canongoe, and cavelly russooms, or other charges, they shall be consolidated in the pottahs into one specific sum of money or quantity of grain; and in the event of claims being instituted by proprietors of land, on engagements in which the rents or revenues may not be so consolidated, such claimants shall be non-

suited with costs, before the udalut of the zillah ; from and after
the expiration of two years, subsequently to the time when the
permanent assessment of the land revenue may have been fixed.—
Sec. VI, *Reg.* XXX, 1802.

Proprietors, or farmers of land, shall not levy any new assessment or tax on the Ryots, under any name, or under any pretence : exactions, other than those consolidated in the pottah, or
otherwise authorized by the Government, shall, upon proof, *before
the collector—Cl.* 1, *Sec.* II. *Reg.* V, 1822,—subject the proprietor
or farmer to a penalty equal to three times the amount of each
exaction.—*Sec.* VII.—*Ibid.*

Whenever the penalties referred to in Sec. VII, Reg. XXX of
1802, shall be levied, the amount of the exaction shall be returned to the ryot, together with such further portion of the penalty
as may appear a reasonable compensation for the injury sustained :
provided however that such penalties shall be held in deposit
during the period limited for appeal by Cl. 1, Sec. XVI of this
Regulation.—*Sec.* VII, *Reg.* V, 1822.

Under-farmers and cultivators of land shall be free to demand,
of proprietors or farmers of land, pottahs for the descriptions of
land they may respectively occupy ; and where proprietors or
farmers of land may refuse, or delay, to execute, or cause to be
executed, pottahs so demanded, such proprietors or farmers of
land shall, after the expiration of six months, (calculating from
the settlement of the permanent land revenue on their estates) be
liable to prosecution *before the collector Cl.* 1, *Sec.* II, *Reg.* V *of*
1822 ; and shall, on proof of such refusal or delay, be also liable
to pay such damages as the collector shall adjudge to be equal to
the trouble and expence incurred by the under-farmers, or cultivators, in consequence of such refusal or delay.—*Sec.* VIII, *Reg.*
XXX, 1802.

Where disputes may arise respecting rates of assessment in
money, or of division in kind, the rates shall be determined according to the rates prevailing in the cultivated lands, in the year
preceding the assessment of the permanent jummah on such
lands ; or where those rates may not be ascertainable, according
to the rates established for lands of the same description and
quality as those, respecting which the dispute may arise—*Sec.*
IX,—*Ibid.*

Sec. VII, Reg. XXX of 1802.—Sec. VII, Reg. V of 1822, makes it clear that authority
in *this* case has been transferred to the Collector.
Sec. VIII, Reg. XXX of 1802.—And it would appear to be in this instance also, for
Cl. 2, Sec. VIII, Reg. V of 1822, authorizes Collectors to inflict, in the cases therein
referred to, the *same* penalty as in Sec. VIII, Reg. XXX of 1802.

Where under-farmers or ryots may refuse to exchange mutual engagements in writing, with proprietors or farmers of land, defining the terms on which such under-farmers or ryots are to hold their lands ; and may persist in such refusal, for the space of one month after the prescribed pottahs may have been offered, in presence of witnesses, by the proprietors or farmers of land such proprietors or farmers of land shall have power—*after making application to the Collector and obtaining his leave for that purpose—Cl. 1, Sec. VIII, Reg. V of 1822,*—to grant the lands of the under-farmers or ryots so refusing to other persons. —*Sec. X, Reg. XXX, 1802.*

If the collector on examination find the rates of the pottah tendered by the proprietor or farmer to be just and correct, the under-farmer or ryot shall be ejected under the Collector's order, unless he assent to the terms ; but if the rate shall exceed the just rate prescribed, an order shall be issued by the Collector to the proprietor or farmer prohibiting the ejectment, and requiring the issue of a pottah within one month from the delivery of the order to him, under penalty for delay as provided in Section VIII, Regulation XXX of 1802.—*Cl. 2, Sec. VIII, Reg. V, 1822.*

Discharges of rent in money, or in kind, received by proprietors or farmers of land, over and above the amount or quantity which may have been specified in the mochulka of the persons paying the same, shall be considered to have been extorted; and discharges, so taken by extortion, shall be repaid, together with a penalty of double the amount of the value, with costs.—*Sec. XI, Reg. XXX, 1802.*

Pottahs executed for one year shall be renewable at the expiration of the Fusly ; but shall be considered in force until renewed. Unless pottahs be renewed within two months after the commencement of the ensuing Fusly, they shall be considered in force, and binding, on the respective parties throughout the Fusly ; provided such delay may not have been produced by the actual refusal of either party to execute the engagement.—*Sec. XII.—Ibid.*

Where estates, or parts of estates, may be sold or transferred, for the liquidation of arrears of rents or revenues due to Government, such pottahs as may have been granted by the former proprietor shall cease to have effect, at the end of the Fusly in which such lands may be sold ; and new pottahs shall be issued by the purchasers of such estates, from the commencement of the following Fusly.—*Sec. XIII.—Ibid.*

Under-tenants, under-farmers, and Ryots, shall be entitled to receipts from proprietors or farmers of land, for all discharges made in money, or in kind ; and where they may have paid the whole rent or revenue, proprietors and farmers of land shall grant to them receipts in full: persons to whom receipts may be refused shall, on proof of the same in the udalut of the zillah, be entitled to, and shall receive, damages from the party refusing such receipts, to an amount equal to double the sum paid, with costs of suit.—*Sec.* XIV, *Reg.* XXX, 1802.

Nothing contained in this regulation shall be construed to prohibit proprietors of land from granting, without the sanction of Government, or its officers, to persons not being British subjects, or Europeans, or descendants from Europeans, leases or pottahs of land, for any term of years, or in perpetuity, on such terms as may be mutually agreed, for the erecting of dwelling houses, or buildings for carrying on manufactures, or other purposes ; and for offices attached to such houses, or buildings, or for gardens ; nor from granting pottahs for clearing and bringing waste lands into cultivation. Pottahs bonâ fide granted for these purposes shall be binding on all future proprietors, notwithstanding the estates including such lands may have been sold to liquidate arrears of revenue due to Government ; unless it may be proved in a Court of Judicature that the lands were not waste when granted in lease, but collusively granted, or fraudulently obtained. —*Sec.* XV.—*Ibid.*

In cases of claims to lands or crops, in districts permanently settled or otherwise, the validity of which claims may depend on the determination of an uncertain and disputed boundary or landmark, and also in cases of disputes respecting the occupying, cultivating and irrigating of land which may arise between the proprietors, or renters and their ryots, in those districts only where the land revenue is fixed, either permanently or for a term of years, persons having such claims may prefer them in person or by vakeel, to the collector of the zillah in which the lands may be situated.—*Cl.* 1, *Sec.* IV, *Reg.* XII, 1816.

The plaint, if for land shall contain as accurate a description as can be obtained of the land claimed, its position, boundaries, extent, and the value of its estimated annual produce ; also whether it be subject to the payment of rent or revenue, or whether it be exempt from any charge on these accounts; also the time when the cause of action arose, the name and residence of the person or persons complained against, and all material circumstances which may elucidate the transaction.— *Cl* 2.—*Ibid.*

If the plaint be for water, it shall with regard to the land to be watered, state the above particulars, and in addition thereto the custom of the village relative to the irrigation of the land in question.—*Cl. 3, Sec. IV, Reg.* XII, 1816.

The provisions of Sec. IV, Reg. XII, 1816, shall be extended to all disputes between ryot and ryot, respecting the occupying, cultivating and irrigating of lands in districts whether permanently settled or otherwise.—*Sec.* XVIII, *Reg.* V, 1822.

The collector on receiving a complaint preferred under the preceding Section, shall issue a summons to the, defendant, containing a short abstract of the complaint, and shall require the defendant to appear at the cutcherry of the collector, in person or by vakeel, on a day specified, to make answer to the complaint. The summons shall be attested by the seal of the collector and his official signature, or that of his assistant, and shall be served by a single peon of the collector's establishment.—*Cl.* 1, *Sec.* V, *Reg.* XII, 1816.

The collector's peon shall require the defendant to affix his signature to the summons in acknowledgment of its having been duly served, and in the event of the defendant refusing to affix his signature thereto, the peon shall call upon some of the village officers or neighbours of the defendant, to witness such refusal and to attest the endorsement of it, which he shall make on the summons and shall return the same to the collector on or before the day fixed for such return.—*Cl. 2.—Ibid.*

If a defendant against whom a summons may issue shall abscond, or is not after diligent search to be found, or shall shut himself up in his own, or in any house or building, or retire to any place, so that the process cannot be served upon him, and the peon shall return that on such account he has not been able to serve or execute the process, or if he shall refuse to acknowledge the service of the summons, on return being made in the mode prescribed in the preceding Clause, the collector shall cause a writing in the language of the district, to be stuck up in some conspicuous part of his cutcherry, containing a copy of the summons and a notice that if the party shall not appear on a day to be specified (which shall not be less than fifteen days from the time that the notice may be fixed up), the collector will proceed without further notice to refer the cause with the consent of the plaintiff, to be tried and determined by a punchayet of the district, in which the disputed lands may be situated, without the appearance or answer of the defendant. The collector shall likewise order a copy of the summons and notice to be fixed up with all practicable despatch on the outer door of the house in which the defendant may have usually dwelt, or in some conspicuous place in the village, or other place in which he may have generally resided. The peon serving the summons shall return the order with an endorsement, stating at what times and places the summons may have been fixed up.—*Cl.* 3, *Sec.* V, *Reg.* XII, 1816.

If the defendant shall appear by the time limited in the notice, the collector shall proceed to investigate the cause of his absence, or the circumstance of his refusal to sign the summons, and if it shall appear to the satisfaction of the collector, that the conduct of the defendant has been contemptuous, he is empowered to punish such contempt by imposing a fine on the defendant, according to the circumstances of the case, not exceeding ten rupees, and if such fine be not immediately paid, or security given for the payment within a reasonable time, the collector shall punish such defendant by committing him to the zillah jail or by keeping him in custody in the cutcherry or village choultry for a period not in any case exceeding fifteen days, or until the fine shall be paid.— *Cl.* 4.—*Ibid.*

On the appearance of the defendant, if he shall appear according to the first summons or by the time limited in the notice, the collector shall cause the plaint to be read over to the defendant in presence of the plaintiff, and shall demand whether he admit, or deny the truth of the complaint. If the defendant shall acquiesce in the truth of the complaint, the collector shall record such acquiescence at the foot of the plaint and require the defendant to attest the same with his signature in the presence of witnesses, not being servants of the collector's establishment, who shall also attest the same, and the document shall be countersigned by the collector, who shall return the document to the complainant, together with an order to the tahsildar or principal native revenue officer of the district, or village moonsiff, to transfer the lands described in the plaint to the plaintiff, or if the plaint include crops grown on such lands, to cause the crops or the value of them to be restored to the plaintiff by the defendant, or if the plaint be for water, to order the water to be distributed as required in the plaint, and no other proceedings shall be necessary in the cause.—*Cl.* 5.—*Ibid.*

If the defendant shall deny the truth of the plaint, the collector shall enquire of the parties whether they mutually consent to have the cause investigated and decided by a village punchayet, and upon their agreeing in writing to have the matter investigated and decided by the punchayet of any particular village, the collector shall immediately forward the petition or plaint with an order to the moonsiff of that village to assemble a punchayet without delay, to investigate and determine the suit.—*Cl.* 6.—*Ibid.*

If either the plaintiff or defendant shall object to the reference of the cause to be tried and determined by a village punchayet, and either of them shall desire in writing that it may be referred to be tried and decided by a district punchayet, the collector, whether the other party agree to such reference or not, shall forward the plaint to the moonsiff of the district in which the disputed property may be situated, with an order to assemble a punchayet within fifteen days from the receipt of such order, to investigate and determine the suit.—*Cl. 7, Sec. V, Reg.* XII, 1816.

If neither of the parties shall agree to the reference of the suit to a district punchayet, the suit shall be dismissed, and the parties shall be at liberty to seek redress from the zillah court or any competent jurisdiction.—*Cl. 8.—Ibid.*

Village and district punchayets are hereby authorized to hear and determine such suits as may be referred to them by the collectors of zillahs under this Regulation, through the village and district moonsiffs.—*Sec. II.—Ibid.*

Plaintiffs and defendants shall be allowed to employ a relative, a servant or a dependant to act in their behalf in suits which may be brought before the collectors of zillahs under this Regulation, under the same provisions as are prescribed by Clauses second and third, Section XIV, Regulation VI, 1816, for suits before the district moonsiffs.—*Sec. III.—Ibid.*

The punchayets shall be assembled according to the rules prescribed for assembling village and district punchayets, and their proceedings, in cases referred under this Regulation, shall be conducted according to the general rules enacted in Regulations V and VII, 1816, for their guidance, with the following qualifications.—*Cl. 1, Sec. VI.—Ibid.*

When only one of the parties shall appear before the district moonsiff, the punchayet shall be formed upon the challenge of such party only, and shall proceed to try the suit without requiring the agreement specified in Clause second, Section IV, Regulation VII, 1816 —*Cl. 2.—Ibid.*

When the decree has been framed and two copies of it prepared, it shall be read in the presence of the parties, and the two copies shall be sealed up in a packet and delivered to the moonsiff, who shall forward it to the collector sealed as he received it.—*Cl. 3.—Ibid.*

Decrees of the village and district punchayets in suits which may be referred to them by the collectors under this Regulation, shall not be carried into execution until confirmed by the collector, nor shall they be set aside for any other cause than gross partiality, on the part of the punchayet.—*Cl. 4.—Ibid.*

The collector shall detain the packet in the state in which he received it, for twenty days, and if in that time no charge of gross partiality shall be preferred by either party against the punchayet, he shall open the packet and confirm the decision, by affixing his seal and signature to each of the two copies, and he shall return them to the moonsiff from whom he received them.—*Sec.* VII, *Reg.* XII, 1816.

The moonsiff, on receiving the copies of the decree confirmed by the collector, shall summon the parties and deliver to each of them a copy of the decree.—*Cl.* 1, *Sec.* VIII.—*Ibid.*

If either the plaintiff or defendant shall fail to appear in person or by vakeel to receive a copy of the decree, or having attended shall refuse to receive a copy, the moonsiff shall cause to be endorsed on the copy intended for such party, such omission or refusal and the date. The moonsiff shall attest the same with his signature, which shall be witnessed by any two credible witnesses. The copy so endorsed shall be deposited in the records of the district moonsiff or the village curnum as the case may be, to be delivered to the party afterwards claiming it.—*Cl.* 2.—*Ibid.*

If either of the parties shall, within the prescribed period of twenty days, charge the punchayet with gross partiality, and if the partiality charged against the punchayet shall be established to the satisfaction of the collector, by the oaths *or solemn affirmations*, of two credible witnesses at the least, he shall in every case, whatever the amount or value of the suit may be, submit his proceedings, with his opinion on the case, to the *civil judge of the zillah*, who, provided the charge be proved by such proceedings to *his* satisfaction, shall annul the decision, and the parties shall be at liberty to have recourse to another punchayet or to any other competent jurisdiction.—*Cl.* 1, *Sec.* IX.—*Ibid.*

Provided however that where the decision of a second punchayet shall agree with the decision of a former punchayet in the same suit it shall be final.—*Cl.* 2.—*Ibid.*

If the partiality charged against the punchayet shall not be proved to the satisfaction of the collector, he shall confirm the decree as prescribed in Sec. VII, of this Regulation, and shall levy a fine from the party making such groundless charge not exceeding one hundred rupees.—*Cl.* 3.—*Ibid.*

Decrees of village and district punchayets in cases referred to them under this Regulation, shall be carried into execution on the written application of the party in whose favor the decree may be given, by the collector, or by the tahsildar or principal native revenue officer of the district, by causing the boundary, when the suit relates to a disputed boundary, to be marked out in the presence of the village moonsiff and curnum, and two or more of the principal inhabitants ; and in all other cases, by causing the land to be given up, or the water to be distributed, as prescribed by the decree.—*Sec.* X, *Reg.* XII, 1816.

Suits instituted before the collectors under this Regulation, shall be exempt from all stamp duties, and shall be liable only to such charges as are specified in Regulation V, of 1816, if decided by a village punchayet, or to such charges as are specified in Regulation VII, of 1816, if decided by a district punchayet.—*Sec.* XI.—*Ibid.*

The village and district moonsiffs shall include in their monthly reports all decisions of punchayets in suits referred to them under this Regulation.—*Sec.* XII.—*Ibid.*

A copy of this Regulation shall be lodged with and preserved by each village curnum for the information of the village moonsiffs.—*Sec.* XIII.—*Ibid.*

The collector shall have authority to refer all disputes respecting arrears of rent or revenue, or respecting rates of assessment in money or kind, or of division in kind, as well as all questions of the right of occupancy or possession of lands or crops, which may be brought before him under this Regulation, to a district or village punchayet for decision ; provided both parties agree to that mode of settlement.—*Cl.* 1, *Sec.* XV, *Reg.* V, 1822.

The collector shall have authority in cases of disputes which may be brought before him under this Regulation to exercise the powers vested in village and district moonsiffs under Regulations V and VII, of 1816.—*Cl. 2.—Ibid.*

When suits respecting disputed lands and crops may be referred to a punchayet, the collector on the application of either party, shall have authority to put one party immediately in possession and maintain him in it till a decision shall be given.—*Sec.* XVII.—*Ibid.*

Collectors of the land revenue, *their subordinates or assistants, Sec.* III, *Reg.* VII, 1828—are hereby authorized to take primary cognizance of all cases, in which persons of any of the several descriptions hereinafter specified shall be accused, or suspected of having wilfully committed, or allowed to be committed, any of the acts of malversation particularized in Clause second of this Section ; and on proof of the guilt of the accused or suspected per-

Cl. 1, Sec. XV, Reg. V, of 1822.—The S. U. in para. 25, of their letter of 20th December 1824 above quoted, expressed their opinion " that questions involving the determina-" tion of *permanent* right were intended by this Clause to be brought under the cogniz-" ance of the Collector."

Cl. 2, Sec. XV, Reg. V, of 1822.—That is, he can assemble the Punchayet, &c.

sons, to inflict on them such punishments as by this Regulation the said collectors are authorized to adjudge.—*Cl.* 1, *Sec.* II, *Reg.* IX, 1822.

The several classes of the offences cognizable by collectors under this Regulation, are declared to be as follows, viz.:

1st. Exacting or corruptly receiving either directly or through the means or agency of any other person, any money or other valuable consideration, for doing or procuring to be done any public or official act for which no such payment or gift could be lawfully demanded or received ; or for the purpose, or under pretence of obtaining or securing some undue gain, benefit or advantage, to the giver of such money or other valuable consideration.

2d. Levying extra and unauthorized cesses or extra collections of any kind not sanctioned by the Regulations, nor by the orders of Government, and intended for the private and personal use and profit of the persons levying or causing the same to be levied.

3d. Embezzling or fraudulently misappropriating the public money.   •

4th. Making false or fraudulent entries in the public accounts or other records, either in regard to the receipt or expenditure of public money in any of the departments under the collector's superintendence, or concerning the extent, value, classification or assessment of land.

5th. Knowingly and wilfully falsifying, destroying, or concealing public accounts or vouchers or documents of any kind immediately relating to the receipt or expenditure of the public money.—*Cl.* 2.—*Ibid.*

The classes or descriptions of persons in regard to whom the collectors shall have authority to exercise the powers of summary investigation, decision and punishment, granted to them by this Regulation, are declared to be as follows, viz. :

1st. All the native servants of the collector's public establishments.

2d. All head inhabitants, curnums and their Gomastahs or persons doing the duty for them, and all other village officers and servants within their respective collectorates.

3d. All persons not on the public establishment, whether being in the private service of a collector, sub-collector, or assistant to a collector, and pretending to act under his or their authority, or whether assuming the character of public officers, or acting or pretending to act under the authority or on the behalf of revenue servants or village officers, who shall in any way interfere in the collection or disbursement of the public money, or who shall demand or receive money as public revenue, or as 'for revenue purposes, or shall exact or receive money or other valuable consideration under pretence of procuring some public act to be done, or some undue advantage to be given by public officers to the persons from whom such money or other valuable consideration shall have been taken.—*Cl. 3, Sec. II, Reg. IX, 1822.*

The jurisdiction vested in collectors, subordinate collectors, and assistant collectors by Regs. IX, of 1822, and VII, of 1828, of the Madras code, in cases of embezzlement of public money, and of the falsification, destruction, or concealment of any public account, record, voucher, or document relating to public money, shall extend to cases of the embezzlement of any public property, or the falsification, destruction, or concealment of any public account, record, voucher, or document relating to any public property, by any person of any of the classes described in the third Clause of Section II, of the said Regulation IX, of 1822.—*Sec. I, Act XXXVI, of 1837.*

All provisions of either of the said Regulations IX, of 1822, and. VII, of 1828, which apply to cases of the embezzling any public money, shall apply to cases of the embezzling any public property whatever, by persons of any of the classes described in the third Clause of Section II of the said Regulation IX, of 1822 ; and all provisions of either of these Regulations, which apply to the falsification, destruction, or concealment of any public account, record, voucher, or document, relating to public money, shall apply to cases of the falsification, destruction, or concealment of any public account, record, voucher or document, relating to any public property whatever, by persons of any of the said classes.—*Sec. II.—Ibid.*

Collectors shall have power to summon before them as witnesses, all persons whose evidence may appear necessary to the due investigation of the cases referred to in this Regulation, as well for as against the accused or suspected persons, and to require the production of documentary evidence. The summonses to be issued by collectors for this purpose shall bear their official seal and signature, and shall specify the time and place of the witnesses attendance, and if reference to documentary evidence be required, the summonses shall contain a requisition to the witnesses in whose possession they may be, to bring such documents along with them.—*Cl. 1, Sec. III, Reg. IX, 1822.*

If any person, after being duly summoned, shall not attend at the time and place appointed, or having attended and taken the oath *or solemn affirmation* required, shall refuse to give evidence, the collector, if it be proved to his satisfaction that the evidence of the person not attending, or refusing to give evidence, is material to the case, shall communicate the same by means of the government pleader, to the *subordinate* judge of the zillah to the jurisdiction of which such person may be amenable ; *who* is hereby directed and required to proceed against such person not attending or refusing to give evidence, in the same manner as if he had not attended or had refused to give evidence in *his own* court.—*Cl.* 2, *Sec.* III, *Reg.* IX, 1822.

If any witness whose evidence is required by a collector shall reside out of the jurisdiction of the zillah to which the collector is amenable, the collector shall transmit written interrogatories to the *subordinate* judge of the zillah in whose jurisdiction the witness may reside, who shall procure the written answers of the witness to such interrogatories, in the manner prescribed *by Act* VII, 1841, and shall return the same to the collector ; whenever a witness may be examined on interrogatories in conformity with the foregoing rule, whether on behalf of the Government or of the accused, the opposite party shall have the right of transmitting cross interrogatories at the same time, and the answers of the witness thereto shall be taken and returned in like manner.—*Cl.* 3. —*Ibid.*

The investigations which collectors are authorized to make under this Regulation shall be summary. Witnesses shall be examined on oath, *or solemn affirmation, Act* V, 1840. All documents produced in evidence shall be endorsed by the collector with his signature or initials, and marked with the date of their production ; a summary of the defence shall be recorded, and the decision of the collector, with a brief statement of the grounds on which it is formed, shall be entered on the proceedings.—*Sec.* IV.—*Ibid.*

Collectors will transmit such periodical or occasional reports of judgments passed under Section IV, Reg. IX, 1822, as the Board of Revenue may direct ; and it shall be competent to the Board of Revenue, whenever they may see fit, to order that any such judgment be not carried into execution, and to pass such further order on the case as to them may seem equitable and just.—*Cl.* 2, *Sec.* II, *Reg.* III, 1823.

When persons of any of the descriptions mentioned in Clause third, Section II, of this Regulation, shall be convicted before a collector, on an inquiry conducted under this Regulation, of any of the offences of the 1st, 2d or 3d class specified in Clause second of that Section, the collector shall have authority to sentence them to pay any sum not exceeding twice the amount of the money ascertained to have been extorted, unduly received, embezzled or misappropriated.—*Cl.* 1, *Sec.* V, *Reg.* IX, 1822.

After a judgment has been passed by a collector for the payment of money under the foregoing Clause, the person against whom such judgment has passed shall be kept in custody until that judgment shall have been satisfied, first, in the collector's cutcherry, and afterwards, if necessary, in the zillah jail as hereinafter provided.—*Cl.* 2.—*Ibid.*

The judgments of collectors for the recovery of money under the preceding Clause shall be executed in the same manner as decrees of the courts of udalut by a warrant under the official seal and signature of the collector which shall specify the name of the person, against whom the judgment has passed, the date of the judgment on the collector's proceedings, and the amount to be levied. In the execution of this warrant, the property of the defaulter shall be seized wherever, or in whose possession soever it may be found. If property, which there is good reason to believe belongs to the defaulter, be claimed by any other person, the same shall nevertheless be attached by the officer charged with the execution of the warrant. If the property so attached be moveable, it shall be brought before the collector, or if not moveable, a full report thereof shall be made to the collector who will hold a summary inquiry on the claim preferred, or refer such inquiry to a punchayet. If the property be proved to belong *bona fide* to the defaulter, a particular account of its nature and value shall be entered on the collector's proceedings, after which he shall order it to be sold in like manner as the rest of the property, attached under the warrant of execution.—*Cl.* 3.—*Ibid.*

When any of the beforementioned persons shall be convicted of any of the offences of the 4th and 5th class specified in Clause second, Section II of this Regulation, the collector shall impose such fine not exceeding 500 rupees, as may appear reasonable, and in default of payment of such fine, he shall further sentence the offender to imprisonment for a period not exceeding 12 months, or until the said fine shall have been paid.—*Cl.* 4.—*Ibid.*

Collectors are empowered, at their discretion, to refer for investigation to their sheristadars and deputy sheristadars, when detached from the huzzoor cutcherry, and also to their tahsildars, within their respective tahsildaries, all cases of a petty nature cognizable by themselves under Regulation IX, 1822.—*Cl.* 1, *Sec.* IV, *Reg.* VII, 1828.

Native officers employed under the preceding Clause shall have the same powers as are granted to collectors by Clause first, Section III, Regulation IX, 1822; but witnesses shall not be examined by them on oath, *or solemn affirmation.—Cl. 2, Sec. IV, Reg. VII, 1828.*

If any person duly summoned by them shall not attend as required, or attending shall refuse to give evidence, or if any person whose evidence is required shall reside out of the limits of the collectorate, the native officer employed shall report the circumstance to the collector, who shall proceed thereupon in the manner required by Clauses second and third, Section III, Regulation IX, 1822. —*Cl. 3.—Ibid.*

Native officers employed under this Section shall take down in writing all the evidence given before them, and shall transmit their original proceedings to the collector; who shall thereupon pass sentence, or order further evidence to be taken, if he deem it necessary; provided always, that collectors shall not have authority to pass sentence against a party convicted on an inquiry by any of the native officers abovementioned of any of the offences of the 1st, 2d or 3d class specified in Clause second, Section II, Regulation IX, 1822, adjudging him to pay a sum exceeding 50 rupees, or to impose a fine exceeding that amount upon a party convicted, on such an inquiry, of any of the offences of the 4th or 5th class specified in the same Clause and Section.—*Cl. 4.—Ibid.*

In cases where no examination of witnesses may be necessary, as where money actually delivered in charge to a public servant has been embezzled or is not forthcoming when called for, and the amount embezzled has been clearly ascertained by reference to the public accounts of the cutcherry, collectors shall make in writing a demand of the specific amount due by such public servant, and on his refusing or neglecting to satisfy the demand, shall proceed to recover the amount by distraint and sale of the defaulter's property, and if necessary, by imprisonment of the defaulter's person, in the same manner as for the recovery of arrears of revenue.—*Sec. VI, Reg. IX, 1822.*

Whenever a collector shall be about to institute an inquiry under this Regulation, if he shall have good reason to believe that the accused or suspected person has concealed or collusively transferred, or is about to conceal or collusively transfer his property for the purpose of evading such order or judgment as may eventually be passed after such enquiry, the collector is hereby authorized to call on such person to give security to such amount as he may consider sufficient to provide for the fulfilment of the judgment that may be eventually passed; and in default of good and sufficient security being given as required, he shall be authorized to attach the property of the accused or suspected person, and to

hold the same in attachment until judgment shall have been passed in the said inquiry. The warrant of attachment to be issued
in such cases shall follow the property of the accused or suspected
person wherever, or in whose possession soever it may be found;
in the event of property seized under this Section being claimed
by any other person, the collector shall proceed as directed in like
cases in Clause third, Sec. V, of this Regulation.—*Sec.* VII, *Reg.*
IX, 1822.

In all cases where an accused or suspected person has refused or
neglected to deposit security according to the collector's requisition
as provided in Sec. VII, and in all cases where a judgment has
passed under the provisions of Cl. first, Sec. V of this Regulation,
as well as where a defaulter has failed to satisfy the public demand
against him made under the provisions of Sec. VI of this Regulation, it shall be competent to a collector to issue a proclamation,
requiring all persons holding property belonging to the defaulter
to surrender the same to him within a specified period, not being
less than fifteen days; after the publication of such proclamation,
and after the expiration of such specified period, any person who
may be convicted before the *Subordinate* judge, (who is hereby empowered to take cognizance of such cases,) of having fraudulently
concealed or collusively received such property, shall be sentenced
by him to pay a fine not exceeding three times the amount of the
value of the property so fraudulently concealed or collusively
received by such person, and to be imprisoned until such fine be
paid; the *Subordinate* judge shall levy the amount of the fine by the
usual process, and in the event of the full amount of the fine not
being realized, shall commit the offender to confinement in the
zillah jail; provided however, that the period of confinement under this Section shall iu no case exceed twelve calendar months.—
Sec. VIII.—*Ibid.*

If information on oath or *solemn affirmation* shall be given
before a collector that revenue papers and accounts respecting
frauds or embezzlements in the public revenue have been fraudulently concealed and deposited in any particular premises, he shall
be competent to issue warrants under his own official seal and
signature addressed to one or more public officers of his establishment, commanding search to be made on the premises for the
discovery of such papers or accounts; search warrants thus issued,
shall be executed between sun-rise and sun-set only, and where
practicable, in the presence of two or more respectable inhabitants
of the village in which the house or place authorized to be
searched may be situated; a full and perfect list of all papers
and other things whatsoever seized in virtue of such warrants,

shall be made out in duplicate on the spot, both copies shall be signed by the officer executing the warrant and by the inhabitants or witnesses present, one copy of such list shall be given to the occupier of the house, or some person on his behalf, and the other shall be annexed to the warrant when returned to the collector. Provided however, that nothing contained in these rules shall be construed to authorize any but females to enter the *zenana* or apartments of the women, in houses belonging to those classes whose women do not ordinarily appear in public.—*Sec.* IX, *Reg.* IX, 1822.

Whenever it may be necessary to sell property in satisfaction of an order or judgment of the collector under the provisions of this Regulation, the sale shall be conducted by the tahsildar or other public servant to whom the collector may delegate that duty, and the rules of Sections XXI, XXII, XXV, XXVI and XXVII of Regulation XXVIII of 1802, as far as they relate to the notification, publicity and fairness of such sales, shall be adhered to by the officer 'conducting the sale, who, if he shall neglect to observe those rules as far as they apply, and shall knowingly permit any unfair dealing either in the appraisement or sale of such property, shall be liable to be fined by the collector in such amount as may suffice to make good the loss sustained in consequence of the unfair practices which he may have so permitted, and in default of payment of such fine, shall be committed to the zillah jail by the collector for a period not exceeding one year, or until such fine shall have been paid.—*Sec.* X.—*Ibid.*

A discretionary authority shall be vested in collectors, subject to the approval and sanction of the board of revenue, to pay to persons from whom money has been exacted or unjustly received, the whole or such part of the sum recovered under the provisions of this Regulation as may appear proper on consideration of the circumstances of the case; provided moreover, that such persons shall be entitled in all cases to receive back, whatever they may have so given to a public servant of Government, if they shall inform the collector, subordinate-collector or assistant, of such exaction or undue receipt of money, within two months after its payment or delivery by the said informants.—*Sec.* XII.—*Ibid.*

Collectors are authorized to keep under restraint any persons against whom they may have instituted an inquiry under the provisions of this Regulation, either by placing peons over the dwelling house of any such persons, to prevent their escape, or, if necessary, by confinement in the cutcherry; and if judgment be given against such persons, then to continue the restraint until the amount adjudged has been paid by them, or the amount realized by sale of the property attached in satisfaction of the order or judgment.—*Cl.* 1, *Sec.* XIII, *Reg.* IX, 1822.

In the event of no property of a person, against whom an order or judgment has been passed under this Regulation, being forthcoming, or not sufficient to pay the amount due by him, the collector shall forward the defaulter or offender to the subordinate zillah court, and shall at the same time furnish the government vakeel of the said court with instructions to present a motion to the judge for his confinement until the amount due, which shall be distinctly stated in the said motion, shall have been discharged, or until the collector shall again move the court for his release. The judge shall receive such motion whether in or out of court, and shall order the confinement of the party accordingly, and the judge shall not discharge him from confinement, except on his paying the full amount mentioned in the collector's motion, or on application from the collector.—*Cl.* 2.—*Ibid.*

Whenever a person against whom a judgment or order shall have passed under the provisions of Section V, or Section VI, Regulation IX, 1822, shall conceive himself aggrieved by such decision, he shall be at liberty, at any time within three months from the date of such judgment or order, to present to the collector a petition of appeal addressed to the board of revenue, which petition the collector shall forthwith forward to the board. The petition shall be written on unstamped paper and shall state the grounds on which the petitioner deems himself aggrieved, and the redress or relief to which he considers himself entitled.—*Cl.* 1, *Sec.* VI, *Reg.* VII, 1828.

On receipt of such petition, the board of revenue, after making such inquiry as they may judge necessary, will either direct the relief prayed for by the petitioner to be granted, or will report the case for the orders of the Governor in Council; or will simply reject the petition by endorsement under the hand of their secretary, referring the party complaining to seek redress, if he thinks proper, in the established courts of udalut.—*Cl.* 2.—*Ibid.*

In cases reported by the board of revenue for the orders of the Governor in Council, in which it shall appear to the Governor in Council that further investigation is necessary, he will appoint one or more commissioners to revise the original proceedings, and will order the commission to sit at such place as may appear to be most convenient; and the provisions of Section XV, Regulation IX, 1822, shall be applicable to such commission.—*Cl.* 3.—*Ibid.*

The commission so appointed shall be vested generally with the same powers as zillah courts under the Regulations in force so far as such powers are necessary to the full and efficient discharge of the duties to be executed. The proceedings of the commission are to be governed by the rules and maxims of justice, and in all points not expressly provided for in this Regulation, the provisions contained in the general Regulations are to be observed as far as they may be consistent and applicable.—*Cl.* 2, *Sec.* XV, *Reg.* IX, 1822.

The commission shall call for and examine the proceedings and evidence recorded by the collector on the summary inquiry which preceded, and on a full consideration of the whole of the evidence, shall decide whether the judgment or order passed by the collector and appealed from, was just and equitable, or if otherwise, in what particulars it was erroneous; and shall order the repayment, with reasonable interest, of any sum which had been adjudged by the collector to be due and payable, but which the commission shall find not to have been so due; and if any property had been sold in satisfaction of such order or judgment of the collector, the commission, in revising the order or judgment, shall determine the amount of compensation to be paid on account of such property so sold; and shall further have authority to adjudge such reasonable costs and charges as may appear sufficient to compensate the complainant for any loss or injury sustained, or for unjust detention of the complainant, or for actual charges or expenses incurred.— *Cl.* 3.—*Ibid.*

When the proceedings shall have been closed, or as soon afterwards as circumstances will admit, the commission shall forward the whole of the proceedings and evidence, with the final judgment on the case, to the Governor in Council.—*Cl.* 4.—*Ibid.*

The decisions of commissions under this Regulation shall be final; but it shall rest with the Governor in Council to determine, in the case of compensation being awarded under the foregoing Clause, whether the amount shall be paid from the public treasury, or whether, (as in cases where the proceedings of the collector on the primary inquiry shall appear to have been unfair and unjustifiable, or where he may appear to have been culpably negligent in regard to the mode of disposing of the complainant's property,) the whole or any part of such compensation shall be made good by the collector who conducted the primary inquiry and the proceedings, in execution of the summary judgment.—*Cl.* 5.—*Ibid.*

If the petition of appeal from a summary judgment of a collector passed under this Regulation be presented before the property which may have been attached has been sold, such property, or any part that may still be unsold, shall be held in attachment pending the appeal; and where the property attached may be sufficient for the security of the amount adjudged by the collector on the primary inquiry, or where the party appealing may give good and sufficient security for the ultimate fulfilment of the collector's judgment, he shall be released from confinement, pending the investigation by the commission.—*Cl.* 6, *Sec.* XV, *Reg.* IX, 1822.

If the decree of the commission confirm the judgment of the collector, the decree shall be executed in like manner as the decree of a court of udalut ; and if the amount finally adjudged be not paid, the appellant and his sureties, where he may have given the security of others, shall be committed to the zillah jail, by an order of the commissioner or commissioners, bearing his or their signature, and specifying the amount to be levied ; and such order shall be a sufficient warrant to the judge to receive such persons into the zillah jail, and to keep them there until the amount decreed against them be fully paid ; or until the collector, under the orders of the board of revenue or of government, apply for their release.—*Cl.* 7.—*Ibid.*

No suit grounded on the summary proceedings of a collector under this Regulation, either in the form of an original complaint against such collector on account of any supposed injustice in conducting such proceedings, or of an appeal from his judgment, shall be received by any court of udalut, unless the plaint or petition is accompanied by the order referred to in *Clause second,* *Section* VI, *Reg.* VII, 1828, remitting the party complaining to seek his redress in the courts of udalut.—*Sec.* XVI.—*Ibid.*

In modification of Sec. XVI, Reg. IX, 1822, it is hereby provided, that no suit, either in the form of an original complaint, or of an appeal, shall be received in any court of udalut under that Section, unless the plaint or petition is accompanied by the order referred to in Cl. 2, Sec. VI, Reg. VII, 1828, under the hand of the Secretary to the Board of Revenue, and is preferred within three months from the date of the delivery of the order.—*See.* II, *Reg.* III, 1832.

The date of the delivery of the order is to be certified by the officer delivering it, by an endorsement on the petition on which the order is written.—*Sec.* III.—*Ibid.*

All claims to the possession of, or succession to, hereditary village, or other offices in the Revenue and Police departments, or to the enjoyment of any of the emoluments annexed to such offices, shall in the first instance be adjudicable by the Collector of the district in which the claim has arisen or may arise.—*Cl.* 1, *Sec.* IV, *Reg.* VI, 1831.

It shall be competent to the Collector to require the attendance of any of the resident native inhabitants of his district, to aid him as assessors in investigating and determining the claims brought before him under the preceding Clause ; and every person neglecting or refusing to attend when called upon for this purpose, shall be liable, at the discretion of the Collector, to a fine not exceeding fifty rupees, the payment of which shall be enforced, if necessary, by the ordinary process of distraint for arrears of Revenue. —*Cl.* 2.—*Ibid.*

It shall be competent to Collectors, at their discretion, to refer the claims brought before them under Clause first of this Section to the native assessors for investigation.—*Cl.* 3.—*Ibid.*

It shall be competent to Collectors, to require and enforce the attendance of all witnesses whose evidence may be necessary in the investigation of claims under the foregoing Clauses, and for this purpose the Collectors shall have the same powers as are vested in the Zillah Judges by Section VII, Regulation III, 1802, the general provisions of which Section, so far as they may appear applicable, shall be observed by the Collectors in all investigations held by them under this Regulation.—*Cl.* 4.—*Ibid.*

Any witness examined by the Collectors or by the native assessors under this Regulation, who shall be guilty of a wilful and corrupt breach of his oath, shall be liable to prosecution for perjury, and on conviction before the Session Court shall be subject to the penalties prescribed for perjury committed before the ordinary Courts of Judicature.—*Cl.* 5.—*Ibid.*

From every decision passed by the Collectors on claims brought before them under Clause first, and from every order of the Collectors imposing a fine under Clause second of the preceding Section, an appeal shall lie to the Board of Revenue, provided such appeal be made within three months from and after the date of the Collector's decision or order.—*Cl.* 1, *Sec.* V.—*Ibid.*

It shall however be competent to the Board of Revenue whenever they may see fit, to admit an appeal preferred after the time limited in the foregoing Clause.—*Cl.* 2.—*Ibid.*

Sec. IV, Reg. VI, 1831.—By Section III of this Regulation, which see at page 154, the ordinary Civil Courts are prohibited receiving or trying any such suits are herein specified.

The decisions or orders of the Board of Revenue on all appeals made to them under the preceding Section, shall be final and conclusive; provided, however, that it shall be competent to the Governor in Council to revise and modify such orders and decisions, whenever he may deem it necessary for the ends of justice.—*Sec.* VI, *Reg.* VI, 1831.

Nothing contained in this Regulation shall be construed to affect in any way the office of Kurnum established by Regulation XXIX, 1802, in districts of which the Land Revenue has been permanently fixed: or to be any wise applicable to the public institutions referred to in Regulation VII, 1817, or to the trustees, managers, or superintendents of those institutions.—*Sec.* VIII. —*Ibid.*

CHAPTER VI.

MILITARY COURTS OF REQUESTS, *Native*—ACT XI. 1841, &c.

I. All Regulations and parts of Regulations concerning Military Courts of Requests are repealed; provided always that nothing in this Act contained shall be held to alter or affect the jurisdiction of a single Officer duly authorized and appointed under the Rules in force in the Madras and Bombay Presidencies for the trial of small suits in Military Bazars at Cantonments and Stations occupied by the troops of those Presidencies respectively, or the trial by Punchayet of suits against Military persons according to the Rules in force under the Madras Presidency.

II. Subject to the aforesaid proviso, within the territories of the East India Company actions of debt and other personal actions against Native Officers, Soldiers and other persons amenable to the Articles of War for the Native Forces in the Military Service of the East India Company, or residing within any Station or Cantonment, and carrying on any trade or business in a Military Bazar, shall be cognizable before a Military Court and not elsewhere, provided the value in question shall not exceed 200 Rupees, and the defendant was a person of the description above mentioned, when the cause of action arose, and when the suit was instituted. Provided that no suit shall be brought before any Military Court under this Act to determine any dispute of caste, or concerning any right to real property.

No person residing within the limits of any Military Cantonment and carrying on trade therein, or who shall have been a trader at any Military Cantonment, shall be allowed to recover in any

---

Military Courts, &c.—These fall within the scope of this work as having a special and limited jurisdiction in certain cases of a civil nature, and inasmuch, as under the circumstances specified in Sec. XVII, an appeal lies from them to the Sudder Udalut.

Sec. I.—" Military Bazars."—Defined in Sec. III, Reg. VII, 1832, as " Stations designated as such in General Orders of Government, within such limits as may from time to time be fixed by order of Government; plans whereof shall be deposited with the Magistrate of the district."—See also Sec. XXXVIII, Reg. VII, 1832, and note thereon, under ' Commissariat Officer.'

Sec. II.—" Amenable to Articles of War."—Those in force at Madras when this Act was passed were contained in Reg. V, of 1827, they were superseded by Act XX, of 1845, which was repealed by Act XIX, of 1847, which contains the present Articles of War.

Military Court of Requests for the Native Troops of the East India Company, held within any such Cantonment, any debt contracted in the way of trade, or for the loan of money, within any such Cantonment, by any person subject to the jurisdiction of such Court, unless the person seeking to recover the debt shall, at the time of contracting thereof, have been registered, as a Military Bazarman within any such Cantonment.—*Sec.* I, *Act* XII, 1842.

All persons serving with any part of the army and receiving public pay in any capacity, menial servants, and other camp followers of every description, shall be subject to the provisions of Act No. XI of 1841, in like manner as enlisted soldiers.—*Sec.* II. —*Ibid.*

All officers and soldiers, all drivers, farriers, trumpeters, and drummers; all unattested recruits; hospital attendants, sub assistant surgeons, native doctors and dressers; all artificers and labourers, suttlers, followers, public and private, or others attached to, or serving with any part of the army, are to be governed by these articles, and subject to trial by Courts Martial.—*Sec.* VII, *Art:* 157, *Act* XIX *of* 1847.

No suit of the nature and limited amount specified in *Sec.* II, *Act* XI, 1841, shall be admitted in any of the civil courts, against any person belonging to any of the military classes specified in *Acts* XI, 1841, XII, 1842, *and* XIX, 1847; unless it be averred in the plaint that the defendant was not of any of these classes when the cause of action arose, or when the suit was instituted. In that case, when the usual notice shall be served on the defendant, if he shall have been of the description specified when the cause of action arose, as well as when the suit was instituted, he shall obtain and deliver to the civil officer by whom the notice is served, a certificate of the kind provided for in the following Section; which certificate shall be received by the civil court, which issued the notice, as proof of the facts declared in it.--*Cl.* 1, *Sec.* XXII, *Reg.* VII, 1832.

Sec. VII, Act XIX, 1847.—This is the latest and most comprehensive description of ' persons amenable to the Articles of War,' and consequently within the provisions of Act XI, of 1841.

Cl. 1, Sec. XXII, Reg. VII, 1832.—This Section applied to suits to be brought before the Military Courts of Requests constituted under Reg. V, of 1827, now repealed; as however Act XI, of 1841, though it repeals all parts of prior Regulations affecting such Courts, enacts that the suits contemplated by it shall be tried in the Military Courts, and ' *not elsewhere*' it may be presumed, that the legislature intends the course indicated in this Section to be observed in cases where doubt may exist, or be started, as to the nature of the suit.

The persons ' specified,' were originally enumerated in Sec. XIII, of this Regulation, but new definitions have since been given.

If the defendant shall not deliver such certificate, he shall either attend pursuant to the notice; or in default thereof, be dealt with by the civil court, in the manner prescribed by the Regulations.—*Cl.* 2, *Sec.* XXII, *Reg.* VII, 1832.

If the defendant, on being served with the usual notice by the civil court, shall maintain that the debt for which he is sued is of the description or amount cognizable by a military court, or by the officer in immediate charge of the police under this Regulation, he shall attend pursuant to the notice; or in default, be dealt with, by the civil court, according to the Regulations. On his attendance and producing the certificate provided for by Section XXIII of this Regulation, the civil court shall immediately make such summary inquiry as may appear necessary, to ascertain whether the debt is or is not, of the nature and amount specified in *Sec.* II, *Act* XI, 1841, *or in Cl.* 3, *Sec.* XX, *Reg.* VII, 1832, and the decision of the civil court on this point shall be final, so far as to determine whether the suit shall be entertained by it, or not.—*Cl.* 3.—*Ibid.*

Clause second Section XXV, Regulation XIII, 1816, shall be applicable to suits dismissed under this Section.—*Cl.* 4.—*Ibid.*

A certificate in the form F. in the Appendix to this Regulation, shall be granted, on application of officers or soldiers, by the officer commanding their regiment; or on application of persons of any of the other military classes specified *as above,* by the officer in charge of the military police at military bazar stations, and elsewhere by the officer in charge of the department to which they belong.—*Sec.* XXIII, *Reg.* VII, 1832.

III. The Commanding Officer of any Station or Cantonment, or Officer Commanding any portion of Troops in the field, is authorized to convene such Military Courts. And such Courts shall be composed, according to the orders of the Commander in Chief for the time being of the Presidency within which the Station or Cantonment is situate, or, in the absence of such orders, according to the discretion of the Convening Officer, either of not less than three European Commissioned Officers, or of not less than three Native Commissioned Officers, and, in the latter case,

---

Cl. 4, Sec. XXII, Reg. VII, 1832.—That is the sudder udalut may authorize the return of the whole. or a portion of the stamp duty which may have been paid on the institution of a suit thus dismissed.

Sec. XXIII, Reg. VII, 1832.—Form F. " I hereby certify that (here enter name caste, " age, rank, trade or profession) was (a native officer or soldier) or a military person of the " description specified in Sec. II, Act XI, 1841, (or Sec. I, Act XII, 1842,) on the " day of   18   (here enter the date of *the cause of action* having arisen), " and that he continued to be so on the   (here enter the date *of the institution of* " the suit."

with an European officer of not less than five years standing, to superintend and record the proceedings. Provided that if there be not a sufficient number of Officers to constitute a Court at the Station or Cantonment where any cause of action may arise, or where the defendant may be residing, the suit shall be determined at the nearest Station or Cantonment where a Military Court can be duly constituted as aforesaid.

IV.   Such Military Courts shall be convened monthly, and shall be holden on some convenient day before the issue of the pay for each month.

V.   The forms of proceeding in every such Court shall be conformable to the usages observed on trials before Courts Martial held for the Native Troops in the service of the East India Company as far as the same are applicable.   And any such Court shall have the like power of summoning witnesses as is possessed by Courts Martial.   Provided always, that every such Court shall have the power of examining the parties to any suit, and of requiring or dispensing with their attendance at its discretion.   And every such Court shall have the like power of taking the examinations of absent parties and witnesses as is possessed by the Civil Courts of the East India Company, under Act No. VII. of 1841, provided that the depositions taken under a Commission issued by any Military Court of Requests shall be receivable in evidence before any such Court subsequently held; Provided also that Commissions may be issued by Military Courts of Requests under this Act, pursuant to the provisions of Act No. VII, of 1841, notwithstanding the Courts to which the Commissions may be directed, are not situate beyond the jurisdiction of such Military Courts.

VI.   Witnesses omitting to attend, refusing to give evidence, or committing perjury, and persons suborning witnesses to commit perjury, shall be tried and punished, if amenable to Articles of War, by a Court Martial, subject to all the Rules contained in such Articles of War for the punishment of such offences in regard to trials for Military offences; and if not amenable to Articles of War, they may be tried and punished in the nearest of the Courts of the East India Company for the administration of Criminal Justice (whether such Court have ordinarily jurisdiction over such person in Criminal matters or not) in like manner as if such offences had been committed in regard to any trial before such nearest Court.

VII.   Any person, Civil or Military, European or Native, using menacing words, signs, or gestures, or otherwise interrupting (whether being personally present or not,) the proceedings of any Military Court of Requests shall be punishable, if amenable to Articles of War by a Court Martial, or if not amenable to Articles of War, in the nearest of the Courts of the East India Company for the administration of Criminal justice (whether such Court have ordinarily jurisdiction over such person in Criminal matters or not,) in like manner as if the offence had been committed in regard to any proceeding of the Court to which it is so referred.

VIII.   A record shall be kept of proceedings in every case tried before any Military Court of Requests.   And such record shall contain the substance of the evidence given, and the nature of such evidence as may have been rejected on the ground of its not being legally admissible, or relevant, or on other grounds, and the same shall be signed by the Members of the said Court. And such record or a copy thereof shall, with as little delay as is practicable, after the conclusion of the proceedings, be transmitted by the European President, or Superintending Officer of every such Court to the Officer Commanding the Station or Cantonment.

IX.   Where a demand shall exceed the amount of 200 Rupees, or where several separate demands shall exceed such amount, no more shall be recoverable from any one defendant by the same plaintiff or plaintiffs than the sum of 200 Rupees only—and the judgment in respect of any demand in a Court of Requests shall be a bar to the recovery of the same demand or of any other or further demand for the same cause of action in any other Court whatever, provided that the liability accrued before the time of instituting the suit in the Military Court— and it shall be competent for every such Military Court to investigate any counterclaim alleged by any defendant.   And it shall be competent for every such Military Court to allow the interest for money agreed on between the parties, provided the same does not exceed the usage of the country in ordinary money transactions.   And every contract made after the passing of this Act upon which a demand for debt exceeding 20 Rupees is founded, not being money due for goods bought and delivered, shall be in writing and expressed in the language of the defendant and signed by him, or on his behalf by some other person than the plaintiff. Provided that it shall not be competent to any Court of Requests to admit any suit for a debt which has accrued upwards of six years, unless a direct promise to pay, made within six years of the commencement of the suit, be proved.

X.   On failure of either of the parties to a suit to attend either personally or by representative, or to produce his witnesses according as he shall be required by any Military Court of Requests, such Court on being satisfied that the party has been duly apprized of what is required of him, may proceed to the termination of the suit in his absence. And if the decree in any such case shall be against the plaintiff, it shall not be competent for him to commence a new suit for the same cause of action.

XI. It shall be lawful for the Commanding Officer to whom the proceedings have been transmitted as aforesaid to return the same for revision either by the same or another Military Court of Requests. And in every such case the second decree shall be final, unless for error in points of law, when the same shall be transmitted to the Commander in Chief, who shall have power to annul the proceedings without prejudice to any future suit. Provided always that in the case of any new trial the Court may receive evidence which was not adduced at the first trial.

XII. Every plaintiff shall prefer his claim in writing and shall deliver the same to the Station Staff-Officer. The claims shall be entered in a Schedule by the Station Staff-Officer, which Schedule is to be sent to Adjutants of Corps or Heads of Departments two days at least before the assembly of the Court, and the Adjutants or Heads of Departments shall be responsible that the defendants belonging to their respective Corps or Establishments have been duly summoned.

XIII. Every decree of any Military Court of Requests shall be published in the Station Orders before the same is executed.

XIV. The execution of decrees of Military Courts of Requests may be either general or special, according to the sentence of the Court. Provided always that the Commanding Officer may, notwithstanding the direction of the Court, order that the execution shall be general or special at his discretion.

XV. In cases in which the execution is to be general, the debt if not paid forthwith, shall, under the authority of the Commanding Officer in writing to be signed by him, be levied by seizure and public sale of such of the Debtor's Goods (under which term are included houses or other erection within the limits of

---

Sec. XV, Act XI, 1841.—" Provisions of Act II, of 1840."—This prescribed that upon a party being sentenced by court martial to imprisonment, it should " be the duty of every judge, magistrate, sheriff, or other officer in charge of any jail, to give effect to such sentence, on the offender being delivered into his custody : and on being furnished with a copy of the sentence by the officer commanding the division, garrison, regiment, or detachment, as the case might be, to which the offender belonged"—it is now superseded by Sec. III, Act XIX, 1847, Article 84, which re-enacts its substance in the same words.

Stations and Cantonments) as may be found within the limits of the Station or Cantonment, or elsewhere ; and if sufficient Goods are not to be found, the debtor, if not a Soldier, shall be arrested and imprisoned in any Civil Goal near to the Station or Cantonment, (for which purpose the provisions of Act No. II, of 1840 shall be applicable) or in any other convenient place of confinement situate within the limits of the Station or Cantonment, for the space of two months, unless the debt be sooner paid, and his Goods, if found within the limits of the Station or Cantonments or elsewhere at any subsequent time, shall be liable to be seized and sold in satisfaction of the debt. And if the debtor be a Soldier and the debt be not liquidated by sale of his Effects, Accoutrements and Necessaries excepted, an order may be issued for payment of the residue by monthly deduction from the pay issued to the debtor under the Rules which follow.

XVI. Where the execution is to be special, the debt shall be satisfied out of the pay and allowances of the debtor and not otherwise. And a certificate of the decree and direction or order thereon certified under the hand of the Commanding Officer and signed by him, shall be a sufficient authority for making such stoppages. Provided always that no more than one-half of the pay and allowances of any Commissioned Officer, or than one-fourth of the pay and allowances of any non-Commissioned Officer or Soldier shall be stopped in any one month.

XVII. In places beyond the Frontier of the Territories of the East India Company, actions of debt and other personal actions may be brought before such Military Courts as aforesaid against persons so amenable as aforesaid for any amount of demand: Provided that such Military Courts beyond the Frontier shall be composed of European Officers—and provided, that if the amount of claim shall exceed 200 Rupees an appeal shall lie to the Court of Sudder Udalut of the nearest Presidency, according to the rules in force with regard to appeals from subordinate Civil Courts.

CHAPTER VII.

MILITARY COURTS OF REQUESTS—*European*, 12th and 13th VICTORIA, CAP. 43.

I. * * * Nothing in this Act contained shall in any manner impeach or affect any Articles of War or other matters made, enacted, or in force, or which hereafter may be made, enacted, or in force under the authority of the Government of India, respecting officers or soldiers being natives of the East Indies, or other places within the limits of the said Company's Charter.

II. The provisions of this Act shall apply to all persons belonging to any of the Forces of the *East India* Company who are or shall be commissioned or in pay as officers, or who are or shall be listed or in pay as Non-Commissioned Officers or Soldiers, or who are or shall be serving or hired to be employed in the Artillery or any of the Trains of Artillery, or as Master Gunners or Gunners, or as Conductors of Stores, or who are or shall be serving in the Department of Engineers, or in the Corps of Sappers and Miners or Pioneers, or as Military Surveyors or Draftsmen, or in the Ordnance and Commissariat Departments, and to all Storekeepers and other Civil Officers employed under the Ordnance, and to all Apothecaries, Veterinary Surgeons, Medical Storekeepers, Hospital Stewards, and others serving in the Medical Department of the said Forces, and to all licensed sutlers and followers in or of any of the said Forces, and that all such persons shall be at all times subject to all the penalties and punishments mentioned in this Act, and shall in all respects whatsoever be holden to be within the intent and meaning of every part of this Act.

' Military Courts, European.'—Courts of Requests assembled under Act XI of 1841, have no jurisdiction over European British Subjects whose cases are reserved to those constituted by the Sections here given of 12th and 13th Victoria, Cap. 43, which being Queen's Courts established by Act of Parliament, act independently of the Sudder Udalut, under the laws made for their guidance.

' Sec. II.—That is, it applies to all those herein specifically mentioned *in addition* to those falling under the general description of ' Officer or Soldier' to which the Act in its 1st Section is generally declared applicable.

LXVI. In all places where the said Company's Forces now are or may be employed, or where any body of Her Majesty's Forces may be serving with the Forces of the said Company, situate beyond the jurisdiction of any Courts of Requests or other Courts for enforcing small demands established at the Cities of *Calcutta, Madras,* and *Bombay* respectively, actions of debt, and all personal actions against officers, all persons licensed to act as sutlers to any corps or detachments, or at any Station or Cantonment, persons resident within the limits of a Military Cantonment, or other persons amenable to the provisions of this Act, not being Soldiers, shall be cognizable before a Court of Requests composed of Military Officers, and not elsewhere, provided the value in question shall not exceed four hundred Company's Rupees and that the defendant was a person of the above description when the cause of action arose, which Court the Commanding Officer of any Camp, Garrison, or Cantonment is hereby authorized and empowered to convene ; and the said Court shall in all practicable cases consist of five Commissioned Officers and in no instance of less than three; and the President thereof shall in all practicable cases be a Field Officer, and in no case be under the rank of a Captain ; and every Member shall have served five years as a Commissioned Officer; and the President and Members assisting at any such Court, before any proceedings be had before it, shall take the following oath, which oath shall be administered by the President of the Court to the other Members thereof, and to the President by any Member having first taken the oath ; (that is to say)

  ' I ——— swear that I will duly administer Justice according to the evidence in the matters that shall be brought before me

      ' So help me God.'

And all witnesses before any such Court shall be examined in the same manner as in the case of a trial by Court Martial ; and it shall be competent for such Court, upon finding or awarding any debt or damage, either to award execution thereof generally, or to direct specially that the whole or any part thereof shall be stopped and paid over to the plaintiff, out of any part not exceeding one half of any pay or allowance, or out of any other public money which may respectively be coming to the defendant in the current or any future month or months, or to direct the same to be so

---

Sec. LXVI.—Persons amenable to this Act—*See Section II, and Note thereon.*

" *Same manner as Court-Martial.*"—i. e. on oath or solemn affirmation as the case may be ; and the penalties of perjury follow the breach of it.

" Imprisoned"—he cannot be sent to a Civil Jail, as a party amenable to Act XI of 1841, can under Section XV, of that enactment.

paid by instalments; and in all cases where the execution shall be awarded generally, the debt if not paid, forthwith, shall be levied by seizure and public sale of such of the defendant's goods and property as may be found within the Camp, Garrison, or Cantonment, under a written order of the Commanding Officer, grounded on the judgment of the Court; and all orders of such Commanding Officer as to the manner of such sale, or the person by whom the same shall be made, or otherwise respecting the same, shall be valid and binding ; and any goods and property of the defendant found within the limits of the Camp, Garrison, or Cantonment, to which the defendant shall belong at any subsequent time shall be liable to be seized and sold in like manner, in satisfaction of any remainder of such debt or damages ; and if any question shall arise whether any such effects or property are liable to be taken in execution as aforesaid, the decision and order of the said Commanding Officer shall be final and conclusive with respect to the same ; and if sufficient goods shall not be found within the limits of the Camp, Garrison, or Cantonment, then any public money, or any part not exceeding one half of the pay or allowances accruing to the defendant, shall be stopped, in liquidation of such debt or damage; and if such defendant shall not receive pay as an Officer, or from any public department, but be a sutler, servant, or follower, he may be arrested by like order of the Commanding Officer, and imprisoned in some convenient place within the Military Boundaries for any period not exceeding two months, unless the debt be sooner paid ; and the said Commanding Officer shall not, nor shall any person acting on his orders in respect of the matters aforesaid, incur any liability to any person or persons whomsoever for any act done by him in pursuance of the provisions aforesaid ; and in cases where the said Court shall direct specially that the whole or any part of the debt or damages shall be stopped and paid out of part of any pay or allowances, or out of any public money, the same shall be stopped and paid accordingly, in conformity with such direction ; provided always, that nothing herein-before contained shall enable any such action as aforesaid to be brought in the said Court by any Officer or Soldier against any Officer.

CHAPTER VIII.

OFFICER IN CHARGE OF POLICE—MILITARY PUNCHAYETS, REG. VII. 1832, &c.

The Regulations at present in force at any Presidency by which the office and powers of Commissariat Officers, or Officers in charge of the Police, or Superintendents of Bazaars are defined and controlled; or by which Punchayets are constituted and guided;— are hereby declared to be in full force, and the same shall continue to be observed at the several Presidencies respectively.—*Sec.* VII, *Art.* 156, *Act* XIX, 1847.

XXI. Clause 3. At all Military Bazaar Stations, suits for the recovery of any debt not exceeding twenty rupees, in which the defendant at the time the cause of action arose, as well as at the period of the institution of the suit, was a native non-commissioned Officer or Soldier, or belonging to any of the Military classes specified in *Acts* XI, 1841, XII, 1842, *and* XIX, 1847, *which see at p.* 90, shall be brought before the Officer Commanding who shall, by a written order, refer them to the Officer in immediate charge of the Police under this Regulation; and the officer in charge of the said police is hereby vested with authority to investigate, decide and determine all such suits.

Clause 4. The Officer in immediate charge of the Police under this Regulation, previously to acting under the preceding Clause, shall *make and subscribe a solemn declaration* according to the Form E. in the Appendix to this Regulation, before the Commanding Officer who is hereby authorized to *receive* the same.

Officer in charge of Police.—That is the Senior Commissariat Officer at the Station vested with Police powers under Sec. IV. of this Regulation, or other Officer appointed specially under Sec. XXXVIII, which see below.

Sec. VII, Act XIX, 1847.—This power was also saved to these functionaries by Act XI, 1841.

Sec. XXI, Reg. VII, 1832, Cl. 3.—Military Bazaar Stations, see note on Sec. 1, Act XI, 1841.

In regard to course of procedure where doubt may exist, or be stated as to the nature of the suit, whether thus cognizable, or by the Civil Courts, see Sec. XXII, under Military Courts of Requests at p. 90 and note thereon.

Cl. 4.—Solemn affirmation—formerly oath, which was dispensed with by Act XXI, 1837, the Form E. is omitted as being at hand in every office when required.

XXXVII.   First.   During the temporary absence of the Officer in immediate charge of the Police under this Regulation, such other Military Officer as may be nominated by the Commanding officer of the station, shall exercise the duties assigned by this Regulation to Officers in charge of the said Police.

Second.   The person so nominated, previously to entering on the duties of his office shall make and subscribe *solemn affirmations* similar to those prescribed in Sections IV. and XXI, of this Regulation, before the Commanding Officer who is hereby authorized to *receive* the same.

XXXVIII.   It shall be competent to the Governor in Council, at any time, by an order in Council, communicated to the civil authorities, and published in General Orders to the army, to declare all or any part of this Regulation, which may now specially apply to Commanding Officers at Military Bazaar Stations only, to be applicable to Commanding Officers at any other Military Stations, besides Military Bazaar Stations.   The limits of such jurisdiction shall, however, previously be defined by the government, and plans thereof shall be deposited with the Magistrate of the district; and where there may be no Commissariat Officer on the spot, a Military Officer shall be appointed by the Government to take immediate charge of the Police, under this Regulation, subject to the orders of the Officer Commanding the Station, and to exercise all or such part of the powers vested by this Regulation in the Officer in immediate charge of the Police, as the Government, in each case, may specially delegate to him.

VIII.   First.   Officers in immediate charge of the Police under this Regulation, shall have power to summon any person resident within Military limits, as a witness before themselves, or before punchayets assembled by them, under this Regulation ; provided always, that no woman shall be summoned whose rank or caste may render it improper to require her attendance.   When the evidence of such woman may be required, the Officer in immediate charge of the Police under this Regulation, shall require her to furnish her deposition in writing duly attested ; the deponent shall state in her deposition that she is prepared to *make solemn affirmation* to the truth of it, if required.

Second.   When Officers in charge of the Police under this Re-

---

Sec. XXXVII.—The affirmation required by Sec. IV, has reference to his Police functions.

Sec. VIII.—Sec. V, Act XI, 1841, gives to Military Courts of Requests the power of obtaining the depositions of absent parties and witnesses under Act VII. of 1841, no provision appears to have been made for the conduct of the Officer in charge of the Police in such cases.

gulation, shall require the attendance of witnesses residing without Military limits, the summons shall be sent to the principal native officer of the village in which the witness resides, to be served by him, unless there be a European Civil Officer in the magistracy, on the spot, in which case it shall be sent to him to be served ; if the witness reside more than four miles beyond such limits, the Officer Commanding shall send the summons to the nearest European Civil Officer in the magistracy, with a letter in the Form contained in the Appendix (C.) to this Regulation. The Civil magisterial Officer shall immediately countersign the summons, and cause it to be served, endorsed, and returned accordingly.

X. Witnesses resident beyond Military limits attending to give evidence before Officers in immediate charge of the Police under this Regulation, shall be entitled to receive batta at the rate of not less than one, or more than four annas per day; the rate to be fixed by the said Officer with reference to the rank and circumstances of each witness, the batta shall be paid daily or otherwise, as it may be applied for, and in all civil suits the sum so paid shall invariably be recovered as the cost due from the parties: the party cast paying the same in the proportion which the sum decreed against him may bear to the sum sued for.

XI. First. Any witness summoned by an Officer in immediate charge of the Police under this Regulation; who shall neglect or refuse to attend, or to give his testimony, or to sign or mark his deposition, if required, shall be liable to be fined by the said Officer in a sum not exceeding 200 Rupees ; provided always that in the event of such circumstance occurring before a punchayet assembled under this Regulation, a written communication thereof shall be made by them to the Officer in immediate charge of the Police. In addition to payment of the fine, the said witness, when forthcoming, may, by order of the Commanding Officer, be committed to close custody, until he shall consent to give his evidence, and, if required, to sign or mark his deposition.

Second. If the fine be not paid forthwith, the amount thereof shall be levied by seizure and public sale of such goods of the offender as may be found within the Military limits ; or if sufficient property be not found within these limits, an application shall be made by the Commanding Officer to the *Subordinate Judge or Principal Sudder Ameen* within whose jurisdiction his property may be situated according to the Form D. in the Appendix to this Regulation.

Sec. XI.—Form D. omitted as at hand in office.

Third. The *Subordinate Judge or Principal Sudder Ameen* shall levy the amount specified in such application from any property belonging to the offender which may be found within the jurisdiction of his Court, and shall communicate the result of his proceedings, and remit the amount levied to the Commanding Officer.

XII. Whatever person having made oath, or *solemn affirmation* before an Officer in charge of the Police under this Regulation, shall wilfully and deliberately depose falsely touching any point material to the issue of the cause pending, such person, if subject to the Rules and Articles of War for the government of the native army under this Presidency, shall be dealt with according to those rules and articles: and if not subject to the same, shall be sent by the Commanding Officer, as provided in Sec. XXXIV, to the nearest Subordinate Criminal Court, together with the original deposition on which the perjury is assigned, duly signed and certified, and the witnesses who can prove the fact which falsifies the deposition, and also the witnesses who can prove the wilful and deliberate giving of the deposition. *The Judge presiding in such Subordinate Criminal Court* shall dispose of the case under Sec. IX, Reg. X, 1816; on conviction before the *Session Court* such person shall be liable to the punishment provided for perjury by Cl. 1, Sec. III, Reg. VI, 1811.

XXIV. Officers in immediate charge of the Military Police shall have authority to summon punchayets, for the decision of suits for sums of money, or other personal property, without limitation as to amount or value, provided the defendant in the suit was a Native Officer or Soldier or belonging to one of the other Military Classes specified, (*See Sec.* XXI, *Cl. 3d, and note thereon*) at the period when the cause of action arose, as well as at the institution of the suit, and provided both parties consent, in writing, to this mode of decision.

XXV. Each party shall nominate two Members of the punchayets, and the Officer in charge of the Military Police shall nominate one additional Member, who shall be unobjected to by the two parties.

XXVI. First. The punchayet shall be assembled by the written summons of the Officer in charge of the Military Police, and shall proceed in the same manner as district punchayets under Regulation VII, 1816, with the exception specified in this Regulation.

Sec. XII.—Sec. VI, Act XI of 1841, makes the like provision for the case of perjury before a Military Court of Requests.

Second. The usual moochulka of the parties, to abide by the award of the punchayet, shall be witnessed and dated by the Officer in charge of the Police, and filed in his office; and the punchayet shall make to him all such communications and reports, as district punchayets are required to make to district moonsiffs, and also deliver to him their proceedings and two copies of their award.

Third. The Officer in charge of the Military Police, on receiving, from the punchayet, a list of the witnesses, and a notification of the day fixed for the trial, shall require the attendance of the witnesses in conformity with Section VIII, of this Regulation.

Fourth. If a punchayet shall report to the Officer in charge of the Military Police that the parties, or either of them, have failed to attend, in person or by vakeel, at the time fixed for the trial, the said Officer shall cause to be affixed, in some conspicuous situation, in the village or other place where the defaulting party may reside, a notice, specifying that the suit will be tried on a given day, which shall not be less than five days from the date of such notice.

Fifth. If a punchayet shall report to the Officer in charge of the Military Police, that a witness has refused or neglected to attend, or to give his testimony, or to sign his deposition, the Officer in charge of the Military Police shall proceed respecting such witness, agreeably to Section XI, of this Regulation.

Sixth. If a punchayet shall report to the Officer in charge of the Military Police, that a party or witness has been guilty of gross disrespect to them, the said Officer may impose a fine on such party or witness, proportioned to his situation and circumstances in life, but in no case exceeding ten rupees; to be commuted, if not paid, for imprisonment, in no case exceeding five days.

Seventh. The Officer in charge of the Military Police, on receiving the award of a punchayet assembled under this Regulation, shall summon the parties before him, and, having declared the decision of the punchayet, shall deliver a copy to each party, endorsing thereon the date of the delivery.

Eighth. If either party shall neglect or refuse to attend, or to receive a copy of the award, the Officer in charge of the Military Police shall endorse on the copy intended for such party, his neglect or refusal, with the date thereof, and attest it with his official

Sec. XXVI, Cl. 3.—Section VIII, see it above.
Sec. XXVI, Cl. 5.—Section XI, see it above.

signature, and retain the copy, to be afterwards delivered to the party, if he should claim it.

XXVII. First. No appeal shall be permitted from decisions passed by punchayets under this Regulation ; but if the punchayet shall be guilty of gross partiality, it shall be at the option of either party to bring the matter, by petition upon stamped paper of the prescribed rate, according to the amount of the suit, before the *Civil* judge of the zillah, within whose jurisdiction the punchayet may be assembled.

Second. The petition shall not be received, unless it be presented, with the award complained of, within thirty days after the date on which copies of the award may have been furnished or tendered to the parties.

Third. If the petition be received, and the partiality charged against the punchayet shall be established to the satisfaction of the judge, by the oaths *or solemn affirmation*, of two credible witnesses at the least, he shall, in every case, whatever the amount or value of the suit may be, *of his own authority, Sec.* XXII, *Act* VII, 1843, annul the decision.

Fourth. Petitions to the *Civil* judge of the zillah, under this Section, shall be presented by the parties in person, or by an authorized vakeel of the Court, to whom a fee of four annas of a rupee shall be allowed, and no more, and the parties shall not be subjected to any other charge whatever.

XXVIII. First. If within thirty days from the date of the delivery or tender to the parties of the award by the punchayet, a petition shall be received by the *civil* judge of the zillah, alleging that the punchayet has been guilty of gross partiality, the judge shall give information thereof to the Officer Commanding the Station at which the punchayet was assembled, by a letter in the Form G. in the Appendix to this Regulation.

Second. The Commanding Officer, on receiving a letter in the foregoing Form, shall order execution of the punchayet's award, to be staid, till a further communication be made to him by the Civil Court.

Third. When the charge has been examined and finally decided upon, the judge shall communicate the result to the Commanding Officer by a letter in the Form H. in the Appendix to this Regulation.

XXIX. When the award of a punchayet shall be annulled by

Sec. XXVIII. Cl. 1 and 3.—Forms G. and H. omitted as at hand in office.

the *civil judge of the zillah*, the parties shall be at liberty to bring their dispute, by written consent of both, before a fresh punchayet, or by complaint of either before any other competent tribunal; provided always, that if a second punchayet come to the same decision as the first, the second decision shall be final.

XXX.   Members of punchayets assembled under this Regulation shall be liable to prosecution in the zillah *civil* Court, for corruption in the discharge of their trust, conformably to the provisions of Section XVIII, Reg. VII, 1816.

XXXI.   Officers in charge of Military Police, and punchayets assembled, under this Regulation, shall not refuse to receive any document whatever, on account of its not being written on stamped paper.

XXXII.   Officers in immediate charge of the Police, and punchayets assembled under Section XXIV of this Regulation, shall not decree interest above twelve per cent per annum, even where more may have been stipulated; nor interest to an amount exceeding the principal; nor compound interest; except where a former bond has been cancelled and a new one entered into for principal and interest consolidated, in which case they may decree interest on the amount of the new bond, as on principal money.

XXXIII.   First.   Decisions in civil suits passed by Officers in immediate charge of the Police under this Regulation, or by punchayets assembled, under its provisions, shall, on the application of the party in whose favor the judgment is given, be carried into execution, by the Officer in charge of the said Police, under the orders of the Commanding Officer, in the manner prescribed by *Sections* XIV, XV, *Act* XI, 1841: Provided that no award of a punchayet shall be carried into execution until forty days after the date on which copies of it were delivered or tendered to the parties: Provided also, that when the amount or value awarded by a punchayet shall not have been paid by the party cast, and cannot be realized from any property or effects belonging or due to him within the Military limits, application may be made by the Commanding Officer to any zillah *civil* judge, within whose jurisdiction property belonging to the defaulter may exist, to realize the residue; and the said judge shall levy the amount from any property of the defaulter within his jurisdiction, remitting the amount, and communicating the result, to the Commanding Officer, meantime, such defaulter shall be arrested and imprisoned for two months, as above provided, according to *Sec.* XV, *Act* XI, 1841, and, at the expiration of the said two months, he shall be liable to be sent by the Commanding Officer to the nearest *zillah civil* judge, who, if the plaintiff pays the usual batta for his prolonged confinement in jail, shall proceed regarding him, as against other civil debtors.

Second. Persons sent under the preceding Clause shall be accompanied by an authenticated copy of the award of the punchayet, and shall be sent in the mode prescribed by Section XXXIV, of this Regulation.

XXXIV. First. Whenever under the provisions of this Regulation, it shall be necessary to forward any person to a Criminal or Civil Court, to a European Civil Officer of the magistracy, or to a Native Officer of Police under them, the Commanding Officer shall send him under proper custody, accompanied with a paper in the English language to the European Officers, and a paper in the Native language to the Native Officers, in duplicate, according to the Form J. in the Appendix to this Regulation.

Second. The Civil Officer to whom the said paper is addressed, shall certify on the back of one of the papers, whether the persons and documents specified in it have been duly received ; and the copy so endorsed shall be returned to the person who delivered it ; the other paper shall remain with the Civil Officer.

Third. The Civil Officers shall receive all persons thus sent to them ; and shall proceed concerning them according to the General Regulations.

XXXV. First. Officers Commanding at Military Bazar Stations are hereby vested, within the limits of their authority, with power to remove nuisances, and to prevent all future encroachments upon the streets of the Bazars and Pettahs within their jurisdiction, by houses, pandals, and other buildings.

Second. But nothing contained in this Regulation shall be construed to authorize Commanding Officers to dispossess proprietors of land, or of houses, situated within the limits of any Military Bazar Station; provided always, that the occupation of ground, which, in case of dispute, the Civil Courts have settled to be exclusively the property of Government, when once allotted to Bazars, shall be subject to all such Regulations as are now, or may be hereafter, established, by General Orders of Government.

XXXVI. Whenever natives shall die without heirs, or ab-

Sec. XXXIV.—Form J. omitted as at hand in office.
Sec. XXXVI.—" Subordinate Judge or Principal Sudder Ameen" in the original, Zillah Judge or Assistant Judge.—The Sudder Udalut ruled on the 9th Oct. 1843, that the duties prescribed in Cl. 7, Sec. XVI, Reg. III, 1802, devolved under Act VII of 1843 on the Subordinate Judge or Principal Sudder Ameen.

scond, and in either case leave property within the limits of any Military Bazar Station, the Commanding Officer of that Station shall send a correct inventory of the property to the nearest *Subordinate Judge*, or *Principal Sudder Ameen*, as the case may be, who shall proceed respecting it agreeably to Clause seventh, Section XVI, Regulation III of 1802.

XXXIX. First. Whenever it may be necessary to execute, within the limits of a Military Station at which one corps or more may be quartered, process of arrest issuing from any Civil or Criminal Court (Her Majesty's Supreme Court at Madras only excepted) the Officer charged with the execution of such process of arrest shall carry it to the Commanding Officer, or Senior Officer in the Station, who shall immediately endorse it with his signature, and use his utmost endeavors to cause the person or persons therein named to be discovered, and if within the limits of the Station, to be forthwith arrested and delivered, according to the exigence of the process, to the Civil Officer charged with the execution thereof.

Second. But nothing contained in the foregoing Clause of this Section, shall be construed to prevent the direct service by the Civil Officers, in the usual way, of notices, summonses, subpœnas, or other process of mere citation, without arrest; or require any communication to the Commanding Officer, or any endorsement by him on such notice or process not involving personal arrest.

XLI. At all Stations beyond the frontier, and in all Detachments in the Field beyond the frontier, the Officer in charge of the General Camp or Field Detachment Bazar, respectively, is hereby vested with authority to investigate, decide and determine all suits of the amount and nature specified in Clause third, Section XXI; provided the defendant, at the time the cause of action arose, as well as at the period of the institution of the suit, was of the description therein specified. The said Officers, previously to exercising these functions, shall *make* and subscribe *solemn declaration*, similar to that contained in Clause fourth of the said Section, before the Officer Commanding, who is hereby authorized to *receive* the same.

XLII. First. In Civil suits to any amount or value, not cognizable under the preceding Section, nor by *Military Courts of Requests under Act* XI *of* 1841, nor by any of the Civil Courts

---

Sec. XXXIX, Cl. 2.—But the F. U. in the C. O. 30th April 1842, A. declared that it was nevertheless desirable that in every practicable case such summonses, &c. should be executed through the Commanding Officer, or other Military Authority.

under this Government; wherein the defendant, at the time the
cause of action arose, was a Native Officer or Soldier, or of any of
the other Military classes specified in *Acts* XI *of* 1841, XII *of*
1842, *and* XIX *of* 1847, and at the time of the institution of
such suit continued so to be, at any Station beyond the frontier,
or with any Detachment in the Field beyond the frontier; it is
hereby declared that it shall be competent to the Officer Commanding such Field Station or Detachment, by mutual consent of
the parties, to refer the same for decision to a native punchayet,
consisting of five persons, of whom each party shall nominate two
Members, and the Commanding Officer the fifth; and power is
hereby vested in such punchayets to try, decide and determine all
such suits.

Second. The decision of the said punchayet shall be carried
into effect by the Commanding Officer, unless either party, within
ten days after the passing of their award, present to him in writing,
a charge of gross partiality against the punchayet. In such cases
an appeal shall lie from the award of such punchayet to the tribunal specified in the following Clause.

Third. In the suits specified in Clause first, where the defendant may altogether refuse to refer the claim upon him to the decision of a punchayet, or where having consented thereto, and an
award having been passed, a charge of partiality may be preferred
against the punchayet within the period before stated, the Officer
Commanding shall immediately assemble a court martial, to be
composed of not fewer than five experienced European Officers including the President, who shall not, on any occasion, be below
the rank of a Captain, and in all possible instances, shall be a
Field Officer; and power is hereby vested in such courts martial
to try, decide and determine all such suits. The decisions of such
courts to be final, and judgment thereupon to be carried into
effect, under the orders of the Officer Commanding.

CHAPTER IX.

SUDDER AMEEN.

No person whatever shall by reason of place of birth or by rea-son of descent be incapable of being a Principal Sudder Ameen, or Sudder Ameen.—*Sec.* III, *Act* XXIV, 1836.

Every British born subject of the Queen, or descendant of such British born subject, who shall be appointed a Principal Sudder Ameen or Sudder Ameen, shall in respect of all Acts done by him as such Principal Sudder Ameen, or Sudder Ameen, be liable to the same proceedings, as well Criminal as Civil, and shall be amenable to the same tribunals, as if he were not of British birth or descent.—*Sec.* IV.—*Ibid.*

It shall be competent to the Court of Sudder Udalut of Fort St. George, with the sanction of the Governor in Council, to augment or diminish at discretion, the number of Sudder Ameens within that Presidency.—*Sec.* I, *Act* XXIX, 1836.

Such parts of any of the Regulations in force as authorize the Sudder Ameens within the Presidency of Fort St. George to re-ceive any fee or commission for judicial duties performed by them are repealed.—*Sec.* II.—*Ibid.*

Every Sudder Ameen shall previously to entering upon the ex-ecution of the duties of his situation, *make and subscribe a solemn affirmation* according to the Form prescribed in No. 1 of the Ap-pendix to this Regulation, before the Judge of the Court to which he may belong.—*Sec.* V, *Reg.* VIII, 1816.

No person whatever shall, by reason of place of birth or by rea-son of descent, be in any civil proceeding whatever exempt from the jurisdiction of the Courts of the Sudder Ameens in the terri-tories subject to the Presidency of Fort St. George.—*Sec.* I, *Act* III, 1850.

Sudder Ameen.—Appointment, and removal of servants on his establishment rests with Civil and Session Judge. S. U. 31st August 1843.

Sudder Ameen at Sircy may remove or suspend without reference to judge, subject to appeal. S. U. 9th October 1843.

Sec. V, Reg. VIII, 1816.—Form omitted, as at hand in all courts.

The Sudder Ameens are to hold their courts at the Station where the *zillah civil*, or *subordinate court is held*, in a room belonging to the court house, or in such convenient place as the said court may direct.—*Sec.* VI, *Reg.* VIII, 1816.

The Sudder Ameens are themselves to investigate the suits *pending before* them in a public court room, and are not to allow their Officers, servants or dependants, or any other person to interfere therein.—*Sec.* IX.—*Ibid.*

All causes *filed by*, or referred to the Sudder Ameens, shall be pleaded either by the parties in person, or by an authorized vakeel of the court to which the Sudder Ameens may respectively belong. The said courts will assign to the court of each Sudder Ameen, such a number of authorized vakeels as may appear necessary. The whole of the Regulations in force regarding the authorized vakeels of the zillah civil, and subordinate courts, shall be applicable to the authorized vakeels employed in the courts of the Sudder Ameens.—*Sec.* X.—*Ibid.*

The provisions of Section VIII, Reg. VI, 1816, are hereby declared applicable to the office of Sudder Ameens.—*Sec.* XIII.—*Ibid.*

The civil actions and criminal prosecutions under Clauses 1 and 2, Section VIII, Reg. VI, 1816, with respect to district moonsiffs, and as extended by Section XIII, Reg. VIII, 1816, with respect to Sudder Ameens, shall be brought before the zillah courts established under this Act.—*Sec.* XXIII, *Act* VII, 1843.

Whenever a Sudder Ameen may be guilty of any gross act of misconduct, *the civil judge of the zillah*—*Sec.* XVI, *Act* VII, 1843, —is authorized to suspend him from his office : but he shall report the circumstances of the case, without delay, for the final determination of the court of Sudder Udalut.—*Sec.* VI, *Reg.* III, 1833.

Sudder Ameens are competent to decide any original suits for land exempt from the payment of rent in money or in kind, either to Government or to any individual representing Government and receiving its dues, the annual produce of which land shall not exceed *seventy-five* rupees ; and for land subject to the payment of rent in money or in kind, either to Government or to any individual representing Government and receiving its dues, the annual produce of which land shall not exceed *seven hundred and fifty* ru-

---

Sec. X, Reg. VIII, 1816.—*Filed by* or referred to.—Under this Section as originally enacted, Sudder Ameens received only such suits as were referred to them, they now *file* directly such suits as may be preferred to them, within their competency under Act IX of 1844, but they may still have certain suits *referred* to them by the civil judge under Sec. XVIII, Act VII, 1843.

Sec. XIII, Reg. VIII, 1816.—Sec. VIII, Reg. VI, 1816.—See at page 20.

pees; or for other real property not of the description above specified, or for sums of money or other personal property, the value or
amount of which shall not exceed *two thousand five hundred* rupees.—*Sec.* VII, *Reg.* VIII, 1816.

Suits within the competency, of a Principal Sudder Ameen or a
Sudder Ameen to decide shall ordinarily be instituted in the
courts of those Officers respectively.—*Sec.* I, *Act* IX, 1844.

The civil judge may however withdraw such suits from the
court in which they have been instituted, and try them himself or
refer them for trial to any other court subordinate to his authority,
and competent in respect to the value of the suit, whenever he
may see sufficient reason for so doing.—*Sec.* II.—*Ibid.*

Whenever there shall be more than one Principal Sudder
Ameen, or more than one Sudder Ameen attached to the court of
any civil judge, and not having any special local jurisdiction, it
shall be the duty of such judge to appoint from time to time the
several moonsiff's divisions which shall constitute the special local
jurisdiction of each of such Principal Sudder Ameens, and Sudder
Ameens, and that each of such Principal Sudder Ameens and
Sudder Ameens, shall be empowered to take cognizance of all
such suits as are mentioned in Section I, of this Act, provided the
landed or other real property to which the suit may relate shall be
situated, or in all other cases the cause of action shall have arisen,
or the defendant at the time when the suit may be commenced
shall reside as a fixed inhabitant within the limits of such local
jurisdiction as aforesaid.—*Sec.* III.—*Ibid.*

In referring suits for trial to Sudder Ameens, the judge shall
generally refer such cases as are likely to involve questions of
Hindoo law to the *Hindoo* Sudder Ameens, and of Mahomedan law
to the *Mahomedan* Sudder Ameens.—*Sec.* VIII, *Reg.* VIII, 1816.

The Sudder Ameens in trying causes which may be referred to
them by the zillah civil judge, *or which may be filed in their courts,*
are to be guided by the same rules as are prescribed for the trial
of suits before the zillah judges.—*Sec.* XIV.—*Ibid.*

Sudder Ameens shall have authority to order execution of the
decisions passed by them, according to the rules for the execution

---

Sec. VII, Reg. VIII, 1816.—" *Competent to decide*" in the original, " judges are authorized to refer," &c., but thus altered under Act IX, 1844, the jurisdiction was extended
as marked by the italics, by Sec. III, Reg. II, of 1821.

Sec. III, Reg. VIII, 1816.—" Suits mentioned in Sec. I."—i. e., those " within their
competency."

Sec. VIII, Reg. VIII, 1816.—This is now inapplicable to its original purposes, but may
guide a judge acting under Sec. XVIII, Act VII, 1843.—See note on Sec. X, of this
Regulation.

of decrees applicable to courts to which they are attached, and to issue all process relative to the causes and proceedings before them under their own official seal and signature, and to realize fines imposed by them without reference to any superior officer.—*Sec.* XXV, *Act* VII, 1843.

Principal Sudder Ameens and Sudder Ameens are hereby prohibited from giving judgment in any case before the decree is drafted; and the period limited for appealing from their decrees shall be computed from the dates on which those decrees are passed. The date on which the period will expire shall be certified at the end of the decree under the signature of the Officer who passed it, and shall be registered and proclaimed in the same manner as directed in respect of decrees of European Courts.—*Sec.* IV, *Reg.* VI, 1828.

So much of all decrees as consists of the points to be decided, the decision thereon, and the reason for the decision, which shall be passed by Principal Sudder Ameens, Sudder Ameens, or Moonsiffs, shall be written originally in the vernacular language of such Principal Sudder Ameen, Sudder Ameen, or Moonsiff, and signed by such Principal Sudder Ameen, Sudder Ameen, or moonsiff at the time of pronouncing such decision; and, in case such vernacular language shall not be the same as the vernacular language commonly used in the Court, wherein the suit to which the decree relates, shall have been instituted, shall be translated into such last mentioned vernacular language, and the translation shall be incorporated in the decree.—*Sec.* III, *Act* XII, 1843.

CHAPTER X.

PRINCIPAL SUDDER AMEEN.

For qualifications and liabilities See Secs. III, IV, *Act* XXIV, *of* 1836, *under
" Sudder Ameen."*

The appointment of Principal Sudder Ameen shall rest with the Governor in Council.—*Sec.* III, *Reg.* VII, 1827.

No person whatever shall, by reason of place of birth, or by reason of descent, be in any civil proceeding whatever excepted from the jurisdiction of the *Principal Sudder Ameens,* in the territories subject to the Presidency of Fort St. George.—*Sec.* II, *Act* XI, 1846.

The original jurisdiction of a Principal Sudder Ameen is co-extensive as to amount and value with that of a Subordinate Civil Court presided over by an European Judge.—Sec. IV, *Act* VII, 1843.

Principal Sudder Ameen.—These functionaries were originally termed native judges, and their courts were constituted and regulated by Reg. VII, of 1827: they received this designation by Act XXIV, 1836.—Sec. I, Act VII, of 1843, which see under zillah civil court, abolished their courts as then existing and re-established them, on a new footing, for the purpose of replacing, where located, the then existing zillah courts. They now perform, with a few specified exceptions, exactly the same duties as the subordinate judges, constituted and appointed for a similar purpose under the same Regulation.

They have the power of dismissing and suspending vakeels and servants of their courts, without reference to civil and session judge, subject of course to appeal.—S. U. 9th October 1843. 10 such courts are now established viz. at,

Chingleput.	Cuddalore.
Nellore.	Masulipatam.
Trichinopoly.	Coimbatore.
Tinnevelly.	Vizagapatam.
Cochin.	Tellicherry.

In the event of there being more than one P. S. A. in a zillah. See Sec. III, Act IX, of 1844, at page 113, under " Sudder Ameen."

Sec. IV, Act VII, 1843.—" *Original jurisdiction, &c.*" that is, under 10,000 Rupees. See this Section in extenso under " Subordinate Zillah Court." Like that tribunal a Principal Sudder Ameen has no ordinary and direct appellate jurisdiction ; he may be authorised to receive appeals from district moonsiffs under the special circumstances mentioned in Clause 2, Sec. VIII, Act VII, of 1843, which see under " Appeals," but in general receives and tries such only as may be referred by the civil judge, under Clause 3, of that Section.

Every Principal Sudder Ameen previously to entering on the duties of his office, shall make and subscribe before the Governor in Council, or before any person whom the Governor in Council may commission to administer it, a solemn declaration similar to that which is directed by Section XIII, Reg. II, of 1802, to be made and subscribed by the Judges of the Zillah Courts.—*Sec. IV, Reg. VII, 1827.*

Such Provisions of the Law as relate to the Seal, Pleaders, Jurisdiction, and Ministerial Establishment, and proceedings generally of the Subordinate Civil Courts, shall be applicable to the Courts of the Principal Sudder Ameens.—Sec. V.—Ibid.

It shall not be competent to a *Principal Sudder Ameen* to receive an appeal from the decision of any European Officer of Government.—*Sec. VIII.—Ibid.*

In every zillah in which there is a Subordinate Court constituted according to Reg. VII, of 1827—*i. e. presided over by a Principal Sudder Ameen*—such appeals shall lie to the Zillah Civil Court.—*Sec. VI, Act VII, 1843.*

No Principal Sudder Ameen shall be competent to issue any precept to any Collector, Subordinate, or Assistant Collector or other European Officer of Government.—*Sec. IX, Reg. VII, 1827.*

In all cases in which a Principal Sudder Ameen has occasion to call upon a Collector, Subordinate Collector, or Assistant Collector, or other European Officer of Government, to do any thing in any matter before his Court, he shall transmit to such Officer an Extract from the Proceedings of the Court containing a brief Abstract of the case and specifying what is required to be done by him, with a request that he will comply therewith, and that he will return an answer stating what he has done within a certain time, and such Officer shall comply with the requisition so conveyed to him, in the same manner as if it had been accompanied by a precept from the Zillah Judge.—*Cl. 1, Sec. VII, Act VII, 1843.*

If such Officer does not comply with such requisition the Prin-

---

Sec. IV, Reg. VII, 1827.—An oath was originally required but is now dispensed with under Act XXI, of 1837, which prescribes the making of a solemn declaration, form of which see under Zillah Civil Court.

Sec. V, Reg. VII, 1827.—In the original certain Sections of Regulation I, of 1827, are specified, but these have themselves been since altered and modified, so that this enactment has in effect, force as above. As to the passing and promulgation of decrees by Principal Sudder Ameens, see Sec. IV, Reg. VI, 1828, at page 114, under " Sudder Ameen."

Sec. VIII, Reg. VII, 1827.—Principal Sudder Ameens were originally prohibited by Sec. VII, of this Regulation, from taking cognizance of any suits in which any European Officer of Government was a *party*, that Section was repealed by Sec. V, Act VII, 1843, and such suits are now cognizable by Principal Sudder Ameens under Act XI, of 1836, and by Sudder Ameens and district moonsiffs under Act III, of 1850. This Section only forbids receipt of an *appeal* from a *decision*.

cipal Sudder Ameen shall report the case to the Zillah Judge, who shall proceed thereon as if the requisition had been made by a precept from himself.—*Cl. 2, Sec.* VII, *Act* VII, 1843.

The recommendation of persons for the office of district moonsiff within the jurisdiction of the Principal Sudder Ameen, shall remain with *the Civil Judge of the Zillah.*—*Sec.* X, *Reg.* VII, 1827.

It shall not be competent to any Principal Sudder Ameen to suspend or fine a district moonsiff.—*Sec.* XI.—*Ibid.*

It shall be the duty of a Principal Sudder Ameen to report to the *Civil Judge of the Zillah* every instance of misconduct or neglect of duty in the district moonsiffs, within his jurisdiction, which may come to his knowledge.—*Sec.* XII.—*Ibid.*

It shall not be necessary that any document prepared in a Principal Sudder Ameen's Court, shall be accompanied with a translation in the English language.—*Sec.* XIII.—*Ibid.*

Collectors, Subordinate, or Assistant Collectors, shall not in any case send persons for confinement to the Principal Sudder Ameen, but to the Zillah Civil, or Subordinate Judge as heretofore.—*Sec.* XIV.—*Ibid.*

Principal Sudder Ameens are hereby authorized and required to perform the duties of Register of Deeds, as prescribed in Regulation XVII, of 1802.—*Sec.* V, *Reg.* XI, 1831.

All powers vested by Regulation XI, of 1832, of the Madras Code in *Subordinate* Zillah Judges shall be vested in every Principal Sudder Ameen within the Territories subject to the Government of the Presidency of Fort St. George, in respect of all hidden Treasure of any of the kinds specified in Section II, of that Regulation, which may be found within his jurisdiction ; and all rules applicable to such Judges, shall be applicable to every such Principal Sudder Ameen in respect of such Treasure.—*Act* XII, 1838.

Sec. XI, Reg. VII, 1827.—Direct communication between these functionaries is requisite and unavoidable where the former have jurisdiction over the latter.—S. U. 9th October 1843.

Sec. XIV, Reg. VII, 1827.—No Principal Sudder Ameen having charge of a jail—as where the Subordinate Criminal Court is presided over by a Principal Sudder Ameen, the jail is placed under charge of the Session Judge by Sec. XLVIII, Act VII, 1843.

CHAPTER XI.

SUBORDINATE ZILLAH COURT.

The Governor in Council of Fort St. George is empowered by an order in Council to replace the existing Civil Zillah Courts by Courts constituted according to Regulations I, and VII, of 1827, at his discretion.—*Sec.* I, *Act* VII, 1843.

Each *Subordinate* Court constituted, according to this Regulation, *under Act* VII, *of* 1843, shall be superintended by an Officer denominated " *Subordinate Judge*" of the Zillah in which it may be stationed; and previously to entering on the duties of his office the *Subordinate Judge* shall make and subscribe, before the Governor in Council, or before any person whom the Governor in Council may commission to administer it, a solemn declaration similar to that which is directed by Section XIII, Regulation II, of 1802, to be made and subscribed by the Judges of the Zillah Courts.—*Cl.* 1, *Sec.* III, *Reg.* I, *of* 1827.

The Subordinate Judges shall use *a Circular Seal one inch and three quarters in diameter bearing an inscription in English*; and

---

Sec. I, Act VII, 1843.—According to Regulations I, and VII, of 1827.—i. e. presided over by " Auxiliary" or as now termed " Subordinate" Judges, or Principal Sudder Ameens respectively. By those Regulations the courts so constituted were vested with all the powers of the then existing Zillah Courts, the rules for the guidance of the Subordinate Zillah Courts are therefore to be sought in Regs. II, and III, of 1802,—as are also those for the proceedings of the Zillah Civil Courts in the exercise of their jurisdiction in original cases.

The " Order in Council" was issued on the 28th July 1843, and established nine Subordinate Courts constituted according to Reg. I, of 1827, that is presided over by an European Judge of the Covenanted Civil Service, viz., in the Zillahs of,

Bellary.	Cuddapah.
Chittoor.	Rajahmundry.
Combaconum.	Madura.
Salem.	Mangalore.
Calicut.	

Cl. 1, Sec. III, Reg. I, 1827.—" Declaration similar," &c.—i. e. the same as now made by the Judges of the present Zillah Civil Courts which see under that head.

also in the character and language of the district. " The Seal of the Subordinate Court in the zillah of——."—*Cl.* 2, *Sec.* III, *Reg.* I, 1827.

A sufficient number of pleaders shall be appointed to each *Subordinate* Court under the provisions contained in Regulation XIV, of 1816, and such establishment of ministerial officers as may appear necessary shall also be attached to each court.—*Sec.* IV. —*Ibid.*

The same power and authority as is now vested in Zillah Judges, and subject to the same rules and restrictions, shall be exercised by the *Subordinate* Judges, within the limits assigned to the local jurisdiction of their Courts respectively.—*Cl.* 1, *Sec.* V.—*Ibid.*

The original jurisdiction vested in the Provincial Courts of appeal in suits for an amount or value less than 10,000 Company's Rupees, shall be transferred to the Subordinate Zillah Courts instituted according to Regulations I, and VII, of 1827.—*Sec.* IV, *Act* VII, 1843.

If the plaintiff in a *Subordinate Zillah Court*, shall state his cause of action as not exceeding *ten* thousand Company's Rupees, and the defendant shall, in answer, deny such statement, and allege the produce, amount, or value, to be such as to render the suit not cognizable by the *Subordinate* Zillah Court, under this Regulation; the Judge of that Court, previously to entering upon any investigation of the merits of the cause, shall make such enquiry as may appear necessary, to ascertain whether the suit be, or be not, receivable, in the *Subordinate* Zillah Court ; and shall pass an order accordingly ; leaving either party, who may be dissatisfied therewith, to prefer a summary appeal therefrom, to the *Zillah Civil* Court, whose decision shall be final upon the question, whether the suit be cognizable, or not, in the *Subordinate* Zillah Court ; but no such objection to the plaintiff's statement of the cause of action shall be received from the defendant, unless offered, in the first instance, in answer to the plaint: nor shall any appeal from the

---

Cl. 2, Sec. III, Reg. I, 1827.—" A Seal," in the original " of the same form and dimen-" sions as the seal directed by Sec. XIV, Reg. II, of 1802, to be used by the Zillah " Courts,"—which are therefore here entered, the above quoted Section also prescribes that " the seal of each Court remain in custody of the Judge."

Sec. IV, Reg. I, 1827.—This as well as Section III, and Sections V, VIII, and IX, of the same Regulation, which see below, are equally applicable to Principal Sudder Ameens.

Sec. IV, Act VII, 1843.—In addition to the original and appellate jurisdiction which he exercises in common with the Principal Sudder Ameen, the Subordinate Judge may take cognizance of appeals, against decisions of European Officers of Government, i. e, Collectors, &c., acting under their special judicial powers, whereas when the Subordinate Court is presided over by a Principal Sudder Ameen, such appeals are by Sec. VI, Act VII, of 1843, reserved to the Zillah Civil Courts.

order of the *Subordinate* Zillah Judge, in such cases, be open to the *Zillah Civil* Court, unless preferred within one month, after the order appealed from is passed; or unless sufficient reason be assigned, to the satisfaction of the *Zillah Civil* Court, why it was not preferred within that period.—*Cl.* 1, *Sec.* IV, *Reg.* XII, 1809.

The petition of appeal from the order of a *Subordinate* Zillah Judge, declaring a suit admissible, or not admissible, in the *Subordinate* Zillah Court, may be preferred at the option of the appellant, either to the Court passing the order appealed from, or to the *Zillah Civil* Court, and, in the former case, the *Subordinate* Zillah Judge shall immediately transmit the petition, with all papers and proceedings relative thereto, for the determination of the *Zillah Civil* Court, until the receipt of which, no further proceedings upon the cause shall be held in the *Subordinate* Zillah Court.—*Cl.* 2.—*Ibid.*

No *stamp duty* shall be demandable upon the summary appeals referred to in this Section. And the *Zillah Civil* Courts shall award to the pleaders employed therein, such proportion of the established fees for pleaders, not exceeding one-fourth, as may appear adequate to the service performed by them, to be paid by the party who may have misrepresented the ·cause of action.— *Cl.* 3.—*Ibid.*

Whenever the Subordinate Judge may require an exposition of the law in original suits or appeals pending before him, he shall transmit a written abstract of the case to the *Civil Judge of the Zillah* for the purpose, *if it be a question of Mahomedan law*, of its being referred for the opinion of the Mahomedan law officer attached to the Zillah Court, *or if it be one of Hindoo law*-of its being transmitted to the Sudder Udalut, for the opinion of the law officers of that Court.—*Sec.* VIII, *Reg.* I, 1827.

All the provisions of the Regulations which are now in force, or may hereafter be enacted, for the guidance of the Zillah Judges in their proceedings and decisions, and generally in all matters relating to the discharge of their functions, whether ministerial or judicial shall as far as consistent with this Regulation, be applicable to the *Subordinate* Judges appointed under this Regulation,

---

Sec. IV, Reg. XII, 1809.—The principle of this enactment is now applicable to the Subordinate Zillah Courts, whether constituted under Reg. I, or VII, of 1827.

Sec. VIII, Reg. I, 1827.—' Exposition of law.'—This is equally applicable to all Courts subordinate to the Civil Court. The Sudder Udalut ruled, on the 11th November 1845, " that under the operation of Sec. XXIV, Act VII, 1843, the office of Pundit Sudder " Ameen in the Mofussil was no longer recognized." A Mahomedan Law Officer still remains attached to the Civil and Session Court under Sec. XXXI, Act VII, 1843.

and the Subordinate Officers attached to their Courts shall be subject to, and be guided by the same rules as are or may be established in respect to Officers of the same description employed in the Zillah Courts.—*Sec. IX, Reg. I,* 1827.

Sec. IX, Reg. I, 1827.—The comprehensive directions of this enactment are equally applicable to Principal Sudder Ameens.

CHAPTER XII.

ASSISTANT JUDGE.

It is hereby enacted, that the Governor in Council of Fort St. George may appoint an Assistant Judge to any Zillah Court, to whom the Judge shall have authority to refer any appeals which may be depending before him, excepting appeals from the Subordinate Courts constituted according to Regulation I, or Regulation VII, of 1827, and such Assistant Judge shall be empowered to try and dispose of cases so referred to him, under the rules applicable to the Judge.—*Act* VII, 1843. *Sec.* LII.

" Assistant Judge."—There is only one such Officer at present, viz. the Assistant Judge in the Zillah of Mangalore.

CHAPTER XIII.

GOVERNMENT AGENTS.

From and after the 1st day of December 1839, the operation of the rules for the administration of Civil Justice, shall cease to have effect, except as hereinafter mentioned, in the undermentioned tracts of country at present included in the districts of Ganjam and Vizagapatam.—*Sec.* II, *Act* XXIV, 1839.

The administration of Civil Justice * *· * within the tracts of country specified in the foregoing Section, which are now included in the district of Ganjam, shall be vested in the Collector of Ganjam, and within those which are now included in the district of Vizagapatam, in the Collector of Vizagapatam, and shall be exercised by them respectively, as Agents to the Governor of Fort St. George.—*Sec.* III.—*Ibid.*

It shall be competent to the Governor in Council of Fort St. George, by an Order in Council, to prescribe such rules as he may deem proper for the guidance of such Agents, and of all the Officers subordinate to their control and authority, and to determine to what extent the decision of the Agents in Civil Suits shall be final, and in what suits an appeal shall lie to the Sudder Udalut. —*Sec.* IV.—*Ibid.*

Upon the receipt of any appeal from a decree of either of the Agents, under the rules to be prescribed as aforesaid, the Court of Sudder Udalut shall proceed to try and determine it in the same manner as appeals from the Zillah Civil Courts.—*Sec.* VI.—*Ibid.*

It shall be competent to the Governor in Council of Fort St. George, by an Order in Council, to make from time to time, with the previous sanction of the Governor General of India in Council, such alterations in the limits of the tracts within the aforesaid districts placed under the jurisdiction of the said Agents respectively, as he may deem expedient.—*Sec.* VIII.—*Ibid.*

From and after the 1st day of September 1843, the administration of Civil Justice, within the district of Kurnool, shall vest in such Agent to the Governor of Fort St. George, as shall be appointed by the Governor in Council of Fort St. George, and shall be exercised by the said Agent, with the aid of such Assistants as may be appointed by the said Governor in Council.—*Sec.* I, *Act* X, 1843.

Sections II, IV, and V, of Act X, of 1843, *provide in the case of Kurnool, exactly the same as IV, VI, and VIII, of Act XXIV, of* 1839, *above given, respectively do in the cases of Ganjam and Vizagapatam.*

It shall be lawful for the Governor General in Council, by an Order in Council, to remove from the jurisdiction and superintendence of the Collectors of Ganjam or Vizagapatam, exercised by them as Agents to the Governor of Fort St. George under Act XXIV, of 1839, any portion of the tracts of country specified in Section II, of the last mentioned Act, and to place any such portion under the jurisdiction and superintendence of such Officer (to be called the Agent for the suppression of Meriah Sacrifices) and his subordinates, as shall, from time to time, be appointed by the Government of Fort St. George in that behalf.—*Sec.* III, *Act* XXI, 1845.

It shall be lawful for the Governor General in Council, by an Order in Council, to remove from the operation of the general Regulations and Laws, any portion of Zillah Rajahmundry, and to place any such portion under the jurisdiction and superintendence of such Officer (to be called the Agent for the suppression of Meriah Sacrifices) and his subordinates, as shall be appointed by the Government of Fort St. George in that behalf.—*Sec.* IV.—*Ibid.*

All such Agents and their Subordinates as shall be appointed under this Act, shall, in the exercise of their jurisdiction and superintendence, be guided by such instructions as they may from time to time, receive from the Government of India through their respective Government.—*Sec.* V.—*Ibid.*

It shall be competent to the Governor General in Council, through the Governments of the aforesaid Presidencies respectively, to prescribe such rules as he may deem proper for the guidance of such Agents and Subordinates, and to determine to what extent the decision of the said Agents in Civil Suits shall be final, and in what Suits an appeal shall lie to the Sudder Udalut, * * * —*Sec.* VI.—*Ibid.* ·

Sec. I, Act X, of 1843.—" Kurnool."—In the original, Kurnool and Bunganapilly, but so much as related to Bunganapilly was repealed from 1st January 1849, by Act XXV, of 1848.

CHAPTER XIV.

ZILLAH CIVIL COURT.

The Governor in Council of Fort St. George, is empowered by an Order in Council to abolish the Provincial Courts of Appeal and the Civil Zillah Courts, now existing in that Presidency, and to establish new Zillah Courts to perform the Civil functions now performed by the said Provincial Courts; and to replace the existing Civil Zillah Courts, by Courts constituted according to Regulations I or VII of 1827, at his discretion.—*Sec.* I, *Act* VII, 1843.

Every Zillah Court established under this Act, shall be superintended by one Judge, who shall be styled Civil and Session Judge of the Zillah.—*Sec.* II.—*Ibid.*

The Zillah Courts established under this Act, shall exercise within the limits assigned to them respectively, by the Order in Council by which they are constituted, the same Civil jurisdiction as is now exercised by the Provincial Courts of Appeal, except the original jurisdiction vested in those Courts in suits for an amount or value less than 10,000 Company's Rupees, and shall be vested with the same authority, and shall be subject to the

---

Zillah Civil Court.—I have endeavoured under this head to embrace such enactments only, as specially concern this tribunal, viz., those which constitute it, and define its local, ad valorem, or personal jurisdiction; or which prescribe Acts of supervision, or modes of procedure, peculiar to itself: those general rules for the conduct of Suits, Original and Appeal, for the issue of process, the execution of decrees, &c., which govern, as far as they may be applicable, *all* the judicial tribunals of the country will be found under those heads respectively.

Sec. I, Act VII, 1843.—The Order in Council was issued on 28th July 1843, and established 20 Zillah Courts—as follows, viz:

1.	Bellary.	11.	Trichinopoly.
2.	Cuddapah.	12.	Combaconum.
3.	Chittoor.	13.	Madura.
4.	Chingleput.	14.	Tinnevelly.
5.	Cuddalore.	15.	Coimbatoor.
6.	Nellore.	16.	Salem.
7.	Guntoor.	17.	Mangalore.
8.	Masulipatam.	18.	Calicut.
9.	Rajahmundry.	19.	Tellicherry.
10.	Chicacole.	20.	Honore.

same rules and restrictions as such Provincial Courts of Appeal, except as hereinafter mentioned.—*Sec.* III, *Act* VII, 1843.

In any Zillah in which the Governor in Council of Fort St. George deems it unnecessary to establish a Subordinate Civil Court constituted according to Regulation I or VII of 1827 it shall be competent to the said Governor in Council by an Order in Council to authorise the Civil Judge to exercise the Civil jurisdiction assigned to such Courts besides the proper Civil jurisdiction of the Zillah Court.—*Sec.* XLV.—*Ibid.*

It shall be lawful for the Governor General in Council, by an Order in Council, to authorise the Governor in Council of Fort St. George at any time to change the stations of Zillah Courts, and the limits of their local jurisdiction, and to abolish any of the Zillah Courts which shall be first established under this Act, and to establish new Zillah Courts in any parts of the Presidency of Fort St. George.—*Sec.* LIII.—*Ibid.*

Every *Civil Judge* previous to entering upon the execution of the duties of his office is to *make* and subscribe the following *solemn declaration* before the Governor in Council or any person whom he may commission to administer it.

I,   A. B. appointed Judge of the Civil Court of the Zillah of
                  solemnly declare that I will administer justice conformably to the Regulations that have been or may be passed by the *Legislature*, according to the best of my ability, knowledge, and judgment; without fear, favor, promise or hope of reward; that I will not receive directly or indirectly, any present, or nuzzer, either in money or effects of any kind from any party or person whomsoever, on account of any suit to be instituted, or which may be depending, or has been decided in the Court of which I am appointed a Judge; that I will not knowingly permit any person or persons under my authority, or in my immediate Service, to receive directly or indirectly any present or nuzzer, in money or effects of any kind from any party or person whomsoever, on account of any suit to·be instituted. or which may be depending, or has been decided in the Court; that I will render a true and faithful account of all sums of money that may be paid into the Court, or disbursed from it; that I will not be concerned, directly

---

Sec. III, Act VII, 1843.—Jurisdiction in cases of inferior amount was transferred to Subordinate Courts constituted under Reg. I, or VII, of 1827, by Sec. IV, Act VII, of 1843, which see under Subordinate Court at page 120.

Sec. XLV, Act VII, 1843.—This was done in the case of Masulipatam, from 1st January 1849, by proclamation in Fort St. George Gazette under date 12th December 1848, page 1233. The Court of the Principal Sudder Ameen was abolished and the Civil and Session Judge directed to act as herein provided.

or indirectly, in the purchase of goods or commodities in the British dominions under the Presidency of Fort St. George, for the purpose of remitting money to Europe, or in any commercial transactions; and that I will not derive, directly or indirectly, any emoluments or advantages from my Station, excepting such as the orders of Government do or may authorize me to receive.—*Sec* II, *Reg.* IV, 1802.

The *Zillah Civil* Courts are to use a Circular Seal two inches in diameter with an inscription to the undermentioned effect in *English, and in the language of the district. The Seal of the Zillah Court of——.Sec.* V,—*Ibid.*

The Subordinate Officers and Vakeels who shall be appointed to the Zillah Courts established under this Act shall be subject to the same rules as *were* applicable to the Subordinate Officers and Vakeels of the Provincial Courts of Appeal.—*Sec.* L, *Act* VII, 1843.

The Governor in Council of Fort St. George shall direct what Law Officers shall be appointed to the Zillah Courts established under this Act, and shall order the manner of their appointment and such Officers shall be subject to the same rules as the Law Officers of the Provincial Courts of Appeal.—*Sec.* LI.—*Ibid.*

In suits which may be instituted in the Zillah Civil Court, if the plaintiff shall state his cause of action to exceed *ten* thousand Company's Rupees, and the defendant shall, in answer, deny such statement, and allege the produce, amount, or value to be such as to render the suit cognizable by a *Subordinate* Court, in the first instance; the *Zillah Civil Judge* shall cause such enquiry to be made, as may appear necessary, to ascertain whether the suit be cognizable in the *Subordinate* or *Civil* Court, under the provisions of this Regulation; and the determination of the *Zillah Civil* Court, upon this point, shall be final; provided. that no such objection to the plaintiff's statement of the cause of action, shall be received from the defendant unless offered, in answer to the plaint in the first instance.—*Cl.* 1, *Sec.* V, *Reg.* XII, 1809.

In the cases provided for in this Section, if the *Zillah Civil* Court determine that the suit is cognizable in the *Subordinate*

Sec. II, Reg. IV, 1802.—An oath was originally required but solemn declaration in writing substituted by Act XXI, of 1837.

The prescribed declaration " must invariably be made, before some Court of Justice in the Provinces"—G. O. G. March 20th, 1849.   Fort St. George Gazette 1849, page 351.

Act VII, 1843—Sections L and LI.—The existing laws affecting these functionaries will be found under their respective heads.

Sec. V, Reg. XII, 1809.—This, as originally enacted, related to the Provincial Courts ; by " Subordinate Court" must be here understood a Court constituted either according to Regulation I, or VII, of 1827.

Zillah Court, the *stamp duty* paid by the plaintiff shall be returned to him ; and he shall be left to institute his suit, de novo, in the *Subordinate* Court. If any pleaders shall have been employed in the *Zillah Civil Court*, that Court shall adjudge to them such proportion of the established fee, not exceeding one-fourth, as *it* may judge adequate, to be paid by the plaintiff.—*Cl. 2, Sec.* V, *Reg.* XII, 1809.

The Zillah Civil Courts are empowered to try and determine, in the first instance, any suit or complaint, or any matter whatever of a Civil nature, which may be transmitted to them, for that purpose, by the Sudder Udalut ; and to *execute or cause execution of* the decree which they may pass, *as provided in Sec.* XIV, *Act* VII, *of* 1843.—*Sec.* VI, *Reg.* IV, 1802.

It shall be competent to the Judges of the Zillah Civil Courts to refer execution of decrees of the Sudder Udalut and of their own Courts to the Subordinate Judges, or Principal Sudder Ameens of their Zillahs respectively, who shall proceed therein under the rules prescribed in the general Regulations applicable to such cases: provided that an appeal shall lie from any order passed by a Subordinate Judge, or Principal Sudder Ameen, under such reference, to the Zillah Civil Court in the first instance, and secondly a special appeal to the Sudder Udalut.—*Sec.* XIV, *Act* VII, 1843.

All other processes issued by the Sudder Udalut, and directed to the Zillah Court, or originating in the Zillah Court, shall be served under the orders of the Zillah Judge, by the proper Officer of the Court.—*Sec.* XV.—*Ibid.*

The *Zillah Civil* Courts are empowered to receive any original suit or complaint, which may be cognizable in any *Subordinate Zillah* Court within their respective jurisdictions, and to command the Judge of such Court, by a precept under the seal of the Court, to receive the suit or complaint and to proceed to hear and determine it; provided proof shall be previously made, to their satisfaction, that the Judge refused or omitted to receive or proceed in it. If the Plaintiff shall refuse or neglect to proceed in the suit or complaint, for the space of six weeks after the order of the *Zillah Civil* Court may be received by the *lower* Court, the Judge is authorized to dismiss it, notwithstanding the order of the *Zillah Civil* Court. In such cases, the Judge, within one week

---

Sec. VI, Reg. IV, 1802.—This Section has not been repealed, though greatly modified by subsequent enactments and practice—in a case which a Civil Judge might be personally disqualified from trying, from interest, &c., perhaps the Sudder Udalut might under this Section direct its trial in another Civil Court, as in Criminal cases is done under Reg. III, of 1827.

after the dismission of the suit, is to certify to the *Zillah Civil Court* under his hand and the seal of the Court, that the suit or complaint has been dismissed, and the grounds of the dismission.— *Sec.* VII, *Reg.* IV 1802.

The *Zillah Civil* Courts are empowered to receive any petitions respecting suits or matters that may be depending, or have been decided, in any *Subordinate Zillah* Court within their respective jurisdictions; and provided it shall be proved, to their satisfaction that the petition was presented, or that due means were used to effect its being presented to the Judge, and that he refused, or omitted, to receive it and proceed on it; or, in the last mentioned case, that undue means were used by any of the Officers of the Court to prevent the petition being presented, the Court is empowered to issue a precept under the seal of the Court, commanding the Judge to receive the petition, and to proceed respecting it according to the Regulations.—*Sec.* VIII.—*Ibid.*

It shall be competent to the Zillah Judge to receive a summary Appeal from the orders of any Principal Sudder Ameen, or Sudder Ameen rejecting any original suit cognizable by him and all rules applicable to summary Appeals from orders dismissing original suits on the ground of any default shall be applicable to the summary Appeals given by this Act.—*Sec.* IV, *Act* IX, *of* 1844.

The Zillah Civil Courts shall not require the *Subordinate Courts* to furnish them with translates of any proceedings or papers written in the country languages.—*Sec.* XXXI, *Reg.* IV, 1802.

In cases in which it shall appear to the *Zillah Civil Judges* that the Judges of the *Subordinate Zillah Courts* have been guilty of negligence or misconduct in the discharge of their duty, they are to report the circumstances to the Sudder Udalut.—*Sec.* X.—*Ibid.*

Sec. VII, Reg. IV, 1802.—By " Subordinate Court" must be here understood, either the Court of the Subordinate Judge, or Principal Sudder Ameen, a similar power is given to the Zillah Judge in cases of original suits rejected by Principal Sudder Ameen or Sudder Ameen by Sec. IV, Act IX, 1844, which see below.

Sec. X, Reg. IV, 1802.—This Section was specially repealed by Sec. II, Reg. II, of 1810, the repeal of which by Act XIII, of 1843, though now itself repealed by Act XXXVII of 1850, must according to Sections XX and XXI, Reg. I, of 1802, be held as having revived so much of the original Regulation as may not be inconsistent or incompatible with that, or subsequent Acts. Act XXXVII of 1850, provides for the regular trial of charges of serious " Official Misconduct," but it does not indicate any course to be pursued in cases where it may appear to a Superior that a Subordinate has been guilty of such negligence or misconduct as renders it his duty to report the circumstances to the higher authorities, as the latter part of this Section does: and it would appear to be a good and legal guide for procedure in cases which certainly might arise; especially when viewed in connection with Sec. XXXIX, Reg. V, of 1802, prescribing the course to be taken by the Sudder Udalut on receipt of such reports, and which is evidently only modified by the subsequent enactment, the latter part thereof being in constant use by that Court.

In suits or complaints which may be transmitted by the Sudder Udalut to be tried and determined by the *Zillah Civil Courts*, and also in appeals from the decisions of the *Subordinate Courts within their jurisdiction*, except as to hearing witnesses and receiving evidence, the *Zillah Civil Courts* are to proceed in the same manner, and with the like powers and authority, and subject to the same restrictions, limitations and exceptions, as are prescribed to those Courts.—*Sec.* XI, *Reg.* IV, 1802.

In every Zillah in which there is a Subordinate Court constituted according to Regulation VII of 1827, the Zillah Court shall take cognizance of the appeals which by Sec. VIII, of that regulation are reserved from the jurisdiction of such Court.—*Sec.* VI, *Act* VII, 1843.

Whenever a Sudder Ameen may be guilty of any gross act of misconduct, *the Zillah Civil Judges, Sec.* XVI, *Act* VII, 1843, are hereby authorized to suspend him from his office ; but they shall report the circumstance without delay, for the final determination of the Court of Sudder Udalut.—*Sec.* VI, *Reg.* III, 1833.

All parts of Regulations VI, and VII, 1816, in which the Zillah Judge is mentioned, shall be understood as applicable to the Judges of the Zillah Courts established under this Act, excepting Section LVI, Regulation VI, 1816, which shall be applicable to the Subordinate Judges and Principal Sudder Ameens, as extended by Section V, Regulation III, of 1833. And all parts of Regulation VI, of 1816 in which the Provincial Court is mentioned, shall be understood as applicable to the Sudder Udalut.—*Cl.* 1, *Sec.* XVII, *Act* VII, 1843.

Provided, that District Moonsiffs may be employed by Subordinate Judges and Principal Sudder Ameens, as well as by Judges of Zillah Courts, in the manner and for the purposes specified in Sections LX, and LXI, Regulation VI, 1816.—*Cl.* 2.—*Ibid.*

When a Zillah Judge sees reasons for calling up under Section LIV, Regulation VI, 1816, any cause that may be depending before a District Moonsiff, he may refer it for trial to the Subordi-

---

Sec. VI, Act VII, 1843.—" Appeals reserved," &c.—i. e. Appeals from *decisions* of European Officers of Government.—See Sec. VIII, Reg. VII, of 1827, and note thereon at page 116, under Principal Sudder Ameen.

Cl. 1, Sec. XVII, Act VII, 1843.—" Excepting Sec. LVI, Reg. VI, 1816, which shall be applicable," &c.—That is, a Subordinate Judge or Principal Sudder Ameen may refer to any district moonsiff within their jurisdiction, any original suit which may be filed in their own Courts, but which is within the competency of a moonsiff as extended by Sec. V, Reg. III, of 1833. The Civil Judge has no need of this power, as no suit within the competency of a moonsiff can be filed in his Court.

Cl. 2, Sec. XVII, Act VII, 1843.—" Purposes specified," &c.—i. e., in execution of decrees, or realization of fines.

nate Judge, or Principal Sudder Ameen, of the Zillah, or to a Sudder Ameen, or another District Moonsiff.—*Sec.* XVIII, *Act* VII, 1843.

When a District Moonsiff shall forward to a Zillah Judge, under Clause 2d, Section III, Regulation I, 1829, a suit instituted in his Court, in which he is directly or indirectly a party, or otherwise personally interested, the Judge may refer it for trial either to a Sudder Ameen, or another District Moonsiff.—*Sec.* XIX.—*Ibid.*

The Judges of Zillah Courts may refer to the Subordinate Judges, and Principal Sudder Ameens, applications for the executions of decisions of District Punchayets preferred under Section XVII, Regulation VII, 1816.—*Sec.* XX.—*Ibid.*

It shall be competent to Judges of Zillah Courts to pass orders of their own authority on complaints preferred under Section XI, Regulation VII, 1816, according to Clause 4 thereof.—*Sec.* XXI. —*Ibid.*

The Zillah Judge shall be competent to receive and pass orders of his own authority on complaints preferred under Section XXVII, Regulation VII, 1832.--*Sec.* XXII.—*Ibid.*

Civil Actions and Criminal prosecutions under Clauses 1 and 2, Section VIII, Regulation VI, 1816, with respect to District Moonsiffs, and as extended by Section XIII, Regulation VIII, 1816, with respect to Sudder Ameens, shall be brought before the Zillah Courts established under this Act.—*Sec.* XXIII.—*Ibid.*

Prosecutions against Magistrates and their Assistants under Sec. XLIII, Reg. IX, 1816 shall be instituted in the Zillah Courts established under this Act.—*Sec.* XXXVIII.—*Ibid.*

No Judge, Magistrate, Justice of the Peace, Collector, or other person acting judicially shall be liable to be sued in any Civil

---

Sec. XVIII, Act VII, 1843.—The Sudder Udalut ruled on the 10th October 1843, that he may not try it himself—as he may, a suit called up from a Principal Sudder Ameen or Sudder Ameen under Sec. II, Act IX, 1844, which see at page 113, under Sudder Ameen.

Sec. XXI, Act VII, 1843.—" Complaints under," &c.—i. e., upon a charge of partiality being established to his satisfaction against a district punchayet, he may himself annul the decision.

Sec. XXII, Act VII, 1843.—He may proceed in like manner in the case of a similar charge against a Military Punchayet.

Sec. XXVIII, Act VII, 1843.—Magistrates under Sec. LIII, Reg. IX, of 1816,—as other judicial functionaries, under other parts of the Regulations—were liable to Civil prosecution for Acts done in their official capacity in opposition to any established Regulation, or without their jurisdiction; but by Act XVIII, of 1850, they are protected from such suits unless it can be shown that their error was intentional, and that they did not in good faith believe themselves to be acting within their jurisdiction.

The said Act itself is inserted in this place, as not only giving due protection to those open to prosecution, but as a necessary guide to the Courts before whom such suits may be brought.

Court for any act done by him in the discharge of his judicial duty, whether or not within the limits of his jurisdiction, provided, that he at the time, in good faith believed himself to have jurisdiction to do or order the act complained of: and no Officer of any Court or other person bound to execute the lawful warrants or orders of any such Judge, Magistrate, Justice of the Peace, Collector, or other person acting judicially, shall be liable to be sued in any Civil Court for the execution of any warrant or order which he would be bound to execute, if within the jurisdiction of the person issuing the same.—*Act* XVIII, 1850.

CHAPTER XV.

SUDDER UDALUT.

The Court of Sudder Udalut shall consist of a chief judge, being a member of Council, but not the Governor, nor the Commander in Chief, and of three Puisne Judges, to be selected from among the Company's covenanted civil servants.—*Sec.* III, *Reg.* III, 1807.

The Governor in Council is empowered whenever he may deem it expedient to appoint additional judges to the Sudder Udalut.—*Sec.* IV, *Reg.* III, 1825.

In future Acts, generally applicable to all the Presidencies, the term, "Sudder Court," shall be deemed applicable to the Courts respectively of the highest civil and criminal jurisdiction, as the case may be, of all the Presidencies.—*Act* VIII. *of* 1842.

The Chief Judge, and each of the Puisne Judges of the Court of Sudder Udalut, previously to entering upon the execution of the duties of their offices, shall make and subscribe, the solemn declaration prescribed for the Judges of the Courts of Appeal, by Section II, Regulation IV, 1802.—*Sec.* V, *Reg.* IV, 1806.

The Court of Sudder Udalut, constituted by Regulation III, 1807, shall possess all the powers vested in the Court of Sudder Udalut by *Regulation* V. *of* 1802, and shall perform all the duties required to be performed by that Court, under the existing Regulations, and any other Regulations which may be passed and promulgated in the mode prescribed by *the legislature.*—*Sec.* VI—*Ibid.*

In cases for which no specific rules may exist, the Sudder Udalut is to act according to justice, equity, and good conscience. —*Sec.* XXX, *Reg.* V, 1802.

Sudder Udalut.—As in the case of the other tribunals, I have endeavoured to embrace under this head such enactments only as concern the Sudder Udalut especially, viz. those relating to its constitution, peculiar jurisdiction and procedure, &c.

The Rules relative to Appeals, whether Regular, Special, or Summary, and such Laws as are of general application in the conduct of Judicial business, will be found under the proper heads.

Sec. V, Reg. IV, 1806.—For form of declaration see under " Zillah Court." At p. 128,

The Register of the Sudder Udalut, *his Deputy and Assistants*, are to be appointed by the Governor in Council: previous to entering upon the execution of the duties of their respective offices, they shall *make*, and subscribe the following *solemn declaration* before a Judge or Judges of the Court.—*Cl.* 1, *Sec.* III, *Reg.* XII, 1802.

The Register to the Sudder Udalut, his Deputy and Assistants, are to perform all such official Acts as may be prescribed to them by the Judges of the Court, who are empowered to assign to all ministerial officers attached *thereto*, the particular duties or business to be performed by them respectively.—*Sec.* V.—*Ibid.*

The *Register of the Sudder Udalut*, after the rising of the Court is to procure all Acts of the Court to be executed. *His Deputy and Assistants* are to assist in performing the abovementioned duty, * * in the manner, and conformably to the rules which the Judges of the Court may think it proper to prescribe..—*Sec.* XI.—*Ibid.*

The Court is to use a circular seal, two inches and a quarter in diameter, with an inscription to the following effect, in the Persian, Telinga and Tamul language and character: " The seal of the Sudder Udalut." The Court is to be held in a large and convenient room at Fort Saint Géorge; and to sit de die in diem, as the dispatch of business may require; and is empowered to make such reasonable adjournments as may be deemed expedient consistently with the business. No rule, order, proceedings, or decree, is to be made, but on Court days; and in open Court.— *Sec.* III, *Reg.* V, 1802.

The orders passed on petitions presented to the Court of Sudder Udalut shall be written in English, and shall have annexed or subjoined to them a translation in one of the current languages of the country.—*Cl.* 4, *Sec.* XV, *Reg.* XV, 1816.

The Sudder Udalut is empowered to receive any original suit or complaint which may be cognizable in any *subordinate zillah* court, and to command the judge of such court, by a precept under the seal of the court, and attested by the register, to receive the suit or complaint; and to proceed to hear and determine

Cl. 1, Sec. III, Reg. XII, 1802.—" Declaration"—the same as that of the Judges, mutatis mutandis. When this Regulation was enacted, Registers were attached to all the Zillah Courts, those offices are now abolished, and it remains applicable only to the Register of the Sudder and Foujdaree Udalut and his Assistants. The Regulation also provided for the reception of, and procedure in, charges of corruption, &c. against ministerial servants of the Courts, covenanted and uncovenanted—as respects the former it has been superseded by Act XXXVII, 1850. So much of it as concerns the Native uncovenanted servants, will be found under the head of " ministerial officers."

it; provided proof shall be previously made to their satisfaction, that the judge refused or omitted to proceed in it; and that the complainant applied to the *zillah civil court ;* and that such court omitted or refused to command the judge to receive or proceed in it under Section VII. Regulation IV, 1802. If the plaintiff shall refuse, or neglect, to proceed in the suit or complaint for the period of six weeks, after the order of the Sudder Udalut may be received by *such* Court, and notified to the complainant, the judge is authorized to dismiss it, notwithstanding the order of the Sudder Udalut. In such cases, the judge, within one week after the dismission of the suit or complaint, is to certify to the Sudder Udalut under his hand and the seal of the Court, that the suit or complaint has been dismissed, and the grounds of the dismission. —*Cl.* 1, *Sec.* IV, *Reg.* V, 1802.

The Sudder Udalut is vested with authority to receive any petitions respecting suits, or matters that may be depending, or have been decided, in any *Subordinate Zillah* Court; and provided it shall be proved to their satisfaction that the petition was presented to the Judge of such Court, and that he refused or omitted to receive it, and proceed on it; and that the complainant applied to the *Zillah Civil* Court, and that such Court omitted or refused to grant the precept specified in Section VIII, Regulation IV, 1802; the Court are empowered to issue a precept under the seal of the Court, and attested by the register, commanding the Judge to receive the petition, and to proceed respecting it, according to the regulations.—*Cl.* 2.—*Ibid.*

The Sudder Udalut is empowered to receive any appeal from a decision of a *Subordinate Zillah* Court, which may be cognizable in any Zillah Civil Court; and to command such Zillah Civil Court, by a precept under the seal of the Court, and attested by the register, to receive the appeal, and to proceed to hear and determine it: provided proof shall be previously made to their satisfaction, that the Zillah Civil Court omitted or refused to receive or proceed in it. If the appellant shall refuse or omit to proceed in the appeal for the period of six weeks, after the order of the Sudder Udalut may be received by the Zillah Civil Court, and

---

Sec. IV, Reg. V, 1802.—This enables the Sudder Udalut to afford a *special* remedy, in the event of the Zillah Civil Court, to which a Summary Appeal against the Act of the Subordinate Court lies, under Cl. 3, Sec. V, Reg. XV, 1816, neglecting or refusing to interfere with, or over-rule the proceeding of the lower Court.

notified to him, the said Court is empowered to dismiss it, notwithstanding the order of the Sudder Udalut. In such cases the Zillah Civil Judge, within one week after the dismission of the appeal, is to certify to the Sudder Udalut, under his hand and the seal of the Court, that the appeal has been dismissed; and the grounds of the dismission.—*Cl.* 1, *Sec.* V, *Reg.* V, 1802.

The Sudder Udalut is vested with authority to receive petitions respecting appeals, or matters that may be depending, or have been decided, in any Zillah Civil Court; and provided it shall be proved to their satisfaction, that the petition was presented to the said Court, and that the Judge refused or omitted to receive it; the Court is empowered to issue a precept under the seal of the Court, and attested by the register commanding the Judge to receive the petition; and to proceed respecting it according to the regulations.—*Cl. 2.—Ibid.*

If it shall at any time appear to the Sudder Udalut that from the pressure of business in any of the *Zillah Civil Courts*, suits amounting to *ten thousand rupees and upwards, being the amount fixed for appeals to the Queen in Council*, can be more conveniently or expeditiously tried in the first instance by the Sudder Udalut, than by the Zillah Civil Court before which they may be depending, it shall be competent to the Sudder Udalut, to order the transfer of all or any of such suits from the Zillah Civil Court, to the Sudder Udalut. In the transfer and trial of such suits, the Sudder Udalut shall be guided by the same provisions, as are prescribed for the conduct of the *Zillah Civil Courts* regarding the transfer and trial of original suits exceeding *ten* thousand rupees in amount or value depending in the Zillah *Civil* Courts.—*Sec.* II, *Reg.* XV, 1816.

The Sudder Udalut is prohibited corresponding by letter, with parties in suits, on process or matters depending before them, or coming within their cognizance. If a party in a suit, or any person amenable to the jurisdiction of the Court, shall have any matter to represent to the Court, he is either to appear in the Court in person and represent the matter in writing, or to make

Cl. 1, Sec. V, Reg. V, 1802.—This Section as far as it goes, seems nearly identical with Cl. 2, Sec. V, Reg. XV, 1816, but it is not thereby repealed, and may be held to warrant a different procedure in the only case—that of " omission to receive and proceed"—to which it refers; Sec. V, Reg. XV, of 1816—which will be found under " Summary Appeals," authorizes the reception of a *Summary* Appeal by the Sudder Udalut, setting forth such refusal, or *other* grounds, but this enactment provides for the *Appeal* or *Petition itself* being *received* by the Sudder Udalut, and transmitted for reception to the lower Court.

Sec. II, Reg. XV, 1816.—This has not been repealed—though it is perhaps considered obsolete by the Sudder Udalut—if in force, it must apply to that Court and the Civil Courts.

the representation in writing through an authorized vakeel; the Court are to pass whatever order upon the representation may appear to them proper, consistently with the Regulations; and to cause a copy of the order to be delivered to the person making the representation, or to his vakeel, under the seal of the Court, and attested by the register.—*Sec.* VI, *Reg.* V, 1802. •

In matters which the Sudder Udalut may be empowered by any Regulation to try in the first instance; and also in appeals that may be preferred to the Court from decisions of the *Zillah Civil Courts* (except as to hearing witnesses and receiving evidence); the Court is to proceed in the same manner, and with the like powers and authority, and subject to the same restrictions, limitations, and exception, as are prescribed to *such* Courts.—*Sec.* VII.—*Ibid.*

The *Sudder Udalut* are empowered to confirm or reverse, in whole, or in part, all decrees from which they are, or may be authorized, to receive appeals: and to make such further order on all such decrees, as justice, equity, and good conscience may require; and award such costs to either party as they may deem reasonable.—*Cl.* 3, *Sec.* IX.—*Ibid.* •

All process both to parties and witnesses, and every rule or order for the execution of a decree or final order, and every other order whatever, which may issue from the Sudder Udalut, is to be written or printed in such of the languages of the country, as the Court may direct; and sealed with the seal of the Court, and signed by the register. All such process, rules, and orders, which are to be served or executed on any parties, witnesses, or persons, (exclusive of the parties, vakeels, or persons in actual attendance on the Court) are to be directed to the *Civil* Court of the *Zillah* —*Sec.* XIII, *Act* VII, 1843—in which the cause of action shall . originally have arisen, or in which the lands may be situated, or the parties may be, or reside. Every such process, rule, and order, is to limit a certain time in which it is to be served, executed, and returned to the Sudder Udalut.—*Sec.* XIII.—*Ibid.*

In all cases in which process, either to a party or witness, and all process whatever, and every rule or order, for the execution of any decree or final order, or any order relating to a cause depend-. ing in the Sudder Udalut, may be directed by such Court to any *Zillah Civil* Court—*Sec.* XIII, *Act* VII, 1843—the Court to

---

Sections XIII, XIV, Reg. V, 1802.—On receipt of such order the Zillah Civil Judge may, if for execution of Decree, refer it for execution to a Subordinate Judge or Principal Sudder Ameen, under Sec. XIV, Act VII, 1843: if otherwise, he must cause it to be executed through the officers of his own Court, under Sec. XV, of the same Act.

which the process may be directed is to execute the order contained in the process, rule, or order: and return it so executed within the time limited; or return to the Sudder Udalut good and sufficient reason why it has not been served or executed. When any process, rule, decree. or order, for the execution of any decree or final order, or any order whatever, shall be transmitted by the Sudder Udalut to a *Zillah Civil* Court to be served or executed; the return to such process, rule, order, or decree, is to be made by the Court, either by endorsement on the process, rule, order, or decree; or to be written on a paper firmly annexed to it; and if the return be made in the last mentioned manner, there is to be an endorsement on the process, rule, order, or decree, referring the Sudder Udalut to the return contained in such annexed paper: and the Court is to cause a copy of the process, rule, order, or decree, together with the return to it, to be deposited amongst the records of the Court. And in all cases in which the Sudder Udalut may transmit any order or process to be served, or executed, by a *Zillah Civil* Court, against a party in a cause, and the party on whom it is to be served or executed, is not, after diligent search, to be found, or shall have absconded, or shut himself up in his own or any house or building, or retired to any place so that the process cannot be served upon him; the Court to which the process may be directed is to cause to be fixed up, in some conspicuous part of the room in which the Court may be held, a writing in the language of the district in which the Court may be situated, containing a copy of the order or process; and a notice, that if the party shall not obey the exigence of it within the time limited, the Sudder Udalut will, without further notice, process, or order, proceed exparte to hear, try, and determine the cause to which such process or order may relate: and the Court is likewise to cause a copy of such writing, to be fixed up with all practicable dispatch, on the outer door of the house in which the party may have commonly dwelt, or in some conspicuous place in the village in which he may have usually resided; and to return to the Sudder Udalut, in the manner before directed, how he has executed the process.—*Sec.* XIV, *Reg.* V, 1802.

If a *Zillah Civil* Court to which any process rule or order of the Sudder Udalut may be transmitted, for the purpose of being served, or executed, on any party, shall return that the party has absconded, or shut himself up in his own or any house or building, or retired to any place so that the process could not be served upon him, or that he was not, after diligent search, to be found; and that they had caused the writing to be fixed up, in the places

and manner directed; and the party shall not appear and obey
the exigence of the process rule or order; the Sudder Udalut is
to proceed exparte to try and determine the cause in which the
process rule or order, shall have issued; in the same manner as
if the party had appeared and obeyed the exigence of the process.
—*Sec.* XV, *Reg.* V, 18: 2.

The Sudder Udalut is empowered, in cases of appeal, in which
it shall appear to them that the original suit has not been sufficiently investigated, in the *Zillah Civil* Court or for any other
cause that may be deemed reasonable by the Court, either to receive such further evidence as they may think necessary for the
just determination of the suit, and give judgment upon it; or, to
refer the suit back to the *Zillah Civil* Court in which it originated,
accompanied by such special directions to the Zillah Civil Court,
with regard to the new evidence *it is* to receive respecting it, as
may be deemed by the Court most conducive to justice, and the
convenience of the parties and witnesses. But in every case in
which the Sudder Udalut may exercise the power above vested in
them, they are to enter upon the record of the trial their reasons
for having exercised it. In cases in which the Court may judge
it proper to receive such further evidence themselves, they are empowered, according as they may deem most conducive to justice
(respect being had to the nature of the cause and the evidence)
either to examine the witnesses to be produced, vivâ voce, in open
Court; first causing the witnesses to be sworn, *or placed on solemn
affirmation*, and their depositions to be reduced into writing, and
signed by the deponents respectively; or, to authorize their register to swear the witnesses *or place them on solemn affirmation*, and
take their depositions, and to cause the deponents to sign them,
and to authenticate them with their signatures. The register, in
such case, is to examine the witnesses in the presence of both
parties, or their vakeels, who are to be at liberty to put any questions to the witnesses that they may think proper; and the questions, with the answers to them, are in the same manner to be
reduced into writing, signed, and authenticated. But if due
notice be given to the parties, or their vakeels, of the examination of any witness or witnesses before the register, and he or
they shall not attend at the time of the examination, the register
is to proceed in the examination as before directed, and the depositions are to be received as good and authentic evidence.—*Sec.*
XVI.—*Ibid.*

Sec. XVI, Reg. V, 1802.—Similar provisions in respect of *Remand* are made by Sec.
X, Act VII, 1843, which see below—this Section, in addition thereto, prescribes the course
to be followed in the event of the Court not seeing fit to *remand.*

If a witness duly summoned by the Court of Sudder Udalut of Fort St. George shall not attend, or shall refuse to give evidence, in the manner prescribed by the existing law, that Court may impose on such witness a fine not exceeding five hundred rupees, and commit him to the jail of the Zillah Court nearest to the Presidency, until he shall consent to give his evidence in the manner prescribed. And if the said witness shall not pay the fine imposed on him, it shall be lawful for the said Court of Sudder Udalut to direct him to be kept in confinement for a further term not exceeding three months.—*Cl. 2, Sec.* I, *Act* XV, *of* 1835.

If any person shall be guilty of contempt of the Sudder Udalut in open Court, the Court may immediately punish the offender by fining him in a sum not exceeding five hundred rupees, or by committing him to custody in the jail of the Zillah· Court nearest to the Presidency, for a term not exceeding six months.—*Sec.* II.—*Ibid.*   •

If it shall appear to the Court of Sudder Udalut that any person has been guilty of wilful and corrupt perjury in any matter depending in that Court, that Court may immediately commit the offender to custody, and transmit him to the *Subordinate Criminal Court* of the Zillah nearest to the Presidency in order to his being brought to trial before the *Session Court in such Zillah ;* and such person shall be dealt with in the same manner, as if the perjury had been committed within the limits of the local jurisdiction of such *Session Court.*—*Sec.* III.—*Ibid.*

In such suits as by any Regulation may be authorised to be tried in the first instance before the Sudder Udalut, and in appeals that may be heard by that Court, no proceedings are to be held, nor any acts whatever done, either on behalf of the plaintiff or defendant, or the appellant or respondent, excepting by the plaintiff or defendant, the appellant or respondent, respectively ; or, by a vakeel admitted to plead in the Court under the established Regulations ; nor by any vakeel, before his vukalutnamah shall have been filed in the Court : and no persons excepting such parties, or their witnesses, or such vakeels, shall be heard, vivâ voce, in any stage in the cause.—*Sec.* XX, *Reg.* V, 1802.

The Sudder Udalut is empowered, in every case in which a sum of money is decreed to be paid by a zemindar, independent talookdar, or other actual proprietor of land ; to issue an order to the proper *Zillah Civil* Court, to execute the decree; in the same manner as *such* Court is authorized to execute decrees, by which a sum of money may be decreed to be paid, by any of the descriptions of persons abovementioned.—*Sec.* XXI.—*Ibid.*

The petition of appeal, pleadings, depositions, and exhibits in

the Sudder Udalut, are to be numbered, marked, dated, and signed by the Register; in the same manner as the complaint, pleadings, depositions, and exhibits, are ordered to be numbered,
marked, dated, and signed by the *Judge* in the Zillah Courts.
The decrees are to be signed by the Judges present in the Court
when the decrees may be passed, and attested by the Register.—
Sec. XXVIII, *Reg.* V, 1802.

The Court of Sudder Udalut shall be an open Court, and holden
as directed in Sec. III, Reg. V, 1802. The ordinary sitting of
the Court shall be held before *one or more of the Puisne Judges.*
But the Chief Judge shall attend and preside when a difference of
opinion between the *Puisne* Judges, or any special case or business may in his judgment require it. In the event of a difference
of opinion when the three *Puisne* Judges are present in Court, the
voices of the majority shall determine the question. But if a difference of opinion should arise when two Judges only are present
in Court, the question shall be postponed, for adjudication, until
the third Judge can attend. The Judge who may be absent
when any such case shall occur, is to be duly advised of the same
by the Register of the Court; and the presiding Judge shall instruct the Register to summon a special sitting of the Court, for
the adjudication of the question, or order it to be brought forward
at the next sitting of the Court, when all the Judges shall be present. Every decree of the Sudder Udalut, shall be signed by the
Judges present at the passing of such decree. All other orders of
Court, as well as all process issued from the Sudder Udalut shall
be signed and issued by the Register, under such instructions as
now are in force, or as may be prescribed by the Court for his
guidance in conformity to Section V, Reg. XII, 1802.—*Sec.* VII,
Reg. IV, 1806.

It shall be competent to a single Judge of the Court of Sudder
Udalut to exercise all the powers at present vested in two or more
Judges of that Court, under the restrictions contained in the re-
maining Clauses of this Section.— *Cl.* 1, *Sec.* IV, *Reg.* VIII, 1831.

It shall not be competent to such single Judge to reverse or alter any order or decision which may have been passed by one or
more Judges of the Court.— *Cl.* 2.—*Ibid.*

It shall not be competent to such single Judge to reverse or alter any order or decision of a Subordinate Court.— *Cl.* 3.—*Ibid.*

It shall be competent to a single Judge of the Sudder Udalut to
hold a sitting of Court on all matters within the cognizance of

---

Cl. 3, Sec. IV, Reg. VIII, 1831.—He may confirm, or remand for revision, under Sec-
X, Act VII, 1843, but he is still precluded from reversing or altering, by this Section.

that Court, and to pass orders or judgments in conformity to the Regulations, subject to the following provisions.—*Cl.* 1, *Sec.* X, *Act* VII, 1843.

On the hearing of any appeal from the decision or order of any Court of inferior jurisdiction, in any case, regular or miscellaneous, if a single Judge of the Sudder Udalut shall be of opinion that no sufficient ground has been shewn to impugn the correctness or justice of such decision or order, it shall be competent to such single Judge, without reference to the order of the file, to confirm the same without requiring the attendance of the opposite party, and with or without a revision of the whole proceedings, as the nature of the case may appear to require, and to communicate the order of confirmation, through the Court from whose judgment the appeal was made, to the opposite party, with a view to enable such party to take immediate measures for the execution of the decree.

On the other hand, if a single Judge shall be of opinion that the decision or order appealed against ought to be altered, or reversed, as being manifestly unjust or at variance with some Regulation in force, or in opposition to the Hindoo or Mahomedan Law, or other Law applicable to the case, or as having been passed without sufficient investigation of the merits, or as grounded on an assumption obviously erroneous, or irrelevant with reference to the points at issue, it shall likewise be competent to a single Judge to issue an injunction pointing out the irregularity, illegality, or other defect, apparent in the proceedings, decision, or order, appealed against, and requiring that the Court by which the same may have been held, or passed, shall revise the case, and proceed thereon in such manner as may appear conformable to justice and to the Regulations.—*Cl.* 2, *Sec.* X, *Act* VII, 1843.

A single Judge of the Sudder Udalut may exercise his discretion in calling for the proceedings of the Lower Courts, or such parts of them as may appear necessary, and may further order a report in English, or in the vernacular language commonly used in the Court, as the occasion may render advisable, on any points requiring explanation, prior to passing a determinatian on the case or matter in appeal.—*Cl.* 3.—*Ibid.*

It shall further be competent to a single Judge to direct, that the execution of any judgment or order passed by any inferior Court, in all cases in which that measure may appear to him expedient, may be stayed until a final decision has been passed thereon.—*Cl.* 4.—*Ibid.*

Any provisions of existing Regulations which require inferior Courts to furnish the Sudder Udalut with translations of papers, written in the vernacular languages of the country, which they may transmit to that Court in appeals and other cases are rescinded.—*Sec.* XII, *Act* VII, 1843.

* * * The Court of Sudder Udalut is directed to report to the Governor in Council all instances of wilful neglect of duty, or aggravated misconduct, by a covenanted servant of the Company, employed in any of the Civil Courts ; whether in a judicial, or ministerial capacity; and whether such neglect or misconduct may have been reported to the Court of Sudder Udalut, or may otherwise appear from the proceedings and papers before the Court. But if the case should appear to the Court to involve an error of judgment only, or a slight default, for which an admonition from the Court may be deemed a sufficient correction ; the Court of Sudder Udalut, in the former case, is authorised to notice the error for the information and guidance of the party who may have committed it ; or, in the latter case, to advise him of his default, and to admonish him accordingly.—*Sec.* XXXIX, *Reg.* V, 1802.

In all instances wherein a precept issued by a *Zillah Civil Court* to a *Subordinate Court,* shall appear to *the Judge thereof* to be contrary to, or unwarranted by the existing Regulations, he is authorised to state to the *Zillah Civil Court,* in what respect he considers *its* precept· to be in deviation from the Regulations, and suspend execution till receipt of a second precept in reply to his objections.   But if the second precept of the *Zillah Civil Court,* in reply to the objections of the *Judge of the Subordinate Court* shall confirm the first precept in whole or in part, and shall require *him* to execute the same without further reference, he shall immediately comply with such requisition.   In case however, the second precept of the Zillah Civil Court should not satisfy the Judge of the *Subordinate Court* that the Regulations have been rightly construed by the Zillah Civil Court he is at liberty, at the same time that he certifies the execution of the order of the Zillah Civil Court, to request that it will transmit copies of its precepts to him, and his returns thereto, with such other papers as may be necessary for the information of the circumstances of the case, to the Court of Sudder Udalut; and the Zillah Civil Court shall accordingly transmit such papers, as requested, without any unnecessary delay.   Provided nevertheless that nothing in this Regulation be understood to authorise *the Judge of any Subordinate Court* to question the propriety of any order issued by

---

See. XXXIX, Reg. V, 1802.—The former part of this Section has been superseded by Act XXXVII, of 1850, the latter is still in constant use.—See Note on Sec. X. Reg. IV, 1802, page 131.

a Zillah Civil Court, in cases clearly left to the discretion and judgment of the Zillah Civil Court by the Regulations: the reference to them, and eventually to the Courts of Sudder Udalut, meant to be authorised by this Regulation, being confined to cases in which the sense of the Regulations, from a difference of construction, or otherwise, may appear doubtful and uncertain.—*Sec.* II, *Reg.* XXII, 1802.

In all instances wherein a reference to the Court of Sudder Udalut, may be made under the preceding rule, the determination of *that* Court, *which is* empowered to prescribe the forms and conduct to be observed by the *Zillah Civil and Subordinate Courts*, in all cases provided for by the Regulations, agreeably to their construction thereof, is to be held final and conclusive.—*Sec.* III.— *Ibid.*

Should any doubt occur to the Sudder Udalut, with respect to the meaning of any part of the Regulations; or should it appear to them, on occasion of any reference from the Zillah Civil or Subordinate Courts that the Regulations do not sufficiently provide for the case submitted to their decision, they are * * * to report the circumstances of it to the Governor in Council.—*Sec.* IV.—*Ibid.*

One part of a Regulation is to be construed by another, so that the whole may stand.—*Sec.* XIX, *Reg.* I, 1802.

If any Regulation shall be passed differing from a former Regulation, either wholly or partially, the new Regulation is to be considered as a virtual repeal of the old one as far as it may differ from the latter, provided that the new Regulation be couched in negative terms, or by its matter necessarily imply a negative.— *Sec.* XX. *Reg.* I, 1802.

If a Regulation that rescinds another Regulation, is itself afterwards rescinded, the original Regulation is to be considered as re-

---

Sec. II, Reg. XXII, 1802.—This enactment has respect to all the Courts, but as affecting official subordination and control—it seemed more appropriate to place it under the head of the superior and controlling Court.

Sec. IV, Reg. XXII, 1802.—In the original the *intention* of the report was explained to be, that in the former case an explanatory, or in the latter, a new, Regulation might be passed, and although this power is no longer possessed by the Governor in Council the Section is retained as still indicating the course to be taken by the Sudder Udalut—leaving it to the Government to take such measures to procure remedy as may be fit.

Sections XIX, XXI, Reg. I, 1802.—Reg. I, of 1802, has ceased to be operative in respect of legislation since the passing of the Statute 3 and 4, William IV, c. 85, of which the 43rd Section vests in the Governor General in Council, the power of making laws for the several Presidencies—these Sections are retained as the guide of the Sudder Udalut in the construction of the enactments of the Madras Government from 1802 till 1834, when local Regulations ceased to be enacted.

vived, without any formal declaration to that purpose.—*Sec.* XXI, *Reg.* I, 1802.

The Court of Sudder Udalut subject to the orders of Government, shall from time to time, as circumstances require, prescribe the forms, and fix the periods, for the transmission of all reports, registers, or other statements to be furnished by the Civil Courts, European or Native, under this Presidency.—*Sec.* III, *Reg.* IX, 1828.

It shall be competent to the Court of Sudder Udalut of Fort St. George, with the sanction of the Governor in Council, to augment or diminish at discretion the number of Sudder Ameens within that Presidency.—*Sec.* I, *Act* XXIX, 1836.

The Court of Sudder Udalut are hereby empowered to permit, from time to time, the Judges of the Civil Courts under the Presidency of Fort St. George to adjourn their respective Courts : and in like manner themselves to adjourn ; so that such occasional adjournments of any Court shall not collectively exceed two months in each year.—*Sec.* III, *Reg.* III, 1816.

The Zillah Civil Judges shall recommend to the Sudder Udalut the persons whom they may deem fit for the office of District Moonsiff ; but no person shall be authorised to officiate as a District Moonsiff without the previous sanction of the Sudder Udalut.— *Sec.* VI, *Reg.* VI, 1816.

No District Moonsiff shall be removed from his office, unless the Sudder Udalut shall be satisfied that there is sufficient cause for his removal.—*Cl.* 4, *Sec.* VII.—*Ibid.*

BOOK II.

REGULAR SUITS.

Trial and Decision of, &c.

CHAPTER I.

The Zillah Courts are to be held in a large and convenient room in the city or place at which they are respectively established, three days in every week, or oftener if the state of the business shall render it necessary. Whenever the judge of a Zillah Court, from indisposition or other cause, shall be prevented from holding a Court three days in each week, as above required, he is at the expiration of the week to report the cause of the court not being so held to the Sudder Udalut. This report is not to be made when the Court may be shut pursuant to orders from the Sudder Udalut under *Regulation* III, 1816. No rule, order, proceeding, or decree, shall be made, but on Court days, and in open Court.—*Sec.* XIV, *Reg.* II, 1802, *and Sec.* IV, *Reg.* IV, 1802.

The orders passed in Miscellaneous Petitions presented to a *Subordinate Zillah* Court shall be written in the current language of the district in which such Court is stationed ; and English translations of such orders shall be furnished on the special application of the parties presenting the petitions.—*Cl.* 3, *Sec.* XV, *Reg.* XV, 1816.

The orders passed on Petitions presented to the *Zillah Civil Courts,* * * * shall be written in English, and shall have annexed or subjoined to them a translation in the *current language of the district.*—*Cl,* 4.—*Ibid.*

Sec. XIV, Reg. II, 1802.—By " Zillah Courts" throughout this Book must be understood, where not otherwise specified, the Zillah Civil Courts, Subordinate Courts and the Courts of the Principal Sudder Ameens—Sec. XXIII, of this Regulation prescribes the course to be adopted by the Judges in applying for leave and the Government in granting it, but as a mere rule of office, in which circumstances and practice have made great alterations, it has not been inserted.

The judges ·of the Zillah Courts are prohibited from corresponding by letter with parties in suits, process or matters depending before them, or coming within their cognizance. If a party in a suit or a person amenable to the jurisdiction of the Court, shall have any matter to represent to the Court, he is either to appear in the Court in person and represent the matter in writing, or make the representation in writing through an authorized vakeel. The Court is to pass whatever order upon the representation may appear to it proper, consistently with the regulations, and to direct a copy of the order to be delivered to the person making the representation or to his vakeel, under the seal of the Court and attested by the *signature of the judge.* The Judges of the Zillah *Subordinate* Courts are also prohibited from corresponding by letter with the *Zillah Civil* Courts respecting any cause or matter before those Courts, or upon any matters whatever, on which they may not be specially empowered so to correspond. When a Subordinate Judge *or Principal Sudder Ameen* shall have occasion to communicate to the *Zillah Civil* Court any information that may be required from him by the Court, or which he may deem it necessary to submit to the Court, respecting any matter or cause that may be before it, he is to certify it to the Court by a writing under his official seal and signature.—*Sec.* XX. *Reg.* II, 1802.

The Zillah Civil Courts are also prohibited from corresponding by letter with the Judges of the *Subordinate* Zillah Courts, respecting any cause or matter before them, or upon any matters whatever on which they may not be specially empowered so to correspond. When they shall have occasion to issue an order to the Judge of any *Subordinate* Zillah Court, or require information from him, on the subject of any suit or matter before them, the Court is to issue a precept, under its seal and the signature of the Judge, commanding the *Subordinate* Judge to execute the order, or requiring him to furnish the information ; and the Judge to whom the precept may be directed is to perform the exigence of it, or return good and sufficient reason why he has not done it.—*Sec.* IX. *Reg.* IV, 1802.

In cases coming within the jurisdiction of the Zillah Courts, for which no specific rule may exist, the Judges are to act according to justice, and equity, and good conscience.—*Sec.* XVII. *Reg.* II, 1802, *and Sec.* XXXIV. *Reg.* IV, 1802.

Sec. XVII, Reg. II, and Sec. XXXIV, Reg. IV, 1802.—Where a double authority is thus quoted, it is to be understood that the 1st quoted enactment is that which referred to the late Zillah Courts, and the 2d that which regulated, in exactly similar terms, the practice of the late Provincial Courts, and that the law is now applicable under the new system to all the Courts of the Zillah.

No Judge, Assistant Judge, Principal Sudder Ameen or District Moonsiff, shall sit on the trial of any cause in which he may be directly or indirectly a party, or may be otherwise personally interested: neither shall he sign a decree passed in such cause by the Court of which he is a Judge.—*Cl.* I, *Sec.* III. *Reg.* I, 1829.

, Every Zillah Judge, Principal Sudder Ameen, Sudder Ameen or District Moonsiff shall, whenever a suit in which he may be directly or indirectly a party, or may be otherwise personally interested, shall be instituted before him, or be referred to him, or be depending in his Court when he takes charge thereof, *forward the record to the Court to which in ordinary cases an appeal lies from his decisions.*—*Cl.* 2 & 3.—*Ibid.*

The jurisdiction of the Zillah Courts shall extend to all Civil suits arising within the districts and places that are or may be included in the Zillahs in which they are respectively established. —*Sec.* III. *Reg.* II, 1802.

No person whatever shall, by reason of place of birth, or by reason of descent, be, in any Civil proceeding whatever, excepted from the jurisdiction of any of the Courts hereinafter mentioned, that is to say. The Court of Sudder Udalut, the Court of the *Zillah Civil or Subordinate Judges*, of the Assistant Judges, and of the *Principal Sudder Ameens* in the Territories subject to the Presidency of Fort St. George.—*Sec.* II. *Act* XI, 1836.

The Zillah Courts are empowered to take cognizance of all suits and complaints respecting the succession or right to real or personal property, land rents, revenues, debts, accounts, contracts, partnerships, marriage, caste, claims to damages for injuries, and generally of all suits and complaints of a civil nature, provided the landed or other real property to which the suit or complaint may relate, shall be situated, or, in all other cases, the cause of action shall have arisen, or the defendant at the time when the suit may be commenced shall reside as a fixed inhabitant, within the limits of the Zillah over which their jurisdiction may extend.— *Sec.* V. *Reg.* II, 1802.

The Zillah Courts are prohibited hearing, trying, or determining the merits of any suit whatever for the discharge of the private debts of any native Prince, Rajah, Zemindar, Polygar, or other in-

---

Sec. III, Reg. II, 1802.—" All Civil Suits" i. e. all within their competency as to value, respectively.

Sec. II, Act XI, 1836.--Similar jurisdiction has now been given to Sudder Ameens and District Moonsiffs by Act III, 1850.

dependent landholder, who did not at the time of entering into such engagements stand amenable to a Court of Justice, or some public authority, for their discharge.—*Sec.* VIII. *Reg.* II, 1802.

If a suit shall have been instituted in a Court of Udalut of any Zillah in which it may have been cognizable, no other Zillah Court is to entertain a suit for the same cause of action. On proof being made in the Court in which the second suit may be commenced, that a prior suit for the same cause of action has been instituted in another Zillah Court competent to try it, the court in which the second suit may be brought is to dismiss it, with costs to be paid by the party so suing. And if any person shall have commenced a suit in any Zillah Court, and whilst that suit is depending, or after a decree may be passed in it, shall commence another suit in any other Zillah Court for the same cause, or if any person shall commence a suit in any Zillah Court which shall appear to the Judge to be frivolous, vexatious, or groundless, he is not only to dismiss the suit with such costs as he may deem it equitable to award against the plaintiff, but is to fine him in such amount as he may think proper, upon a consideration of the nature of the case, and the situation and circumstances in life of the offender, and commit him to close custody until he pays the fine.—*Sec.* IX.— *Ibid.*

The Zillah Courts are prohibited from entertaining any cause which, from the production of a former decree, or the records of the Court, or other instrument, shall appear to have been heard and determined by any former Judge, Superintendent of a Court, Collector, or other public officer having competent jurisdiction or authority. If any doubt should arise respecting the competency of the former jurisdiction or authority, the Judges are to report the circumstances to the Sudder Udalut, and wait the instructions of that Court.—*Sec.* X.—*Ibid.*

The Zillah Courts are prohibited from interfering in any respect in any cause or matter of a criminal nature, declared cognizable by the Magistrates of the several Zillahs, the Session Courts, or the Foujdaree Udalut, or any other Courts for the trial of cases of a criminal nature, that now exist or which may be hereafter established; excepting for contempt and perjuries committed in open Court, as prescribed in Sections VIII and XXII, Regulation III, of 1802.—*Sec.* XI.—*Ibid.*

The Zillah Courts are not to receive or entertain any suit, under any pretence whatever, relating to any land, house, tenement, or hereditament, nor a dispute regarding the boundaries of lands, houses, tenements, or hereditaments, situated within the town of Madras, or the limits of the Supreme Court of Judicature at Madras, which for the purpose of this rule is declared to be bound as follows. That the southern limits shall be the southern bank of the Saint Thomé River, as far as the road leading to the Long Tank ; that the limits shall then be continued in a northern direction, along the bank of the Long Tank, and from thence along the bank of Nungumbaukum Tank, as far as the village of Chettapet, upon the banks of the Poonamally River ; that the limits shall be continued, in the same direction, to the villages of Kilpaukum and Peramboor, and that, from the latter village, it do take an eastern direction to the sea, so as to include the whole village of Tandearpetta; also that no lands, situated to the southward of the Saint Thomé River, or to the westward, of the bank of the Long Tank, or of the Nungumbaukum Tank, shall be considered within the limits of the said town of Madras ; but that all the lands included in the said villages of Chettapet, Kilpaukum, Peramboor, and Tandear, shall be considered within the said limits. Nor shall the Zillah Courts entertain any suit whatever against a person who may be a resident of Madras, or of any place within the said limits, at the time the suit may be instituted. The Courts are commanded not to intermeddle with or take cognizance of the suits abovementioned, which are to be considered entirely exempt from their jurisdiction. But the prohibitions contained in this section are not to be construed to extend to preclude the Zillah Courts entertaining any suit concerning marriage, or caste, in which no money or other valuable thing may be demanded or decreed, although the cause of action shall have arisen, or the defendant may reside, or shall have resided at the time the suit commenced, within the limits of the Supreme Court.—*Sec.* XII. *Reg.* II, 1802.

The Courts are prohibited hearing, trying, or determining the merits of any suit, against any person or persons, to regain the possession of lands, or grounds, or other real property, situated within either the five Northern Circars, if the cause of action shall have arisen previous to the acquisition of these provinces, by the Company's government, which for this purpose, shall be reckoned from the twenty-sixth day of February, 1768.—*Cl.* 1, *Sec.* XVIII.—*Ibid.*

The said period, (of the twenty-sixth of February 1768,) shall be held equally applicable as to the purposes aforesaid, in respect to the town and district of Cuddalore, the Jageer lands, or other Territories, at that time subject to the jurisdiction of the Company's Government.—*Cl.* 2.—*Ibid.*

In cases not falling within the above descriptions, and where the country, town, or district may have accrued to the possession of the

Company's Government, at any time subsequent to the said twenty-sixth of February 1768, the date of the particular acquisition shall in every instance become the period beyond which no civil suit or cause of action shall be cognizable by the Udalut Courts; provided, however, that the date of such acquisition shall not exclude from the cognizance of the Courts any suit where the cause of action may have arisen within twelve years, antecedent to the date of enacting this regulation; all suits where the cause of action may have arisen within twelve years, antecedent to the passing of this law, are hereby declared equally cognizable by the Udalut Courts, notwithstanding the country, town, or district, in which the cause of action shall have arisen, may not at that time have been subject to the Company's Government.—*Cl.* 3.—*Sec.* XVIII. *Reg.* II, 1802.

The *Zillah* Courts are prohibited hearing, trying, or determining the merits of any suit whatever, against any person or persons, if the cause of action shall have arisen twelve years before any suit shall have been commenced on account of it, unless the complainant can shew by clear and positive proof, that he had demanded the money or matter in question, and that the defendant had admitted the truth of the demand, or promised to pay the money; or that he directly preferred his claim within that period, for the matter in dispute, to a Court of competent jurisdiction or person having authority (whether local or otherwise for the time being) to hear such complaint, to try the demand, and shall assign satisfactory reasons to the Court why he did not proceed in the suit, or shall prove that either from minority, or other good and sufficient cause, he was precluded from obtaining redress. But from this rule are excepted, all claims founded on bonds, which shall have been in a course of payment by instalments, or of which any proportion shall have been paid within twelve years previous to the institution of the suit; and also all claims on mortgages, the period for rendering which obsolete and unactionable is to be determined by the laws of the country.—*Cl.* 4.—*Ibid.*

The Courts of Udalut are hereby prohibited from taking cognizance of any claim to hereditary or personal grants of money or of land revenue, however denominated, conferred by the authority of the Governor in Council in consideration of services rendered to the state, or in lieu of resumed Offices or privileges, or of Zemindaries or pollams forfeited or held under attachment or management by the Officers of Government, or as a yeomiah or charitable allowance, or as a pension; and also of any claim for the recovery or continuation of, or participation in, such grants, whether preferred against private individuals or public Officers, unless the plaint is accompanied by an order signed by the chief, or other Secretary to Government, referring the complaining party to seek redress in the established Courts of Udalut.—*Cl.* 1, *Sec.* II, *Reg.* IV, 1831.

The power to decide on such claims is reserved exclusively to the Governor in Council, after due investigation by such persons and in such manner as he may deem fit.—*Cl.* 2.—*Ibid.*

The grants mentioned in Section II, Regulation IV, of 1831, of the Madras Code shall not be liable to attachment or sequestration in satisfaction of any decree or order of any Court whatever. —*Act* XXIII, 1838.

The provisions of Regulation IV, of 1831, of the Madras Code, relating to grants of money or land revenue made by the British Government, shall be extended to all similar grants within the territories subject to the Presidency of Fort St. George, which, having been made by any native government, have been confirmed or continued by the British Government.—*Act* XXXI, 1836.

All emoluments derived from lands, from fees in money or grain, or from other sources, which have been annexed by the state to hereditary village and other Offices in the revenue and Police departments *shall be* inalienable from such offices by mortgage, sale, gift, or otherwise ; *and* all transfers which may hereafter be made thereof by the holders of such offices, shall be null and void ; and such emoluments shall not be liable to attachment or other process in satisfaction of decrees of Court.—*Sec.* II, *Reg.* VI, 1831.

Claims to the possession of, or succession to, hereditary village or other offices in the revenue and Police departments, or to the enjoyment of any of the emoluments annexed thereto, shall not be cognizable by the ordinary Courts of judicature.—*Cl.* 1, *Sec.* III. —*Ibid.*

In suits regarding succession, inheritance, marriage, and caste, and all religious usages, and institutions, the Mahomedan laws with respect to Mahomedans, and the Hindoo laws with regard to Hindoos, are to be considered as the general rules by which the Judges are to form their decisions. The Mahomedan and Hindoo law officers of the Courts are to expound the law of their respective persuasions, in cases in which recourse may be required to be had to it. The Judge of the Zillah Court may further refer cases for the opinion of the Law Officers of the *Sudder Udalut*, through the medium of the *Register* of that Court ; but no reference is to be made

---

Cl. 1, Sec. III, Reg. VI, 1831.—Such suits are cognizable by Collectors in virtue of the powers given to them by Sections IV, VIII, of this Regulation, which see under " Collector" at page 87.

by the Judges to any individual not acting in a public and responsible capacity; yet this shall not prohibit parties in a suit submitting law opinions, quoting or referring to authorities in support of their claims.—*Cl.* 1, *Sec.* XVI, *Reg.* III, 1802.

In addition to the authority granted to Zillah Judges by Clause first, Sec. XVI, Reg. III, 1802, to refer cases and questions for the opinion of the law officers of the Sudder Udalut through the Register of that Court, they are hereby declared competent *in like manner* to refer cases and questions whether arising in their own Courts, or in the Courts of Sudder Ameens, or transmitted by district Moonsiffs * * * .—*Sec.* II, *Reg.* III, 1828.

So much of any law or usage now in force within the territories subject to the Government of the East India Company, as inflicts on any person forfeiture of rights or property, or may be held in any way to impair or affect any right of inheritance, by reason of his or her renouncing, or having been excluded from the Communion of any religion, or being deprived of caste, shall cease to be enforced as Law in the Courts of the East India Company, and in the Courts established by Royal Charter within the said territories.—*Sec.* I, *Act* XXI, 1850.

No rights arising out of an alleged property in the person and services of another as a slave shall be enforced by any Civil or Criminal Court or Magistrate within the Territories of the East India Company.—*Sec.* II, *Act* V, 1843.

No person who may have acquired property by his own industry, or by the exercise of any art, calling, or profession, or by inheritance, assignment, gift, or bequest, shall be dispossessed of such property, or prevented from taking possession thereof, on the ground that such person, or that the person from whom the property may have been derived, was a slave.—*Sec.* III.—*Ibid.*

Sec. XVI, Reg. III, 1802.—" The Office of Hindoo Law Officer" in the Zillah Courts was virtually abolished under Sec. XXIV, Act VII, 1843, as ruled by the S. U. 11th November 1845. Zillah Judges desiring an exposition of Hindoo Law for themselves, or for Courts below them, upon reference made to them under this enactment, can now transmit questions to the Hindoo Law Officers of the Sudder Udalut only. A Mahomedan Law Officer is still attached to the Civil and Session Court under Act VII, 1843, to whom questions arising in their own Courts or those below them may be put.

Sec. II, Reg. III, 1828.—See Note on Section XVI, Reg. III, 1802.

Sec. I, Act XXI, 1850.—This modifies Section XVI, Reg. III, 1802, a claim affecting inheritance, in which according to Hindoo or Mahomedan Law, a party would be defeated in consequence of his having embraced another religion, or having forfeited it according to the rule of those persuasions—is not now to be disposed of according to that Law, in reference to such bar or hindrance; but according to the rules thereof, supposing such impediment not to exist.

Sec. II—III, Act V, 1843.—This enactment is also a modification of Section XVI, Reg. III, of 1802, it overrules anything to the contrary which may exist in the Hindoo or Mahomedan code.

The Judges of the Zillah Courts are strictly enjoined not to order, or allow of, a report of any matters of fact relating to any cause depending before them, with a view to the passing of a decree, to be made to them, by any officer of the Court, or any other person: excepting in cases in which special authority for that purpose may be given to the Courts by any regulation. This rule, however, is not to be construed to prevent a Judge referring any question arising on the Mahomedan or Hindoo law, to the *Mahomedan Law Officer of the Court, or the Law Officers of the Sudder Udalut.* When a reference of this nature is deemed necessary, a statement of the facts, on which the question of law may arise, is to be made out in writing, and signed by the Judge of the Court, and *submitted to the proper Law Officer,* for his opinion on it. A blank is to be left for the answer of the law Officer, on the same paper on which the question is stated, or on a paper firmly annexed to it. The answer is to be attested with · the signature of the Law Officer, and the dates on which the questions may be stated to him, and the answer may be given, are to be specified.—*Sec.* XVII. *Reg.* III, 1802.

In cases of disputed property regarding lands, houses, or their limits or boundaries, in which the Court may deem a local investigation proper, the Court is to appoint an Ameen ; who is to be sworn, *or subscribe solemn affirmation,* to make a true and faithful report to the Court, of the several matters which he may be directed to investigate ; and not to take, or receive, directly or indirectly, from either party, any gratuity, reward, or consideration, besides the sum which may be allowed to him by the Court. The Ameen is to be ordered to make his report in writing, subscribed with his name, and to deliver it into Court, on a certain day, which is to be specified in his commission. The report is to be received by the Court as evidence in the cause, with regard to the matters which the Ameen may be commissioned to investigate, and no other. The Court may order such sum to be paid to the Ameen as may be thought reasonable, for his trouble; and the amount is to be added to the costs, and paid by the person against whom the decree may be passed. But the Court is to be careful that expenses are not unnecessarily incurred by the Ameen by delay, or other means.—*Sec.* XVIII.—*Ibid.*

The plaintiff is to pay the charges of summoning the defendant, and his own witnesses ; and of all process attended with expense which may be issued in his behalf, previous to the decision of the suit.—*Sec.* XIX.—*Ibid.*

The Judges of the Zillah Courts are to order the causes depending in their respective Courts to be brought on for trial, according to the order in which they may be filed : except in cases in which it may be otherwise directed by any regulation ; or in which the Judge may think it proper for special reasons, which he is to state at large upon the record of the trial, to bring on the cause before its turn. The causes for the trial of which a day may be appointed by the Judge *are to be entered in a book*, and, on the day fixed, called for trial, in the order in which they may have been entered. A paper containing a list of the causes, and the day appointed for the trial of them, is to be fixed up, in some conspicuous part of the Court room, seven days previous to the day for trial.—*Sec.* XX, *Reg.* III, 1802.

If any person shall be guilty of contempt of Court, in open Court ; or of undue arrogations of the authority of the Court ; or of illegal exertions of judicial authority in his own cause ; the Court is immediately to punish the offender by fining him in a sum not exceeding two hundred Rupees, and by keeping him in custody, until the fine shall be paid. The Courts are to regulate the amount of the fines which they may impose under this Section according to the situation and circumstances in life of the offenders.—*Sec.* XXII.—*Ibid.*

Any person who shall set up a fictitious claim to property attached in satisfaction of a decree of a Judicial Court, or who may introduce a false allegation or allegations into a petition presented to a Zillah Civil Court, or to the Courts subordinate to it, with a fraudulent design, shall be punishable to the extent provided in Section XXII, Regulation III, 1802.—*Sec.* II, *Reg.* I, 1832.

It shall be lawful for any Court by which any person shall be, or shall have been committed to custody under the authority of Section XXII, Regulation III, 1802, of the Madras Code to liberate such person when such Court shall be of opinion, that the confinement has been sufficient for the punishment of his offence, and no person shall, under the authority of the said Section, be kept in custody for a term exceeding two months.—*Act* VI, 1836.

All persons whatsoever, whether generally amenable to the Courts of the East India Company or otherwise, using menacing gestures or expressions, or otherwise obstructing justice in the presence of any Zillah Magistrate, Joint Magistrate, or other Officer under a Magistrate empowered to try Criminal cases, or any superior or inferior Court, Civil or Criminal, of the East India Company, shall be liable to be fined by the authority whose proceedings are obstructed, to any amount not exceeding 200 Rupees, or, in case such fine be not paid to be imprisoned for any period not exceeding one month. Provided, that from the award of punishment in such cases an appeal shall lie, if preferred within one month, to the authority, Civil or Criminal, appointed by Law to hear appeals in all other cases from the decisions of the Officer by whom the fine was imposed ; and provided also, that notwithstanding any thing in this Act, it shall be lawful to indict any person amenable to Her Majesty's Supreme Courts, as for a misdemeanor in any of the cases aforesaid sustainable before this Act, if no proceeding shall have been had against the offender in the Court where the offence was committed, but not otherwise.—*Sec.* I, *Act* XXX, 1841.

If a witness or any person shall be guilty of wilful and corrupt perjury in any cause or matter depending in Court, the Judge is immediately to commit the offender to close custody to take his trial before *the Session Court of the Zillah.*—*Sec.* VIII, *Reg.* III, 1802.

Act XXX, 1841.—European British Subjects are punishable under this Act.

Sec. VIII, Reg. III, 1802.—" Commit to take his trial, &c." i. e. he must send him to the Subordinate Criminal Court for committal.

CHAPTER II.

INSTITUTION OF SUIT—PROCEEDINGS, &c.

Upon any person, either by himself, or his vakeel duly appointed, preferring a written complaint on account of any matter declared cognizable by the Zillah Courts, to the proper Zillah Court, the Court *may under circumstances specified in Cl.* I, *Sec.* IV, *Reg.* II, *of* 1811, *q. v. inf:* issue a summons upon the defendant, containing a short account of the nature of the demand, and requiring the defendant either to accompany the Officer who may be deputed to serve the summons, to appear in person before the Court, or to deliver to him good and sufficient security to appear and answer to the complaint on the day appointed, either in person or by vakeel. The person who may become security for the appearance of the defendant is further to bind himself to be responsible for the personal attendance of the defendant whenever it may be required by the Court, and in the event of his not being able to produce him either whilst the suit is depending, or at any time before the final decree in the cause is executed, to be answerable for such sum as may be adjudged against the defendant. The summons is to be served on the defendant by the Nazir, or his inferior Officer, if he can be found; and in the event of his not giving the required security, the Nazir or Officer is to take his person into custody: and bring him before the Court. The Nazir is to return the summons on the day appointed, with an endorsement specifying in what manner he has executed it. If the defendant shall appear either in person or by vakeel, the Court is to fix a day according to its discretion for him to answer to the complaint, and, if it shall deem it reasonable so to do, may at any time allow the defendant a further period for delivering his answer. And if the defendant shall appear in person, and shall not have given the security abovementioned for his appearance and attendance, the Court is to require him to give it, and in the event of his refusing or omitting to comply with the requisition he is to be committed to close custody until he shall have given the security, or performed the decree of Court.—*Sec.* V, *Reg.* III, 1802.

The following form of security bond, or an instrument to the following effect, is to be executed by the sureties for the appearance of defendants in the Zillah Courts required by Section V, of this regulation:

" Whereas a suit has been instituted in the —— Court of the Zillah of   by   plaintiff, against   defendant; and whereas I   inhabitant of   , have voluntarily become security for the appearance of the said defendant to answer to the above suit, and perform all such orders as may be passed thereupon, until the final decree on it shall have been carried into execution; I do therefore hereby engage and bind myself, my heirs, and successors, that the said defendant shall appear in person, or by vakeel, to make answer to the plaint against him in the suit aforesaid on the   , being the day on which his appearance has been required in the said Zillah Court; and further that the said defendant shall personally attend at the said Zillah Court, whenever the same may be required by the Judge thereof, at any time whilst the above suit is depending before *the said Court, or an Appellate Court,* or before the final decree which may be passed thereupon, by the above Courts respectively, shall be fully and completely carried into execution; in default of which, and in the event of my not producing the said defendant when called upon, I will be answerable for such sum as may be adjudged against him; and for the performance of whatever order or decree may be passed against him on the suit abovementioned."—*Sec.* XXIX, *Reg.* III, 1802.

If a defendant against whom a summons may issue, shall abscond, or is not after diligent search to be found, or shall shut himself up in his own, or in any house or building, or retire to any place so that the process cannot be served upon him, and the Nazir shall return that on such account he has not been able to serve or execute the process, the Judge is to cause a writing in the language of the country where the Court may be held, to be struck up in some conspicuous part of the room in which the Court may assemble. The writing is to contain a copy of the summons and a notice, that if the party shall not appear on a day to be fixed (which shall not be less than fifteen days from the time that the summons may be fixed up) the Court will proceed, without further notice, to try and determine the cause, without the appearance, or answer, of the defendant. The Court is likewise to order a copy of the summons, and notice, to be fixed up, with all practicable dispatch, on the outer door of the house in which the defendant may have usually dwelt; or in some conspicuous place in the village, or other place, in which he may have generally resided. The Nazir is to return the order with an endorsement, stating at what times, and places, the summons and notice may have been fixed up. The return of the Nazir is to be filed in the Court, and to form a part of the record of the trial. If the defendant shall not appear at the time limited in the notice, or if a defendant who may have been served with a summons shall not appear, or if having appeared, he shall refuse to give answer, or make other default, or admit the truth of the plaintiff's bill of complaint, the Court, on examining the allegations of the plaintiff only, and the depositions of his witnesses, is to decree and give judgment; in the same manner as if the defendant had appeared, answered, and entered into proof.—Sec. XIII, Reg. III, 1802.

If a defendant for whose appearance security may have been taken shall not appear, or having appeared, shall refuse to give answer, the plaintiff is permitted to institute a suit against the sureties on their engagement, and is to be entitled to recover from them whatever he may prove to be due to him from the defendant; or he may proceed against the defendant, in the same manner as defendants are directed to be proceeded against who have been served with a summons, and have not appeared, or have refused to give answer.—Sec. XIV.—Ibid.

But upon the institution of a civil suit in the mode prescribed by the regulations, in any Zillah Court, the general first process against the defendant, instead of the summons and requisition of security for appearance prescribed by Section V, Regulation III, 1802, shall be a notice only, containing a short statement of the demand, with a requisition to attend in person, or by Vakeel, and to deliver an answer to the plaint, on or before a certain day, to be specified in the notice.—Cl. 1, Sec. II, Reg. II, 1811.

If the defendant have an accredited agent at the place where the Court is held, expressly empowered, either by a clause in his general moktarnamah, or by a separate moktarnamah granted for that purpose, to receive, on behalf of his constituent, notices or other judicial processes, which may not be especially ordered to be served personally, by an Officer of the Court; the notice to be issued, under the preceding Clause, shall be tendered to such agent, to be communicated by him to his principal; and the agent's acknowledgment, to be indorsed upon it, shall be accepted as a sufficient service of it, if he be desirous of giving such acknowledgment, in preference to the notice being served on the person of his principal, by an Officer of the Court.—Cl. 2.—Ibid.

If the defendant shall not have an accredited agent at the place where the Court is held, or if he shall not have expressly authorized his agent to receive notices of the above description; or if such agent shall decline receiving the notice for communication to his constituent, and the defendant be resident within the jurisdiction of the Court; it shall be served on him, through the Nazir of the Court, by a single chupprassy, or peon, who shall require only the acknowledgment of the defendant to be endorsed upon it; or if he be absent from his usual place of residence, the acknowledgment of his principal agent, or of any person acting for him during his absence. If the defendant be resident within the jurisdiction of any other Zillah Court, than that in which the suit may have been instituted, the notice shall be transmitted to the Judge of the Zillah in which the defendant may reside, to be served in the manner above directed. If the defendant be neither resident within the jurisdiction of the Zillah Court in which the suit may be instituted, or of any other Zillah Court, and the suit shall notwithstanding be cognizable, either in claims to landed or other immoveable property, from the property claimed being situated within the jurisdiction of the Court; or, in other cases, from the cause of action having arisen within its jurisdiction; the notice, if the suit be for land or other immoveable property, shall be served upon the defendant's agent or representative in charge of such property; and in other suits, the Judge shall cause notice of the claim to be conveyed to the defendant, in such manner as may appear most certain and convenient, according to the circumstances of the case.—*Cl.* 3, *Sec.* II, *Reg.* II, 1811.

If a defendant to whom a notice may have been issued, as directed in the preceding Section, shall abscond, or is not after diligent search to be found, or shall shut himself up in any house or building, or retire to any place, so that the notice cannot be served upon him, the Judge, on receiving the Nazir's return to this effect, shall issue a proclamation, as directed in similar cases, when a summons cannot be served upon a defendant, by Section XIII, Regulation III, 1802. If the defendant shall not appear in person or by Vakeel, by the time limited in such proclamation, or if a defendant, who may have been served with a notice, as directed in the preceding Section, shall not appear in person or by Vakeel, within the time specified; or if, having appeared, he shall refuse to answer the plaint, or make other default; the Court as provided in the section abovementioned, shall proceed to try the cause exparte; and, after examining the plaintiff's evidence in support of his claim, shall give judgment, in the same manner as if the defendant had appeared, answered, and entered into proof. —*Sec.* III, *Reg.* II, 1811.

If a defendant, after receiving the notice prescribed in Section II *of this Regulation* shall attend in person, or by Vakeel, and deliver his answer to the plaint, and no reason shall subsequently appear to the Court for requiring security for his appearance, during the trial of the suit, he shall be allowed to defend the cause, to its termination, without being called upon for such security.   But if the Judge shall be satisfied, by sufficient proof, that there is reason to believe the defendant intends to abscond, and withdraw himself from the jurisdiction of the Court, he may, either on the institution of the suit, or at any time whilst the suit is depending in the Zillah Court, issue process against the defendant, requiring him to give security for his appearance, as prescribed on the issue of summons by Section V, Regulation III, 1802, under penalty of being committed to close custody, until such security be given, or the decree of the Court be complied with, as provided in the abovementioned Section ; or until an attachment of property shall have taken place, to secure the execution of the ultimate judgment in the cause, under the provision made by the following Section of this Regulation.—*Cl.* 1, *Sec.* IV, *Reg.* II, 1811.

The security bond, to be executed in such instances, shall in substance correspond with that prescribed in Section XXIX, Regulation III, 1802 ; and in fixing the extent of the security to be required, the Judge shall exercise his discretion, with respect to the responsibility of the surety or sureties to be found by the defendant, for his personal attendance when required, as specified in Section V, of Regulation III, aforementioned ; and, in the first instance, whatever may be the claim of the plaintiff, shall demand from the defendant such security only as may appear necessary to secure his appearance during the trial of the suit.   Provided that if, at any time in the course of the trial, the security so taken from the defendant shall appear to the Judge insufficient, he is authorized and required to take such further security, as he may think necessary to secure the appearance of the defendant ; and if judgment be given against the defendant in the Zillah Court, the Judge shall immediately proceed to execute such judgment in conformity to the regulations ; or, if the case be appealable, and an appeal be lodged in the mode prescribed by the Regulations, shall, as the case may be, stay such judgment, on receiving good and sufficient security, or enforce it, according to the rules established in the existing Regulations.—*Cl.* 2.—*Ibid.*

In any case if the Judge be satisfied, by sufficient proof, that there is ground to apprehend the defendant means to dispose of the property in his possession, by any private transfer, or to cause the public sale of any disputed land, by withholding the assessment upon it, or to move any personal property from the jurisdiction of the Court, whilst the suit against him is depending, for the purpose of avoiding the execution of an eventual judgment

against him ; the Judge is authorized to call upon the defendant
for malzaminy security, in 'such sum as may appear sufficient to
make good the ultimate judgment of the Court; and in the event
of such security not being given (within a reasonable time to be
allowed for that purpose), to cause the attachment of any land,
effects, or other property belonging to, or possessed by, the defendant, to the amount or value of the cause of action, in the suit
depending; or the attachment of which may be deemed necessary,
to secure the execution of the judgment to be passed in the cause.
—Cl. 1, Sec. V, Reg. II, 1811.

The attachment, in such cases, shall be made by a written order
of the Court, to be read and proclaimed upon the spot, and to be
affixed in some conspicuous situation at the place where the property is situated ; after which, any private alienation of the
property sequestered, whether by sale, gift, or otherwise, during
the continuance of the attachment, shall be deemed illegal and
void, and any unauthorized removal of the property so attached,
during such period, with a view to oppose or evade the sequestration, shall be punishable, on proof, as an act of resistance to the
process of the Court; according to the provisions in force concerning resistance to the process of the Civil Courts. In suits for
landed property of considerable value, wherein it may appear necessary, for the purposes of justice, to divest the defendant from
the management of the land until the suits be decided, or malzaminy security be given, the attachment shall be made through the
Collector of the district in which the land is situated, as prescribed by Clause ninth of Section XII, Regulation IV, 1802, in appeal
cases wherein neither the appellant nor respondent may be able to
give security for staying the execution of the decree. But in other
cases, the attachments which may be ordered under the present
rule, shall not, without special cause, to be recorded on the proceedings of the Court, remove the defendant or his representative
from the possession and management of the land, or other property
attached, until a decision be passed in the cause before the Zillah
Court; nor be understood to preclude any act of the defendant,
or his representative, relative to such property, which may be consistent with the object of the attachment.—Cl. 2.—Ibid.

Upon the decision of the suit, the Judge shall pass such further
order relative to the property attached, as may be just and conformable with the judgment given in the cause. If the decree be
against the defendant, all right and interest possessed by him in
the property attached, (saving arrears of rent or revenue due from
land, and any other bonâ fide claims which may be entitled to
satisfaction in preference to the decree,) shall be held answerable

for the execution of the judgment, in the mode prescribed by the regulations. But if the plaintiff's claim be dismissed, or be not, in any considerable proportion, established against the defendant, all expense and loss to the defendant, which may arise from the attachment, of his property in consequence of such claim, shall be reimbursed to him by the plaintiff, as part of the costs of suit. —*Cl. 3, Sec.* V, *Reg.* II, 1811.

Whenever any property may be attached by order of a Zillah Court, under the provisions contained in the foregoing Section, the trial of the cause shall be proceeded on, and brought to a conclusion, as speedily as possible, without regard to the order of time, with respect to other depending causes in which it may have been instituted. The attachment shall also be taken off on the delivery of sufficient malzaminy security, at any time previous to the decision of the cause in the Zillah Court.—*Sec.* VI.—*Ibid.*

The provisions contained in the two preceding Sections shall be held equally applicable to the *Zillah Civil* Courts, and, Sudder Udalut, in all cases wherein an attachment of property, made by a *Subordinate* Zillah Court, may be continued during the trial of an appeal before a *Zillah Civil* Court, or the Court of Sudder Udalut ; or in which those courts may judge it proper to order an attachment of property, in default of security being given, as required, either by the appellant, or respondent, in any depending appeal.—*Sec.* VII.—*Ibid.*

When personal bail, or security for money or other property may be demandable from a party in any original civil suit, or appeal, and he shall tender a deposit of money, or pf promissory notes, or other obligations of government, or any other sufficient money security, to the amount required ; such deposit shall be accepted, instead of hazirzaminy or malzaminy securities, and shall be carefully kept by the treasurer of the court ; to be restored, or disposed of as the Court may direct, on the termination of the cause, or whenever the purpose, for which the deposit is made, shall have been accomplished.—*Sec.* VIII.—*Ibid.*

Every process, rule, order or decree of the Zillah Courts (with the exception contained in this Section) is to be immediately served or executed without application to any person, or the interference of any individual whomsoever, according to the requisition of it, within the limits of the special jurisdiction of each Court. But in every case in which the defendant shall be a Hindoo, or Mahomedan woman of a rank, or quality, which, according to the customs and usages of the country, would render it improper to compel her to appear in an open Court of justice, the Judges of the Zillah Courts are not to issue any compulsory process against her, to compel her to appear and make answer; but are to issue a summons, requiring her to appear in person, or by vakeel, at a certain time to be named in the summons, in the Zillah Court, and answer to the complaint and abide by the orders which the Court may think proper to pass in the cause. The summons is to be directed to the Nazir of the Court, and is to contain a short account of the nature of the demand or complaint; with a notice that, if the defendant shall not appear as required by the summons at the time specified in it, or having so appeared, shall not answer the complaint at the time which may be fixed by the Court, or make any other default, the Court will proceed to try and determine the cause in the same manner as if the defendant had appeared, answered, and done what she is authorized or required to do, in defence of the suit. The summons is further to command the Nazir to deliver a copy of it to the Dewan or some principal servant of the defendant. The Nazir is not to have recourse to compulsion to enforce the summons, but is to serve it in the manner herein directed and no other. The Nazir is to return the summons on the day appointed for the appearance of the defendant with an endorsement, specifying in what manner he has executed it; and, if he has not executed it, the reason why it has not been executed. If the defendant should appear in person, or by vakeel, the Court is to fix a certain day, according to its discretion, for her to answer to the complaint; and appoint a day for the parties to deliver in their pleadings; and the Court is to try and determine the cause in the same manner as suits instituted against persons not being women of the abovementioned description. Upon the summons being issued, if the Dewan or other principal servant of the defendant shall abscond, or otherwise act so that the summons cannot be served upon him, or shall not after diligent search and enquiry be found, the judge, upon the return of the summons, and proof being made before him on oath, *or solemn affirmation*, of the fact, is to proceed against the defendant, in the same manner as he is directed to proceed against a defendant who after diligent search cannot be found, or shall have absconded, or otherwise acted so that he could not be served with a summons. If a female defendant on whom no summons can be served, after the prescribed notice has been issued, shall not appear as required, or appearing, shall neglect or refuse to answer, or make other default, or admit the truth of the complaint; the Court, on examining the allegations of the plaintiff only and receiving the depositions of his witnesses, is to decree and give judgment; in the same manner as if the defendant had appeared, answered, and entered into proof.—*Sec.* XV, *Reg* III, 1802.

CHAPTER III.

PLEADINGS.

No complaint is to be received but from a plaintiff, nor any answer to a complaint but from the defendant, or their respective Vakeels duly empowered. Nor is any person to be permitted to do any act, or to be heard vivâ voce in any stage of a cause, excepting the plaintiff or defendant, or their Vakeels or witnesses.—*Sec.* II, *Reg.* III, 1802.

Every complaint that may be presented to any *Zillah Civil, or Subordinate Court,* is to state precisely the matter of complaint. If it be concerning a zemindarry, or an independent or a dependent talook, or any landed property being lakheraj (exempt from the payment of revenue to government) or malguzarry (subject to the payment of revenue to government) it is to state the amount of the annual produce of the land according to the most accurate estimate which the claimant may be able to procure. To obviate all doubt respecting what is meant by the annual produce of lakheraj and malguzarry lands, it is declared to be the aggregate of the sums that may have been paid under the regulations by the dependant Talookdars, under-farmers, and ryots, on account of the year in which the claim may be preferred, and that would be payable by them, were the claimant to be put into possession of the lands during that year. If the complaint is for a house, garden, tank, or any real property not being malguzarry or lakheraj land, or any valuable thing, or relating to marriage or caste, or for damages for any injury, it is to state according to the nearest estimate the exact sum of money, or the amount in which the plaintiff may be endamaged. The complaint is also to specify the name of the person complained against, the time when the cause of action arose, and is to be signed by the complainant, or his Vakeel duly authorized. The complaint is to be signed and numbered and dated in the order in which it may be received, by the Judge of the Court, and is to be registered in a book by a native officer of the Court, whose particular duty it shall be to copy and register complaints. Every complaint, answer, reply, and rejoinder, is to be written in the language and character of the country wherein the Court may be held.—*Sec.* III.—*Ibid.*

When the defendant has delivered in his answer to the complaint, the plaintiff is to reply to it on the next Court day. The plaintiff shall not introduce in his reply any matter not contained in his complaint. He shall either acknowledge the answer of the defendant to be true, or simply and shortly deny the truth of such of the facts in the answer as he intends to dispute; or simply deny the truth of all the facts contained in it, or the competency of the answer. The defendant is to rejoin to the reply on the same day. He shall not introduce in his rejoinder any matter not contained in his answer. He shall simply deny the truth of the reply of the plaintiff, or the parts of it which he means to dispute, and aver the truth or competency of his own answer; and no further pleadings whatever are to be admitted in the cause. But if from mistake, inadvertence, or other cause, the plaintiff shall have omitted to insert in his complaint any thing material to the suit, the Court, on the omission being represented either by the plaintiff or his Vakeel, *if upon a perusal of the pleadings previously filed, and from a consideration of the circumstances alleged by the parties it shall deem it just and proper.—Cl.* III, *Sec.* VII. *Reg.* XV, 1816: *may* allow the plaintiff to prefer a supplemental complaint in which he is to state the matter omitted. And the defendant to deliver an answer to the supplemental complaint on a day to be fixed for that purpose. And the plaintiff and defendant to reply and rejoin in the same manner, as on the original complaint, but no other. In like manner, if the defendant from mistake, inadvertence, or other cause, shall have omitted to insert in his answer any thing material to his defence, the Court upon his representing the omission, either in person or by his Vakeel, *may, if it see fit,* permit the defendant to deliver in a supplemental answer. The plaintiff and defendant are to reply and rejoin in the same manner as on the original answer. But no more than one supplemental complaint, or one supplemental answer, is to be received by the Court.—*Sec.* V, *Reg.* III, 1802.

When a defendant in an original Civil suit shall refuse, or neglect to file a rejoinder within the period prescribed for that purpose, the Court, after recording such refusal or neglect, shall proceed in the trial of the suit, in the same manner as if a rejoinder containing a general denial of the claim had been regularly filed.—*Cl.* 2, *Sec.* VII, *Reg.* XV, 1816.

When the rejoinder has been filed, *or neglect or refusal to file recorded as provided in Cl.* 2, *Sec.* VII, *Reg.* XV, 1816, the Court, either immediately, or on a fixed day (eight days notice of which is to be given to the parties) as soon after the pleadings are closed as the business of the Court will permit, is to examine the truth of the complaint or claim by the oaths of the parties, if they mutually consent to that mode of examination; and *by oath, or solemn affirmation* of the witnesses who may be produced by them, if they have any witnesses to produce.—*Sec.* VI, *Reg.* III, 1802.

In the trial of original regular suits, as well as in the trial of appeals in such suits, the prescribed pleadings shall be completed and read in open Court, before any exhibits are filed, or witnesses summoned in support of the allegations of either of the parties; unless special and sufficient reason be assigned for taking the immediate deposition of a witness, without waiting until the pleadings are completed and read in open Court.—*Cl.* 1, *Sec.* X, *Reg.* XV, 1816.

If from the pleadings in the case the points at issue cannot be clearly ascertained, or if from any other reason further explanations may be requisite, the Courts shall on the day on which the suit may be first brought to a hearing, make such enquiries from the parties, or their pleaders, as may appear necessary, with a view to ascertain the precise object of the action, and the grounds on which it is maintained, and shall record the result on their proceedings.—*Cl.* 2.—*Ibid.*

The Court shall then consider and record the point or points to be established respectively by the plaintiff, and by the defendant, and shall proceed to take the evidence which may be adduced by either party upon such points, in the manner prescribed by the rules in force.—*Cl.* 3.—*Ibid.*

In like manner, if proof shall be required on any other points in the course of the trial, such points shall be recorded on the proceedings, and the proper party shall be called upon for the requisite evidence; and no exhibit shall be filed, or witness summoned, unless expressly declared to be in proof, or refutation of some point, upon which the Court may have directed that evidence should be taken.—*Cl.* 4.—*Ibid.*

Sec. VI. Reg. III, 1802.—" Oaths of the parties." This I presume was merely intended to allow of parties under certain circumstances making affidavit to the truth of their pleadings, and would authorize their making solemn affirmation in like case—but there is another mode of examination " by oath of parties on mutual consent" which is not unfrequent in practice and partakes of the nature of ordeal—one party agreeing to swear, according to a particular *form*, to the truth or falsehood of an allegation, and the other to allow a Decree to be made accordingly.

Cl. I, Sec. X. Reg. XV. 1816.—" Prescribed Pleadings." A European or a Native Judge may accept any translation of a pleading or miscellaneous address coming judicially before him, which may have been prepared by the party from whom such address may emanate. The responsibility of acting thereon will of course rest with the functionary accepting the translation, who as a matter of duty should ascertain that it be correct.—Cir. Lr. S. U. 18th November 1844.

In order that the parties in a suit, or their authorized pleaders, may be fully prepared to file their exhibits, and to name their witnesses, as well as to furnish any explanations of the case, which may be required, at the time when the suit may first be brought to a hearing, the several Courts are enjoined carefully to attend to those provisions in the Regulations, which require that eight days previous notice shall be given to the parties, of the day on which the Court may propose to bring the suit to a hearing.—*Cl.* 1, *Sec.* XII, *Reg.* XV, 1816.

For this purpose it shall be sufficient for the Court to affix, in some conspicuous place in the Court room, a notification, specifying the number of the suit, the names of the parties and of the vakeels respectively entertained in the suit, together with the date on which it may be intended that such suit shall be brought to a hearing before the Court, and such notice shall be held and considered to be in force until the suit can be brought to a hearing, either on the day fixed or any subsequent day.—*Cl.* 2.—*Ibid.*

If either of the parties in a suit, which may be brought to a hearing, after due notice shall have been given in the manner above prescribed, shall not be prepared to file his exhibits, or the names of his witnesses, or to furnish any explanations of the case which may be required by the Court, and shall not assign sufficient and satisfactory reason for the delay, the Courts are authorized to impose upon such party such fine as may appear just and proper: provided that the fine shall in no instance exceed one-fourth of the *stamp duty paid on institution of the suit*, if a similar neglect shall occur a second time, after due notice shall have been given of the day fixed for the case being again brought forward, the Courts are authorized either to impose a second fine, under the limitation above prescribed, or to proceed as in other cases of default.—*Cl.* 3.—*Ibid.*

If a plaintiff or appellant in any Court shall at any time, neglect to proceed in his suit or appeal for six weeks, the suit or appeal shall be dismissed; and it shall not be necessary to give the plaintiff or appellant any notice previous to dismissing his suit or appeal. The suit or appeal shall be dismissed, as of course, after the expiration of six weeks without any proceeding on the part of the Court, or of the defendant, or otherwise, or assignment of any reasons, unless the plaintiff or appellant, or his representative in case of his death, upon special application, shall have previously satisfied the Court of the propriety of allowing further time. The Court shall record upon the proceedings the reasons at large for allowing further time in all cases in which further time may be allowed, but it shall not be necessary to specify the reasons for refusing any application for further time.—*Sec.* I, *Act* XXIX, 1841.

In all cases in which a suit or appeal is dismissed under the preceding Section, the Court shall award to the defendant or respondent the costs he may have incurred in the suit or appeal. But such dismissal shall be no impediment to the institution of a new suit or appeal, where the party is not precluded by lapse of time, or period of appeal, or otherwise than by the mere circumstances of having instituted the suit or appeal dismissed, and of such dismissal ; and such dismissed suit or appeal shall not prevent lapse of time under the law of limitations being incurred.—*Sec.* II. —*Ibid.*

No appeal shall lie against the decision passed in accordance with the provisions of the preceding Clauses of this Act, other than a summary appeal on the fact of default.—*Sec.* III.—*Ibid.*

Every default of a plaintiff or appellant in all suits or appeals, shall be held to be cured whenever the opposite party, passing over the default, shall have taken any step in the suit or appeal, and whenever the Court shall have passed judgment in the suit or appeal, whether such opposite party shall or shall not have taken any such step.—*Act* XVII, 1847.

CHAPTER IV.

EVIDENCE—WITNESSES—EXHIBITS.

No person shall by reason of any conviction for any offence whatever be incompetent to be a witness in any stage of any cause, civil or criminal before any Court in the territories of the East India Company.—*Act* XIX, 1837.

" EVIDENCE, &c."—Unless there be special enactment to the contrary, the Courts adhere, so far as local circumstances will admit, to the principles of the English Law of Evidence, a few memoranda regarding which may perhaps be usefully inserted in this place—the fullest information is to be found in Mr. Phillip's able treatise on this subject.

Act XIX, 1837.—Removes a ground of incompetency, which the English Law recognizes, and reduces the objections which can be taken to the competency of a witness to three, viz. :

    1. Defect of Understanding.
    2. Want of Religion.
    3. Interest.

DEFECT OF UNDERSTANDING may be either original and natural, as in Idiots—or may have supervened, as in the Insane—or may arise from immaturity, as in Children. An Idiot is wholly and always incompetent—an Insane person may during lucid intervals become competent—Children are incompetent or otherwise according to the degree of understanding they may be found to possess, without reference to any fixed age : a sine quâ non being that they be found capable of being examined upon oath, or solemn affirmation.

WANT OF RELIGION.—The witness must believe in a God, by whom truth is enjoined and falsehood punished—further enquiry as to his religious opinions, or belief in the peculiar tenets of the particular religion he ostensibly professes, is neither necessary or allowable.

INTEREST.—A witness may be interested for himself, or from relation to the Suitor—it is a general rule that a party to the record in a Civil Suit cannot be a witness for himself, or a joint Suitor—and this holds in the Courts of this country, except in so far as it is relaxed by Section VI, Regulation III, 1802, which allows Plaintiff and Defendant to be examined on oath, on mutual consent. As to ordinary witnesses the general rule is, that they are competent unless they can be shewn to have a direct interest in the event of the particular Suit—what constitutes such direct disqualifying interest must be left in great measure to the discretion of the presiding Judge, in the particular case, and it may be remarked that of late years the Courts have endeavoured as far as possible to let the objection go to the *credit*, rather than to the *competency* of the witness.

All objections, save as above, must be to the credit, not to the competency of witnesses.

In estimating credit due to a witness consider all such circumstances as may be within knowledge, and may conduce to formation of opinion on any of the following points.

    1. His knowledge of the facts.
    2. His disinterestedness.
    3. His integrity.
    4. His veracity.
    5. His oath, and his probable regard to it.

The production of a Government Gazette of any Presidency, containing an Act purporting to have been passed by the Governor General in Council, shall be held in all Courts sufficient proof that such Act has been so passed.—*Act* X, 1835.

To procure the attendance of witnesses, the Zillah Courts, on the requisition of the plaintiff or defendant, or their respective vakeels, are to issue a summons to the witnesses whom the parties may name (provided they may not be Hindoo or Mahomedan women of a rank or quality which, according to the manners and customs of the country, would render it improper to compel them to appear in a Court of justice) specifying at whose request the

---

So much of **WITNESSES**—in respect of **EVIDENCE** is to be remembered—
That the best procurable is always to be taken.
That hearsay is no evidence, except in certain cases.
That it may be of three kinds.

> 1st. Admissions.
> 2nd. Presumptions.
> 3rd. Proofs.

ADMISSIONS.—Bonâ fide admissions are in general a highly satisfactory species of Evidence : there may be cases in which they are made with ulterior views.

PRESUMPTIONS—or circumstantial evidence—may be either violent or probable : *violent* where certain consequences *necessarily* attend certain facts ; *probable* where they *usually* do so. And there are also " Presumptions of the Law," or matters which it takes for granted unless the contrary be proved—as " that every man is aware of the consequences of his own act," &c.

PROOFS—Are either written or Parol.

WRITTEN PROOFS—Are either public Records, or instruments of a private nature. Of these originals must be produced if practicable, and why not, be satisfactorily shewn before copy be admitted : unless in cases in which copies are directed by law to be received as evidence, as is the case with public Records generally : the value of written proof *differs* in *degree* or value according to various circumstances.

PAROL PROOFS—Or oral evidence—in this there can be no *degree*, it is admissible at all, only in matters within the knowledge of the witness, and must, as to each fact deposed to, be absolutely true or false, it is not admissible in lieu of written evidence when procurable.

As a general rule of evidence—communications made on the faith of the professional confidence which a client reposes in his legal adviser are not required or allowed to be revealed in a Court of Justice to the prejudice of the client—Clause 2, Section X, Regulation XV, of 1816, might, if acted on without due caution, seem to trench on this law, it is well to bear this rule in mind while acting thereunder.

HEARSAY EVIDENCE—Is that which does not derive its effect solely from the credit to be attached to the witness himself, but rests also in part on the veracity and competency of some other person, from whom the witness may have received the information—as a general rule it is inadmissible, but it may be considered and valued according to circumstances in certain cases, and indeed in some *must* be greatly relied on, as in cases of Pedigree—matters of Public Interest—Ancient possession, Dying Declarations, &c.

SECONDARY EVIDENCE—By Secondary Evidence is meant—such as implies the existence of primary, or more original information, of the same fact—as if a party offer a copy of a Deed or Will where he ought to produce the original ; and it is inadmissible unless it be shewn that the primary cannot be had—as that it is in the hands of an adverse party, or lost, or destroyed, without default of the party ; then the copy is admissible as the " *best evidence attainable.*"

It is also a general rule of evidence that if a party prove the substance of the issue, it is enough ; he need not prove immaterial averments which might be expunged from the record—without affecting his right—this rule has to be borne in mind in recording points under Clause 3, Section X, Regulation XV, of 1816.

summons may have been issued, and requiring them to appear in the Court on a day to be named in the summons, and there to depose concerning the matter in dispute between the parties. If a witness so summoned shall not attend on the day appointed, or attending shall refuse to give evidence or to subscribe his deposition as hereafter required, the Judge, in the first case, if it shall be proved to his satisfaction on oath *or solemn affirmation* that the witness was material to the cause, is to issue an order to the Nazir to seize and bring the witness before the Court, and is to impose on such witness, not having attended, or refusing to give evidence, a fine not exceeding five hundred rupees, and to commit him to close custody, until he shall consent to give his evidence, and sign his deposition. If a witness who may attend pursuant to a summons shall have incurred any expense in consequence of his being required to appear, the Court is to award to him such sum, for his charges, as may appear to it reasonable, whether he be examined or not. If the sum so awarded shall not be paid immediately, or secured to the witness to the satisfaction of the Court, the party at whose requisition the witness may have been summoned is not only to lose the benefit of his testimony, but the Court, after the decree in the cause shall be passed, is to confine such party until he shall discharge the sum awarded to the witness. The Zillah Courts are to administer to parties consenting to be examined on oath, *and to witnesses not exempted from taking an oath under Act V, of* 1840, such oaths as may be considered most binding on their consciences according to their respective religious persuasions.— *Sec.* VII, *Reg.* III, 1802.   Para 1, *and Sec.* XX, *Reg.* IV, 1802.

Deponents of the Hindoo or Mahomedan persuasion within the territories of the East India Company shall, instead of any oath or declaration, now authorized or required by law, make affirmation to the following effect :

" I solemnly affirm in the presence of Almighty God, that what I shall state shall be the truth, the whole truth, and nothing but the truth."—*Sec.* I, *Act* V, 1840.

The deposition of every witness who may appear in Court is to be taken vivâ voce in open Court, in the language in which he is most conversant ; and shall be reduced into writing in the language of the country in which the Court may be held. Where the witness shall desire it, his deposition shall be reduced into writing in the language in which his parole evidence was given. The deposition is to be subscribed by the witness, with his name or mark. Every exhibit or written evidence (excepting exhibits that may be proved by such absent witnesses as are hereafter mentioned) is to be produced in open Court at the trial ; and if disputed, is to be duly proved by the examination of witnesses sworn *or affirmed* as above directed, whose depositions are in the same manner to be reduced into writing and signed. Every exhibit is to be marked with some letter or number, to identify it; and the letter or number is to be referred to in the deposition proving it. All exhibits proved by witnesses not present in Court are, in the same manner, to be marked and referred to in the depositions proving them; and are to be endorsed and minuted as having been read at the time they may have been read in the Court.—*Sec.* VII, *Reg.* III, 1802. Para 3.

In the event of any witness being a Hindoo or a Mahomedan woman of a rank or quality, which, according to the customs and manners of the country, would render it improper to compel her to appear in a Court of justice, *or being otherwise exempt, either absolutely by law, or at the discretion of the Court, from personal appearance in Court, their evidence shall be taken in the manner prescribed by Act VII, 1841, q. v. infra.*—*Sec.* VII, *Reg.* III, 1802. Para 4, *and Sec.* XIX, *Reg.* IV, 1802.

But if the personal attendance of a party in a suit, or a witness (provided the party, or witness, be not a woman of a rank or quality, which, according to the customs and manners of the country, would render it improper to compel her to appear before the Court of justice) who may be resident at any distance whatever beyond the limits of the jurisdiction of the Court, shall be deemed by the Judge trying the cause to be indispensably necessary, he is to address the Judge of the Court, in the jurisdiction of which the person whose attendance is required may reside, requesting him to order him to attend; and the Judge so addressed is directed to comply with the requisition, without further delay than may be necessary in the event of the attendance of such person, before the Court of the Judge to whom the application may be made, being indispensable, in consequence of his being either a party or a witness in a suit depending before the Court.—*Sec.* VII, *Reg.* III, 1802. Para 5, and *Sec.* XIX, *Reg.* IV, 1802.

If any exhibit or written evidence is offered to a Zillah Court, in a cause depending before it, and the Judge of the Court shall think it just and proper to reject it, he is to endorse upon it the word " Rejected," together with the names of the parties in the cause, and the name of the party who produced the document, the date on which it may be rejected, and his reasons for not admitting it, (which may be written either upon the document rejected, or on a paper to be annexed to it) and to subscribe his name to the endorsement, and return the document with his reasons so written, to the person who produced it.—*Sec.* VII, *Reg.* III, 1802. Para 6.

The Judges of the Zillah Courts are authorized to employ any of their principal native officers, in taking down the depositions of witnesses whom they may not have time to examine *vivâ voce* themselves; provided that such depositions be taken in open Court in the presence of the parties, or their authorized pleaders, whose attestations shall be subscribed to all depositions so taken, in testimony of their having been present; and if any dispute or question shall arise, in the course of taking the evidence of a witness so examined, the Judge shall immediately, or as soon as practicable, hear and enquire into the same, in the presence of the witness, and of the parties, or their pleaders, and shall pass such order thereupon as may appear to him proper.—*Sec.* XXII, *Reg.* VII, 1809, *and Sec.* VIII, *Reg.* XII, 1809.

It shall be lawful for any Court within the territories of the Government of the East India Company, and the several Judges thereof, in every civil proceeding depending in such Court, upon the application of any of the parties to such proceeding, to order the examination, upon interrogatories or otherwise, before any Officer of any such Court, or other person or persons named in such order, of any witnesses within the jurisdiction of the Court where the proceeding shall be depending, or to order a commission to issue to any other Court for the examination of witnesses at any place or places out of such jurisdiction upon interrogatories or otherwise, and by the same or any subsequent order or orders to give all such directions for taking such examinations as well within the jurisdiction of the Court wherein the proceeding shall be depending as without, as may appear reasonable and just; provided always, that any Court to whom any such commission shall be directed, shall take the examination in open Court in all cases where witnesses are able to attend in Court and are not exempted from attendance by law, absolutely, or at the discretion of the Court. Provided also that such commissions as aforesaid for the examination of witnesses out of such jurisdiction may be directed otherwise than to some Court, under special circumstances which may appear to the Court issuing the commission to render such special direction expedient. Provided also that all commissions issued and orders made by any Court of the East India Company, and which are required to be executed within the local limits of any of Her Majesty's Supreme Courts, shall be directed in manner hereinafter mentioned.—*Sec.* II, *Act* VII, 1841.

When any order shall be made for the examination of witnesses within the jurisdiction of the Court wherein any such proceeding as aforesaid shall be depending by the authority of this Act, it shall be lawful for the Court or any Judge thereof, in and by the first order to be made in the matter, or any subsequent order, to command the attendance of any person to be named in such order, and to direct the attendance of any such person to be at his own place of residence, or elsewhere, if necessary or convenient so to do, and to produce all necessary documents and papers. And the wilful disobedience to any such order shall be deemed a contempt of Court, and punishable as in other cases of refusing or neglecting to give testimony. Provided always that every person whose attendance shall be required under this Act. shall be entitled to the like payment for expenses and loss of time, as upon attendance in Court in cases where such expenses are now allowed.—*Sec.* III, *Act* VII, 1841.

It shall be lawful for every Court or person authorized to take the examination of witnesses by an order or commission issued in pursuance of this Act, and they are hereby authorized and required, to take all such examinations upon oath, or affirmation where an affirmation is admissible or required upon a trial, and if upon such oath or affirmation any person making the same shall wilfully and corruptly give any false evidence, every person so offending shall be deemed and taken to be guilty of perjury, and every person causing or procuring another person to commit the offence of perjury hereby defined shall be guilty of subornation of perjury. —*Sec.* IV.—*Ibid.*

Before any order or commission for the examination of any witness under this Act shall be issued, the Court or Judge issuing the same shall be satisfied that there is good reason for believing that the witness will be unable to attend at the usual time for examination, by reason of absence from the jurisdiction, sickness, or other cause allowed by law. And before granting any such commission, the Court granting the same shall make particular enquiry as to the present residence of the witness whose deposition is to be taken under such commission, and as to the Court of the same degree as the Court granting such commission, or of inferior degree to such Court, which may be nearest to the place of residence of the witness, and the commission shall ordinarily be directed to such Court of equal or inferior degree as may most conveniently execute the same. Provided however that if there be doubt as to which is the most convenient Court of equal or inferior jurisdiction, such commission may be directed to the Judge having jurisdiction within the district within which the commission is to be executed. And the Judge shall at his discretion execute the commission in his own Court, or direct it to any Subordinate Court within his district, which shall have the same effect for all the purposes of this Act as if the commission had in the first instance been directed to such Subordinate Court. And no deposition taken under this Act, except as hereinafter mentioned, shall be read in evidence without the consent of the party against whom the same may be offered, unless it be proved that the deponent is beyond the jurisdiction of the Court, or dead, or unable from sickness or infirmity, to attend to be personally examined, or distant without collusion more than 50 coss from the place where the Court is held, or exempted by law, absolutely or at the discretion of the Court, from personal appearance in Court, or unless the Court shall at its discretion dispense with the proof of any of the above circumstances, or shall authorize the deposition of any witness being read in evidence notwithstanding proof that the causes for taking such deposition have ceased at the time of reading the same; and after the witness shall be produced, and shall have delivered his testimony, it shall be lawful for the Court at its discretion to authorize the reading of the deposition. And all depositions taken under this Act, being duly certified, may be read, at the discretion of the Court, without proof of the signature to such certificate.—*Sec.* V, *Act* VII, 1841.

Any Court other than one of Her Majesty's Courts, or any Judge thereof, may issue such commissions as aforesaid, and such orders as are indicated in the Second and Third Sections of this Act to be executed within the local limits of the jurisdiction of any of Her Majesty's Courts; and all such commissions and orders, except when directed otherwise than to a Court, shall be directed to a Court of Requests having jurisdiction within such limits, or any part thereof.—*Sec.* VI.—*Ibid.*

Such commissions and orders as aforesaid may be issued for execution under this Act within the territories of Princes and States in alliance with the East India Company; and all persons within such last mentioned territories being in the service of the East India Company are hereby required to pay obedience thereto, and for disobedience thereof shall on being found within the jurisdiction of the Court, or Judge issuing any such commission or order, be punishable in like manner, as if such offence had been committed within such jurisdiction; and for giving false testimony under the same shall be punishable by any Court of Justice within the territories of the East India Company.—*Sec.* VII.—*Ibid.*

Whenever the evidence of any absent witness shall be required out of the jurisdiction of the Court in which the proceedings for which the evidence is wanted may be pending, and the commission shall be directed to any Court, such Court may punish the wilful disobedience of any such order as aforesaid as a contempt, notwithstanding it shall not itself have made such order, with the same amount of punishment as in other cases of refusing or neglecting to give testimony.—*Sec.* VIII, *Act* VII, 1841.

Sec. VIII, Act VII, 1841.—' *Absent witnesses.*'—It is frequently necessary to send interrogatories to be put to witnesses in Ceylon to which this Act of course does not apply : —they are forwarded through the Secretary to Government who obtains the answers in communication with the Government of Ceylon—the Sudder Udalut under date 12th June 1850, directed that such interrogataries should always be accompanied with translations in English.

CHAPTER V.

PROCESS—ISSUE OF—RESISTANCE TO, &c.

All orders and process of the Court which may be directed to be served, or executed, on any person, are to be written, or printed, in the *language of the country where the Court shall be held ; Cl.* 1, *Sec.* XV, *Reg.* XV, 1816, and are to be sealed with the seal of the Court, and signed by the Judge. When a summons or any process is issued against a defendant, or a witness, in a cause, or any other person who may not reside or be present at the place at which the Court may sit, and for the serving or executing of which a peon, or peons, may be necessary ; each peon is to be paid by the party in whose behalf the summons or process may issue, four annas per day for his subsistence ; excepting in districts where custom may have fixed the subsistence money of peons at a lower rate ; in which case the lower rate, and no more, is to be paid. The name of each peon deputed to serve the process, the amount of his subsistence money, and the number of days for which he is to receive it, are to be endorsed on the writing. No greater number of peons than two are to be deputed to serve or execute any process of the Courts ; and one peon only is to be sent, excepting in cases in which the Judges may think two peons necessary.—*Sec.* XXI, *Reg.* III, 1802.

The summonses and other processes issued by the several Courts, shall be written or printed in one of the current languages of the country.—*Cl.* 5, *Sec.* XV, *Reg.* XV, 1816.

It is to be understood that the country language in which the processes, *and* orders, are to be written, shall be the language most familiar to the party or parties concerned ; and if a party shall be desirous of having a persian translation of an order, instead of a

---

Process.—The rules relative to notices and summonses, necessary on the " Institution of a suit" will be found under that head in Book II, Chapter II, as being rather forms connected therewith, than orders of a Court requiring certain things to be done in consequence of its decisions.

Sec. XXI, Reg. III, 1802.—A peon detained in village where sale may be held should receive usual batta at discretion of the Judge. For serving process at the Sudder Station he should also have the usual batta,—Cir. Ext : S. U. 8th July, 1844. Paras 4 & 5.

copy or translation thereof in one of the current languages of the country, the Court passing the order, shall comply with his application to that effect.—*Cl.* 6, *Sec.* XV, *Reg.* XV, 1816.

Every process, rule, order, or decree of the Zillah Courts. *With exception of those requiring to be issued to Hindoo or Mahommedan women of rank upon the institution of suit against them,* is to be immediately served or executed without application to any person, or the interference of any individual whomsoever, according to the requisition of it, within the limits of the special jurisdiction of each Court.—*Sec.* XV, *Reg.* III, 1802.

When a decree, *shall be referred by a Zillah Civil Court to a Subordinate Court for execution under the provisions of Sec.* XIV, *Act* VII, *of* 1843. Return is to be made by the Judge of the *lower* Court either by endorsement on the decree, or to be written on a paper firmly annexed to it; and if the return be made in the last mentioned manner, there is to be an endorsement on the decree referring the *Zillah Civil Court* to the return contained in such annexed paper, and the Judge is to cause a copy of the decree together with the return to it, to be deposited among the records of his Court, * * * * *.—*Sec.* XVI, *Reg.* IV, 1802.

If a Zemindar, independent Talookdar, or other actual proprietor of land, or a dependent Talookdar, shall resist or cause to be resisted any process, rule, order, or decree of a Zillah Court *or of the Sudder Udalut,* the Court, on proof of the resistance being made by oath, to its satisfaction, is to cause the offender to be summoned to answer to the charge. If the offender shall abscond, or shut himself up in his own or any house, or in any building, or retire to any place so that he cannot be served with the summons, the Court is to proceed against him in the manner directed with regard to other persons absconding or acting as above specified, so that they cannot be served with the process of the Court. If the offender shall not appear within the prescribed time, or if he shall appear, and, after receiving his answer to the charge and hearing the evidence which he may produce in his defence, it shall be proved to the satisfaction of the Court that he is guilty of the charge; the Court is to decree that the offender shall, from the date of the decree, forfeit his zemindarry, talook, or other estate in which the resistance may have been made; or, if the resistance shall have been made out of the limits of the estate of the offender, the zemindarry, talook, or other landed property that he

---

Sec. XVI, Reg. IV, 1802.—This Section, as originally enacted, contained provisions relative to other processes than decrees, which the late Zillah Courts were required to execute for the Provincial Courts—it remains in force only so far as given above, in respect of decrees.

may possess within the jurisdiction of the Court the process of which may have been resisted. If the cause shall not be appealed to *a Court competent to receive an* appeal within the time limited for preferring appeals to such Court in the established Regulations, the Court is immediately to forward a copy of its decree and proceedings respecting the charge, to the Governor in Council. If the offender shall appeal within the prescribed period, and the *appellate* Court should confirm the decision of the *lower* Court, and the cause shall not be *further* appealable; or, if it shall be *further* appealable, and the offender shall not lodge an appeal within the time limited for preferring appeals to that Court, in the established Regulations; the *appellate* Court is immediately to forward a copy of their decree and proceedings in the appeal, and of the decree and proceedings of the *lower* Court, to the Governor in Council. If an appeal shall be received from the decision of *a Zillah Civil* Court, and the Sudder Udalut should confirm the decree of that Court, they are immediately to transmit a copy of their decree, and proceedings, and of the decrees and proceedings received from the *Zillah* Court, to the Governor in Council. No appeal shall lie in this case to the Sudder Udalut, unless the annual produce of the lands of the offender which may be adjudged forfeited (calculating according to the amount paid and payable to the offender by the dependent talookdars, under-farmers, and ryots on account of the year in which the decree may be passed) shall exceed one thousand rupees. In the event of an appeal from the decree of the *Zillah* Court being presented to the Sudder Udalut, and the admission or rejection of the appeal depending upon the produce of the lands for the year before mentioned exceeding, or falling short of, one thousand rupees, the Court of Sudder Udalut is to order the *Zillah* Court to obtain the necessary information regarding the produce; and, after receiving their report, admit, or reject, the appeal, according as they may deem equitable. It shall be at the option of the Governor in Council, after the receipt of a decree adjudging the estate of any person forfeited under this Section, either to order it to be executed, or to commute the forfeiture for such fine as, upon a consideration of the situation and circumstances in life of the offender, he may think adequate to the offence for which the decree may be passed. In the event of the Governor in Council commuting the forfeiture for a fine, the Court which shall have transmitted the decree and proceedings to him, upon receiving notice of the fine that he may impose, is to levy the amount of it by the same process as is prescribed for enforcing decrees of the Court. In cases wherein a decree for the forfeiture of an estate or farm may be passed and transmitted to the Governor in Council, the decree in question shall not be deemed final until confirmed by the Governor in Council; and shall not be carried into execution until notice of his confirmation be received. In the event of the Governor in Council ordering the decree to be executed, the Court is to issue a precept, under the seal of the Court and the signature of the *Judge*, requiring the collector of the revenue of the Zillah to depute an Ameen, with a proper establishment of Officers, whose allowances are to be specified in the precept, to sequester the lands and collect the rents and revenues. If the lands of the offender shall be deemed by the Court too inconsiderable to admit of their being charged with the expense of an Ameen, they are to direct a precept to be issued to the collector of the Zillah, to order the nearest Tahsildar, or any other Officer who may be employed under him in the business of the collections, to take charge of the lands. The Officer is to perform the duties prescribed to Ameens in such cases, and under the same restrictions and penalties.—*Sec.* XXIII, *Regs.* III & IV, 1802, *and for S. U. Sec.* XXIV, *Reg.* V, 1802.

If the decree adjudging the lands of the offender forfeited shall be confirmed under Section XXIII, *or in case of the Sudder Udalut stand good*, it shall be at the option of the Governor in Council either to confer the rights which the offender possessed in the lands on his heirs, upon their agreeing to make good all sums whatever that may be due from him to Government on account of the lands forfeited, and to pay the fixed public revenue assessed upon them, or, if the property forfeited be a dependent talook, the revenue payable from it to the proprietor within whose estate it may be situated; or to order the lands to be disposed of at public sale under the rules prescribed for the sale of land so forfeited.—*Sec.* XXIV.—*Ibid, and for S. U. Sec.* XXV, *Reg.* V, 1802.

If a farmer of land, holding a farm immediately of Government, shall resist, or cause to be resisted, any process, rule, order, or decree which may at any time issue from any Zillah Court; *or from the Sudder Udalut*, on proof of the resistance being made by oath, *or solemn affirmation* to its satisfaction, the Court is to cause the of-

---

Sec. XXIII, of Regs. III & IV, 1802.—Similar provisions, mutatis mutandis, are made for the conduct of the Sudder Udalut in like cases, by Section XXIV, Regulation V, of 1802, which, as well as Sections XXV, XXVI, and XXVII, of the same Regulation in like manner correspond with Sections XXIV, XXV, and XXVI, respectively, of Regulations III and IV, of 1802, which govern the Subordinate and Zillah Courts—and it did not therefore appear necessary to re-print them under " Sudder Udalut." It is only requisite to observe that when such a decree is made by the Sudder Udalut itself, all which relates to appeal is of course superfluous. The Sudder Udalut is " immediately to forward a copy of its decree to the Governor in Council," the other proceedings ordered are identical. A Principal Sudder Ameen or Subordinate Judge, using the above Sections, should quote as from III of 1802, a Civil Judge from IV of 1802, and the Sudder Udalut from V of 1802.

fender to be summoned to answer to the charge. If the offender shall abscond, or shut himself up in his own or any house or building, or retire to any place, so that he cannot be served with the summons; the Court is to proceed against him in the manner directed with regard to other persons absconding, or otherwise acting as above specified, so that they cannot be served with the process of the Court. If the offender shall not appear within the prescribed period, or if he shall appear within the limited time, and, after receiving his answer to the charge, and hearing the evidence which he may have to produce in his defence, it shall be proved to the satisfaction of the Court that he is guilty of the charge, the Court is to decree the lease cancelled from the expiration of the revenue year of the district in which the decree may be passed. *If the decree be by the S. U., or if by another Court and* the offender shall not appeal to a Court *competent to receive an* appeal within the time limited for preferring appeals to that Court, the Court is immediately to transmit to the Governor in Council, a copy of the decree and of all the proceedings respecting the charge. If the offender shall appeal within the prescribed period, and the *appellate* Court should confirm the decision of the *lower* Court, and the cause shall not be *further* appealable, or, if it shall be *further* appealable, and the offender shall not lodge an appeal within the time limited for preferring appeals to that Court; the *appellate* Court is immediately to forward a copy of their decree and proceedings in the appeal, and of the decree and proceedings of the *lower* Court, to the Governor in Council. If an appeal from the decision of *a Zillah Civil* Court shall be admitted, and the Sudder Udalut should confirm the decree of the *Zillah* Court, they are immediately to transmit a copy of their decree and proceedings, and of the decrees and proceedings received from the *Zillah* Court, to the Governor in Council. An appeal shall not lie to the Sudder Udalut, unless the revenue payable to Government by the offender for the year in which the decree may be passed, on account of the lands, the lease for which may be adjudged annulled, shall exceed one thousand rupees. It shall be at the option of the Governor in Council, after the receipt of a decree adjudging the lease of a farmer annulled under this Section, either to order the decree to be executed, or to commute the forfeiture of the lease for such fine as, upon a consideration of the situation and circumstances in life of the offender, he may think adequate to the offence for which the decree may be passed; or, if the offender shall not be desirous of being continued in his farm, to fine him as above prescribed, and compel him to retain the farm during the remainder of the lease, and to hold him and his surety responsible for the discharge of their engagements until the term of them shall expire. If a fine shall be imposed upon the offender, the Court which shall have transmitted the final decree and proceedings to the Governor in Council, upon receiving notice of the fine, is to levy the amount of it by the same process as is prescribed for enforcing decrees of the Court. In cases wherein a decree for the forfeiture of the lease of the offender may be passed and transmitted to the Governor in Council, the decree in question shall not be deemed final until confirmed by the Governor in Council, and shall not be carried into execution until notice of his confirmation be received. If the lease of the offender shall be annulled, and a balance shall be due from him to Government at the close of the year in which the lease may be cancelled, both he and his surety are to be held responsible for the payment of it, and the collector of the revenue of the Zillah is empowered to proceed against them for the recovery of it, agreeably to the rules in that respect established. The offender is permitted to prosecute, in the Courts of the Zillah in which the farm may be situated, the dependent talookdars, under-farmers, and ryots, in the lands included in the farm, for any arrears of rent or revenue that may be due from them to him, on account of the period during which his lease remained in force.—*Cl.* 1, *Sec.* XXV, *Regs.* III *and* IV, *of* 1802, *and for S. U. Sec.* XXVI, *Reg.* V, 1802.

In all cases of resistance to the process of any Zillah Court, if the Judge of the Court, whose process may have been resisted, shall be of opinion that a fine to Government will be a more proper and adequate punishment for the offence, than a forfeiture of the offender's estate or farm under the provisions contained in this, and Sections XXIII and XXIV, he is authorized, instead of the decrees of forfeiture so directed, to adjudge the offender to pay such fine to Government as may appear proper, upon a consideration of his situation and circumstances in life, and the offence of which he may be convicted; as provided with regard to persons not being land-holders or farmers of land by Section XXVI, and subject to the provisions in that Section for an appeal from the judgment of the Court.—*Cl.* 2.—*Ibid.*

If any person not being a zemindar, independent talookdar, or other actual proprietor of land, or a dependent talookdar or a farmer of land holding a farm immediately of Government, shall resist, or cause to be resisted, any process, rule, order, or decree, which may at any time issue from a Court of Udalut established in any Zillah, *or from the Sudder Udalut*, on proof of the resistance being made by oath *or solemn affirmation* to its satisfaction, the Court is to cause the offender to be summoned to answer to the charge. If the person for whom the summons may be issued shall abscond, or shut himself up in his own or any house, or building, or retire to any place so that he cannot be served with the summons; the Court is to proceed against him in the manner directed with regard to other persons absconding, or otherwise acting as above specified, so that they cannot be served with the process of the Court. If the offender shall not appear within the prescribed period; or if he shall appear within the limited time, and after receiving his answer, and hearing the evidence which he may have to produce in his defence, it shall be proved to the satisfaction of the Court that he is guilty of the charge, the Court is to adjudge the offender to pay such fine to Government, as may appear to it proper, upon a consideration of his situation and circumstances in life, and the offence for which the decree may be passed. If the offender shall not prefer an appeal to *a Court competent to receive one*, within the time prescribed for lodging appeals, the Court is to proceed to levy the amount by the same process by which it is empowered to carry its decrees for sums of money into execution. If an offender *sentenced by a Subordinate Court*, should appeal to the *Zillah Civil Court* within the prescribed time, and the Civil Court should confirm the decision of the *lower* Court, the rules regarding appeals to the Sudder Udalut, from the decisions of the Zillah Civil Courts, for sums of money, are to be held applicable to decisions which may be passed by the *Zillah Civil Courts* under this Section. If the *Zillah Civil Courts* should confirm the decisions of the *lower* Court, and the offender shall not prefer an appeal to the Sudder Udalut within the time prescribed for lodging appeals, the Court is to proceed to levy the amount by the same process by which it is empowered to carry its decrees for sums of money into execution.—*Sec.* XXVI, *Regs.* III *and* IV, 1802, *and for S. U. Sec.* XXVII, *Reg.* V, 1802.

If the fine imposed *by a Zillah Civil Court* shall not exceed five thousand rupees, or if it shall be above that sum, and the offender shall not prefer an appeal to the Sudder Udalut within the time prescribed for lodging appeals, the Court is to proceed to levy the amount, by the same process by which it is empowered to carry its decrees for sums of money into execution.—*Sec.* XXVI, *Reg.* IV, 1802.

" Whereas it is expedient that the Sudder Dewany Udalut, and
" Nizamut Udalut, or other provincial Courts, however denomi-
" nated, exercising the highest jurisdiction within the provinces
" respectively subject to the Governments of Fort William, Fort
" St. George and Bombay, should have power and authority to exe-
" cute process of arrest, either civil or criminal, within the towns
" of Calcutta and Madras, and the town and island of Bombay,

" notwithstanding the jurisdiction of His Majesty's Courts estab-
" lished at those places respectively ; be it therefore enacted, that
" it shall and may be lawful for the said Court of Sudder Dewany
" and Nizamut Udalut, or other provincial Courts aforesaid, to exe-
" cute, or cause to be executed upon all persons subject to the
" jurisdiction of such Courts respectively, all manner of lawful pro-
" cess of arrest, within the respective limits of the towns of Cal-
" cutta and Madras, and of the town and island of Bombay, in the
" same manner as the said Courts respectively may, by virtue of
" any power now vested, or hereafter to be vested in them, law-
" fully execute, or cause to be executed, such process in any place
" situate without the said limits ; any Act, Charter, or other mat-
" ter or thing whatsoever to the contrary notwithstanding: pro-
" vided always, that all such process which shall be executed with-
" in the limits aforesaid, shall be in writing, and shall have under-
" written or endorsed thereon, or otherwise annexed thereto, a
" translation·thereof, or of the substance thereof, in the English
" language and character, signed by one of the Judges of the
" Court from whence the same shall issue."—*Sec.* CXIII, *Cap.*
155, 53*d Geo: 3d.*—In. *Sec.* II, *Reg.* II, 1820.

Any writ, warrant, or other process issued by any Court, Judge,
or Magistrate in the territories beyond the local limits of the Supreme Courts of Calcutta, Madras, and Bombay, respectively, may .
be executed within those limits in manner following:—A copy of
such writ, warrant or other process, authenticated as such by the
attestation of the Court, Judge, or Magistrate signing or issuing
the same, accompanied by a certified translation in the English
language, shall be presented to any Judge of Her Majesty's
Courts, who may thereupon, under his hand and signature, endorse and direct the same to be executed within the local limits of
any of Her Majesty's Courts by the Sheriff, or by any justice of
the peace, according to the nature of such writ, warrant or other
process.—*Sec.* I, *Act* XXIII, 1840.

Upon the delivery of every such writ, warrant, or process, so
endorsed as aforesaid, to any such Sheriff as aforesaid, every such
Sheriff shall make a memorandum of the date of such delivery
and shall execute such writ, warrant, or process in like manner as
if the same had originally issued from any of Her Majesty's

Sec. II, Reg. II, 1820.—Under this law processes from the Mofussil used to be executed through the Sudder Udalut. Act No. XXIII, of 1840, has established a different
course of proceeding with respect to *them*—but this law is unrepealed, and the Sudder
Court at Madras may still execute, or cause to be executed, *their own* process within the
limits of the Supreme Court. The Court would otherwise be unable to act efficiently
under Act XV, of 1835.

Courts, and had been delivered at the date as appearing by the memorandum ; and such Sheriff shall make no distinction as to priority or otherwise between the execution of any writ, warrant, or other process originally issued from any of Her Majesty's Courts, and the execution of any writ, warrant, or other process under this Act. But every writ, warrant, and other process, whether original or endorsed as aforesaid, shall, amongst each other, be subject to the same rules touching the mode and order of execution as are now established in respect of writs, warrants, and other process originally issued from Her Majesty's Courts of Justice.—*Sec.* II, *Act* XXIII, 1840.

Every such Sheriff shall be liable to be proceeded against in Her Majesty's Courts of Justice for all matters touching the execution of any writ, warrant, or other process executed under this Act, in like manner as if the same had originally issued from any of Her Majesty's Courts of Justice. And all persons and property seized or detained under any writ, warrant, or process executed by virtue of this Act, shall be dealt with in like manner as if such persons or property had been seized or detained under the like writ, warrant, or other process issued from any of Her Majesty's Courts of Justice.—*Sec.* III.—*Ibid.*

All persons disobeying or obstructing the execution of any writ, warrant, or other process endorsed under this Act, shall be punishable in Her Majesty's Courts of Justice, in like manner as if the same had issued from such Courts: provided always, that in the case of process for the attendance of witnesses, Her Majesty's Courts shall be governed by the like rules, touching expenses and other matters, as are established in regard to subpœnas issued from such Courts.—*Sec.* IV.—*Ibid.*

In the case of persons seized or detained by virtue of any writ, warrant, or other process executed, under the authority of this Act, by any justice of the peace or by any Sheriff, it shall be the duty of every such Sheriff or Justice of the Peace, if so required by the endorsement of the Judge, to deliver the party in custody to such authority or persons as shall be particularly specified in such endorsement, and who shall have been charged with the execution of the writ, warrant, or other process by the authority originally issuing the same, and for that purpose to cause the party in custody to be conveyed to any place within the Company's territories beyond the local limits of the jurisdiction of Her Majesty's Courts.—*Sec.* V.—*Ibid.*

In the case of any writ, warrant, or other process required to be endorsed under the authority of this Act, it shall be lawful for the Judge who shall be required to endorse the same, to remit the same for amendment to the authority issuing the same, if the same shall appear to be defective in any matter of form.—*Sec.* VI, *Act* XXIII, 1840.

In the case of any writ, warrant, or other process required to be endorsed under the authority of this Act, for the seizure or detention of any person, it shall be lawful for the Judge who shall be required to endorse the same to direct by endorsement that bail (the amount and number of sureties to be specified in such endorsement) may be taken; and for this purpose to call for such documents and to make such inquiry as he shall think proper.—*Sec.* VII.—*Ibid.*

CHAPTER VI.

DECREES—PREPARATION OF.

When the parties have been heard, and the witnesses on both sides examined, and the exhibits received and considered, the Judge is to give judgment according to justice and right; and is to order costs to be paid to the party in whose favor the decree may be made.—*Sec.* IX, *Reg.* III, 1802.

The Judges of the Zillah Courts are invariably to state in every decree the grounds on which they may pass it.—*Sec.* XVI, *Reg.* II, 1802.

The Judges of the Zillah Courts are to insert in their decrees the names of the witnesses whose depositions may have been taken, the title of every exhibit read in the cause, and the amount of the annual produce of the land, or the sum of money, or the value of the property, or thing, decreed. The decree is to be sealed with the seal of the Court, and signed by the Judge, and dated on the day on which it may be passed.—*Sec.* XXVII, *Reg.* III, 1802.

The Zillah Courts are not to pass a decree in any suit, concerning the succession or right of inheritance to a zemindary, talook, land, house, or other real property, to which there are more claimants than one, who by the Hindoo or Mahomedan law, (respect being had to the religion of the claimants) would be entitled to a portion of the property, excepting the property be, by the decree, adjudged to all the claimants in the proportions to which they may be respectively entitled.—*Sec.* XIX, *Reg.* II, 1802.

The decrees passed by the *Subordinate and Civil Zillah Courts*, and by the Sudder Udalut shall be written in English.—*Cl.* 2, *Sec.* XV, *Reg.* XV, 1816.

An abstract of every decree *passed by the Court of Sudder Udalut, or by the Zillah Civil Courts, or by the Courts of the Subordinate Judges,* containing a succinct statement of the grounds of judgment, shall, on the day of the promulgation of the decree, be entered in the diary of the Court passing the decree: and every

---

Sec. XXVII, Reg. III, 1802.—In decrees, and all papers submitted to Sudder Udalut, the corresponding English is to be given for every native date; and all native terms or expressions are also to be explained in English; and paragraphs of the decree are to be numbered.

party in the suit wherein the decree is passed, shall be entitled to be furnished with a copy of that abstract, on application for a copy thereof ; or with a translation of that abstract in a current language of the district or country, on application for such a translation.—*Sec.* II, *Act* XXXV, 1837.

If the decree shall be given against the defendant or respondent, and the whole of the money or property which may be demanded by the appellant or plaintiff shall be decreed to him, a sum equal to the whole of the fees of his pleader shall be adjudged to the plaintiff or appellant, in addition to the other costs which may be awarded to him; but if only a part of the money or property claimed is decreed to the plaintiff or appellant, a sum bearing the same proportion to the money or to the value of the thing decreed, as the fee did to the demand stated in the plaint or appeal, is to be decreed and added to the costs which may be awarded to the plaintiff or appellant.—*Cl.* 1, *Sec.* XXVI, *Reg.* XIV, 1816.

If the suit of the plaintiff or appellant shall be dismissed, whether upon an investigation of the merits, or otherwise, the plaintiff or appellant, is to be charged with the fees of his own pleader and with those of the defendant or respondent.—*Cl.* 2.—*Ibid.*

Provided, however, that if in any instance the payment of the pleaders fees, according to the preceding rules, should not appear to be just and equitable, the Courts of Civil Judicature may exercise their discretion in charging the fees of the pleaders to the parties respectively, in such proportions as may appear equitable and proper, under a consideration of all the circumstances of the case.—*Cl.* 3.—*Ibid.*

Act XXXV, 1837.—At the commencement of every appeal decree, a statement should be entered showing the nature of the claim preferred, the grounds on which it was made, and the manner in which it was disposed of in the Lower Courts. At the end of every copy of a decree and also of the abstracts or documents mentioned in Section II, Act XXXV, of 1837, a note is to be entered in *English* in the following *words* and *order* :

> Sealed and signed—*here enter date,*
> Term of special appeal expires „
> Copy applied for............ „
> Copy ready............... „
> Copy furnished............. „

Delay not attributable to party—(enter No. of days.)
Appeal time with reference to Sec. III, Act XXXV, of 1837, will expire (enter date.)
In all decrees in which notification as to appeal time is written in English, a similar one in the language of the district, is to be written immediately below it.—Cir. Lr. S. U. 5th September 1849.

Cl. 1, 2, 3, Sec. XXVI, Reg. XIV, 1816.—Though under Act I of 1846 parties are left to make their own arrangements as to remuneration with their pleaders, yet these Clauses were left unrepealed, and remain in force as guides in settling costs, to be paid by the party cost, under Section VII of that Act. Whatever arrangements may have been made between the successful party and his vakeel, costs at the old rate, as laid down in Section XXV Regulation XIV of 1816, which see under " Pleaders," are to be awarded.

property ; such decrees shall be stayed, or enforced, in cases of appeal, according to the rules now established, with the following addition thereto.—*Cl.* 1, *Sec.* XII, *Reg.* XII, 1809.

The security to be given by appellants, for staying the execution of decrees appealed from in cases of money, or other moveable property ; or by respondents, when such decrees are carried into execution during an appeal, shall be sufficient, in addition to the amount or value adjudged, to cover the interest that may be expected to arise upon the amount payable under the decree, if confirmed in appeal, according to the provision for adjudging interest in such cases, made by Section XXXV, Regulation IV, A. D. 1802.—*Cl.* 2.—*Ibid.*

The Judges of the several Courts, by which security may be taken from appellants or respondents, for performing the decrees to be passed on appeals, are enjoined to be particularly careful in ascertaining that the security received, is good and sufficient, and they are required in all cases to cause the Nazir or other Officers, by whom the property of the sureties may be ascertained, to deliver in as accurate a statement as can be obtained of such property, with a full report of the enquiry made respecting it ; informing him, at the same time, that he will be held responsible for any wilful misrepresentation, in his statement or report.— *Sec.* XIII.—*Ibid.*

The following provisions are enacted in addition to the Rules now in force regarding the security to be required from parties for the execution of decrees of the Civil Courts, or for staying the execution of judgments in the civil suits during an appeal in such suits.—*Cl.* 1, *Sec.* XIII, *Reg.* XV, 1816.

All persons who may enter into security bonds for the purposes mentioned in the preceding Clause, are prohibited from transferring, or from causing to be transferred, by sale, gift, mortgage or otherwise, any land or other immoveable property belonging to them and specified in the schedule of property on which their security may have been accepted, until the object of their security shall have been completely fulfilled.—*Cl.* 2.—*Ibid.*

This prohibition however shall not be construed to affect the legality of any private transfer or mortgage of such property, in cases in which the amount of any demand on the surety which may eventually arise under the terms of the security bond, shall be duly discharged by him ; but it is hereby declared, that no private transfer, or mortgage of such property which may be made by a surety in the interval between the execution of the security bond and the final and complete enforcement of the judgment, shall be considered to bar the prior right of the Court to hold the whole or any part of such property answerable in the first instance for the amount of any demand upon it, which may eventually arise under the terms of the security bond and which may not be duly discharged by the surety.—*Cl.* 3, *Sec.* XIII, *Reg.* XV, 1816.

Such parts of the Regulations as are construed to require, that the decrees passed in civil suits shall be executed and enforced by the Courts without any application for that purpose from the parties, are hereby declared subject to the following modifications.—*Cl.* 1, *Sec.* XIV, *Reg.* XV, 1816.

The execution of decisions passed by village punchayets and district punchayets, which may be required to be carried into effect by the Zillah Judge, under Regulations V and VII of 1816, shall be subject to the modifications of this Section.—*Cl.* 2.—*Ibid.*

The Zillah Courts, and the Sudder Udalut, shall not be required to carry into execution any decree, which may be passed in original suits or in appeals, except in conformity with the following rules and provisions.—*Cl.* 4.—*Ibid.*

Any party who may be desirous of obtaining the execution of a decree shall appear either in person or by an authorized pleader, before the Court by whom such decree may have been passed, and shall present a petition written on the stamped paper prescribed in Section XX, Regulation XIII of 1816, praying for the execution of the decree.—*Cl.* 5.—*Ibid.*

The petition shall state the number of the suit, the names of the parties, the date and substance of the decree, whether any appeal has been preferred or admitted from the decision, and whether any, and what, adjustment of the matter in dispute has been made between the parties subsequently to the decree ; it shall further contain a statement of the specific amount due to the petitioner under the decree, whether on account of costs of suit or otherwise, and the name of the individual or individuals, against whom the enforcement of the decree is solicited.—*Cl.* 6. —*Ibid.*

The Court, after causing the purport of the petition to be compared with the decree contained in the original record of the suit, shall proceed to execute the same, in conformity with the pro-

---

Cl. 5, Sec. XIV, Reg. XV, 1816.—The duty of executing Decrees passed by the late Zillah Courts lies with Sub-Judge, or Principal Sudder Ameen.—Cir. Ext. S. U. 23d October 1843.

Decrees revised by lower Court under Cl. 2, Sec. X, Act VII, 1843, should be executed by the lower Court passing them, with whom the record will be.—Cir. Ext. S. U. 5th March 1844.

visions which are now in force or which may be hereafter enacted.—*Cl.* 7, *Sec.* XIV, *Reg.* XV, 1816.

Provided however, that if the suit shall have been tried exparte, or that an interval of more than one year shall have elapsed between the date of the decree, and the application for its execution ; or that the enforcement of the decree shall be solicited against individuals being heirs or representatives of the original parties in the suit, or against one only of several individuals equally affected by the decree, or if there shall appear reason to believe that the matter in dispute has been adjusted by the parties subsequently to the decree, either by the voluntary surrender of the thing adjudged, or by the payment of the sum decreed either in whole or in part, by instalments or otherwise, it shall be competent to the Court, instead of proceeding to the immediate enforcement of the decree, to issue a notice to the party, against whom execution may be sued out, requiring him to shew cause within a limited period to be fixed by the Court, why the decree should not be executed against him. If upon such notice the party shall not attend in person or by Vakeel, or shall not shew sufficient cause to the satisfaction of the Court, why the decree should not be forthwith executed, the Court will cause the judgment to be satisfied according to the rules in force. If the party shall attend in person or by Vakeel, and shall offer any objection to the enforcement of the decree, the Court shall issue such order, after a due consideration of the circumstances of each case, as may appear just and proper.—*Cl.* 8.—*Ibid.*

The preceding rules shall not be construed to prevent the Courts from issuing process of execution, for the purpose of recovering any fees or costs which may be due to Government, * * * In such cases, as well as in suits in which a party may have been

---

Cl. 7, Sec. XIV, Reg. XV, 1816.—The various causes assigned for non-execution of Decrees may generally be classed as follows—

    1. Warrant returned........No effects.
    2.   do.   ....No further effects.
    3.   do.   ....Parties not found.
    4.   do.   ·   ....Creditors not proceeding.
    5.   do..   ....Parties agreed.
    6.   do.   ....No purchasers.
    7.   do.   ....Other claimants.
    8. .... Sale ordered.
    9. ....Property attached waiting orders.
    10. ....Process not issued.

In the six first cases no further proceedings can be adopted towards the execution of the Decree without renewed exertion on the part of the judgment creditor ; within six weeks therefore after such return, the application should be struck off the list, leaving it of course optional to the creditor to make fresh application at any future time, should he see fit to do so. In respect of the other cases the Courts must use their best exertion to expedite the execution of the Decree,—Cir. Lr. S. U. 5th May 1849.

allowed to plead in formâ pauperis, the Court shall proceed without any application from the parties, to enforce execution of the judgment, so far as relates to the recovery of the amount of fees or costs due to Government.—*Cl.* 9, *Sec.* XIV, *Reg.* XV, 1816.

If a defendant in a suit in a Zillah Court shall be committed to close custody at the instance of the plaintiff, either whilst the suit is depending, or after the decree shall have been passed, the Judge at the time of the commitment of the defendant, is to make an order on the Plaintiff, for the payment of whatever monthly allowance he may think reasonable for the subsistence of the defendant; upon a consideration of his rank and situation in life, and the circumstances of the plaintiff. The allowance is not to exceed four annas, nor be less than one anna per day; and is to be made payable to the Nazir, who is to give monthly receipts for it to the plaintiff, dated on the day on which the money may be paid. The first payment is to be made immediately upon the confinement of the defendant; and every subsequent payment at the expiration of the next and following month, calculating from the day on which the Defendant may be confined. If the Plaintiff shall neglect or refuse, to pay the prescribed allowance, for the space of one month, after any payment may become due, the Nazir is to report the omission or refusal in writing, under his signature to the Judge. Upon receipt of the report, the Judge is to cause it to be notified to the Plaintiff by a writing in the language of the country in which the Court may be held, to be fixed up in some conspicuous place in the Court room, that if he shall not, within one month after the date of the notice, pay the sums in arrear, together with the allowance for one month in advance, the Court will release the defendant. If the Plaintiff shall not. make the payments required by the notice, the Court is accordingly to discharge the Defendant from custody. Plaintiffs are not to be required to pay any thing to Defendants who may be committed to custody for disobedience to an order of the Court.—*Sec.* X, *Reg.* III, 1802.

A question having arisen, whether the amount paid for the subsistence of persons in confinement, under judgments of the Civil Courts, as prescribed by Section X, Regulation III, 1802, is to be repaid by the party confined, on his release; it is hereby explained that such repayment is to be made, in common with the re-imbursement of other costs of suit and process, when any

---

Cl. 9, Sec. XIV, Reg. XV, 1816.—Such process was also allowed, by this Section as originally enacted, to be issued for recovery of fees due to a party in a suit, but by Section VIII, Act I, of 1846, it was enacted that such demands should not be enforced otherwise than by regular suit.

property may be forthcoming from which the amount can be levied. But when no property can be pointed out for the reimbursement of the subsistence money paid to prisoners, they shall not be detained in confinement, for the repayment of such money only.—*Sec.* XII, *Reg.* II, 1811.

Doubts having been entertained whether any of the established Civil Courts are competent to provide, in their decrees, for the payment, by instalments, of money adjudged by them, or to make such provision, in cases of indigence, at any period after passing their decrees; it is hereby declared, that the Civil Courts, in general are restricted from granting indulgence of time, in the satisfaction of a final judgment, when property, from which such judgment can be satisfied, (whether belonging to the party against whom the judgment is given, or to his surety or sureties for the performance of such judgment) may be forthcoming; unless the party in whose favour the decree is passed shall consent to waive his right of immediate enforcement, under an engagement for gradual payment, or otherwise; or unless a short postponement of the sale of property shall, under any particular circumstances appear just and equitable. But when no property may be pointed out from which the judgment can be enforced, and the party against whom it is passed, or his surety, if he have given any, may be willing to engage (under sufficient malzaminy or hazirzaminy security, as one or the other may be tendered, or required) for the liquidation of the amount due, by instalments, within such period, as the Court passing the final decree or entrusted with the execution of it, shall deem reasonable and proper, it shall be competent to the Court, by which the final judgment is given, or to any superior Court revising the proceedings of an inferior Court, to accept the engagement so offered, and to cause execution of the decree in conformity therewith, so long as the conditions of it shall be duly fulfilled. In such cases, if the person delivering the accepted engagement shall have been taken into custody, he shall be immediately discharged, and shall not be liable to further arrest in execution of the judgment to which such engagement may refer, except on failure to perform the terms of it; nor shall any interest be chargeable, in such instances, beyond what may be provided for, in the engagement.—*Sec.* X.—*Ibid.*

For the relief of the insolvent debtors and their sureties, who may be in confinement, for the satisfaction of the decrees of the Civil Courts, and may have no means of discharging the amount demandable from them, by instalments or otherwise, the Judges, of the Zillah Subordinate Courts, the *Zillah Civil Courts*, and the Court of Sudder Udalut, are empowered, on receiving from the

person of persons confined, in such cases, a statement upon oath
or solemn affirmation, containing a full and fair disclosure of all
property belonging to them, whether in land, money, or effects,
or of whatever description; and whether held in their own names,
or in the names of any other persons, or jointly with others; to
cause enquiry to be made, for the purpose of ascertaining the
truth of such statement, or the validity of any objections thereto,
which may be offered by the party at whose instance the prisoner,
or prisoners, may be in confinement; and if the result of such
enquiry shall satisfy the Court, that the statement of property so
delivered is true and faithful, and that the persons confined possess no other means of discharging the amount demandable from
them, and the property included in the statement, or such part
thereof as the Court may deem it proper to sell, in satisfaction of
the judgment passed, shall be given up for sale; the Court, on
receiving such surrender of property, may cause it to be sold, in the
mode prescribed by the regulations; and may order the release of
the person or persons in confinement, either with, or without,
hazirzaminy security, for his or their appearance when required.
Provided, however, that nothing in this Section, which is meant to
grant relief in cases of real inability and fair dealing only, shall
entitle any debtor or surety, under the judgment of any Civil Court,
to be released, without full satisfaction of such judgment, if he shall
be guilty of any fraudulent concealment of property, or shall
have committed any manifest fraud or misdemeanor which may
appear to the Court to render him an improper object of the relief
intended for persons acting with good faith, and willing to surrender all the property in their possession for the benefit of their
creditors. Nor shall release from confinement, in any instance, under this Section, prevent the creditor from bringing to sale (by application to the Court) in full payment of the sum adjudged due
to him, any property which may be subsequently possessed by the
party released; or from causing such party to be again confined,
until the judgment be fully satisfied, when it may appear, by sufficient proof, that he had fraudulently concealed any property actually belonging to, and known to have been possessed by him,
either in his own name, or that of others in his behalf at the time
of his discharge. Provided further that all proceedings held, and
orders passed, by the judges of the *Zillah Subordinate Courts* under the discretion vested in them by this Section, shall, on representation of the parties affected thereby to the *Zillah Civil Courts*
be open to the revision and determination of those Courts; and,
in like manner, all orders passed by the *Zillah Civil Courts* under
this Section, shall be open to the final decision of the Sudder
Udalut.—*Sec.* XI, *Reg.* II, 1811.

BOOK III.

SPECIAL SUITS.

CHAPTER I.

REVENUE SUITS.

Suits preferred in the Zillah Courts for arrears of rent or revenue from under-farmers or ryots, or their sureties, where no pottah has been granted, shall be dismissed with costs, unless it shall be proved to the satisfaction of the Judge that a pottah had been tendered and refused, or that both parties had agreed to dispense with the use of pottah and moochulka.—*Sec.* IX, *Reg.* V, 1822.

Where a collector may demand a sum of money from a proprietor or farmer of land as an arrear of revenue, and where such proprietor or farmer may deny, by a writing ·to that effect addressed to the collector, the justness of the claim in whole, or in part, but in order to prevent any further process being issued against him may discharge the demand in full; the proprietor or farmer shall be at liberty to sue the collector in the *Subordinate Court* of Udalut of the Zillah, for the recovery of whatever money may have been unduly exacted; the Court shall give judgment in favour of the complainant for all such sums as he may have paid beyond the

---

Revenue Suits.—This term may be thought equally applicable to those ' Suits respecting matters of Revenue' in which the Collector is vested with judicial powers, and the regulations relative to which will be found in Book I, Ch. V, pp. 49—68—but by " Revenue Suits" is here meant Suits or matters in which the Revenue Officers are *parties* before the Zillah Courts; the proceedings in which are regulated by special enactment.

It may be held that Suits between Proprietors and farmers of Land and Ryots must be brought in the Zillah Courts—Reg. V of 1822 notwithstanding—See note on Sec. III, Reg. XXVIII—1802 at page 52—and if so, the penal sections of that Regulation therein enumerated, will apply to Subordinate Zillah Courts, and ought to have been in this Chapter, on " Revenue Suits liable to be brought before Zillah Courts."

There is also another description of ' Revenue Suits' which might perhaps have been included in this Chapter, but which, as intimately connected with the " Collectors Revenue Tribunal" have been placed under that head at pp. 66—68—thus Sections XXXV and XL, Reg. XXXVIII, 1802 give an action the right of which is specially reserved by Cl. 1, Sec. II, Reg. V, of 1822—to ryots against landholders or farmers, at whose instance they may be confined as revenue defaulters, or their goods distrained; while under the latter Section landholders or farmers may, if they prefer it, proceed by regular instead of summary suit, or by way of distraint—Sec. XLI of the same Regulation prescribed that such suits shall have priority of decision.

amount due, and shall further adjudge the same to be refunded from the public treasury of the Zillah, with interest at the rate of twelve per cent per annum, from the date of the exaction, to the fulfilment of the decree with costs of suit.—*Sec.* IX, *Reg.* XXVII, 1802.

Where proprietors or farmers of land confined for arrears of revenue, which arrears may not have been adjudged to be due by a judicial decree, may consider the demand not to be warranted by their engagements with Government, they shall have free liberty to prosecute the Collector for such confinement, in the *Subordinate Court* of the Zillah. Where no part of the arrear may be due, the Judge shall release such proprietors, or farmers, and decree such costs and damages against the Collector, as he may deem to be equitable, upon a consideration of the circumstances of the case. Where only a part of the demand may be proved to be due, the Court shall discharge the defaulter, on his paying such part. In both cases, however, the Court shall, previously to the release of such defaulters, take good security from them for the execution of the final decision in appeal, where the cause may be appealed by the Collector. Where Collectors may represent to the Court that an appeal will not be preferred from the decision, or where the appeal may not have been lodged within the time limited for preferring appeals, the Judge shall release the defaulters, without taking such security.—*Cl.* 1, *Sec.* XI.—*Ibid.*

Suits instituted under this Section shall be prosecuted within a reasonable period of time, not exceeding three months in any case, from the confinement of the defaulter: and on failure thereof, the prosecutor shall be non-suited.—*Cl.* 2.—*Ibid.*

Persons confined for arrear of rents or revenues due to Government, shall have liberty to move the *Subordinate Court* of the Zillah, to compel the Collector to shew cause for such continued confinement; where the person making such motion may be confined under the decree of a Court of Udalut and the time prescribed for appealing from the decision may have elapsed, the Judge is not to enter into the merits of the case, but shall simply enquire whether the defaulter has discharged the amount of the decree, and the sums which may have become due from him subsequently to his confinement. Where the defaulter may not be confined under a judicial decree, but under the process which Collectors are em-

Sec. XI, Reg. XXVII, 1802.—" *Subordinate Courts*" in the original " Udalut of the Zillah" *these* functions of which now devolve on the Subordinate Zillah Court, whether presided over by a European Judge or Principal Sudder Ameen ; that is, *either* can entertain a suit against the Collector for an unwarranted *act*, though if the Collector have given a *judicial decision* in any case, under any law authorizing him to do so, no *appeal* will lie from *it* to a Principal Sudder Ameen, under Sec. VI, Act VII, 1843, which see at p. 116.

powered by this Regulation to issue, for the purpose of conveying persons to jail, in order to secure the revenues of Government; and where such defaulter may dispute the demand, the Judge shall not anticipate the merits of the case, but shall leave the defaulter to prosecute the Collector: where however the defaulter, admitting the validity of such demand, may plead the demand having been actually discharged, the Judge shall proceed to investigate the matter of fact. Where it may appear on examination of the defaulter's accounts (which examination shall be considered to be a continuation of the original suit or process, and not a new suit or process), that the demand, for which he may be in confinement, has been liquidated; the Judge shall release the defaulter, on his giving security to make good any sum which the collector may state to be still due from him, in the event of the cause being appealed, and of the sum disputed being awarded in favor of Government. Where the Collector may not object to the adjustment of accounts made by the Court; or where the Collector objecting to the adjustment, the defaulter may omit to give the security above required; or where the Collector may omit to appeal within the time limited for lodging appeals; the Judge shall release the prisoner without taking security. Where the whole or a part of the money for which the defaulter is confined may remain undischarged; or where such defaulter, acquiescing in the adjustment of accounts made by the Court, may have been confined on account of such demand for a term exceeding one year; the Judge shall have power to release him, on his giving good security for payment of the remaining debt, by instalments, during the course of one year after his release. The Collector and the defaulter shall have a right of appeal from the decisions passed by the *Subordinate* Zillah Court, in the event of either of them being dissatisfied with such decision.—*Cl.* 1, *Sec.* XII, *Reg.* XXVII, 1802.

For the better securing to the party a speedy delivery from erroneous, or wrongous imprisonment, such suits shall be conducted by oral process; unless where the party confined shall otherwise desire.—*Cl. 2.—Ibid.*

Where a Collector may proceed to arrest an actual proprietor of land, in the particular cases authorized, or a farmer of land, for

Sec. XII, Reg. XXVII, 1802.—" *Subordinate Court*"—In this Section perhaps, this term must be taken to mean exclusively a Court presided over by a European Judge; because by Section XIV, Act VII, 1843, Collectors cannot send parties for confinement to Principal Sudder Ameens; but although the petitioner under this Section may be in the custody of a Civil Judge, it does not follow that his petition for release from such custody should not be addressed to, and decided upon by the Subordinate Court, though presided over by a Principal Sudder Ameen, a proceeding which would leave to either party an appeal to the Civil Court, as provided in the latter part of the Section.

the recovery of arrears, he shall depute two peons, and no more, with a writing under his official seal, and signature, which writing shall specify the amount of the arrear due from the defaulter, the date on which it became payable, and generally the causes of the arrest, and shall require the defaulter to deliver himself into the custody of the peons, that they may convey him to the jail of the Zillah. The peons shall proceed with the defaulter directly to the jail. On the arrival of the defaulter at the jail, the Collector shall apply to the Court, by motion in writing through the Vakeel of Government, for the confinement of the defaulter; which writing shall become a record of the Court. The motion shall specify the amount of the arrear due from the defaulter, the date on which it became payable, and generally the causes of the arrest. On receipt of the motion, the Judge shall order the defaulter to be confined in the jail of the Zillah, and shall detain him there until he discharge the arrear for which he may have been confined in the first instance, as well as all subsequent arrears which may have accumulated during his confinement; or until the Collector apply to the Court by motion, made as above directed, for his release.

*   *   *   *   *

Where the defaulter may not reside, or not be within the limits of the Zillah, the Collector shall send two peons, with the writing above mentioned, to the Collector of the Zillah in which the defaulter may be, or reside, at that time; and such Collector shall assist to take the defaulter into custody, and to convey him to the jail of the Zillah in which he may be so apprehended. The Collector issuing the writing shall forward to the Vakeel of Government in such Zillah, the prescribed motion for the confinement of the defaulter, so that he may have it ready to present to the Judge on the arrival of the defaulter at the jail. The Collector shall likewise specify, in the writing, the name of the Zillah, to the jail of which the defaulter is to be conveyed. With the above exceptions as to the mode of serving the process, and as to the jail in which the defaulter is to be confined, the other rules contained in this Regulation shall be held equally applicable to the case, as if the defaulter had been confined in the jail of the Zillah containing the lands on account of which the arrear may be due. Suits or complaints which the defaulter may have to prefer against the Collector or his officers, or the Ameen deputed to take charge of his lands, shall be lodged in the Court of the last mentioned Zillah; and the Judge of that Zillah in the jail of which the defaulter may be confined, shall give effect to all decrees or orders which may be transmitted to him by the Judge of the Zillah in

which the suits or complaints of the defaulter may be so lodged.—
Cl. 1, *Sec.* XIII, *Reg.* XXVII, 1802.

Where a Collector may issue the process prescribed against an
actual proprietor of land, on account of arrear of the public revenue ; and where the defaulter may refuse to obey, or resist or
cause to be resisted the peons deputed by the collector, or abscond,
or shut himself up in his own or any other house, or in any building, or retire to any place so that the process cannot be served
upon him ; the Collector who may issue the writing shall move the
Subordinate Court of the Zillah, through the Vakeel of Government in the Court, to arrest the defaulter ; and the Judge shall,
upon receiving the oaths *or solemn affirmation* of two or more credible persons to the truth of the circumstances, require the defaulter, by a publication in writing, to deliver himself into the custody
of the Court within four weeks, calculating from the day following
the date of the publication. The publication, shall be written in
the dialect of the district; it shall be fixed up, as early after the
date of it as may be practicable, at the usual place of abode, or at
the principal Cutcherry in the estate, of the defaulter, in the office of the Collector, and the Court room of the Udalut of the Zillah. The Collector shall continue the Ameen deputed to collect
the rents and revenues of the estate, in the same manner as if the
process issued had been duly served, and obeyed by the defaulter.
Cl. 1, *Sec.* XIV.—*Ibid.*

Where the defaulter may not surrender himself before the expiration of the time limited in the said publication, or where he
may deliver himself up within the prescribed time ; the Judge,
after receiving such answer as may be made for the defaulter,
with the evidence which may be produced in his defence, and
after receiving that which the Collector may adduce in support of
his case, shall, upon proof of the charge, decree the proprietary
right of the defaulter, and of his heirs, in the estate, to be forfeited
to Government. Where the defaulter may not appeal from the decree
of the *Subordinate* Court to the *Zillah Civil* Court, the *Subordinate*
Judge shall transmit, to the Governor in Council, a copy of the
decree, and of all the proceedings in the case. Where the defaulter may appeal to the *Zillah Civil* Court, and where the *appellate*

Sec. XIII, Reg. XXVII, 1802.—The application for confinement under this Section
must be made to the Civil Judge, if there be no European Subordinate Judge, that is to
the Officer in charge of the Jail.

Sec. XIV, Reg. XXVII, 1802.—The powers given to the Subordinate Court by this
and the following Sections, may it would seem be exercised, whether an European Judge
or a Principal Sudder Ameen preside therein : it is only necessary for the latter functionary to bear in mind that if it be necessary to communicate with the Collector, his Subordinate or Assistants, he must proceed as directed in Cl. I, Sec. VII, Act. VII, 1843.

Court may confirm the decision of the *lower* Court, the cause not being appealable to the Sudder Udalut, the *Zillah* *Civil* Court shall forward a copy of the decree and proceedings in *that* Court, and of the proceedings and decree of the *lower* Court, to the Governor in Council. Where an appeal may be received from the decision of the *Zillah* *Civil* Court, and the Sudder Udalut may confirm the decree of the *Zillah Civil* Court, a copy of the decree and proceedings received from the *Zillah* *Civil* Court shall be furnished to the Governor in Council. Where the Judge of the *Subordinate* Zillah Court may give judgment against the Collector, the defaulter shall nevertheless be detained in confinement, in the same manner as if the process prescribed had been duly served ; a copy of the decree and proceedings shall be furnished by the Court, to the Collector, on his application. In this case, the Collector shall not appeal from the decision of the Court, without authority had for that purpose from the Board of Revenue. In the event of such appeal, and if the *Zillah Civil* Court may reverse the decision of the *lower* Court, the cause not being appealable to the Sudder Udalut, the *Zillah Civil* Court shall transmit a copy of the decree and proceedings and decree in the appeal, and of the decree and proceedings of the *lower* Court, to the Governor in Council. Where the Judge of the *Subordinate* Court may give judgment in favor of the Collector, and the decision be reversed in the *Zillah Civil* Court, the Collector shall not appeal to the Sudder Udalut, except by authority had for that purpose from the Board of Revenue. Where appeal may be made to the Sudder Udalut, and the decision of the *Zillah Civil* Court reversed, a copy of the decree and proceedings, and of the decree and proceedings received from the *Zillah Civil* Court, shall be furnished to the Governor in Council. Appeal shall not lie from the *Zillah Civil* Court to the Sudder Udalut, unless the annual produce of the estate of the defaulter, on account of which the arrears may have been demanded, may exceed one thousand Rupees, to be calculated according to the amount paid or payable by the dependent Talookdars, under-farmers, or Ryots, to the defaulter on account of the year in which the decision of the *Subordinate* Zillah Court may pass. To which end, the Collectors shall state generally, in their petitions of appeal, whether the produce of the estate exceeds or not, according to their information and belief, the sum of one thousand Rupees. Where the defaulter may not surrender himself within the prescribed time, or where having surrendered himself within the limited time, the Collector may have stated the produce of the estate to be less than one thousand Rupees, and the defaulter may not deny the truth of the Collector's statement, a cause brought under such circumstances before the *Zillah Civil*

Court shall not be appealable from the decision of *such* Court to that of the Sudder Udalut. Where a defaulter appealing from the decision of a *Subordinate* Zillah Court, may, in his answer to the charge, object to the statement made by the Collector respecting the produce of his estate, the Judge of *that Court* shall proceed to try the objections, and shall pass a decision on them according to equity and justice. Where a cause may, under such circumstances, be afterwards brought before the *Zillah Civil* Court, and no objection be offered by either party, to the decision of the *Subordinate* Zillah Court on the Collector's statement of the produce of the estate, such decision shall be held to be accurate. Where objections to the decision of the *lower* Court may be offered, the *Zillah Civil* Court shall try the objections, and decide on them according to equity and justice. Where an appeal from the decree of the *Zillah Civil* Court may be made to the Sudder Udalut, and the admission or rejection of the appeal depend on the produce of the estate exceeding or falling short of one thousand Rupees, the Court of Sudder Udalut shall examine the decisions of the inferior Courts on this point, and decide whether the cause be, or be not, appealable. Decrees passed under this Section by the *Subordinate* Zillah Courts, or by the *Zillah Civil* Courts, or by the Sudder Udalut, by which the proprietary right of the estate of a defaulter may be judged to be forfeited to Government, shall not be carried into execution, in any case whatever, without an order from the Governor in Council for that purpose. In the event of the Governor in Council commuting the forfeiture for a fine, the Court which may have transmitted the decree and proceedings to the Governor in Council shall, on receiving notice of the fine, levy the amount of it by the usual process for enforcing decrees of the Court; and shall pay the amount to the Collector of the Zillah. The suit which a Collector may institute against a defaulter in the *Subordinate Court* of the Zillah under this Section, as well as the prosecution or defence of any appeal from the decision of such Court which may be made to the *Zillah Civil* Court, or from the decree of the *Zillah Civil* Court to the Sudder Udalut, shall be carried on at the public expense, and be conducted by the Vakeel of Government.—*Cl.* 2, *Sec.* XIV, *Reg.* XXVII, 1802.

Where a decision may have been passed by a *Subordinate* Court of Udalut, in consequence of which the whole or any part of a sum of money demanded, or actually received, by a Collector as an arrear of revenue under this Regulation, from any proprietor or farmer of land, may be adjudged to be not due; the Collector shall be furnished, on application to the Court through the Vakeel of Government, with a copy of the proceedings and decree; but the Collector shall not appeal from the decision of the *Subordinate* Court, nor ultimately from the decision of the *Zillah Civil* Court unless by virtue of written authority from the Board of Revenue, for that purpose, which authority shall be shewn at the time, and lodged together with the appeal. In all cases in which the Board of Revenue may order the Collector to appeal from the inferior to the superior Court, the Collector shall be indemnified by Government for all costs and damages awarded against him by the Courts. —*Sec.* XXI, *Reg.* XXVII, 1802.

Where a Collector may be prosecuted, and the prosecutor, being cast, may be dissatisfied with the decision of the *Subordinate Court* so as to appeal to the *Zillah Civil* Court; the Collector shall appoint one of the Vakeels of the *Zillah Civil* Court to plead the cause. Where the decree of the *lower* Court may be confirmed, or the appellant, being dissatisfied with the decision of the *Zillah Civil* Court, may appeal to the Sudder Udalut, the Collector shall appoint one of the pleaders in the Sudder Udalut to maintain the suit. Where the *Zillah Civil* Court may not confirm the decision of the *lower* Court, the Collector, on application to the *Zillah Civil* Court, shall be furnished with a copy of the proceedings and decrees of both Courts; but the Collector shall not appeal from the decision of either Court, without written authority had and obtained from the Board of Revenue, for that purpose, which authority shall be lodged with the appeal.—*Sec.* XXII.—*Ibid.*

In prosecutions which may be instituted in the Courts of Udalut, against the Collectors, for sums of money demanded or taken, directly or indirectly, for their own use, from any proprietor or farmer of land, or from any surety, or from any purchaser of land; or for any acts done in their official capacity, repugnant to this Regulation, or not warranted by it, or for any acts which may not involve claims to monies received or demanded by him on behalf of Government, in conformity to this Regulation; the suits shall be considered to be entirely of a private nature, between the Collectors and the prosecutors; the Collectors shall defend such suits at their own risk and expense, in the same manner as other individual persons amenable to the jurisdiction of the Courts, not being employed by Government.—*Sec.* XXIII.—*Ibid.*

Collectors shall not derive any pecuniary advantage from suits which they may institute, or which may be instituted against them, in the Courts of Judicature, in their official capacity; with the exception of suits, in which they may be engaged under Section XXIII; the sums awarded to them in which shall be applicable to their own use; but Collectors shall not sustain loss by recovering the debts of Government, in cases in which their conduct may be adjudged, by a final judicial decree, to be conformable to this Regulation.—*Sec.* XXIV, *Reg.* XXVII, 1802.

Security shall not be demanded *from* Collectors for their personal appearance, in any public suit in which they may be engaged under this Regulation: nor shall security be required from them for the payment of costs, or for the performance of the decrees or orders of the Court, in suits which, by this Regulation, are to be conducted by the Vakeels of Government, at the public expense. In suits of a personal nature, Collectors shall give the same security for the payment of the costs, and the performance of the decrees and orders of the Courts, as individual suitors. Where Collectors may refuse or omit to pay, within the limited time, sums of money ordered to be levied from them on account of personal suits, or on account of the costs or damages of such suits, the Court shall levy the amount by the customary process. Where the Court may be unable to obtain payment, the Judge shall state the case to the Governor in Council, in order that the amount may be paid from the public treasury, and deducted from the salaries of such Collectors. In cases where Collectors may omit or refuse to obey the orders or decrees of Courts of Judicature, the Court from which the process may have issued shall have power to fine them, according to the nature of the offence. In the event of Collectors refusing or omitting to pay the fine, the Courts shall state the case to the Governor in Council, in order that the amount may be recovered through the interference of Government.—*Sec.* XXV.—*Ibid.*

Where process or orders may be issued by the Courts of Judicature to Collectors of Zillahs, (in suits instituted under this Regulation) the *Judge* of the Court issuing the process or order shall transmit it, under a cover sealed in the form of a letter, and superscribed with his name and official appellation, and addressed " To the Collector of the Zillah of." The Collector shall acknowledge the receipt of the process, or order, on the day on which he may receive it by a letter addressed " To the *Judge* of the Court of."— *Sec.* XXVI.—*Ibid.*

The instructions which Collectors may transmit to the Vakeels of Government in the Courts, shall be inclosed under a cover sealed, and directed to the Vakeels, and transmitted under a sealed cover, addressed to the *Judge* of the Court in which the cause may be depending, and superscribed with the official appellation of the person dispatching it. The *Judge* shall deliver such instructions sealed to the Vakeel. In like manner the Vakeel shall transmit, through the *Judges* of the respective Courts, the papers and documents they may have to return to the Collectors.—*Sec.* XXVII, *Reg.* XXVII, 1802.

Collectors shall not be liable to prosecution for the official acts of their predecessors. But Collectors engaged in suits for which they are personally answerable, and removed from office, pending such suits, shall carry them on, in the same manner as if they had continued in office.—*Sec.* XXVIII.—*Ibid.*

Where Collectors may die, or be removed from office, their successors shall carry on such process or suits for which the Government may be ultimately responsible, as may be depending in the Courts at the time of such death or removal.—*Sec.* XXIX.—*Ibid.*

CHAPTER II.

SUITS AGAINST GOVERNMENT—OR PUBLIC OFFICERS.

Collectors of the revenue and their assistants and native officers ; the Collectors of the Customs, their assistants, and native officers employed in the collection of the Customs ; the Mint and Assay Masters, and their assistants and native officers ; are hereby declared amenable to the Zillah Court in the jurisdiction of which they may reside, or carry on the public business committed to their charge, for any act or acts, done in their official capacity, in opposition to any established regulation.—*Sec.* VII, *Reg.* II, 1802.

If any person shall consider himself aggrieved under any established Regulation, by an act done by any of the Officers of Government described in Section VII, pursuant to a special order originating with the Governor in Council, or the Board of Revenue, the Officer by whom the Act may be done shall not be liable to be sued for it.   In such cases, Government is to be considered as the defendant, and the person deeming himself aggrieved is to present a petition to the Judge of the Court of Udalut of the Zillah, to which the Officer, by whom the act complained of may have been done, shall be amenable in his public capacity, stating wherein he considers himself injured under the Regulations, and praying that the Governor in Council will order the Court of Udalut in which the cause may be cognizable, to try the points or matters contested, agreeably to the Regulations.   The Judge to whom the petition may be presented, is to forward it immediately to the Governor in Council, who, provided he shall not think it proper to afford the redress solicited by the petitioner, and provided the Courts of justice shall be competent to try the cause, will direct the Court in which it may be cognizable to proceed to the trial of it.   If the Governor in Council shall order the cause to be tried, the Court is immediately to send a written notification of the order to the complainant, and the cause is to be considered as filed in the Court, from the date of the notification.   The Court is then to proceed to try the suit under the

---

Sec. VII, Reg. II, 1802.—This Section declares the liability—Regulation I, of 1823, *which see at p.* 214, prescribes the course of proceeding in such cases.

sáme Rules and Regulations as are prescribed for the trial of suits between individuals. The Officer by whom the Act complained against may have been done, is to carry on the suit under the directions of the Governor in Council, or the Board of Revenue, according to the immediate authority under which he may have acted, and is to issue the necessary instructions to the Vakeel of Government, in the Court in which the suit may be instituted, or subsequently carried in appeal. In the event of Government being cast in any of the Courts, the Officer entrusted with the management of the suit is to send a copy of the Decree, and proceedings of the Court, to the Governor in Council, or to the Board of Revenue, according to the immediate authority under which he may have acted, with a letter stating any objection that he may have to offer to the decision. The board *is* to submit all such decrees and proceedings to the Governor in Council, with their opinion respecting them. The Governor in Council will order an appeal from the decisions that may be transmitted to him under this Section, to be preferred, or not, as may appear to him advisable. The costs and damages that may be awarded against Government in suits instituted under this Section, are to be defrayed from the public treasury.—*Sec.* XV, *Reg.* II, 1802.

Whenever a petition of complaint may be preferred to any Court of Civil Judicature against a Collector, or other public Officer amenable thereto, for Acts connected with his official duties, the Judge of such Court shall receive and file the petition of complaint in the same manner as all other such petitions are received and filed, and shall issue the usual summons thereon.—*Cl.* 1, *Sec.* II, *Reg.* I, 1823.

If the public Officer, on receiving the summons, shall consider the case to be of such a nature as that he may either recommend to the Governor in Council to grant the redress sought by the petition, or request permission to defend the suit at the public expense, he shall immediately instruct the Government Vakeel to appear for him, and to move the Court to grant him such specific time, to put in his answer to the petition, as may be necessary to enable him to make the requisite reference to the Board of Revenue, or other official superior at the presidency, and to receive orders thereon.—*Cl.* 2.—*Ibid.*

Sec. XV, Reg. II, 1802.—Under Section VII, of this Regulation and Regulation I, of 1823, the public Officer can only be sued for acts averred to be done in " opposition to established regulation," *this* enactment prescribes the course to be adopted by individuals considering themselves aggrieved by an act done " *under* a regulation by special order of Government" for which the public Officer cannot be sued.

The Judges of the several Courts are hereby authorized and directed to grant such reasonable time, for the purposes specified in the foregoing Section, to public Officers against whom petitions of complaint may have been filed in their respective Courts ; and, when necessary, to extend the period so granted, on application being made to them by motion in the usual way.—*Sec.* III, *Reg.* I, 1823.

In the event of the redress sought for by the plaint being granted under orders from the superior authority, in consequence of a reference made under Clause second, Section II of this Regulation, the Court in which the suit may have been filed, shall certify the amount of costs incurred by the plaintiff in the institution of his suit, and shall dismiss the cause from the file, on payment being made of such costs, or on the plaintiff's filing a razeenamah in the usual form.—*Cl.* 1, *Sec.* IV.—*Ibid.*

Provided however, that the plaintiff shall not be entitled to receive the costs referred to in the foregoing Clause, if he shall fail to prove to the satisfaction of the Court, on being called upon so to do, that before instituting the suit, he applied to the public Officer for the redress which by his plaint he has sought to obtain, and that his application was refused.—*Cl.* 2.—*Ibid.*

The Collector of Customs, his deputy and assistants, and native officers, employed in the collection of the Customs, at the port ,of Madras, shall be amenable to the Subordinate Court in the Zillah of Chingleput, for any act or acts done in their official capacity, contrary to, or not warranted by, *Act* VI, 1844 ; in the same manner as if they resided, or carried on the public business committed to their charge, within the limits of the jurisdiction of the said Zillah ; and the said Court is accordingly hereby empowered to take cognizance of such suits.—*Sec.* LV, *Reg.* IX, 1803.

Sec. LV, Reg. IX, 1803.—All other Collectors of Customs are amenable to the Courts, under Section VII, Regulation II, 1802, and Section LIII. Act VI, 1844. This Regulation merely indicates the Zillah, to the Courts of which, the Collector of Customs at Madras, shall be held amenable. The Subordinate Court in the Zillah of Chingleput is not presided over by a European Judge, but public Officers are now clearly liable to be sued in the Courts of the Principal Sudder Ameens for " *acts* done in their official capacity," although no *appeal* from their *decisions*, when acting judicially, will lie to those Courts. When Section VII, Regulation VII, 1827, was repealed by Section V, Act VII, 1843, European Officers of Government clearly became liable, in all private matters, to the jurisdiction of the Principal Sudder Ameen's Courts, and it only remained to determine, 1st, whether they should be so for acts done in their public capacity, and 2d, whether appeals should lie from their decisions to Principal Sudder Ameens, which questions appear to be set at rest by Sec. VI, Act VII, 1843, which says that " *appeals* shall *not* lie to Principal Sudder Ameens from the *decisions* of European Officers of Government ;" but which, by its total silence in regard to their *acts* leaves *them* subject to the jurisdiction of the Principal Sudder Ameens, had it been intended to exempt Public Officers from answering for their *acts* in those Courts, it is to be presumed it would have been so specified.

Persons deeming themselves aggrieved by the confiscation of their goods, or by the levying of double duty on such goods, under circumstances which may appear to them not to warrant, conformably to the provisions contained in Act VI, 1844, the confiscation of such goods, or the subjecting them to the payment of double duty, may institute a suit in the *said* Court *at* Chingleput, for the recovery of the value of such goods, if they shall have been confiscated ; or of the amount of the double duty, in the event of double duty having been levied on such goods; together with damages for the loss which such persons may have sustained thereby.—*Sec.* LVI, *Reg.* IX, 1803.   ·

Suits instituted against the Collector of Customs, his Deputy, Assistants, or native officers, shall be tried in the manner prescribed by the Regulations, respecting suits instituted against Collectors of Revenue in Zillahs.—*Sec.* LVII.—*Ibid.*

The Court shall require all persons instituting suits against the Collector of Customs, to give good and sufficient security to prosecute such suits to an issue, and to pay whatever damages may be awarded against them by the decree of the Court, in the event of the suits so instituted proving to be groundless, or litigious : the Court shall not issue process against the Collector of Customs, until the required securities shall have been given.—*Sec.* LVIII.—*Ibid.*

When written process shall be issued, by the *said* Court at Chingleput, against the Collector of Customs at Madras, the *Judge of* the Court shall transmit such process, under a sealed cover, addressed to the Collector, in the form of a letter, and superscribed with his name and official appellation. The Collector shall immediately acknowledge the receipt of the process, by an endorsement to that effect on the instrument, and return it under a sealed cover to the *Judge of* the Court.—*Sec.* LIX.—*Ibid.*

The Collector of Customs, shall report to the Board of Revenue the institution of any suit against him, under this Regulation, and shall receive the orders of the Board of Revenue, to defend the suit, or to make satisfaction to the party, or parties, if the Board of Revenue shall see reason to do so.—*Sec.* LX.—*Ibid.*

The Collector of Customs shall be indemnified for all costs and damages, awarded against him by the Court, in suits defended under the orders of the Board of Revenue.—*Sec.* LXI.—*Ibid.*

If the Collector of Customs shall undertake the defence of any suit, without reporting the same to the Board of Revenue, and receiving their orders thereon, the defence, so undertaken, shall be at the cost and risk of the Collector of Customs ; but it shall be in the option of the Board of Revenue to order the defence, so undertaken by the Collector of Customs, to be conducted on the public account, and at the expense of Government; or in the event of the suit having been decided against the Collector of Customs, to recommend to the Governor in Council, that any part, or the whole, of the costs, and damages, awarded against the Collector of Customs, may be defrayed from the public treasury. —*Sec.* LXII, *Reg.* IX, 1803.

In prosecutions which may be instituted in the *Subordinate* Court at Chingleput, against the Collector of Customs at Madras, for any act or acts done in his official capacity contrary to, or not warranted by, Act VI, 1844 or for any act, or acts which may not involve claims to monies received or demanded by him on behalf of Government, in conformity thereto, such suits shall be considered to be entirely of a private nature, between the Collector of Customs and the prosecutors; the Collector of Customs shall defend such suits at his own risk and expense, in the same manner as other individuals amenable to the jurisdiction of the Court of Chingleput, who may not be employed by Government. —*Sec.* LXIII.—*Ibid.*

The Collector of Customs shall not derive pecuniary advantage from the suits which may be instituted against him, in the *Subordinate* Court of Chingleput, in his official capacity; with exception to the personal suits, of the nature described in the preceding Section: but the amount of the costs and damages decreed against individuals instituting suits against the Collector of Customs, in his official capacity, on the ground of such suits being vexatious and litigious, shall be carried to the credit of Government.— *Sec.* LXIV.—*Ibid.*

Security shall not be demanded from the Collector of Customs at Madras for his personal appearance, in any suit in which he may be engaged, under this Regulation, nor for the payment of the costs and damages that may be awarded against him: if the Collector of Customs at Madras shall omit or refuse to obey any order or decree of the *Subordinate* Court of Chingleput, in any suit instituted against him, under this Regulation, the Court is empowered to fine him, according to the nature and extent of the offence. In the event of the Collector of Customs persisting in refusing to obey the order or decree of the Court, and to pay the fine imposed on him by the Court for disobedience, the Judge shall state the case to the Governor in Council, in order that the decree may be enforced, by deducting from the salary and emoluments of the Collector of Customs, the amount of the costs and damages decreed against him, together with the fine imposed by the Court. —*Sec.* LXV, *Reg.* IX, 1803.

The Collector of Customs at Madras shall have the benefit of appealing from the decisions of the *Subordinate* Court at Chingleput, to the *Zillah Civil* Court; and from the decrees of that Court to the Sudder Udalut and ultimately to *Her Majesty in Council* subject to the rules and regulations prescribed regarding appeals from the decisions of those Courts respectively; (with exception to finding the securities required to be found by individuals:) but in suits which may be defended on the public account, under the orders of the Board of Revenue, the Collector of Customs shall not appeal, without having received their written authority for that purpose.—*Sec.* LXVI.—*Ibid.*

The instructions which the Collector of Customs may transmit to the Vakeels of Government in the Court, respecting suits instituted against him under this Regulation, shall be enclosed under a sealed cover, and directed to the Vakeel, and transmitted under a sealed cover addressed to the *Judge* of the Court, in which the cause may be depending, and superscribed with the official appellation of the Collector. The *Judge* shall deliver such instructions to the Vakeel. In like manner, the Vakeels shall transmit, through the *Judges* of the respective Courts, the papers and documents which they may have to return to the Collector of Customs.—*Sec.* LXVII.—*Ibid.*

The Collector of Customs shall not be liable to prosecution for any act of his predecessor. But in the event of the Collector of Customs being removed from office, during the time while suits, in which he may be engaged, and for which he may be individually answerable, are depending in the Court, he shall carry them on, in the same manner as if he had continued in office.—*Sec.* LXVIII.—*Ibid.*

The Collector of Customs for the time being shall carry on suits for which Government may be ultimately responsible, under the orders of the Board of Revenue.—*Sec.* LXIX.—*Ibid.*

All the Rules contained in this Regulation, respecting the Collector of Customs, are to be considered equally applicable to his Deputy, or Assistant, (being covenanted Servants of the Company), whilst officiating as Collectors.—*Sec.* LXX.—*Ibid.*

It shall be lawful for any Collector of Customs, or other Officer who may be authorized to adjudicate Customs cases, if he shall decide that a seizure of goods made under the authority of this Act was vexatious and unnecessary, to adjudge damages to be paid to the proprietor by the Customs Officer who made such vexatious seizure, besides ordering the immediate release of the goods; and if the proprietor accept such damages, no action shall thereafter lie against the Officer of Customs in any Court of justice on account of such seizure: and if such adjudicating Officer shall decide that the seizure was warranted, but shall deem that the penalty of confiscation is unduly severe, it shall be lawful for him to mitigate the same to the extent of the levy of double duty; and if the said Officer shall adjudge confiscation, it shall further be lawful for him to order that from the proceeds of the sale of the goods, a proportion not exceeding one-half shall be distributed in rewards amongst such Officers as he shall deem entitled thereto, and in such proportion as he may direct to each respectively.—*Sec.* LXII, *Act* VI, 1844.

All Officers of Customs shall, as heretofore, be amenable to the Civil Courts of the Presidency of Fort St. George, by action for damages on account of any executive acts done in their official capacity, at the suit of the parties injured by such acts. Provided, however, that no suit shall lie against a Collector of Customs or other Officer for any judicial award in a matter of Customs passed under the preceding Section of this Act.—*Sec.* LXIII.—*Ibid.*

On a seizure of Salt being reported to the Board of Revenue, they shall immediately take the case into consideration. If they determine that the salt is not liable to confiscation, they shall order it to be released, and the Officer by whose authority the salt shall have been seized (not being a Magistrate) shall be liable to be sued for damages in the Zillah Court, and shall maintain the suit at his own risk and expense; the Board are, however, empowered to indemnify the person, by whose authority the seizure shall have been made, for the consequence of the suit, should they, on a consideration of the circumstances of the case, deem such person entitled to indemnification; or the Board may order the suit to be defended on the part of Government, or grant such indemnification as they may deem equitable to the owners of the salt, reporting to Government the measures they may have adopted, and their reasons for adopting them.—*Sec.* XVII, *Reg.* I, 1805.

Persons deeming themselves aggrieved under this Regulation by any act, or order, done or issued by the Governor in Council, or by the Board of Revenue, or by any of the officers of Government, shall be at liberty to apply for redress, in the manner prescribed in Section XV, Regulation II, A. D. 1802.—*Sec.* XXI, *Reg.* I, 1805.

Any person who shall deem himself aggrieved under this Regulation, *for regulating the Revenue derivable from the monopoly or exclusive sale of Tobacco in the Provinces of Malabar, Canara, and Coimbatore,* by any Act or orders done or issued by the Governor in Council, or by the Board of Revenue, or by any of the Officers of Government, shall be at liberty to apply for redress in the manner prescribed in Sec. XV, Reg. II, of 1802.—*Sec.* XVII, *Reg.* VII, 1811.

In all original suits or appeals wherein Government may be one of the parties, the Court which may pass judgment, whether for or against Government, shall, in addition to the copies of decrees required by the existing Regulations to be delivered to the parties, transmit a copy of the decree as soon as the same can be prepared, to the Secretary to the Government in the judicial department, for the information of the Governor in Council; such copies of decrees are not required to be upon stamped paper, but are to be duly authenticated by the official seal and signature of the Judges by whom the same may have been passed.—*Sec.* XXXI, *Reg.* VII, 1809.

CHAPTER III.

PAUPER SUITS.

Persons, unable by reason of their poverty to defray the expenses of a law suit, shall be admitted to sue as paupers before the several *Zillah Civil* and *Subordinate* Courts, and the Sudder Udalut, *and before Sudder Ameens, Act* IX, 1844, under the rules and subject to the restrictions hereinafter specified.—*Sec.* III, *Reg.* VII, 1818.

It shall be competent to the Zillah Courts to refer, at their discretion, to the district moonsiffs such pauper suits, admitted by them, as may with reference to the value of the cause of action be cognizable by those officers respectively.—*Cl.* 2, *Sec.* III, *Reg.* IV, 1825.

No persons shall be admitted to sue as paupers under this Regulation, if the cause of action shall not exceed *ten* rupees, or if the claim be for damages on account of slander, abusive language, assault, or personal injury.—*Cl.* 1, *Sec.* IV.—*Ibid.*

Suits for the recovery of pecuniary penalties, incurred by any breach of the Regulations, shall be admissible as pauper suits.—*Sec.* II.—*Ibid.*

Every person desirous of being admitted to plead as a pauper in an original suit, shall submit his application under the following rules.—*Cl.* 1, *Sec.* V, *Reg.* VII, 1818.

The applicant shall address himself to one of the constituted vakeels of the Court in which he is desirous of suing, and the vakeel, if he be willing to undertake the conduct of the suit, shall draw out a statement containing a declaration of the nature, extent, and grounds of the demand, and the names of the persons intended to be sued. This statement shall be signed by the applicant, and shall have annexed to it a declaration to be signed by the vakeel, that he has attentively considered the applicant's case, and has carefully perused the documents produced to him in support

---

Cl. 2, Sec. III, Reg. IV, 1825.—By this Clause " Sudder Ameens" also *were* declared competent to have Pauper Suits *referred* to them, but they can now file them direct, under Act. IX, of 1844—District Moonsiffs are still prohibited doing so by Cl. 3, Sec XII, Reg. VI, 1816.

of it, and that he is of opinion that the suit is, (or is not,) sustainable.—*Cl.* 2, *Sec.* V, *Reg.* VII, 1818.

The opinion, which the vakeel is required to give that a suit proposed to be instituted by a pauper is, or is not sustainable, shall be in all cases accompanied by a statement of the grounds, on which such opinion is formed.—*Sec.* IV, *Reg.* IV, 1825.

If the opinion of the vakeel shall be that the case is sustainable, the applicant shall present to the Court a declaration according to the form in the Appendix A, having annexed to it a true and perfect schedule of the property real and personal, of which he is possessed, with the value thereof. The declaration and schedule shall be subscribed by the applicant, and shall be read in open Court and sworn to, *or solemnly affirmed*, by the said applicant. And if any person taking the oath or affirmation hereby appointed, shall thereby commit wilful perjury, and shall be convicted thereof, such offender shall incur the penalties directed by the Regulations to be inflicted for the crime of perjury.—*Cl.* 4, *Sec.* V, *Reg.* VII, 1818.

In cases wherein the opinion of the vakeel may be against the claim of the party wishing to sue as a pauper, it shall be competent to the Court, on application from such party, to take into consideration the grounds of the vakeel's opinion, and should it see fit, to admit the applicant to sue in formâ pauperis.—*Cl.* 2, *Sec.* V, *Reg.* IV, 1825.

In cases wherein the opinion of the vakeel may be in favor of the claim of a party wishing to sue as a pauper, it shall be competent to the Court, after taking into consideration the grounds of that opinion, to reject the application of such party to sue in formâ pauperis.—*Cl.* 3.—*Ibid.*

Whenever the Court may admit a party to sue in formâ pauperis under Clause second, or reject his application under Clause third of this Section, the grounds of such resolution shall be recorded; but no appeal shall be allowed therefrom.—*Cl.* 4.—*Ibid.*

After the declaration and schedule shall have been sworn to, *or solemnly affirmed*, the Court shall fix a day, on which they will admit the applicant to institute his suit as a pauper, unless good cause shall be then shewn against his admission. The day to be so fixed shall be sufficiently distant to admit of the production of evidence by the party complained against, to invalidate the statement of the applicant. And the Court shall, immediately after filing of the statement and schedule, cause a copy thereof to be affixed in some conspicuous place in the Court-room, and shall issue a notice to the person complained against, which notice shall contain the nature and amount of the demand, and the day on which the applicant will be admitted to enter his suit as a pauper, unless good cause be shewn to the contrary.—*Cl. 5, Sec.* V,. *Reg.* VII, 1818.

It is hereby declared competent to the vakeel who has drawn out the application, as well as to the person intended to be sued, to show cause against the applicant being admitted to the benefit of the pauper Regulation.—*Cl. 6.—Ibid.*

Objections to an alleged plea of poverty shall be written on stamped paper of the value prescribed by Section XIX, Regulation XIII, of 1816. The names of the witnesses, who are to prove facts alleged in such objections, are to be mentioned therein ; and if the witnesses so named are not in attendance, the Court are to summon them on an early day.—*Cl.* 7.—*Ibid.*

Nothing in this Section shall be construed to render it imperative on women, or others of such rank and caste, as are by the usages of the country exempted from appearing in Courts of Justice, to appear therein for the purpose of qualifying as paupers ; but such persons may appear by an accredited agent.—*Cl.* 8.—*Ibid.*

On the day fixed the Court shall proceed to hear, and determine upon, all objections that have been entered by the party intended to be sued, or by the vakeel retained by the applicant, either especially to the truth of the schedule exhibited by the applicant, or generally to his admission to the benefit of the pauper Regulation ; and the decision thereon by the Court competent to admit the application of the person, desirous to sue as a pauper, shall in all cases be final.—*Cl.* 9.—*Ibid.*

If no objections are made to the admission of the applicant to sue as a pauper, or if the objections made shall be deemed insufficient, the Court shall take into consideration the amount and value of the property sworn to, *or solemnly affirmed ;* and if they are of opinion, that the applicant could not defray the probable costs of suit without being reduced to great distress, they are to admit him to institute his suit as a pauper.—*Cl.* 10.—*Ibid.*

Every person admitted to sue as a pauper shall, before he be permitted to file any pleading, find two good and sufficient sureties for his appearance, whenever his attendance may be required by the Court. The security bonds shall correspond with the form B, prescribed in the Appendix of this Regulation.—*Sec.* VI, *Reg.* VII, 1818.

Sec. VI, Reg. VII, 1818.—The form B. is omitted as at hand in every Office. The Sudder Udalut have ruled that such bonds may be on unstamped paper, though they are not included in the list of documents exempted in the following Section, and although the Courts in Bengal require that they should be on stamp.

Stamp duty shall not be required from persons who may be admitted to sue as paupers. The plaint, reply, or other pleadings on the part of the pauper, as well as applications on his part for receiving exhibits and summoning witnesses, may be written on unstamped paper. The notice to the defendant, the summons for witnesses and other processes on the part of the pauper, shall be served through the peons on the establishment of the Courts, without any expense to the pauper; and the copy of the decree, as well as copies of orders or proceedings which he may be required to take, shall be furnished to a pauper on unstamped paper.—*Cl.* 1, *Sec.* VII, *Reg.* VII, 1818.

Whenever it shall appear to the Court, before whom a pauper suit is depending, that a witness, whose evidence may be considered to be material to the issue of such suit, is unable to defray the expenses necessary to his appearing before the Court, they are empowered to direct the payment to such witness of such necessary and reasonable expenses, as may be incurred in his attendance before the Court, and to charge the same in their monthly abstract. —*Cl.* 2.—*Ibid.*

On the conclusion of the suit, the Court shall calculate the whole of the costs, which would have been incurred by the plaintiff on account of the several stamp duties, prescribed by Regulation XIII of 1816, and other legal expenses had he not been permitted to sue as a puaper, and shall charge the same· in the decree to the party cast, or to the parties respectively, in such proportions as may be deemed equitable.—*Cl.* 3.—*Ibid.*

Whenever a Court before whom a pauper shall have instituted a suit shall, by their decree declare the said suit to be vexatious or litigious, it shall be competent to that Court to adjudge, that the said pauper do pay a fine not exceeding 200 rupees, and be imprisoned until such fine shall be paid, provided the time of imprisonment do not exceed six months, at the end of which period, or of such shorter period, as the said Court may have fixed in commutation for the said fine, the pauper shall be released.   Provided always that no sum shall be received in payment of the said

---

Cl. 1, Sec. VII, Reg. VII, 1818.—Instruments which ought to have been written on stamp cannot be received as exhibits from a Pauper until penalty be paid, it is immaterial whether parties filing exhibits not prepared in conformity to law, sue in formâ pauperis or not; as the previous breach of the law, whether by themselves or others, san form no ground for an indulgence, which under the circumstances would be unreasonable and illegal : nor do the provisions of Cl. 1, Sec. VII, Regulation VII, 1818, authorize copies of pleadings, proceedings or documents, belonging to *any other* suit, which he may *wish* to take, being given to a Pauper on unstamped paper, the only documents to be furnished on unstamped paper, are such as he may be *required* to take.—Sudder Udalut, 9th August 1841.

fine, until the whole of the fees and costs of suit, which may have been decreed against the said pauper, shall have been paid.—*Sec.* VIII, *Reg.* VII, 1818.

The Courts are empowered and directed to proceed for the recovery of any costs decreed against a pauper, by attachment and sale of any property which may, at any time after the passing of their decree, be discovered to belong to the said pauper.—*Cl.* 1, *Sec.* IX.—*Ibid.*

Courts are empowered to proceed for the recovery of any sums due by the securities of a pauper under the terms of the security bonds, in the same mode as they are directed to proceed in executing decrees of Court.—*Cl.* 2.—*Ibid.*

Whenever a pauper plaintiff against whom a decree has been passed may desire to appeal therefrom, he shall address himself to one of the vakeels of the Court competent to admit the appeal; and the vakeel, if he be willing to undertake the conduct of the appeal, shall draw out a petition setting forth the specific grounds, on which the appeal is preferred, and shall present the said petition within the period prescribed for the admission of regular appeals, together with a copy of the decree appealed from.—*Cl.* 1, *Sec.* X.—*Ibid.*

If the Court shall be of opinion, that an appeal is necessary to correct any error or omission in the original decree, or is otherwise requisite for the ends of justice, they shall admit the appeal on the appellant's producing good and sufficient security for his appearance as prescribed in Section VI, and shall proceed in the investigation under the general rules of appeal. But if the appeal shall not appear to be necessary for the ends of justice, the Court shall reject the petition, and such order of rejection shall be final. Provided however, that such order of rejection shall not bar the said plaintiff's right to appeal on fulfilling the regular conditions of appeal under the Regulations relative to payment of stamp duties and fees.—*Cl.* 2.—*Ibid.*

Plaintiffs in original suits who did not sue as paupers, shall be admissible to appeal in formâ pauperis from the judgments passed in such original suits.—*Cl.* 1, *Sec.* II, *Reg.* III, 1822.

Defendants in original suits shall be admissible to appeal in formâ pauperis from the judgments passed against them in such suits.—*Cl.* 2.—*Ibid.*

The admission of persons to appeal, or defend in appeal, under the foregoing Clauses, shall be in conformity with the Rules prescribed in Sections V and VI, Regulation VII of 1818, for persons desirous of being admitted to plead as paupers in original suits, and subject to the restrictions contained in Section X of that Regulation in respect to the admission of appeals from pauper plaintiffs.—*Cl. 3, Sec.* II, *Reg.* III, 1822.

It shall be the duty of the Court competent to admit the appeals in the cases above provided for, to satisfy themselves, in the event of objections being made by the other party to the admission of the applicant as a pauper, that the property of which the said applicant was possessed at the time when the original suit was instituted, has passed from his hands, or has otherwise been rendered unavailable to him, either by the operation of the judgment from which he is desirous of appealing, or of some other judgments, or generally of causes over which he had no control.—*Cl.* 4.—*Ibid.*

In as much as a pauper plaintiff in whose favour a decree may have passed, will be unable to obtain execution of the said decree pending an appeal, the Court to whom an appeal may be preferred by an original defendant will admit the original plaintiff to defend the appeal as a pauper without further investigation.—*Sec.* XI, *Reg.* VII, 1818.

Courts are hereby empowered to assign one of their constituted vakeels to act on behalf of any person to present his original application or his petition of appeal, or to prosecute any original suit, or to conduct the prosecution or defence of any appeal under the provisions of this Regulation.—*Sec.* XII.—*Ibid.*

It is hereby declared, that the rules contained in this Regulation, are intended to apply to regular suits and appeals only, and not to summary suits, or summary appeals of any description.—*Sec.* XIII.—*Ibid.*

The rules contained in Regulation VII of 1818, with the modifications thereof provided in this Regulation, are hereby declared to be applicable to the admission of special appeals.—*Sec.* III, *Reg.* II, 1822.

CHAPTER IV.

SOLDIERS' SUITS.

Such parts of the Regulations in force as prohibit the Courts of Civil Justice from corresponding by letter with parties in depending suits, or direct that no pleadings shall be received in any Civil cause except from the parties or their authorized pleaders ; such parts of the Regulations in force as require generally, that depending causes shall be brought to trial according to the order in which they may stand on the file ; and such parts thereof as prohibit the Courts from furnishing copies of decrees, or from receiving mokhtarnamahs on any other paper than the prescribed stamped paper, are hereby declared to be subject to the modifications contained in the following Sections of this Regulation.—*Sec.* II, *Reg.* VIII, 1817.

Whenever a native officer or soldier on the military establishment of the Presidency of Fort St. George shall be desirous of instituting a regular or summary suit in any Zillah Court, and shall not be able to obtain a furlough or leave of absence for the purpose of superintending or conducting such suit in person, he shall be at liberty to execute a mokhtarnamah or power of attorney, drawn up according to the form No. 1, in the Appendix to this Regulation, authorizing and appointing any member of his family, or other person, to institute and carry on the suit, and to perform all acts in the original trial of the cause, and eventually in appeal, in the same manner as if the party were himself personally present and consenting.—*Cl.* 1, *Sec.* III.—*Ibid.*

Such mokhtarnamah shall not be required to be written on stamped paper, but shall be executed by the native officer or soldier in the presence of the commanding officer of the corps or detachment, to which he may belong, who shall countersign the same in testimony of its having been voluntarily executed.—*Cl.* 2.—*Ibid.*

The mokhtarnamah so executed is to be transmitted by the com-

---

"Soldiers' Suits"—By Section XXII, Regulation VII, 1832, which see at page 90—Suits under 20 Rupees cannot be instituted in the Civil Courts against Military persons.

Cl. 1, Sec. III,—" Appendix, Form No. 1"—Appendix and Forms omitted as at hand in every office.

manding officer under cover of a public letter drawn up in the form No. 2, of the Appendix, addressed to the *Judge* of the Court in which the suit is to be instituted, and upon the receipt of such letter, a notice shall be issued by the Court for the purpose of procuring the attendance, either personally, or by a constituted vakeel, of the person nominated in the mokhtarnamah.—*Cl. 3, Sec. III, Reg. VIII, 1817.*

If such mokhtar shall refuse to attend the Court in person, or by a constituted vakeel, or shall decline to undertake the trust, or having undertaken it, shall subsequently die, or be prevented by any sufficient cause from discharging the duty confided to him, the Court shall cause information of the same to be communicated to the native officer or soldier, by an extract from their proceedings enclosed in an official letter to be addressed to the commanding officer of the corps.—*Cl. 4.—Ibid.*

If the appointed mokhtar shall attend the Court in person, or by a constituted vakeel, and shall consent to undertake the duty confided to him, the original mokhtarnamah shall be deposited in the Court, and shall form part of the record of the cause. The suit shall be instituted, tried and determined in conformity with the general rules in force for the institution and trial of other similar suits; provided, however, that in all cases where the native officer or soldier, who may be the principal in the suit, shall not be himself present at the time of its decision, an authenticated copy of the decree written on unstamped paper, shall be transmitted by the Court, to the commanding officer of the corps or detachment, for the purpose of its being communicated to the native officer or soldier.—*Cl. 5.—Ibid.*

It is hereby explained that no part of the preceding Clauses, or of the subsequent provisions of this Regulation, is intended to be applicable to claims originating in loans granted by a native officer or sepoy, or in pecuniary transactions of a commercial nature.— *Cl. 6.—Ibid.*

For the purpose of ensuring the due communication to all native officers and sepoys, of the summons or other notice of the institution of suits against them, so as to prevent as far as possible such suits from being brought to trial ex-parte; it is hereby enacted that in all such suits the plaint or petition of appeal shall contain a declaration that the defendant or respondent is a native officer or soldier, and all plaintiffs or appellants who shall knowingly and intentionally omit to make such statement, are hereby declared liable to be fined in such sum as the Court before whom such pleadings may be filed, shall deem equitable, not exceeding one fourth of the stamp duty in each case; and it is further provided, that the plaintiff or appellant shall state in his plaint or petition of appeal, to the best of his knowledge or belief, the particular regiment or corps to which such native officer or sepoy may belong, or in the event of his being unable to specify the same, then it shall be the duty of the Court before whom the suit is filed, to endeavour to ascertain the point.—*Cl.* 1, *Sec.* IV, *Reg.* VIII, 1817.

A notice in the usual form, together with a copy of the plaint or petition of appeal on unstamped paper, enclosed in an official letter drawn up according to the form No. 3, of the Appendix, shall be then transmitted by the Court to the commanding officer of the corps, for the purpose of their being communicated to the native officer or soldier against whom the suit may have been instituted: a similar notice shall be issued, when omitted in the first instance, from ignorance of the defendant's being a native officer or soldier, attached to a regular corps, if at any subsequent period during the trial of the suit it should appear to the Court, that the defendant or respondent is a native officer or soldier as above described.—*Cl.* 2.—*Ibid.*

The commanding officer shall, if practicable, cause the notice to be served on the party to whom it is addressed, and shall then return it to the Court from whom it issued, with the written acknowledgment of the party endorsed thereupon, together with the mokhtarnamah, according to the form No. 1, in the Appendix, if the party should have appointed an attorney to defend the suit in his behalf. If from whatever cause the notice transmitted to the commanding officer cannot be served upon the native officer or soldier, to whom it is addressed, it shall be returned by the commanding officer to the Court from whom it had been received, with information of the cause which had prevented the service of it. In such case of non-service of process, the Court shall make such further reference, or shall adopt such other measures in order to the due service of such process, as may appear to be proper and consistent with the Regulations.—*Cl.* 3.—*Ibid.*

When a native officer or soldier may obtain a furlough for the purpose of instituting or defending a Civil suit in any Zillah Court, he shall be furnished by the commanding officer of the corps or detachment, with an official letter addressed to the *Judge* of the Court in which the suit is to be tried; such letter shall be drawn up according to the form No. 4, of the Appendix to this Regulation, but it shall not give cover to any petition, nor contain any statement or explanation of the merits or circumstances of the case. —*Cl.* 1, *Sec.* V.—*Ibid.*

Such letter shall be delivered in person by the native officer or
soldier to the Court, who are hereby authorized, at the request of
the party, to nominate a vakeel of the Court to aid in preparing
the pleadings, and generally in conducting the prosecution or defence of the suit. The Court shall at the same time cause the native officer or soldier to be duly apprized of the provisions contained in Regulation XIV of 1816, and in any other Regulation in
force, relative to the duties, and established fees of pleaders, and
of the necessity of conforming thereto in the event of his employing a pleader.—*Cl.* 2, *Sec.* V, *Reg.* VIII, 1817.

Nothing contained in the preceding Section shall be construed
to prohibit a native officer or soldier, from pleading his cause in
person, or from employing any authorized pleader of the Court,
instead of applying to the Court to nominate a vakeel to act on
his behalf.—*Sec.* VI.—*Ibid.*

The Zillah *Civil and Subordinate* Courts are hereby authorized
and required to bring to a hearing, without regard to the order in
which they may be filed, all suits in which a native officer or soldier, who may have obtained leave of absence from his corps, may
be a party, and to pass a decision thereon as speedily as may be
consistent with the due administration of justice.—*Cl.* 1, *Sec.* VII.
—*Ibid.*

If the cause cannot be brought to a decision previously to the
expiration of the furlough granted to such native officer or soldier,
the Court before whom the suit may be depending, is hereby vested with a discretionary authority to grant to such native officer or
soldier, an extension of his leave of absence for a period sufficient
to admit of a reference being made to the commanding officer of
the corps, for the purpose of ascertaining whether the furlough
can be prolonged for any further specific period. But whenever
a Judge may exercise the discretionary power above vested in him,
he shall be careful to make the reference immediately in an official
letter to the commanding officer of the corps to which the native
officer or sepoy may be attached.—*Cl.* 2.—*Ibid.*

A native officer or soldier returning to his corps before a final
decision has been passed in his suit, shall be at liberty to leave the
further conduct of the suit, either to a mokhtar duly constituted
under a mokhtarnamah executed according to the form No. 1, in
the Appendix to this Regulation, or to one or more of the established pleaders of the Court empowered to act for him by a regular vakalutnamah.—*Cl.* 3.—*Ibid.*

Whenever any land or other real property belonging to a native
officer or soldier may be attached by a Court of Justice, for the

purpose of realizing the amount of any judgment, fine, or penalty imposed on such native officer or soldier, the Court shall cause notice of the same to be issued in the manner prescribed in Clause second, Section IV of this Regulation, and shall postpone the sale for such definite period as may appear reasonable, for the purpose of affording an opportunity to the native officer or soldier to discharge the amount of the judgment, fine, or penalty.—*Sec.* VIII, *Reg.* VIII, 1817.

Any registered proprietor of an estate paying revenue to Government, who may be entertained as a native officer or soldier on the military establishment under the Presidency of Fort St. George, shall be at liberty to notify to the Collector the rank which he may hold, and the designation of the corps to which he may be attached. A record of such notification shall be inserted by the Collector in the public registers and accounts relative to the estate and its assessment, and in cases in which the estate, or a portion of the estate of a native officer or soldier, who may have made such notification, shall become liable to public sale for the recovery of an arrear of revenue, the Collector shall address an official letter to the commanding officer of the corps, drawn in the form prescribed in No. 5, of the Appendix to this Regulation ; and shall enclose in such letter a written notice, signed and sealed by himself and attested by the principal native officer on his establishment, specifying the amount of the arrear, and the date on which it became due, and requiring that it be paid at the treasury of the Collectorship, within such limited period of time as, on consideration of the distance at which the corps may be stationed, and other circumstances of the case, may appear to be proper and reasonable.—*Cl.* 1, *Sec.* IX.—*Ibid.*

The commanding officer of the corps shall acknowledge to the Collector the receipt of his letter, and shall specify the date on which the notice may have been communicated to the party, or the circumstances which may have rendered it impracticable to make such communication.—*Cl.* 2.—*Ibid.*

If the native officer or soldier shall omit to discharge the arrear within the term specified in the notice, the Collector shall report the circumstances of the case to the Board of Revenue, transmitting at the same time a copy of the notice and of his correspondence with the commanding officer, and shall be guided in his further proceedings by the orders which he may receive in each case from the Board.—*Cl.* 3.—*Ibid.*

Nothing contained in this Regulation shall be construed to authorize the commanding officer of any corps or detachment to correspond with the Civil Courts, or with the Collectors, regarding the merits of any judgment or order, passed by those authorities respectively under the provisions of this Regulation.—*Cl.* 1, *Sec.* X, *Reg.* VIII, 1817.

Nothing contained in this Regulation shall be construed to modify, or to affect the existing rules for the trial of Civil suits, in which persons who may have been discharged from the service, or who may be attached to provincial battalions, or to local or irregular corps, or who may be camp followers, or non-combatant retainers of the army, or who may be relations or members of the family of a native officer or soldier, may be parties : the foregoing provisions of this Regulation are to be considered as strictly and exclusively applicable to native officers or soldiers, who may be entertained in regular corps, and on the actual strength of the army, on the establishment of the Presidency of Fort St. George. —*Cl.* 2.—*Ibid.*

The reduced pay or pension, however called, of any Invalid Officer, Soldier, Sailor or Retainer of the Army or Navy, in the Military or Naval Service of the East India Company, and also any monthly or yearly pension, or pecuniary allowance to any person in consideration of past services and present infirmities, or old age, granted by authority of the Governor General in Council, or of the Governor, or Governor in Council, or Lieutenant Governor, of any Presidency or place within the territories under the Government of the East India Company, and also the pension of any Out Pensioner of Chelsea or Greenwich Hospital, granted by authority of the Commissioners of Chelsea or Greenwich Hospital respectively, and also all money due, or to become due, on account of any such pension or allowance, shall be exempt from seizure, attachment or sequestration by process of any Court within the said territories, at the instance of a creditor for any demand against the pensioner, or in satisfaction of a decree or order of any such Court.—*Sec.* II, *Act* VI, 1849.

All assignments, agreements, orders, sales, and securities of every kind, made by any such pensioner, in respect of any money not payable at or before the making thereof, on account of any such pension, or for giving or assigning any future interest therein, are null and void.—*Sec.* III.—*Ibid.*

This Act shall not apply to any process of any Court established by Royal Charter, issued out of such Court before the passing of this Act ; or to any assignment, agreement, order, sale, or security by any such pensioner, made before the passing of this Act in respect of a Chelsea or Greenwich pension, or a pension or allowance granted in the Presidency of Madras * *.—*Sec.* IV, *Act* VI, 1849.

All the Courts of the East India Company shall receive plaints in original suits, not being suits originating in loans or in pecuniary transactions of a commercial nature upon unstamped paper, when the plaintiff is a native officer or soldier in the Military establishment of the Presidency of Fort William, Fort St. George, or Bombay.—*Sec.* III, *Act* XV, 1845.

The value of any stamp from which a plaintiff may be exempted by the last preceding Section shall be charged in the decree on behalf of Government to the party cast, or to the parties respectively, in such proportions as may be deemed equitable.—*Sec.* IV. —*Ibid.*

If any native officer or soldier shall institute a suit under this Act, in which he is not bonâ fide interested, or not interested to the extent alleged in the plaint, for the purpose of enabling some other person to avail himself fraudulently of the advantages conferred by this Act, such native officer or soldier shall be liable to a fine not exceeding five times the value of the stamped paper which the party interested would have required for the institution of the suit otherwise than under this Act; such fine to be levied in the manner prescribed for the execution of decrees.—*Sec.* V.—*Ibid.*

CHAPTER V.

SUMMARY SUITS.

All Summary Suits authorized by the Regulations (*whether for recovering the possession of land or other property in cases of forcible dispossession, under Regulation* XXXII, 1802, *or for the speedy realization of arrears of rent, under Regulation* XXVIII, 1802) or for any other purpose in which a summary process is sanctioned by the Regulations, shall be cognizable, as heretofore, *in the Subordinate Zillah Courts*, whatever may be the produce, amount, or value of the land or other property in dispute.—*Sec.* VII, *Reg.* XII, 1809.

Sec. VII, Reg. XII, 1809.—" All Summary Suits authorized by the Regulations" this description, if those specially referred to be excluded, as having by Sec. II, Reg. V, 1822, been made cognizable by the Collector, leaves little in this kind to the Subordinate Civil Courts—The law touching such will be found under the head of " Collector" pp. 49—88 and with reference to the doubts entertained, as to with whom—Reg. V, of 1822 notwithstanding—jurisdiction in such cases properly remains, see note thereon at p. 47.

A Summary process to test the validity of an arrear for which a party is confined lies against a Collector under Sec. XII. Reg. XXVII, 1802, which, as an interlocutory proceeding in a " regular Revenue Suit," has been entered under that head at p. 204.

A Summary process for deciding on validity of demands between landlord and tenant, for which the latter may have been arrested, is also given by Sec. XXXIV, Reg. XXVIII, 1802, which see pp. 63—66, where for convenience; and as immediately connected with preceding and following Sections, it has been entered, though perhaps it might more properly have been inserted in this place.

The proceedings directed to be held under Acts. XIX and XX of 1841 are also of a Summary nature, but as those enactments will be found at length under the head of " Administration and Succession" it is not necessary to insert them here.

By Sec. XIII, Reg. VII, 1818, Paupers are debarred, from the institution of Summary Suits of any description.

BOOK IV.

APPEALS.

CHAPTER I.

SUMMARY APPEALS.

It shall be competent to the Sudder Udalut to receive a summary appeal from the orders or decrees of the *Zillah Civil* Courts in all cases, in which the latter may have refused to admit an original suit or appeal regularly cognizable by them; or having admitted such suit, or appeal, may have dismissed it on the ground of delay, informality or other default, without an investigation of the merits of the case.—*Cl. 2, Sec. V, Reg. XV, 1816.*

In like manner it shall be competent to a *Zillah Civil* Court to receive a summary appeal from the orders or decrees of the Subordinate Zillah Courts in cases, in which the latter may have refused to admit an original suit or appeal regularly cognizable by them, or having admitted such suit or appeal, may have dismissed it, without an investigation of the merits on the grounds, of delay, informality or other default.—*Cl. 3.—Ibid.*

It shall be competent to the Zillah *Civil* Judge to receive a summary appeal, from the orders of any Principal Sudder Ameen, or

---

Cl. 2, Sec. V, Reg. XV, 1816.—This and the following enactments relative to Summary Appeals against dismission or refusal of Suits, are so nearly identical with Sections VII and VIII, Reg. IV, 1802—*which sec at p.* 130—and Sections IV and V, of 1802—*at p.* 136 *and* 137—by which the Zillah Civil Courts, and Sudder Udalut respectively, are empowered to command receipt of an original suit, appeal, or petition, refused by the inferior Courts, that they may perhaps be considered as superseded by them—but those enactments have been entered under the heads of Zillah Court, and Sudder Udalut, as not specifically repealed, and as they may be held to confer a *particular* authority on those Courts as explained in the note at p. 138.

This Clause says " *all cases,*" but there is one case in which, when a Zillah Civil Court dismisses a suit as not " regularly cognizable" by it, no Summary Appeal lies to the Sudder Udalut, viz. where an exception to the jurisdiction, arising out of the *value* of the suit, is taken by the defendant in an original suit instituted in the Zillah Court, the determination of the Civil Judge is final on the point under Section V, Reg. XII, of 1809, *which see at p.* 129—but if a like exception be taken in a Subordinate Court, though the Judge thereof is empowered by Sec. IV, Reg. XII, of 1809—*which see at p.* 121—to determine on the point in the first instance, a Summary Appeal from *his* decision will lie to the Zillah Civil Court under Clause 2 of the same Section.

Sudder Ameen, rejecting any original suit cognizable by him ; and all rules applicable to summary appeals from orders dismissing original suits on the ground of any default, shall be applicable to the summary appeals given by this Act.—*Sec.* IV, *Act* IX, 1844.

If any appeal from a decision or order of a district moonsiff, which may have been under this Section referred for decision, or preferred in the first instance to a Subordinate Judge or Principal Sudder Ameen, be dismissed without any decision being come to on its merits, it shall be competent to the party aggrieved by such order of dismissal to prefer a summary appeal from it to the Judge of the Zillah, and it shall be the duty, of the said Zillah Judge to hold such proceeding on such summary appeal as he may consider proper ; and having satisfied himself that the order dismissing the appeal has been passed without sufficient cause, being shewn for such dismissal, it shall be competent for such Zillah Judge to issue his precept to the Court by which the appeal may have been dismissed, requiring that the appeal shall be again admitted on the file, and a decision passed upon it after mature consideration of its merits.— *Cl.* 4, *Sec.* VIII, *Act* VII, 1843.

In all the preceding cases the summary appeal shall be preferred within the same limited period as is prescribed for the admission of regular appeals, and subject to the provisions contained in the following Clauses.— *Cl.* 5, *Sec.* V, *Reg.* XV, 1816.

Sec. IV, Act. IX, 1844.—Cl. 4, Sec. V, Reg. XV, of 1816, which is now obsolete, gave power to the then Zillah Judges to receive like appeals, from a Register or Sudder Ameen so dismissing suits referred to them—Act XVII, 1838 authorized Zillah Judges, Assistant Judges, and Principal Sudder Ameens, to receive such from District Moonsiffs within their respective jurisdictions, but both these enactments are virtually superseded by Cl. 1, Sec. VIII, Act VII, 1843—*which see under appeals*, and which indicates the Zillah Civil Court as the only tribunal competent to receive appeals, either regular or summary, from Subordinate Courts, whether presided over by a European Judge, or Principal Sudder Ameen, or from Sudder Ameens, or District Moonsiffs—except in the particular case specified in the second Clause of that Section, authorizing the receipt of appeals from District Moonsiffs by a Subordinate Judge or Principal Sudder Ameen, when located at distances remote from the station of the Civil Court—By Clause 3, Sec. VIII, Act. VII, 1843, the Civil Judge is empowered to refer appeals (i. e. either regular or Summary) from District Moonsiffs to the Subordinate Judge, or Principal Sudder Ameen : and Cl. 4 of the same Section, which as relating solely to " Summary Appeals" is here inserted, provides for a " Summary Appeal" to the Civil Judge, in case of such referred appeal being improperly dismissed.

Cl. 5, Sec. V, Reg. XV, 1816.—"; Limited period prescribed." i. e, from any inferior Court to Zillah Civil Court 30 days under Sec. VIII, Act VII, 1843 : and from Zillah Court to Sudder Udalut three months : in either case to be calculated as directed in Act XXXV, 1837.

The rules which regulate the admission of appeals in suits, apply to appeals from interlocutory orders, vide C. O. S. U. No. 23 : and upon the principles laid down in Circular Order of the Sudder Udalut dated 20th July 1832, in cases in which petitions may be presented praying for the reconsideration of an interlocutory order, the period which may elapse between the presentation and disposal of such petitions, can alone be added to the ordinary term of appeal—Cir. Inst. S. U. 8th November 1850.

Whenever a party may be desirous of preferring a summary appeal in the cases abovementioned, he shall appear either in person, or by a vakeel duly authorized, before the Court which under the preceding rules may be competent to receive such appeal, and shall present a petition written on the stamped paper prescribed by Section XX, Regulation XIII of 1816, and accompanied by an attested copy of the order or decree passed in the case.—*Cl.* 6, *Sec.* V, *Reg.* XV, 1816.

The party presenting such petition, shall not be liable to the payment of stamp duty; nor shall he be required to furnish any security, except such as may be eventually necessary under the Regulations in force, for staying the execution of the decree, from which the appeal may be preferred.—*Cl.* 7.—*Ibid.*

It shall not be requisite to give any notice to the respondent, or to require his attendance on such summary appeal being preferred, unless in any particular instance the Court may deem it proper to adopt that measure, nor shall any pleadings or proceedings be holden on such summary appeal, excepting such as may suffice to determine whether the suit was or was not rejected or dismissed by the lower Court on sufficient grounds, and in conformity with the Regulations.—*Cl.* 8.—*Ibid.*

If upon such summary proceedings, it shall appear to the Court, that the suit was rejected in the first instance, or after having been admitted was dismissed, without an investigation of the merits upon insufficient grounds, or in opposition to the Regulations, it shall be competent to the Sudder Udalut, and to the Zillah Civil Judges, respectively, to direct the lower Court or Officer from whose order or decree the petition of appeal may have been presented, to receive the original suit or appeal, or to revive it if it shall have been received and dismissed, and to try and determine such cause on its merits, according to the Regulations.—*Cl.* 9.—*Ibid.*

If on the contrary such summary appeal shall be found to be groundless and litigious, the Sudder Udalut, and the Zillah *Civil* Judges, are respectively authorized and required to reject the petition for a summary appeal, and to impose such fine on the litigious appellant, as may appear to be in each instance proportionable

---

Cl. 6, Sec. V, Reg. XV, 1816.—" Party desirous, &c."—Paupers are debarred from a Summary appeal by Sec. XIII, Reg. VII, 1818, and the Sudder Udalut ruled on the 1st July 1850 that a Summary appeal is not open to a Defendant. '

to the condition of the party, and to the circumstances of the case; provided that such fine shall in no case exceed the amount of the stamp duty which would have been payable by the appellant on the institution of such case as a regular suit or appeal. All orders imposing fines, or rejecting petitions of summary appeals, which may be passed under this Clause, by the Sudder Udalut, or by the Zillah *Civil* Judges, shall be final and conclusive.—*Cl.* 10, *Sec.* V, *Reg.* XV, 1816.

CHAPTER II.

REVIEW OF JUDGMENT.

Any persons considering themselves aggrieved by a decree passed in a regular Civil suit or appeal by a *Subordinate or Civil* Zillah Court, from which decree no further appeal may have been admitted by a superior Court, and who, from the discovery of new matter or evidence, which was not within their knowledge, or could not be adduced by them at the time when the decree was passed, or from any other good and sufficient reason, may be desirous of obtaining a review of the judgment passed against them, are at liberty to present a petition for this purpose to the Court, in which the decree in question may be passed; such petition shall be written on stamped paper of the value prescribed in Section XX, Regulation XIII of 1816, and shall be presented within the period of three calendar months, which period shall be calculated according to the provisions of *Sec.* III, *Act* XXXV, 1837. The Courts are nevertheless authorized to admit applications for a review after the period abovementioned, provided that the parties preferring the same shall be able to shew just and reasonable cause, to the satisfaction of the Court, for not having preferred such application within the limited period; in such case, however, the Courts are enjoined to proceed with caution, and to state at large upon the proceedings, their reasons for admitting such applications after the limited period. If the Courts shall be of opinion, that there are not any sufficient grounds for a review, they shall reject the petition, and their order to that effect, shall be final; but if on the contrary, they shall be of opinion, that the review desired, is necessary to correct an evident error, or omission, or is otherwise requisite for the ends of justice, they shall report the same to the Sudder Udalut, transmitting at the same time, a statement of the grounds of their opinion, with a copy of the petition presented to them, and a copy of the decree passed in the case.—*Cl.* 2, *Sec.* VI, *Reg.* XV, 1816.

The Court of Sudder Udalut, in cases referred to them under the preceding Clause, as well as in all cases, in which a petition

---

Cl. 2, Sec. VI, Reg. XV, 1816.—The provisions of this Clause are applicable to Sudder Ameens and District Moonsiffs—C. O. S. U. 7th March 1842, No. 78.

may be presented to them for a revision of their own judgments, which may not have been appealed *to Her Majesty in Council*, or though appealed, the proceedings in which may not have been transmitted to *Her Majesty in Council*, are authorized to grant the review desired, if upon a consideration of the reasons stated, the circumstances of the case shall appear in justice to require it; the Sudder Udalut shall record on their proceedings the grounds upon which a review may be granted by them in each instance, and shall issue any instructions regarding the admission or rejection of new evidence in the case, which they may deem just and proper. —*Cl.* 3, *Sec.* VI, *Reg.* XV, 1816.

The order of a Subordinate or Civil Zillah Court, or of the Sudder Udalut, rejecting the petition for a review in the first instance, or of the latter Court refusing to sanction a review when applied for by a lower Court, shall not be construed to preclude the party from instituting a regular appeal (if the case be appealable) in a competent Court, subject to the conditions and rules prescribed by the Regulations in force for the admission of such appeals.— *Cl.* 4.—*Ibid.*

CHAPTER III.

REGULAR APPEALS.

Appeals shall lie to the Zillah Court from all decrees or orders of Subordinate Civil Courts constituted according to Regulations I and VII of 1827, and of Sudder Ameens and District Moonsiffs in cases in which appeals are now allowable, but such appeals must be preferred within the period of 30 days, to be calculated as prescribed in the existing Regulations.—*C.* 1, *Sec.* VIII, *Act* VII, 1843.

Provided, that whenever a Court constituted according to Regulation I of 1827, or according to Regulation VII of 1827, is established in any Zillah at a place remote from the station of the Zillah Court, the Sudder Udalut, with the sanction of the Governor in Council, may order appeals from the decisions and orders of District Moonsiffs stationed within the limits assigned to such Court, to be preferred to such Court. But it shall be competent to the Zillah Judge, at his discretion, to call up to his own Court, from time to time, appeals received by any such Court, and to dispose of them himself.—*Cl.* 2.—*Ibid.*

Provided also, that the Judge of any Zillah Court may refer to any Subordinate Judge or Principal Sudder Ameen in the Zillah, any appeals from District Moonsiffs which may be filed in the Zillah Court.—*Cl.* 3.—*Ibid.*

Appeals, Regular and Summary, from decisions and orders of the Zillah Courts, shall lie to the Sudder Udalut, under the same rules and restrictions as are applicable to similar appeals to the Sudder Udalut from the Provincial Courts of Appeal.—*Sec* IX.—*Ibid.*

" Regular Appeal."—The Provisions of Law given in this Chapter are, unless specially noted otherwise, of general application to the appellate Courts, whether the Zillah Courts ôr the Sudder Udalut.

Cl. 3, Sec. VIII, Act VII, 1843.—Appeals from Sudder Ameens cannot be referred under this Clause but ' Summary Appeals' from District Moonsiffs may.—Cir. Ext. S. U. 9th November, 1843.

This Clause includes all orders of every description, whether recorded as decrees in regular suits, or merely as orders in matters of a miscellaneous nature.—Cir. Ext. S. U. 14th November, 1843.

Petitions of appeal to the Sudder Udalut must be presented within three calendar months, *or to the Zillah Courts within* 30 *days.—Cl.* 1, *Sec.* VIII, *Act* VII, 1843,—after the day on which the decree may be given, *to be calculated according to the Provisions of Act* XXXV, 1837.

But it shall nevertheless be permitted to *the party desirous to appeal to a Civil Court, or to the Sudder Udalut,* to prefer his petition of appeal after the expiration of the *limited periods,* and the *appellate* Court is authorized to admit the appeal, provided the petitioner can show just and reasonable cause, to its satisfaction, for not having preferred it within the limited period. But whenever a Court shall admit an appeal which may be preferred to it after the limited time, it is to enter upon the record of the trial its reasons at large for admitting the appeal.—*Cl.* 4, *Sec.* XII, *Reg.* IV, 1802.—*Cl.* 5, *Sec.* X, *Reg.* V, 1802.

The limited period for appealing shall be computed from the day on which the decree is sealed and signed, agreeably to Section XXVII, Regulation III of ·1802, of the Madras Code : provided always, that if, within such limited period as aforesaid an application be made by a plaintiff or defendant for a copy of the decree, or for a copy of a translation of the abstract mentioned in the Clause last preceding, or for both a copy of the decree, and a copy or a translation of the abstract, and if the document or documents so applied for be not delivered or tendered on the same day to the party applying, then, for every day of such delay, not attributable to that party, a day shall be added to the period allowed for appealing, in as far as the right of that party is concerned.—*Sec.* III, *Act* XXXV, 1837.

The day on which the time for appealing will expire, shall be certified at the end of every document furnished to any party according to the last preceding Section.—*Sec.* IV.—*Ibid.*

On the day on which any such decree is sealed and signed, the day on which the original limited period for appealing will expire shall be proclaimed in open Court.—*Sec.* V.—*Ibid.*

Where an appeal is intended from *a Subordinate Court to a Zillah Civil Court, or* from a *Zillah Civil Court* to the Sudder Udalut,

---

Cl. 4, Sec. XII, Reg. IV, 1802.—Cl. 5, Sec. X, Reg. V, 1802.—Throughout this Chapter where such double quotations occur, the first is the authority for the Zillah Courts—the latter for the Sudder Udalut. The period for appeal cannot be extended, nor can application for permission to appeal be attended to after the limited period has expired—the only way in which a party can obtain indulgence under this Clause, is by *putting in his appeal petition accompanied* by a motion showing cause why he exceeded the limited period and praying its receipt.

Sec. III, Act XXXV, 1837.—For Sec. II of this Act, relating to the preparation of decree—see under decree, at p. 191.

such appeal *may* be presented in the first instance to the *Court* in which the decree appealed against may have been passed : *which* Court shall on the next Court day, or as soon after as may be practicable, admit the same under the conditions in that respect prescribed.—*Cl.* 1, *Sec.* XII, *Reg.* IV, 1802.—*Cl.* 2, *Sec.* X, *Reg.* V, 1802.

No Judge of the Sudder Udalut shall sit on the trial of any appeal in a cause tried before himself as a Judge of a Zillah Civil Court, neither shall he sign a decree passed on such appeal by the Court of which he is a Judge.—*Cl.* 1, *Sec.* II, *Reg.* III, 1825.

No judicial officer, European or Native, shall try an appeal from any decision passed by himself in any situation which he may have previously held.—*Cl.* 1, *Sec.* II, *Reg.* I, 1829.

Whenever an appeal may be preferred to any judicial officer, European or Native, having appellate jurisdiction, from a decree passed by himself in any former capacity, or whenever such an appeal may be pending in the Court to which he is appointed, at the time when he takes charge thereof, he shall forward the petition of appeal, and all the pleadings, evidence, and documents to the Court to which in ordinary cases an appeal lies from his decisions ; and that Court shall receive and try the appeal in the same manner as other appeals which it is empowered to try.—*Cl.* 2.—*Ibid.*

The removal of the appeal to the higher Court, in these cases, shall no ways affect the stamp duties, which shall be the same as if the appeal had been tried by the Court to which it was first preferred.—*Cl.* 3.—*Ibid.*

Any party who may be desirous of appealing from a judgment passed against him, by a Sudder Ameen, *Principal Sudder Ameen*, *or by a* Judge of any Subordinate Zillah Court, from which a regular appeal may be admissible under the Regulations, shall be at liberty to present his petition of appeal without an authenticated copy of the decree, to the *Court*, in which the decision may have been passed, such petition of appeal shall not be required to contain the specific grounds or reasons of the appeal, but may state shortly that the party being dissatisfied with the judgment, is desirous of appealing from it. The petition must be written on stamped paper according to the rates contained in

---

Cl. 1, Sec. XII, Reg. IV, 1802.—Cl. 2, Sec. X, Reg. V, 1802.—By these enactments parties desirous of appealing were necessitated to prefer their appeals in the Court passing the decree, and by other Clauses of the same Sections—now superseded—were obliged to present therewith an authenticated copy of the decree.

By Sec. VIII, Reg. XV, 1816, it is now optional with parties either so to present their appeals to the Court passing the original decree, in which case they need not present with it an attested copy thereof, or to the appellate Court, when a copy is necessary.

Section XIII, Regulation XIII of 1816, and must be accompanied by the prescribed security for the eventual costs in appeal.—*Cl.* 2, *Sec.* VIII, *Reg.* XV, 1816.

The Zillah Judge, after referring to the decree in the original record of the suit, shall admit the appeal; provided that the petition of appeal and the security required shall have been duly presented in the mode prescribed, within the period limited for the admission of such appeals under the existing Regulations.—*Cl.* 3.—*Ibid.*

The specific objections to the judgment, and detailed grounds and reasons for preferring the appeal, may be stated at the option of the party, in the original petition of appeal, or may be subsequently filed in the Court trying the appeal, as a separate pleading; in the latter case such pleading is to be written on the stamped paper, and according to the rates prescribed for other pleadings in Section XIX, Regulation XIII of 1816.—*Cl.* 5.—*Ibid.*

In like manner any parties who may be desirous of appealing from the judgments passed by the Zillah Civil Courts in suits regularly appealable to the Sudder Udalut, or from the judgments of the Sudder Udalut, in suits which may be regularly appealable to the *Queen* in Council, shall be at liberty to present their petition of appeal without an authenticated copy of the decree to the Court by which the judgment may have been passed, in conformity with the provisions contained in the preceding Clauses of this Section.—*Cl.* 6.—*Ibid.*

Under the preceding rules, parties in suits decided in the first instance in a Zillah Subordinate, or Civil Court, or the Sudder Udalut, will be enabled to prefer an appeal from such decision without the necessity of filing an authenticated copy of the decree; but if any party in a suit, which may be regularly appealable to a Civil Court,

---

Cl. 2, Sec. VIII, Reg. XV, 1816.—" *Court* in which the decision may have been passed" in the original " Judge of the Zillah." The S. U. ruled on the 19th March, 1844, that under the new system established by Act VII, 1843, Subordinate Judges, Principal Sudder Ameens, and Sudder Ameens may receive appeals from their own decrees, for transmission to the appellate Court, without an authenticated copy of the decree, but that if the petitions be presented direct to the civil Court, they must be accompanied by authenticated copy of the decree appealed against—except in the case of Sudder Ameens decrees, of which, as they explained on the 9th March, 1850, no authenticated copies need be presented, whether the appeal be presented to the civil Judge, or to the Sudder Ameen himself.

When brief petition of appeal is sent up under this Clause it should be accompanied by a copy of the decree appealed from.—Cir. Lr. S. U. 28th August, 1844.

Cl. 5, Sec. VIII, Reg. XV, 1816.—" *Separate pleading.*" If this be not filed within six weeks from the admission of the appeal, it is a default, for which the suit is struck off under Act XXIX of 1841. The S. U. ruled on the 19th March, 1844, that this enactment was not affected by Act VII, 1843.

or to the Sudder Udalut, may be desirous, under the option allowed by the Regulations, of presenting his petition of appeal in the Court by which the appeal is to be tried, rather than in the Court by which the decision may have been passed in the first instance, it shall be requisite for such party, to file with his petition of appeal an authenticated copy of the decree.—*Cl.* 7, *Sec.* VIII, *Reg.* XV, 1816.

For the purpose of obtaining an authenticated copy of the decree in such case, the party desiring it shall furnish to the Court by whom the decision may have been passed, one, two, or more sheets, or rolls, of the stamped paper prescribed in Section XXII, Regulation XIII of 1816, as may be necessary for transcribing the decree.—*Cl.* 8.—*Ibid.*

When such stamped paper shall be furnished, the seristadar, or such other principal officer, as may be authorized by the Court to discharge that duty, shall endorse on it the date of its being furnished, the name of the party on whose account it may be presented, and the number of the suit to which it may be intended to be applicable, and shall grant to the party a corresponding receipt for the same on unstamped paper; the copy of the decree shall then be prepared and duly authenticated, and shall be delivered or tendered to the party by whom the stamped paper may have been furnished, or to his vakeel in open Court, and the date of the delivery or tender of such copy shall be also endorsed on the copy—*Cl.* 9.—*Ibid.*

The respective periods, limited by the Regulations for the admission of appeals in such cases, shall be calculated *as prescribed by Act* XXXV, 1837, *which see at page* 242.—*Cl.* 10.—*Ibid.*

The principles of the rules contained in Clauses eighth, ninth, and tenth of this Section, are to be considered applicable to all copies of decrees from which a party may be desirous of preferring a special or a summary appeal, and to all copies of orders passed by the Judges of the Zillah Courts, and by the Sudder Udalut, which those Courts may be required to furnish to parties under the provisions of any Regulation.—*Cl.* 11.—*Ibid.*

Plaintiffs in original suits who did not sue as paupers, shall be admissible to appeal in formâ pauperis from the judgments passed in such original suits.—*Cl.* 1, *Sec.* II, *Reg.* III, 1822.

Defendants in original suits shall be admissible to appeal in forma pauperis from the judgments passed against them in such suits.—*Cl. 2, Sec.* II, *Reg.* III, 1822.

The admission of persons to appeal or defend in appeal under the foregoing Clauses, shall be in conformity with the rules prescribed in Sections V, and VI, Regulation VII of 1818 for persons desirous of being admitted to plead as paupers in original suits, and subject to the restrictions contained in Section X of that Regulation in respect to the admission of appeals from pauper plaintiffs.—*Cl. 3.—Ibid.*

It shall be the duty of the Court competent to admit the appeals in the cases above provided for, to satisfy themselves, in the event of objections being made by the other party to the admission of the applicant, as a pauper, that the property of which the said applicant was possessed at the time when the original suit was instituted has passed from his hands, or has otherwise been rendered unavailable to him, either by the operation of the judgment from which he is desirous of appealing, or of some other judgments, or generally of causes over which he had no control.—*Cl. 4.—Ibid.*

In all authorised cases of appeal the Court in which the decree appealed from may have been passed shall suspend the execution of it during the appeal, provided the party against whom the decree may have been passed shall, at the time of preferring his appeal, or within such reasonable period afterwards as may be fixed for the purpose, deliver the securities required by this and the next following Clause; viz.' if the decree be for a zemindarry, talook, or other land, or for a house or other real property, good and sufficient security, in a sum equal to one year's produce thereof; and in all other cases, good and sufficient security in an amount equal to the sum of money, or value of the thing, decreed, for the performance of the decree which may be passed upon the appeal.—*Cl. 5, Sec.* XII, *Reg.* IV, 1802.—*Cl. 6, Sec.* X, *Reg.* V, 1802.

In all authorized cases of appeal, the party desirous of appealing is, with his petition of appeal, to deliver good and sufficient security for the payment of the costs that may be awarded on the appeal. Without such security, or without proof of inability to find the same as required with respect to paupers by Regulation VII, 1818, no appeal shall be admitted. It is hereby declared that the presenting a petition of appeal without the security required by this Clause, before the expiration of the time limited for appealing, shall not be considered as preserving to the appellant his right of appeal, as far as respects the limitation in question.—*Cl. 6, Sec.* XII, *Reg.* IV, 1802.—*Cl. 7, Sec.* X, *Reg.* V, 1802.

When the securities above required shall have been entered into, the Judge of the *lower* Court is immediately to endorse on the petition, in his own handwriting, the day of the. month and year in which it was presented, and sign it with his name, and cause to be written in the margin of the record, immediately opposite to the decree. of the Court, the word " Appealed," and transmit the petition to the *appellate* Court. The Court is, at the same time, to direct notice in writing to be given to the appellant that, within fifteen days, the proceedings held in the cause appealed will be certified to the *appellate* Court; and that if he shall not proceed in the appeal within six weeks after the petition of appeal shall have been filed in *the appellate* Court, his appeal will be dismissed; unless he shall show reasonable cause, to the satisfaction of *that* Court, for not having proceeded in it.— *C.* 7, *Sec.* XII, *Reg.* IV, 1802.— *Cl.* 8, *Sec.* X, *Reg.* V, 1802.

Notwithstanding the appellants, in causes depending before *appellate* Courts may have entered into the securities required of them by the above Clauses in this Section, those Courts are further authorized, in cases wherein, from delay in the decision, the securities originally so given may afterwards appear insufficient, (in respect to the period of the time the cause has been pending or is likely to remain still undecided) on the application of the respondent or respondents in all such cases, to require any additional security which they may deem necessary, to secure the party who may have obtained a judgment in his favor from any loss, by the non-execution of such judgment during the appeal : and, in default of such further security being given within a reasonable period to be fixed for that purpose, the Courts—*on application of party, Sec.* XIV, *Reg.* XV, 1816—are empowered to direct the judgment in question to be carried into execution, in like manner as if no securities had originally been given by the appellant; provided that, in such cases, good and sufficient security, as prescribed by the Regulations, be given by the respondent previous to his being put in possession of the property in litigation. The supplemental security required in this Clause, as necessary to maintain a depending appeal, is carefully to be distinguished from the securities originally necessary to warrant the cause being appealed; the supplemental security being only demandable by the *appellate* Courts after a lapse of time, the original securities being requirable by the *lower* Courts, previous to the petition of appeal being admitted.— *Cl.* 8, *Sec.* XII, *Reg.* IV, 1802.— *Cl.* 9, *Sec.* X, *Reg.* V, 1802.

As cases may occur wherein neither the appellant, nor the respondent, may be able to give the prescribed securities for staying the execution of the decree, or for the execution thereof in favor of the plaintiff, it is hereby enacted that, in all such cases, the property adjudged shall be held in attachment during the appeal, or until such time as one of the parties may be able to give the required securities, by the Collector of the district wherein the land may be situated, at the expense of the party who may be ultimately declared entitled thereto, under the provisions in that respect established. No attachment, however, is to be made by any Collector in the cases herein supposed, until he shall receive a precept requiring him to make the same, from the Court wherein the original judgment in the cause may have been passed; which precept shall state specifically the property to be included in the attachment, and shall require the Collector to continue the same, till ordered to be withdrawn by a further precept from the Court, to be issued either on the prescribed securities being given by one of the parties, or on the cause being finally determined.—*Cl. 9, Sec. XII, Reg.* IV, 1802.—*Cl. 10, Sec. X, Reg.* V, 1802.

Where a petition for an appeal to an *appellate Court, shall be rejected* on whatever ground by *the Court of original jurisdiction,* such Court shall, on the Court day next ensuing, or as soon afterwards as may be practicable, cause the appellant to be furnished with a copy of their order for rejecting the appeal; and the appellant shall be still at liberty to present his petition of appeal to the *appellate* Court in the mode, and under the restrictions, prescribed by this Section; provided that such petition set forth the previous application made to the *lower* Court, and the rejection of the appeal by that Court, and be accompanied by a copy of the order of rejection, or by a declaration that such copy was applied for ten days after the same was passed, and not obtained.—*Cl. 10, Sec. XII, Reg.* IV, 1802.—*Cl. 11, Sec, X, Reg.* V, 1802.

Where the party desiring to appeal shall neglect, or refuse, to enter into the securities in the manner prescribed in this Section, the Court by whom the decision may have been passed is—*on application of the opposite party, Sec. XIV, Reg. XV,* 1816—to order the decree to be executed.—*C.* 11, *Sec. XII, Reg.* IV, 1802.— *Cl.* 12, *Sec. X, Reg.* V, 1802.

The Judge of the *lower* Court—*with as little delay as possible after receipt of notice from appellate Court, that an appeal has been admitted, S. U.* 19*th March,* 1844—is to certify, under his hand and the seal of the Court, to *the appellate* Court, the record duly made up, and authenticated; including the original complaint, answer, replication, and rejoinder of the parties; the original depositions, exhibits, and every original paper read in the cause. Previous to transmitting the abovementioned papers to the *appellate* Court he is to cause true and faithful copies of all the originals, authenticated by the seristadar, or head native officer of the Court, to be made out and deposited in the Zillah Court, in lieu of the originals. The copies are to be deemed records of the Court; and are to be received in evidence in any other Zillah Court. In cases where any original deposition, or other original proceedings or matter whatsoever, shall have been previously entered in any Zillah Court, in any book which may likewise contain proceedings in other distinct causes, or any other matter so that such original papers cannot be transmitted to the *appellate* Court without the other proceedings or matters; the judge of the *Lower* Court, within the time, and in the manner before directed, is to certify a true and authentic copy of such original papers, and that the original of each copy transmitted is so entered in such book. But he is nevertheless to transmit the original complaint, the original answer, or other separate pleadings of the parties, and the original exhibits which shall have been delivered in or produced by the parties, and read in the course of the cause before the Court, if they be forthcoming, in the manner before required. In cases where any original paper shall have been mislaid or lost, and a copy of it shall have been entered in any book or proceedings the copy is to be deemed the original; and the judge is to transmit a copy of it to the *appellate* Court; and, in like manner, to certify it, and that the original after due search, cannot be found. —*Sec.* XIII, *Reg.* IV, 1802.—*Sec.* XI, *Reg.* V, 1802.

In all instances wherein the plaintiff, in a *Lower* Court, may obtain a judgment in his favor for land, or other real property; and the defendant appealing therefrom to a *Zillah* Court, may be left in possession of the property, under the security prescribed by the

---

Sec. XIII, Reg. IV, 1802. Sec. XI, Reg. V, 1802.—These Sections originally prescribed respectively the course to be pursued by a Zillah Judge on receiving for transmission to the Sudder Udalut, an appeal from his own decree, or that of any Subordinate tribunal in the Zillah: or by a provincial Court on receiving an appeal from its own decree for transmission to the Sudder Udalut; as here modified—they are so far as circumstances admit—applicable to Subordinate Judges or principal Sudder Ameens receiving appeals for transmission to Civil Courts, or Civil Courts for transmission to Sudder Udalut. On the 19th March, 1844, the S. U. ruled that " in all cases the records of the original suits need not be sent till called for by the appellate authority" and by proceedings of 27th June, 1844, explained that the rule was intended to apply to cases appealed from the Civil Courts to itself, as well as from Subordinate tribunals to the Civil Courts—but by proceedings of the 15th February, 1847, the S. U. rescinded the latter order, and directed that " whenever notice may be given to a Court below, of an appeal having been admitted from its decree by the Sudder Udalut, the original record of the suit be forwarded to the Sudder Udalut with the least possible delay after the receipt of such notice—a certified copy being first made, and deposited in the Court. The order of the 19th March, 1844, however remains in force, as respects the Civil Courts and those Subordinate to them, it is usual for the Civil Court to notify the receipt of an appeal to a Subordinate Judge or Principal Sudder Ameen, and the original record is then sent—but copies are *not* made; as obviously unnecessary, now that the Courts are generally under the same roof. The records of the Sudder Ameen are already in the record room of the Civil Court.

regulations; any private transfer of such property by sale, gift, or ótherwise or any mortgage thereof which might be made by such appellant during the appeal to the *Civil* Court, or during a further appeal to the Court of Sudder Udalut, or Queen in Council would, in the event of the judgment against him being confirmed on the appeal, be of course, and is hereby declared to be, null and void : but as malguzzarry lands (lands assessed with the public revenue) are in all cases, by whomsoever possessed, held answerable for the public revenue assessed thereon ; and as according to the general rules established for the collection of the public revenue, such lands, and also lakheraj lands, and other property appertaining to the same state, may become liable to sale by government from the neglect of the party in possession to discharge the revenue due therefrom; by which sale, in cases of appeal, the party to whom the property of the lands is ultimately adjudged, might, notwithstanding, be deprived of it, unless he purchased the same, at the public sale; to obviate all doubt respecting the right of the party making the purchase in such cases, it is hereby declared, that whenever any land or other property, for which a judgment may have been obtained in any of the established Courts of justice, but which, during an appeal from such judgment by the party cast, may be left in the possession of the appellant, shall, while such appeal is pending, or before the ultimate judgment thereon be put in execution, be sold by Government, to make good an arrear of the public revenue due from the appellant; and shall be purchased by the respondent; the party so purchasing, in the event of such property being finally adjudged to him on the appeal, shall be entitled to recover from the appellant, so left in possession, the full amount of his purchase money, and of all expenses attending the purchase so made by him ; with interest thereon at the rate of twelve per cent per annum ; in addition to any other sum which may be adjudged due to him, on account of the profits arising from the land, or other property in question, anterior to the sale. It is further declared, that in the case above supposed, if the respondent shall not have purchased the land, or other property, sold by Government to make good an arrear of public revenue due from the appellant left in possession thereof; and if the ultimate judgment on the appeal be in favor of such respondent, he shall be entitled to recover from the appellant left in possession, the amount of the purchase money paid for the property so sold, and adjudged to the respondent with interest thereon, at the rate of twelve per cent per annum ; in addition to any other sum which may be adjudged to him, on account of the profits arising from the property so sold, anterior to the sale of it : unless the property in question shall have been, directly, or indirectly, purchased by the appellant himself, or in his behalf, at the public sale ; in which case, on clear proof thereof being made by the respondent to whom such property may be ultimately adjudged, he shall be entitled to the possession thereof, and to all profits arising therefrom, as may be directed by the decree in the case, notwithstanding the fictitious sale supposed.—*Cl.* 1, *Sec.* XIV, *Reg.* IV, 1802.

The principles of the rules contained in the preceding Clause, and in Clause Eighth, Section XII, of this Regulation, are to be considered equally applicable to cases in which the plaintiff in a Zillah Court may be put in possession of land, or other property adjudged to him, during an appeal ; in consequence of the defendant's failing to give the securities prescribed : and, generally, to all cases, in which the possession of property may be transferred by the decree of any Court of Justice, from which decree an appeal may be depending in a superior Court ; whether a *Zillah Civil* Court, or the Court of Sudder Udalut, or the *Queen* in Council, in the cases for which an appeal to *her* is provided by *Regulation* VIII, 1818.—*Cl.* 2.—*Ibid.*

The *detailed* petition is to state (respect being had to the matter decreed) the annual produce of the lands, whether lakeraj, or malguzarry, the sum of money, or the value of the property which may be decreed, the name of the person in whose favour the decree may be given, the Court in which it may have been passed, when it was made, what was decreed by it, and whether the decree has been executed, and is to assign some cause special or general for appealing from the decision.—*Cl.* 2, *Sec.* XII, *Reg.* IV, 1802.—*Cl.* 3, *Sec.* X, *Reg.* V, 1802.

In appeals preferred to the Zillah Civil Court, or Sudder Udalut, no acts whatever shall be done on behalf of the appellant or respondent, except by the appellant or respondent themselves, or by a vakeel admitted to plead in the Court under the established Regulations ; nor by any vakeel before his vakalutnamah shall have been filed in the Court ; and no persons, excepting such parties, or their witnesses, or such vakeels, shall be heard *vivâ voce*, in any stage in the cause.—*Sec.* XXII, *Reg.* IV, 1802.—*Sec.* XX, *Reg.* V, 1802.

In all regular suits which may be appealed to a *Zillah Civil* Court, or to the Sudder Udalut, it shall be left to the option of the respondent, either to file an answer to the petition and reasons of appeal, or not, as he may judge proper ; provided however, that if no answer shall be filed by a respondent, it shall be competent to the Court trying the appeal, in all cases in which it may be deemed expedient, to direct the respondent to file an answer to the petition of appeal, or to any particular points in it, which may appear to require an answer or explanation.—*Cl.* 2, *Sec.* IX, *Reg.* XV, 1816.

No·further pleadings beyond the answer of the respondent, shall ᵇe admitted in appealed suits, except the duplicate of the plaint provided for by Clause first, Section XXIV, Regulation XIII, of 1816, or such supplemental pleadings as may be authorized by the Court under the provisions of Clause third, Section VII, of this Regulation.—*Cl.* 3.—*Ibid.*

An appeal not proceeded in for six weeks is to be dismissed, as of course: unless special leave be granted for delay.—*Act* XXIX, 1841.

Whenever an appeal in any Courts shall have been dismissed under the provisions of Act XXIX of 1841, it shall be competent to the Court which shall have dismissed such appeal to readmit the same, if the appellant shall make application for that purpose, on the stamp prescribed for miscellaneous petitions, within three months after the appeal shall have been dismissed, if dismissed by the Sudder Court—and within one month after the Appeal shall have been dismissed, if dismissed by any other Court—and shall satisfy the Court that the dismissal was occasioned by the default of his vakeel or by unavoidable accident.—*Sec.* 1, *Act* XVI, 1845.

No appeal which has been readmitted under this Act, and again dismissed under the provisions of Act XXIX, 1841, shall be again readmitted.—*Sec.* III.—*Ibid.*

On the hearing of any appeal from the decision or order of any Court of inferior jurisdiction, in any case, regular or miscellaneous, if a *Zillah Civil Judge, Subordinate Judge, or Principal Sudder Ameen.*—*Sec.* XI, *Act* VII, 1843, shall be of opinion that no sufficient ground has been shewn to impugn the correctness or justness of such decision or order, it shall be competent to such *Zillah Civil Judge, Subordinate Judge, or Principal Sudder Ameen,* without reference to the order of the file, to confirm the same without requiring the attendance of the opposite party, and with or without a revision of the whole proceedings, as the nature of the case may appear to require, and to communicate the order of confirma-

---

Cl. 3, Sec. IX, Reg. XV, 1816 —" *Duplicate of Plaint*" this can hardly be considered a "*pleading*" being merely a *copy* of the plaint ordered to be made on additional and complementary stamp, when the original has been inadvertently prepared on an insufficient stamp—by this Section in appeals, as in regular suits, the appellate Courts are authorized to admit supplemental pleadings *for the purposes specified in Sec. V, Reg. III, 1802, which see at page 168.*

Act XXIX, 1841.—As this enactment applies also to original suits, and will be found at length at pp. 170—171 it is not here reprinted.

Sec. I, Act XVI, 1845.—" *Default of his Vakeel, &c.*" as regards the curing of defaults, whether in original suits or appeals, see Act XVII, 1847, at page 171.

tion, through the Court from whose judgment the appeal was made, to the opposite party, with a view to enable such party to take immediate measures for the execution of the decree. On the other hand, if *he* shall be of opinion that the decision or order appealed against ought to be altered, or reversed, as being manifestly unjust, or at variance with some Regulation in force, or in opposition to the Hindoo or Mahomedan Law or other Law applicable to the case, or as having been passed without sufficient investigation of the merits, or as grounded on an assumption obviously erroneous, or irrelevant with reference to the points at issue, it shall likewise be competent to *him* to issue an injunction pointing out the irregularity, illegality, or other defect, apparent in the proceedings, decision, or order, appealed against, and requiring that the Court by which the same may have been held, or passed, shall revise the case, and proceed thereon in such manner as may appear conformable to justice and to the Regulations.—*Cl. 2, Sec. X, Act* VII, 1843.

The *Zillah Civil Courts* are empowered in cases of appeal in which it shall appear to them that the original suit has not been sufficiently investigated in the *lower* Court, or for any other cause that may be deemed reasonable by the *Zillah Civil Court*, either *to proceed as authorized by Cl. 2, Sec. X, and Sec.* XI, *Act* VII, *of* 1843 : or to receive such further evidence as they may think necessary for the just determination of the suit, and give judgment upon it.—*Sec.* XVIII, *Reg.* IV, 1802.

If a petition of appeal shall be preferred *to a Zillah Civil Court*

Cl. 2, Sec. X, Act VII, 1843.—This Clause of a Section otherwise applicable only to the Sudder Udalut, and therefore inserted at length at page 144, is extended to the lower Courts by Sec. XI of the same Act : it must be remembered that no reversal or alteration of a decree or order can be made under this enactment; if a Judge be of opinion that such is necessary, he must either remand the case, or call on the respondent to plead, and proceed as usual in regular appeals. See Cir. Ext. S. U. 22d December, 1846.

A regular appeal decree may be passed, notwithstanding this Section, if it seem more adviseable. Cir. Ext. S. U. 12th February, 1844.

Every order or injunction under this Section dismissing or remanding petition of appeal must be considered an appeal decree, and consequently every such appeal should be filed and numbered. Cir. Ext. S. U. 13th February, 1844.

And such injunctions should be entered as decrees in the statements and reports. Cir. Ext. S. U. 5th March, 1844.

Decree revised under this Section takes the place of the old decree, and in its revised form is open to regular appeal. Cir. Ext. S. U. 3d December, 1844.

Sec. XVIII, Reg. IV, 1802.—A similar power to call for fresh evidence in appeal, is given to the Sudder Udalut by Sec. XVI, Reg. V, of 1802, which is given at length at page 141, as containing provisions in regard to the examination of the witnesses by the Register, which are now applicable only to that Court. These enactments being unrepealed there appears no legal objection to the receipt of fresh evidence by an appellate Court; but in practice it is rarely ever done; such evidence if deemed necessary, is always directed to be taken by the lower Court, to which the suit is remanded for its judgment thereon.

against the decision of any Zillah *Subordinate* Court, *or to the Sudder Udalut against the decision of any Zillah Civil Court*, founded on an award of arbitration, it is to be dismissed with costs ; unless it be fully proved to the satisfaction of the Court, by the oaths *or solemn affirmations* of two credible witnesses, that the arbitrators have been guilty of gross corruption, or partiality, in the cause in which they have made the award.—*Sec.* XXVIII, *Reg.* IV, 1802. —*Sec.* XXII, *Reg.* V, 1802.

The petition of appeal, pleadings, depositions, and exhibits in the *Zillah Civil Courts, or Sudder Udalut* Court, are to be numbered, marked, dated, and signed in the same manner as the complaint, pleadings, depositions, and exhibits, are ordered to be numbered, marked, dated, and signed, *in original suits*. The decrees are to be signed by the Judge or Judges present in Court, when the decrees may be passed ; and *in the case of the Sudder Udalut* attested by the register.—*Sec.* XXIX, *Reg.* IV, 1802.—*Sec.* XXVIII, *Reg.* V, 1802.

Where the *Zillah Civil* Courts may confirm the decree of a *Subordinate* Zillah Court, *or where the Sudder Udalut may confirm that of a Zillah Civil Court*, they are to adjudge interest, at the rate of one per cent per mensem, on all sums receivable by the respondent under the decree passed in his favor, from the date of such decree; and are authorized to punish appeals which may appear to them litigious, by a fine to Government, proportionate to the condition of the party, and the circumstances of the case.— *Sec.* XXXV, *Reg.* IV, 1802.—*Sec.* XII, *Reg.* V, 1802.

CHAPTER IV.

SPECIAL APPEALS.

A special appeal shall lie to the Court of Sudder Udalut at Madras, from all decisions passed on regular appeals in the Civil Courts subordinate to *it*, which shall appear to be inconsistent with some law, or usage having the force of law, or some practice of the Courts, or shall involve some question of law, usage, or practice, upon which there may be reasonable doubts.—*Sec. I, Act III, 1843.*

Application for special appeals shall not be admitted unless they are presented to the proper Court as aforesaid, within the period limited for the presentation of regular appeals.—*Sec. II.—Ibid.*

Every application for a special appeal shall be accompanied by copies of the several decrees previously passed on the case.—*Sec. III.—Ibid.*

Every application for a special appeal duly presented to the

Act III, 1843.—Upon the provisions of this Act the Sudder Udalut, in their proceedings of the 17th December, 1849, remarked " that agreeably to the unqualified terms of Section II, Act III of 1843, no application for special appeal can be legally admitted, unless it be presented within the period limited for the presentation of regular appeals," and that the required copies of the previous decisions *must* be exhibited within the same period. A strict interpretation of the law, which exacts that " every application for special appeal shall be accompanied by copies of the several decrees previously passed on the case" might perhaps justify the conclusion that unless the petition praying for special appeal be so " accompanied," that is unless the petition and the copies of decrees previously passed be simultaneously submitted, it cannot be recognized as a legal application for special appeal, but without intending to rule this point, the Court intimate that the documents in question must be invariably exhibited within the period allowed for the presentation of regular appeals, and that failure to observe this injunction will necessarily involve a rejection of the petition praying for special appeal, even though the latter may have been filed within the limitation above mentioned."

* * * " The provisions of the law are imperative, and confer upon the Sudder Udalut, no authority to admit special appeals, not legally instituted within the period allowed by law for the presentation of regular appeals."

By Circular Letter 14th January, 1850, a notice embodying the above construction is directed to be appended to all appeal decrees.

Sec. II, Act III, 1843.—Applications for admission if accompanied by a correct English translation, will be taken up and disposed of by S. U. before those not so accompanied. Cir. Ext. S. U. 30th June, 1847.

Sec. III, Act III, 1843.—For directions as to mode of procuring these copies see Cls. 8, 9, 11, Sec. VIII, Reg. XV, 1816, at p. 245.

proper Court as aforesaid, shall be heard by a single Judge of the Court in the presence of the special appellant, or his vakeel, or agent; and it shall be competent to the Judge, at his discretion, to call for and peruse any document forming a part of the record of the cause, and to summon the opposite party to answer the application.—*Sec.* IV, *Act* III, 1843.

If it shall appear to the Judge that a special appeal is admissible under this Act, he shall pass an order accordingly, and shall at the same time, reduce the point or points to be determined, to writing in English, in the form of a certificate, which shall be translated into the vernacular language in use in the Court, and the special appeal shall then be brought on the file of the Court to be heard and determined in due course. Provided, that it shall not be necessary to call for or refer to any part of the proceedings, the reading of which is not required for deciding the point or points of law stated in the certificate.—*Sec.* V.—*Ibid.*

If it shall appear to the Judge that a special appeal is not admissible under this Act, he shall reject the petition; and his order so rejecting a petition for a special appeal shall be final.—*Sec.* VI. —*Ibid.*

In every case of special appeal admitted as aforesaid, the Court of Sudder Udalut shall determine the point or points, certified as above enacted, and no other point or points of the case whatever.— *Sec.* VII.—*Ibid.*

Provided that when the special ground of appeal may have been incorrectly or incompletely certified, it shall be competent to the Court to amend the certificate. Provided that such amendment shall relate only to the point or points originally stated in the certificate; and it shall not be lawful for the Court to receive or add any new point or points.—*Sec.* VIII.—*Ibid.*

The existing laws and Regulations of the Presidency of Madras relating to special appeals, shall continue in force so far as they are not inconsistent with the provisions of this Act.—*Sec.* IX.— *Ibid.*

No special or second appeal shall be admitted by the Sudder Udalut, unless upon the face of the decree, or of documents exhibited with it (assuming all the facts of the case as stated in the decree), the judgment shall appear to be inconsistent with some established judicial precedent or with some Regulation in force, or with the Hindoo or Mahomedan laws, in cases which are required to be decided by those laws, or with any other law or usage which may be applicable to the case, or unless the judgment shall involve some point of general interest or importance not before decided by the superior Courts.—*Cl.* 1, *Sec.* IV, *Reg.* XV, 1816.

Petitions of special appeal shall be written upon the stamped paper prescribed in Section XIII, Regulation XIII of 1816, with reference to the value or amount of the suit; the petition shall state distinctly the specific ground or grounds under Clause first of this Section, *or Sec.* I, *Act* III, 1843, on which the special appeal is solicited, and shall be presented either by the party in person, or by an authorized pleader of the Court. In the latter case, the petition shall be signed by the pleader, who shall certify on the back of the petition that he has duly considered the grounds stated for admitting a special appeal under *the above enactments*, and believes them to be well founded and sufficient.—*Cl.* 3.—*Ibid.*

If on a consideration of the circumstances of the case the Court shall see reason for admitting a special appeal on any of the grounds stated in the first Clause of this Section, *or Sec.* I, *Act* III, 1843, the appellant shall be required to furnish the prescribed security, within a reasonable period to be fixed by the Court; when the required security shall have been duly furnished, the Court will admit the special appeal, and proceed *therein as prescribed by Act* III, 1843.—*Cl.* 4.—*Ibid.*

If the *Sudder Udalut* shall not see sufficient reason for admitting the special appeal, and shall in consequence *finally* reject the petition, *under Sec.* VI, *Act* III, 1843, the appellant shall not be entitled to receive back the amount or value of the stamp on which the petition may have been written under Clause third; the Court *is*, however, vested with a discretionary authority in any particular instance of hardship, to refund any portion not exceeding three-fourths of the amount of such stamp duty, to the party who may have paid the same, or to his legal representative.—*Cl.* 5.—*Ibid.*

Cl. 1, Sec. IV, Reg. XV, 1816.—Prior to the passing of Act III of 1843, all proceedings in special appeals were regulated by this Section—and so much thereof remains in force as is not inconsistent with, or superseded by the said Act—*this* Clause might appear to be in the latter predicament, but the S. U. on the 11th October 1850, held that certain of its provisions were still in force, under Sec. IX, Act III, 1843. It is presumed therefore that Sec. I, Act III of 1843, does not necessarily comprehend all the grounds on which a special appeal is admissible at Madras—but that any cause, which can be shown within the compass of this Clause is also ground of special appeal.

CHAPTER V.

All persons desirous of appealing from a judgment of the Court of Sudder Udalut to the *Queen* in Council, are required to present their petition of appeal to the said Court of Sudder Udalut, either in person, or through one of the pleaders of that Court, within six calendar months from the date on which the judgment appealed against may have been passed.—*Sec.* III, *Reg.* VIII, 1818.

No stamp duty or Institution fee, shall be payable in respect of any proceeding in any appeal, or in respect of any paper or copy of any paper necessary for any appeal from any Court of the East India Company to Her Majesty in Council.—*Act* XI, 1339.

Any parties who may be desirous of appealing from the judgments of the Sudder Udalut in suits which may be regularly appealable to *Her Majesty in Council*, shall be at liberty to present their petition of appeal without an authenticated copy of the decree *to the Sudder Udalut.*—*Cl.* 6, *Sec.* VIII, *Reg.* XV, 1816:

The Court of Sudder Udalut may either order the judgment passed by them to be carried into execution, taking sufficient security from the party in whose favor the same may be passed, for the due performance of such order or decree as *Her* Majesty, *her* heirs or successors, shall think fit to make on the appeal; or suspend the execution of their judgment during the appeal, taking the like security in the latter case from the party left in possession of the property adjudged against him : but in all cases security is to be given by appellants to the satisfaction of the Sudder Udalut for the payment of all such costs as the said Court may think likely to be incurred by the appeal, as well as for the performance of such order or judgment as *Her* Majesty, her heirs or successors, may think fit to give thereupon, and after receiving such security the Court of Sudder Udalut are to declare the appeal admitted, and to give notice thereof to the appellant and respondent respectively ; that they may take measures, the one to prosecute, the other to

---

" Appeal to *Queen* in Council."—Prior to the passing of this law appeals from the Sudder Udalut lay to the Governor in Council.

defend, the cause in appeal before Her Majesty in her Privy Council, according to the established mode of proceeding in similar cases.—*Sec.* IV, *Reg.* VIII, 1818.

In all cases wherein the Sudder Udalut may admit an appeal to the *Queen* in Council they are to cause two exact copies to be made of all the proceedings held, and judgments or orders given, in the case appealed, including the whole of the evidence and documents, (translated into English, if the original documents be in any of the country languages;) and are to transmit the same as soon as prepared, under their official seal and the signature of their register, to the Governor in Council, for the purpose of being forwarded by the first secure and separate conveyances to Her Majesty in Council.—*Sec.* V.—*Ibid.*

In all cases of appeals to the Queen in Council from judgments delivered by the *Court of Sudder Udalut at Fort St. George*, the expense of preparing two copies of all the proceedings held, and judgments or orders given in the case appealed, including the whole of the evidence and documents, and of translating into the English language such of the aforesaid proceedings as may have been originally drawn out in the country languages, shall be defrayed by the parties prosecuting the appeal.—*Sec.* I, *Act* II, 1844.

The Court of Sudder Udalut is empowered and required to cause the deposit by the appellant, within the time allowed for furnishing security for costs of appeal, of such a sum as shall be sufficient to cover the expense of making the two aforesaid copies, and when such deposit shall have been made, and not till then, to declare the appeal admitted, and to give notice thereof to the appellant and respondent respectively.—*Sec.* II.—*Ibid.*

The register to the Sudder Udalut shall also, on the application of the appellant or respondent, furnish him or them with one or more copies of the proceedings held, and judgments or orders passed on the case appealed; provided however, that the parties on whose application such copies shall be made, shall respectively agree to defray such expense as may be incurred thereby; but not otherwise. And the register is not to deliver to parties copies prepared for their use, without the previous payment of the expense incurred thereby.—*Sec.* V, *Reg.* VIII, 1818.

Sec. IV, Reg. VIII, 1818.—" Security for costs" the amount to be deposited on that account is fixed by the C. O. S. U. No. 21, at 5,000 Rupees; leaving respondent to move for a higher rate in certain cases.

" Established mode of proceeding."—See rules for appeals promulgated by Her Majesty in Council, 10th April, 1838.

In case the judgment appealed from shall have been passed in pursuance of any local Regulation or Regulations enacted by the Governor in Council, or in case any such Regulation shall have been referred to in the judgments passed by any of the Courts wherein the cause appealed from may have been tried and decided, a copy of such Regulation or Regulations, or an extract therefrom, containing all that has reference to the matter at issue, shall be annexed to the several copies of the proceedings prepared in conformity to the preceding Section, whether for delivery to the parties, or for transmission to Her Majesty in Council.—*Sec.* VI, *Reg.* VIII, 1818.

BOOK V.

CHAPTER I.

ESTATES, ADMINISTRATION TO, WILLS, &c.

In all cases of a Mussulman, or other person subject to the jurisdiction of the Zillah Courts, having, at his death, left a Will and appointed an executor or executors to carry the same into effect, and in which the heir to the deceased may not be a disqualified landholder subject to the superintendence of the Court of wards, the executors so appointed are to take charge of the estate of the deceased, and proceed in the execution of their trust according to the Will of the deceased, and the laws and usages of the country, without any application to the Judge of the Court of Udalut, or any other Officer of Government, for his sanction ; and the Courts of Justice are prohibited to interfere in such cases, except on a regular complaint against the executors for a breach of trust or otherwise ; when they are to take cognizance of such complaint, in common with all others of a civil nature, under the general rule contained in Section V, Regulation II, 1802, and proceed thereupon according to the Regulations; taking the opinion of their law Officers upon any legal exception to the executors, as well as upon the provision to be made for the administration of the estate, in the event of the appointed executor being set aside, and generally upon all points of law that may occur ; with respect to which the Judge is to be guided by the law of the parties, as expounded by his law Officers, subject to any modifications enacted by the Governor in Council in the form prescribed by Regulation I, 1802.—*Cl. 2, Sec.* XVI, *Reg.* III, 1802.

Estates, &c.—Regarding succession of property, and collection of debts due to representatives of deceased persons, not British subjects, see below Acts XIX and XX of 1841. The law on this subject, as laid down in Sec. XVI, Reg. III of 1802, must be considered and studied in connection with those Acts, by which it is modified.

Cl. 2 to 7, Sec. XVI, Reg. III, 1802.—These six Clauses correspond respectively with Sections II to VII, Reg. V of 1799, of the Bengal Code.

Cl. 2 to 7, Sec. XVI, Reg. III, 1802 —" *All cases of a Mussulman, &c.*" in the original " *Hindoo*, Mussulman, or other person" but the enactment was rescinded as regards Hindoos by Sec. II, Reg. V of 1829, because " Wills are instruments unknown to the Hindoo law, and have been made totally repugnant to it" and therefore " the empowering

The rules contained in Clauses 3, 4, 5, 6, and 7, Sec. XVI, Reg. III, 1802, respecting the Estates of Hindoos dying intestate are hereby declared equally applicable to the cases of Hindoos dying and leaving Wills.—*Sec.* III, *Reg.* V, 1829.

Wills left by Hindoos within the territories subject to this Government shall have no legal force whatever, except so far as their contents may be in conformity with the provisions of the Hindoo law, according to the authorities prevalent in the respective provinces under this Presidency.—*Sec.* IV.—*Ibid.*

· In case of a Hindoo *dying either with or without a Will, or of a* Mussulman, or other person subject to the jurisdiction of the Zillah Courts dying intestate, but leaving a son, or other heir, who by the laws of the country may be entitled to succeed to the whole estate of the deceased, such heir if of age and competent to take the possession and management of the estate, or if under age, or incompetent and not under the superintendence of the Court of wards, his guardian or nearest of kin who by special appointment, or by the law and usage of the country, may be authorized to act for him, is not required to apply to the Courts of Justice for permission to take possession of the estate of the deceased, as far as the same can be done without violence ; and the Courts of Justice are restricted from interference in such cases, except a regular complaint be preferred ; when they are to proceed thereupon according to the general Regulations.—*Cl.* 3, *Sec.* XVI, *Reg.* III, 1802.

If there be more heirs than one to the estate of a *Hindoo dying either with or without a Will, or of another* person dying intestate, and they can agree amongst themselves in the appointment of a common manager, they are at liberty to take possession : and the Courts of Justice are restricted from interference, without a regu-

---

" of executors to take charge of the estate and proceed in the execution of their trust ac-
" cording to the Will of the deceased, is at variance with the Hindoo law."
The Hindoo law embodies a complete " statute of distribution" from which a testator cannot deviate—any party entitled in distribution may therefore proceed against all and every one hindering him of his right, whether in fulfilment of the wishes of the deceased or otherwise.

Cl. 3, Sec. XVI, Reg. III, 1802.—An adult *Hindoo*, or the natural and lawful guardian of a minor, would take possession of his father's estate, and administer it according to Hindoo law, notwithstanding his father may have left a Will appointing other executors to give effect to another disposition of his property. A *Mussulman* or *other person* in like circumstances only does so in *accordance* with a Will, or in the event of intestacy.

Cl. 4, Sec. XVI, Reg. III, 1802.—Parties in such a case might proceed under Act XIX of 1841.

Cl. 7, Sec. XVI, Reg. III, 1802.—The Subordinate Judge or Principal Sudder Ameen is to take charge of estates under this Clause and of the property of Europeans dying intestate.—Cir. Ext. S. U. 9th October, 1843.

In taking charge of the estates of European Pensioners, it is necessary that copies of any Wills which may be found to have been left by them, should be forwarded to the Superintendent of Pensions.—Cir. Lr. S. U. 22nd January, 1845.

lar complaint, as in the case of a single heir: but if the right of succession to the estate be disputed between several claimants, one or more of whom may have taken possession, the Judge, on a regular suit being preferred by the party out of possession, shall take good and sufficient security from the party or parties in possession, for his or their compliance with the judgment that may be passed in the suit; or, in default of such security being given, within a reasonable period, may give possession, until the suit may be determined, to the other claimant, or claimants, who may be able to give such security; declaring, at the same time, that such possession is not in any degree to affect the right of property at issue between the parties; but to be considered merely as an administration to the estate, for the benefit of the heirs who may, on investigation, be found entitled to succeed thereto.—*Cl.* 4, *Sec.* XVI, *Reg.* III, 1802.

In the event of none of the claimants, to the estate of a *Hindoo dying with or without a Will, or other* person dying intestate, being able to give the security required by the preceding Clause, and in all cases wherein there may be no person authorized and willing to take charge of the landed estate of a person deceased, the Judge within whose jurisdiction such estate may be situated, (or in which the deceased may have resided, or the principal part of the estate may lie, in the event of its being situated within two or more jurisdictions) is authorized to appoint an administrator for the due care and management of such estate; until, in the former case, the suit depending between the several claimants shall have been determined, or, in the latter case, until the legal heir to the estate, or other person entitled to receive charge thereof as executor, administrator, or otherwise, shall attend and claim the same; when, if the Judge be satisfied that the claim is well founded, or if the same be established after any enquiry that may appear necessary, the administrator appointed by the Court shall deliver over the estate to him, with a full and just account of all receipts and disbursements during the period of his administration.—*Cl.* 5. —*Ibid.*

In all instances of an administrator being appointed under this Section, he is, previous to entering upon the execution of his office, to give good security for the faithful discharge of his trust, in a sum proportionate to the extent thereof; and the Judge appointing him is authorized to fix for him (subject to the approbation of the Court of Sudder Udalut, to whom, a report is to be made in such instances) an adequate personal allowance, to be paid out of the proceeds of the estate, and to be a per centage thereupon, after deducting the expenses of management.—*Cl.* 6, *Sec.* XVI, *Reg.* III, 1802.

The *Subordinate* Judges, *or Principal Sudder Ameens*, on receiving information that any *Hindoo has died either with or without a Will, or other* person within their respective jurisdictions has died intestate, leaving personal property, and that there is no claimant to such property, are to adopt such measures as may be necessary for the temporary care of the property ; and to issue an advertisement, in the current language of the country, requiring the heir of the deceased, or any person entitled to receive charge of his effects, to attend for this purpose ; such advertisement to be published on the spot where the property was found, at the *Court House* of the Zillah, and, if ascertainable, at the dwelling place of the deceased ; or, if the deceased were an European, in the *Fort St. George* Gazette: after which, should any person attend and satisfy the Judge, of his title to the property, or to receive charge thereof as executor, administrator, or otherwise, the same is to be delivered up to him ; on repayment of any necessary expense incurred in the care of it. Should no claim be preferred within the twelve months, next ensuing, an inventory of the property, and report of the circumstances of the case, is to be transmitted to the Governor in Council for his orders.—*Cl.* 7.—*Ibid.*

Clause seventh, Section XVI, Regulation III, A. D. 1802, prescribes rules for the guidance of the Zillah Judges, with respect to the charge of the unclaimed assets of estates of Europeans dying intestate.—It being however enacted in Statute XXXIX, George III, Chapter 79, Section 21, that whenever any British subject shall die intestate, and neither a creditor, nor the next of kin shall apply for letters of administration, the *Administrator General* shall administer to the estate of the deceased, it shall be the duty of the *Subordinate* Judges, *or Principal Sudder Ameens*, whenever any British European subject shall die within the limits of their jurisdictions, and no Will shall be found among the effects of the deceased, to report the circumstance without delay to the *Administrator General*; retaining the property under their charge, until letters of administration shall have been obtained by that Officer, or by some other person from the Supreme Court of Judicature ; when the property is to be delivered over to the person obtaining such letters ; or in the event of a Will being subsequently disco-

vered, to the person who may obtain probate of the Will.—*Sec.*
V, Reg. IV, 1809.

No Will made by any person *whose personal property cannot by
the Law of England pass to their representatives without probate or
letters of administration obtained in one of H. M. Supreme Courts
of Judicature* under the age of twenty-one years shall be valid.—
Sec. V, *Act* XXV, 1838.

Provided also, that no Will made by any married woman shall
be valid, except such a Will as might have been made by a married woman before the passing of this Act.—*Sec.* VI.—*Ibid.*

No Will shall be valid unless it shall be in writing and executed in manner hereinafter mentioned; (that is to say) it shall be
signed at the foot or end thereof by the testator or by some other
person in his presence and by his direction, and such signature
shall be made or acknowledged by the testator in the presence of
two or more witnesses present at the same time, and such wit-

---

Sec. V, Reg. IV, 1809.—"*Administrator General.*"—In the original "Registrar of the
Supreme Court"—but the duty has been transferred to an "Administrator General," an
office created in Bengal by Act VII of 1849, and extended to Madras by Act II of 1850.
As the functions of the Mofussil Judge are limited to the communications, herein prescribed, with the Administrator General, the scope of this work does not seem to require
the insertion of those Acts in this place.

It may be useful however to note that, by Sec. XX of Act VII of 1849, the Administrator General is authorized in the event of any British subject dying intestate, upon his
being satisfied that the effects do not exceed 500 Rupees to grant a certificate to "any
person claiming to be entitled to a principal share of the effects of the deceased," enti-
tling him to collect and receive the same—and receipt of the holder of such certificate is a
full and a sufficient discharge to parties paying debts, or making over property to him.

It must be remarked that the term "European British subject" in this Section does
not include European Officers or Soldiers serving in the army.

The rules and articles of war for their Government, ordered by Her Majesty to have
effect from the 1st day of January, 1850—prescribe—*See Sec.* I, *Articles* 29, 30, *and* 31
—the formation of Regimental Committees for the purpose of taking charge of the
estates of such parties, and give certain directions for their conduct therein, referring
them for fuller guidance to the provisions of Act 12th and 13th, Vict. Cap. 43 : in Sections
LX to LXIV of which, are contained complete instructions on the subject—it is only necessary to mention here, that such committee administers to the estate without probate of
Will or Letters of Administration, so far as regards collection of assets, and payment of
debts : and that the Military Secretary to Government deals in like manner with the sur-
plus, if not exceeding 1,000 Rupees. Particular instructions for the guidance of such
"committees of adjustment" are to be found in G. O. G. 22nd April, 1851. No.
79 of 1851.

Act XXV, 1838.—This enactment is identical with the Act of Parliament, 1st Victoria
Cap. 26 : a few Sections only thereof being omitted as wholly inapplicable to this country. It provides for and settles various points of law arising upon the construction and
effect of Wills—but as the decision of such cases do not fall within the jurisdiction of
the Mofussil Courts—it is unnecessary to insert the Act at length. Such Sections however are given as are most likely to be required by individuals for their own guidance and
to be of general use in the provinces—Sections V to VIII of this Act are identical with
Sections VII to X and Sections IX to XX with Sections XIII to XXIV of the Act of
Parliament.

nesses shall subscribe the Will in the presence of the testator, but no form of attestation shall be necessary.—*Sec.* VII, *Act* XXV, 1838.

No appointment made by Will in exercise of any power, shall be valid, unless the same be executed in manner hereinbefore required ; and every Will executed in manner hereinbefore required shall, so far as respects the execution and attestation thereof, be a valid execution of a power of appointment by Will, notwithstanding that it shall have been expressly required that a Will made in exercise of such power should be executed with some additional or other form of execution or solemnity.—*Sec.* VIII.—*Ibi l.*

Every Will executed in manner hereinbefore required shall be valid without any other publication thereof.—*Sec.* IX.—*Ibid.*

If any person who shall attest the execution of a Will, shall at the time of the execution thereof, or at any time afterwards, be incompetent to be admitted a witness to prove the execution thereof, such Will shall not on that account be invalid.—*Sec.* X.—*Ibid.*

If any person shall attest the execution of any Will, to whom, or to whose wife or husband, any beneficial devise, legacy, estate, interest, gift or appointment of or affecting any real or personal estate (other than and except charges and directions for the payment of any debt or debts) shall be thereby given or made, such devise, legacy, estate, interest, gift or appointment, shall so far only as concerns such person attesting the execution of such Will, or the wife or husband of such person or any person claiming under such person or wife or husband, be utterly null and void, and such person so attesting shall be admitted as a witness to prove the execution, or to prove the validity or invalidity thereof, notwithstanding such devise, legacy, estate, interest, gift or appointment mentioned in such Will.—*Sec.* XI.—*Ibid.*

In case by any Will any real or personal estate shall be charged with any debt or debts, and any creditor, or the wife or husband of any creditor, whose debt is so charged shall attest the execution

---

Sec. VII, Act XXV, 1838 —" No form of attestation" i. e., no particular form ; but it is better and safer to use an attesting Clause, meeting all the requirements of the Act, the following is recommended.

Signed by the said A. B. the testator, as and for his last Will and testament, in the presence of us, present at the same time, who, in his presence, in the presence of each other, and at his request, have hereunto subscribed our names as witnesses.

R. F.
G. H.

of such Will, such creditor, notwithstanding such charge, shall be admitted a witness to prove the execution of such Will, or to prove the validity or invalidity thereof.—*Sec.* XII, *Act* XXV, 1838.

No person shall, on account of his being an executor of a Will, be incompetent to be admitted a witness to prove the execution of such Will, or a witness to prove the validity or invalidity thereof. —*Sec.* XIII.—*Ibid.*

Every Will made by a man or woman shall be revoked by his or her marriage (except a Will made in exercise of a power of appointment, when the real or personal estate thereby appointed would not in default of such appointment pass to his or her heir, executor or administrator, or the person entitled as his or her next of kin, under the statute of distributions.)—*Sec.* XIV.—*Ibid.*

No Will shall be revoked by any presumption of an intention on the ground of an alteration in circumstances.—*Sec.* XV.—*Ibid.*

No Will or Codicil, or any part thereof shall be revoked otherwise than as aforesaid, or by another Will or Codicil executed in manner hereinbefore required, or by some writing declaring an intention to revoke the same, and executed in the manner in which a Will is hereinbefore required to be executed, or by the burning, tearing or otherwise destroying the same by the testator, or by some person in his presence and by his direction, with the intention of revoking the same.—*Sec.* XVI.—*Ibid.*

No obliteration, interlineation or other alteration made in any Will after the execution thereof, shall be valid, or have any effect, except so far as the words or effect of the Will before such alteration shall not be apparent, unless such alteration shall be executed in like manner as hereinbefore is required for the execution of the Will; but the Will, with such alteration as part thereof, shall be deemed to be duly executed, if the signature of the testator and the subscription of the witnesses be made in the margin or some other part of the Will opposite or near to such alteration, or at the foot or end of, or opposite or near to such alteration, or at the foot or end of, or opposite to a memorandum referring to such alteration, and written at the end of some other part of the Will. —*Sec.* XVII.—*Ibid.*

Sec. XVI, Act XXV, 1838.—" Codicil."—This should begin thus, " this is the *first* or *second* Codicil—*as the case may be* to the last Will and testament of me———— which Will is dated the ———— day of ————." The attestation of the Codicil runs the same as for the Will inserting " as and for a Codicil to his last Will and testament."

No Will or Codicil, or any part thereof, which shall be in any manner revoked, shall be revived otherwise than by the re-execution thereof, or by a Codicil executed in a manner hereinbefore required, and shewing an intention to revive the same, and when any Will or Codicil which shall be partly revoked and afterwards wholly revoked, shall be revived, such revival shall not extend to so much thereof as shall have been revoked before the revocation of the whole thereof, unless an intention to the contrary be shewn.—*Sec.* XVIII, *Act* XXV, 1838.

No conveyance or other act made or done subsequently to the execution of a Will of or relating to any real or personal estate therein comprised, except an act by which such Will shall be revoked as aforesaid, shall prevent the operation of the Will with respect to such estate or interest in such real or personal estate as the testator shall have power to dispose of by Will or at the time of his death.—*Sec.* XIX.—*Ibid.*

Every Will shall be construed, with reference to the real estate and personal estate comprised in it, to speak and take effect, as if it had been executed immediately before the death of the testator unless a contrary intention shall appear by the Will.—*Sec.* XX. —*Ibid.*

Notwithstanding any thing in this Act contained, any Soldier being in actual Military Service, or any Mariner or Seaman being at Sea, may dispose of his personal estate as he might have done before the making of this Act.—*Sec.* XXIX.—*Ibid.*

Whenever a person dies leaving property, moveable or immoveable, it shall be lawful for any person claiming a right by succession thereto, or to any portion thereof, to make application to the Judge of the Court of the district where any part of the property is found or situate, for relief, either after actual possession

---

Sec. XXIX, Act XXV, 1838.—The Supreme Court at Madras has ruled that this does not apply to commissioned officers—their Wills *must*, under any circumstances, therefore be executed in accordance with the 7th Section of this Act—considerable doubt was entertained, as to the meaning of the term " Actual Military Service" which was set at rest by a G. O. of the Government of India, No. 213 of 1846, dated 7th August, 1846, issued upon legal opinions taken by the Hon'ble Court of Directors, and declaring it to mean " Service in the field" and that all Wills of Soldiers prepared " during ordinary Service" should be signed and witnessed in the mode prescribed by Sec. VII, Act XXV, 1838.

If the signature be made *for* the testator, by some person in his presence and by his direction, as authorized by the Act, the name of the testator should be signed, and the form of the attestation may run thus—

" The above signature was made by A. B. and was acknowledged by the testator C. D., in the presence of us, present at the same time, who have hereunto subscribed our names as witnesses in the presence of the testator, and in the presence of each other."

has been taken by another person, or when forcible means of seizing possession are apprehended.—*Sec.* I, *Act* XIX, 1841.

It shall be lawful for any agent, relative, or near friend, or for the Court of Wards in cases within their cognizance, in the event of any minor, disqualified, or absent person being entitled by succession to such property as aforesaid, to make the like application for relief.—*Sec.* II.—*Ibid.*

The Judge to whom such application shall be made, shall in the first place enquire by the solemn declaration of the complainant, and by witnesses and documents at his discretion, whether there be strong reasons for believing that the party in possession, or taking forcible means for seizing possession, has no lawful title, and that the applicant, or the person on whose behalf he applies, is really entitled, and is likely to be materially prejudiced if left to the ordinary remedy of a regular suit, and that the application is made bonâ fide.—*Sec.* III.—*Ibid.*

In case the Judge shall be satisfied of the existence of such strong ground of belief, but not otherwise, he shall cite the party complained of, and give notice of vacant or disturbed possession by publication, and after the expiration of a reasonable time shall determine summarily the right to possession (subject to regular suit as hereinafter mentioned) and shall deliver possession accordingly: provided always that the Judge shall have the power to appoint an Officer who shall take an inventory of effects, and seal, or otherwise secure the same, upon being applied to for that purpose, without delay, whether he shall have concluded the enquiry necessary for citing the party complained of, or not.—*Sec.* IV.—*Ibid.*

In case it shall further appear upon such application and examination as aforesaid, that danger is to be apprehended of the misappropriation or waste of the property before the summary suit can be determined, and that the delay in obtaining security from the party in possession, or the insufficiency thereof is likely to expose the party out of possession to considerable risk, provided he be the lawful owner; it shall be lawful for the Judge to appoint one or more Curators with the powers hereinafter next mentioned, whose authority shall continue according to the terms of his or their respective appointments, and in no case beyond the determination of the summary suit and the confirmation or deli-

---

Sec. III, Act XIX, 1841.—" Solemn declaration"—it has been ruled that the complainant must appear in person to make this. *See Rep. Sum. case* 13*th April,* 1842, *p.* 26.

very of possession in consequence thereof: provided always, that in the case of land, the Judge may delegate to the Collector, or to his Officer, the powers of a Curator, and also that every appoint-ment of a Curator in respect of any property be duly published.— *Sec.* V, *Act* XIX, 1841.

The Judge shall have power to authorize such Curator, either to take possession of the property generally, or until security be given by the party in possession, or until inventories of the pro-perty shall have been made, or for any other purpose necessary for securing the property from misappropriation or waste by the party in possession. Provided always that it shall be entirely dis-cretionary with the Judge, whether he shall allow the party in possession to continue in such possession, on giving security, or not; and any continuance in possession shall be subject to such orders as the Judge may issue touching inventories, or the secur-ing of deeds or other effects.—*Sec.* VI.—*Ibid.*

The Judge shall exact from the Curator security for the faithful discharge of his trust, and for rendering satisfactory accounts of the same as hereinafter mentioned, and may authorize him to re-ceive out of the property such remuneration as shall appear rea-sonable, but in no case exceeding five per centum on the personal property, and on the annual profits of the real property. All sur-plus monies realized by the Curator shall be paid into Court, and vested in public securities for the benefit of the persons entitled thereto upon adjudication of the summary suit. Provided always, that although security shall be required from the Curator with all reasonable despatch, and, where it is practicable, shall be taken generally to answer all cases for which the person may be after-wards appointed Curator, yet no delay in the taking of security shall prevent the Judge from immediately investing the Curator with the powers of his office.—*Sec.* VII.—*Ibid.*

Where the estate of the deceased person shall consist wholly or in part of land paying revenue to Government, in all matters regarding the propriety of citing the party in possession, of ap-pointing a Curator, and of nominating individuals to that appoint-ment, the Judge shall demand a report from the Collector, and the Collector is hereby required to furnish the same. In cases of urgency the Judge may proceed, in the first instance, without such report, and he shall not be obliged to act in conformity thereto, but, in case of his acting otherwise than according to such report,

---

Sec. V, Act XIX, 1841.—" Appoint Curator"—for forms of Curator's Engagement, Bond, Sunnud, &c.—*See C. O. S. U.* 13*th November*, 1843, *No.* 66.

he shall immediately forward a statement of his reasons to the Court of Sudder Udalut ; and the Court of Sudder Udalut if they shall be dissatisfied with such reasons, shall direct the Judge to proceed conformably to the report of the Collector.—*Sec.* VIII, *Act* XIX, 1841.

The Curator shall be subject to all orders of the Judge regarding the institution or the defence of suits, and all suits may be instituted or defended in the name of the Curator on behalf of the estate.   Provided that an express authority shall be requisite in the sunnud of the Curators appointment for the collection of debts or rents ; but such express authority shall enable the Curator to give a full acquittance for any sums of money received by virtue thereof.—*Sec.* IX.—*Ibid.*

Pending the custody of the property by the Curator, it shall be lawful for the Judge to make such allowances to parties having a *primâ facie* right thereto, as upon a summary investigation of·the rights and circumstances of the parties interested, he shall consider that necessity may require ; taking, at his discretion, security for the payment thereof with interest, in case the party shall, upon the adjudication of the summary suit, appear not to be entitled thereto.—*Sec.* X.—*Ibid.*

The Curator shall file monthly accounts in abstract, and at the period of every three months, if his administration last so long ; and upon giving up the possession of the property, file a detailed account of his administration to the satisfaction of the Judge.— *Sec.* XI.—*Ibid.*

The accounts of any such Curator as is above described shall be open to the inspection of all parties interested ; and it shall be competent for any such interested party to appoint a separate person to keep a duplicate account of all receipts and payments by such Curator.   And if it be found that the accounts of any such Curator are in arrear, or if they shall be erroneous or incomplete, or if the Curator shall not produce them whenever he shall be ordered to do so by the Judge, he shall be liable to a fine not exceeding one thousand rupees for every such default.—*Sec.* XII.— *Ibid.*

After the Judge of any district shall have appointed any Curator, such appointment shall preclude the Judge of any other district within the same Presidency from appointing any other Curator, provided the first appointment be in respect of the whole of the property of the deceased.   But if the appointment be only in respect of a portion of the property of the deceased, this shall not preclude the appointment within the same Presidency of another

Curator in respect of the residue or any portion thereof: Provided always that no Judge shall appoint a Curator, or entertain a summary suit previously instituted under this Act before another Judge ; and provided further, that if two or more Curators be appointed by different Judges for several parts of an estate, it shall be lawful for the Sudder Udalut to make such order as it shall think fit for the appointment of one Curator for the whole property.—*Sec.* XIII, *Act* XIX, 1841.

This Act shall not be put in force, unless the aforesaid application to the Judge be made within six months of the decease of the proprietor whose property is claimed by right in succession.—*Sec.* XIV.—*Ibid.*

This Act shall not be put in force to contravene any public act of settlement. Neither in cases in which the deceased proprietor shall have given legal directions for the possession of his property after his decease, in the event of minority or otherwise, in opposition to such directions, but, in every such case, so soon as the Judge having jurisdiction over the property of a deceased person, shall be satisfied of the existence of such directions, he shall give effect thereto.—*Sec.* XV.—*Ibid.*

This Act shall not be put in force, for the purpose of disturbing the possession of the Court of Wards of any Presidency ; and in case a minor, or other disqualified person whose property shall be subject to the Court of Wards, shall be the party on whose behalf application is made under this Act, the Judge if he determines to cite the party in possession and also to appoint a Curator, shall invest the Court of Wards with the Curatorship of the estate pending the suit, without taking such security as aforesaid ; and in case the minor or other disqualified person shall, upon the adjudication of the summary suit, appear to be entitled to the property, possession shall be delivered to the Court of Wards.—*Sec.* XVI.—*Ibid.*

Nothing in this Act contained shall be any impediment to the bringing of a regular suit either by the party whose application may have been rejected, before or after citing the party in possession ; or by the party who may have been evicted from the possession under this Act.—*Sec.* XVII.—*Ibid.*

The decision of the Judge upon the summary suit under this Act shall have no other effect than that of settling the actual possession ; but for this purpose it shall be final, not subject to any appeal or order for review.—*Sec.* XVIII.—*Ibid.*

Sec. XVIII, Act XIX, 1841.—The Sudder Udalut in Bengal reversed the *illegal* order of a Judge, in a case in which his *legal* order would have been final and not subject to appeal. *See Rep. Sum. cases* 1*st September,* 1846, *p* 83.

It shall be lawful for the Governments of the respective Presidencies to appoint public Curators for any district or number of districts. And the Judge having jurisdiction shall nominate such public Curator or Curators in all cases where the choice of a Curator is left discretionary with him under the preceding provisions of this Act.—*Sec.* XIX, *Act* XIX, 1841.

Whenever a person dies leaving moveable or immoveable property within the local limits of the jurisdiction of any of Her Majesty's Supreme Courts, and such Court shall be satisfied that danger is to be apprehended of the misappropriation and waste of the property before it can be ascertained who may be legally entitled to the succession to such property, it shall be lawful for the said Court to authorize and enjoin the Ecclesiastical Registrar, or one or more Curators to collect such effects, and hold, or deposit, or invest the same in such manner and place, and upon such security, and subject to such orders and directions as the Court may deem expedient.—*Sec.* XX.—*Ibid.*

No debtor of any deceased *Hindoos, Mahomedans, or other persons not usually designated as British subjects,* shall be compelled in any Court of Law to pay his debt to any person claiming to be entitled to the effects of any deceased person or any part thereof, except on the production of a certificate to be obtained in manner hereinafter mentioned, or of a Probate or Letters of Administration, unless the Court shall be of opinion that payment of the debt is withheld from fraudulent or vexatious motives, and not from any reasonable doubt as to the party entitled.—*Sec.* I, *Act* XX, 1841.

The Zillah or district Court within the jurisdiction of which any part of the property of the deceased may be found, shall have authority to grant a certificate under this Act. The applicant in his petition shall set forth his title. The Judge shall issue notice of application, inviting claimants, and fixing a day for hearing the petition, and upon the appointed day, or as soon after as may be convenient, shall determine the right to the certificate, and grant the same accordingly.—*Sec.* II.—*Ibid.*

The certificate of the district or Zillah Judge shall be conclusive

---

Sec. I, Act XX, 1841.—" Certificate"—for form of this, *See C. O. S. U.* 13*th November,* 1848, *No.* 87, observe that the certificate under this Act is granted specially for facilitating the collection of debts on succession, and does not refer to applications for succession to property. The S. U. have ruled that the application for a certificate cannot be made through a friend or agent, as that for relief may be under Act XIX of 1841.

Sec. II, Act XX, 1841.—Petition must be on stamped paper, as any other petition to the Court; but it has been ruled in Bengal that the certificate should be granted on plain paper.

of the representative title against all debtors to the deceased, and shall afford full indemnity to all debtors paying their debts to the person in whose favor the certificate has been granted.—*Sec.* III, *Act* XX, 1841.

The district or Zillah Judge may take such security as he shall think necessary from any person to whom he shall grant a certificate, for rendering an account of debts received by him, and for indemnity of persons who may be entitled to the whole or any part of the monies received by virtue of such certificate, whose right to recover the same by regular suit against the holder of the certificate is not affected by this Act.—*Sec.* IV.—*Ibid.*

The granting of such certificate may be suspended by an appeal to the Court of Sudder Udalut; which Court may declare the party to whom the certificate should be granted, or may direct such further proceedings for the investigation of the title, as it shall think fit. The Court may also upon petition after a certificate shall have been granted by the district or Zillah Judge, grant a fresh certificate in supersession of the certificate granted by the district or Zillah Judge, and such fresh certificates shall not affect any payments made to the person to whom any former certificate may have been granted, without notice that the same has been superseded, but shall entitle the person named therein to receive all monies that may have been recovered under the first certificate from the person to whom the same may have been granted.—*Sec.* V.—*Ibid.*

Every certificate shall give authority to the person to whom the same is granted, throughout the Presidency within which the same is granted, and no certificate subsequently granted in respect of the same property shall be valid or effectual, except as hereinafter mentioned.—*Sec.* VI.—*Ibid.*

A person certified as aforesaid, may be empowered to receive interest on Government Notes, Dividends, or on shares of any Bank or parts thereof, and to negotiate such securities: He may be also empowered to receive a share of such interest or dividend, or to negotiate a share of such securities. But these powers shall only arise by express words in the certificate.—*Sec.* VII.—*Ibid.*

Where a certificate shall have been granted in cases in which such certificate would be valid but for the previous grant of a certificate, all payments made to the person holding the latter certificate in ignorance of the grant of the previous certificate shall be held good against claims under such previous certificate.—*Sec.* VIII.—*Ibid.*

With regard to the property of deceased Hindoos, Mahomedans, and other persons not usually designated by the term British subjects, no certificate in respect of any such property shall be valid, if made after a Probate or Letters of Administration granted in respect of the same, provided assets belonging to the deceased were at the time of his death within the local jurisdiction of the Court granting the Probate or Letters of Administration.—*Sec.* IX, *Act* XX, 1841.

Where a certificate shall have been granted in cases in which certificate would be valid, but for a Probate or Letters of Administration previously granted, all payments made to the person holding the certificate in ignorance of the previous granting of the Probate or Letters of Administration, shall be held good against claims under the Probate or Letters of Administration so previously granted.—*Sec.* X.—*Ibid.*

No Probate or Letters of Administration shall be valid for the purpose of the recovery of debts, or for the security of debtors, after a certificate granted in respect of the same property for which such Probate or Letters of Administration shall have been granted, provided assets belonging to the deceased were at the time of his death within the jurisdiction of the Court granting such certificate.—*Sec.* XI.—*Ibid.*

Where Probate or Letters of Administration may have been granted, in cases in which such Probate or Letters of Administration would be valid, but for the previous grant of the certificate, all payments made in ignorance of the previous grant of the certificate shall be held good against claims under such previous certificate.—*Sec.* XII.—*Ibid.*

Under Act XIX of 1841, Curators may be invested with certain powers which are conferred on persons obtaining certificates under this Act, and which belong to executors and administrators, it is hereby enacted that Curators appointed under the said Act, shall not exercise any powers which, but for that Act, would lawfully belong to such persons obtaining certificates, executors, or administrators, where certificate, Probate, or Letters of Administration, has been actually obtained; but all persons who may have paid debts or rents to a Curator authorized by a Judge to receive the same shall be indemnified, and the Curator shall be responsible for the payment of the same to the person who has obtained a certificate, the executor, or administrator, as the case may be. —*Sec.* XIII.—*Ibid.*

All Probates and Letters of Administration granted by any of Her Majesty's Courts in cases in which any assets belonging to deceased persons were at the time of their deaths, within the local jurisdiction of the Court granting the Probate or Letters of Administration, shall have the effect of Probate and Letters granted in respect of the property of British subjects, but for the purpose of the recovery of debts only, and the security of debtors paying the same, except so far as in this Act provided.—*Sec.* XIV, *Act* XX, 1841.

Nothing in this Act contained shall be held to extend to the property of any person usually designated as a British subject.— *Sec.* XV.—*Ibid.*

In the case of disputes among persons, claiming to be jointly entitled to be proprietors of any public Securities of the East India Company, as the representatives of any deceased person, the District or Zillah Judge, whenever sufficient cause shall be shown to him, and on the request of any such claimant, may grant a certificate of Administration of the personal Estate of the deceased, so far as concerns the said Securities, according to Act XX of 1841, to such person as shall be from time to time appointed by the Governor of Bengal, and Governors of Madras and Bombay in Council respectively, to act as Trustee under this Act ; and shall specify in such certificate the several persons appearing to him to be such proprietors, and their several shares ; and the said Trustee, by virtue of such certificate, shall be entitled to receive and give discharges for the interest accruing due on such Securities ; and shall account for, and pay the sum to the several persons specified in the certificate to be thereunto entitled, according to the shares therein set forth ; and shall be empowered to act in all other respects concerning the said Securities as Agent for such persons ; and shall be entitled to the same rate of commission upon all such transactions as is allowed to the Government Agent for the time being on the like transactions, as Agent of the public creditors of the East India Company, by any Regulations from time to time made by the Governor General of India in Council : Provided nevertheless that the right of any other person to recover the whole or any part of the monies so paid, by regular suit against all or any of the persons to whom the same have been paid, shall not be affected by this Act.—*Sec.* I, *Act* X, 1851.

If any such disputes among persons claiming to be proprietors of public Securities of the East India Company, are not ended within two years from the date of the certificate of Administration granted by any District or Zillah Judge, the said Trustee may apportion the principal sum of the said Securities rateably among the parties appearing from the aforesaid certificate to be proprietors thereof, and may apply for and receive new Securities from the proper officer appointed to issue the same, in the respective names of the several parties certified to be entitled thereto ; provided that such new Securities shall be issued only according to the rules in use for the regulation and issue of such public Securities ; and the receipt of the said Trustee for such new Securities, by endorsement on the old Securities or otherwise, shall be a legal discharge to the East India Company against the disputing parties claiming to be entitled to the several amounts for which such Securities shall be issued : Provided always that, if the amount of any Securities in dispute or any part thereof, shall not be sufficient to admit of their rateable division according to the rules applicable to the issue of such Securities, the said Trustee may sell, and dispose of the disputed Securities, or such part as shall be necessary under this provision, and apportion the proceeds thereof among the parties entitled to receive the same.—*Sec.* II, *Act* X, 1851.

Every such certificate, granted to the Trustee appointed under this Act, shall be taken to supersede and annul any previous certificate given of a half or any other share in the said personal estate, so far as concerns the said Securities.—*Sec.* III.—*Ibid.*

As regards Residents in Foreign States, out of the jurisdiction of British Courts of Justice, a certificate of Administration to personal estates granted by the British representative accredited to that state, or as regards the residents in any district to which Act XX of 1841, does not extend, such certificate granted by the British officer in that district, holding the highest executive authority, shall have the same effect as regards public Securities of the East India Company, as a certificate granted to a Native subject of Her Majesty under the provisions of Act XX of 1841, as amended by this Act.—*Sec.* IV.—*Ibid.*

This Act shall be construed with and as part of Act XX of 1841.—*Sec.* V.—*Ibid.*

CHAPTER II.

ARBITRATION.

In suits that may be brought before any of the Courts of civil judicature concerning disputed accounts, partnerships, debts, doubtful or contested bargains, or non-performance of contracts, in which the cause of action shall exceed two hundred rupees; the Courts are to recommend the parties to submit the decision of the matters in dispute to arbitration.—*Sec.* II, *Reg.* XXI, 1802.

In all suits for money or personal property, the amount or value of which shall not exceed the sum of two hundred rupees; the Courts are empowered, with the consent of the parties, to refer the suit to the decision of one arbitrator. The parties, or their vakeels, upon agreeing to the reference, shall, on or before the next Court day, mutually choose some one common friend or indifferent person, who may be willing to undertake the arbitration. If the parties shall not agree with respect to the person to be appointed arbitrator; or, if the person nominated by them shall refuse to accept the arbitration, and the parties, or their vakeels,

---

Arbitration.—Village moonsiffs are authorized to try suits for personal property not exceeding 100 rupees, as arbitrators under Sections XXVII and XXVIII, Reg. IV of 1816, which see at page 7, as are district moonsiffs, either for real or personal property, under Sections LVII and LVIII, Reg. VI of 1816, which see at page 35. All suits tried by village or district punchayets, under Regulations V and VII, of 1816, respectively, may be said to be decided by arbitration.

Sec. II, Reg. XXI, 1802.—When parties will not consent to arbitration in such cases, the Courts are subjected to very great difficulties; by Reg. VI of 1832, of the Bengal Code, European Judges are empowered to avail themselves of the assistance of respectable natives in three ways.

1st. By referring a suit, or any point or points therein, to a punchayet.

2nd. By constituting two or more such persons assessors.

3rd. By employing them as a jury; and one great use of these powers is pointed out in the following Circular Order Sudder Dewany Udalut, 4th February 1840.

" Whenever occasion may require the examination and scrutiny of native account " books in any Civil case, the European Judges should as far as possible, call in the aid " of assessors for that purpose; in instances, however, where such a course may be " deemed by them inexpedient, recourse should be had to the agency of Ameens, to be " appointed at the expense of the plaintiff or defendant as the case may be, whose duty, " it would be to inspect the books either at the Mahajanams' house or in Court, as might " seem fitting with reference to the circumstances of the case, and the wishes of the par- " ties; and the latter course should also be followed by the native Courts, who are not " authorized to employ assessors for the purpose stated."

It is to be regretted that this excellent law and practice does not extend to Madras— our Ameens under Sec. XVIII, Reg. II, 1802, can only be employed in matters touching limits and boundaries of houses and lands.

cannot agree in the appointment of another person willing to undertake the arbitration; the Court, with the consent of the parties, is to appoint as arbitrator in the cause, the proprietor of the estate in which the cause of action shall have arisen, or the farmer, if the estate be held in farm of Government, or the cauzy of the pergunnah, or the tahsildar, or any other creditable person; provided that the person so to be nominated, by the Court, be not in any respect interested in the matter in dispute. But if the parties cannot agree in the nomination of an arbitrator; or, if the person whom they may nominate shall refuse to accept the trust, and the parties cannot agree upon the appointment of any other person willing to undertake the arbitration, or shall not consent to the appointment of an arbitrator by the Court, the cause is not to be referred to arbitration; but is to be tried by the Court. In the event of the parties, or their vakeels, agreeing in the nomination of an arbitrator, willing to accept the arbitration, or to an arbitrator being appointed by the Court; the person so chosen or appointed, shall be the arbitrator in the cause. The parties, however, in suits of the nature of those described in this Section, are to have the option of chosing two or more arbitrators to decide their cause, in the same manner as the parties in the causes specified in Section II.—*Sec.* III, *Reg.* XXI, 1802.

The Judges of the Courts are enjoined to afford every encouragement, in their power, to persohs of character and credit to become arbitrators; but they are not to employ any coercive means for that purpose, nor to permit any of their public officers, or private servants, to be arbitrators in a cause. In all cases, the Courts are directed to endeavour, but without using any compulsion, to prevail upon parties to submit their cause to the arbitration of one person, to be mutually agreed upon by them. In every case (with the exception of the cases specified in Section III, which the Courts are empowered to refer to one arbitrator with the consent of the parties) the parties are to choose the arbitrators, who are to decide the matter in dispute, without fee or reward.—*Sec.* IV.—*Ibid.*

Whenever a suit shall be submitted to arbitration, the Court in which it may have been instituted, previous to the arbitrator or arbitrators entering on the arbitration, is to cause the parties to execute arbitration bonds, binding themselves to abide by the award, and agreeing that it be made a decree of the Court. The Court is to fix such time as it may think reasonable, upon a con-

---

Sec. IV, Reg. XXI, 1802.—" *Not to permit, &c.*"—Authorized vakeels of the Court may be arbitrators under Sec. XIX, Reg. XIV of 1816, which see under " vakeels."

sideration of the nature and circumstances of the case, for the delivery of the award, and the period so fixed is to be specified in the bonds. If the cause shall be referred to two or more arbitrators, the following provisions are to be made for completing the award, in the event of the arbitrators not delivering it by the limited time, either from disagreement or other cause. If the decision of the suit shall be referred to two or more arbitrators, whether an odd or an even number, the parties are to have the option, of nominating jointly one person as umpire; or, if the number of arbitrators appointed shall be three or more, being an odd number, to agree that the award given by the majority shall be final; or, to permit the arbitrators to nominate an umpire. The name of the umpire, and the time by which he is to make his award, in the event of the arbitrators not delivering it by the limited period, is to be specified in the bonds, which are to be executed before the arbitrators enter upon the enquiry. In the event of an umpire being appointed, and the arbitrators not agreeing in an award by the limited period, their authority is to cease from such period, and the umpire is to give his award.—*Sec.* V, *Reg.* XXI, 1802.

When a cause shall be referred to arbitration, and the bonds specified in the preceding Section shall have been executed, the Court is to transmit, to the arbitrator or arbitrators, a copy of the bill of complaint; and, by a short writing under the seal of the Court, refer to him or them the matters in dispute between the parties. In the trial of the suit, the arbitrators are to investigate the matters in dispute, by hearing the pleadings of the parties, and examining their respective witnesses and documents. The Court is to issue the same process to the parties, and to the witnesses whom the arbitrator or arbitrators, or the parties, may desire to have examined, to appear before the arbitrator or arbitrators, and to administer such oaths, *or solemn affirmations* to the parties and witnesses, as the Court is authorized to administer, in causes tried before it; and persons not attending in consequence of such process, or making any default, or refusing to give their testimony, or to sign their depositions, or being guilty of any contempt to the arbitrator or arbitrators, during the investigation of the suit, are to be subject to the like disadvantages, penalties, and punishments, by order made by the arbitrator or arbitrators, as they would incur, for the same offences, in suits tried before the Court; provided that the arbitrator or arbitrators shall report the order, with the reason for making it, to the Court, and obtain its

---

Sec. V, Reg. XXI, 1802.—Arbitration bonds are exempted from the " stamp duty on exhibits" by Cl. 2, Sec. XVI, Reg. XIII of 1816, which see under " stamps."

consent thereto ; which is to be signified by the Judge or Judges signing the order. In cases in which an arbitration may be held at a considerable distance from the Court, the Court may grant commissions to the arbitrators to administer the proper oaths, or *solemn affirmations* to witnesses, whom they may be desirous of *so* examining.—*Sec.* VI, *Reg.* XXI, 1802.

In cases where arbitrators, or umpires, shall not have been able to complete the award by the limited time, from want of the necessary evidence, or information, or other good and sufficient cause, the Courts are empowered to allow a further time for the delivery of the award. In the first mentioned case, the Courts are to fix a period, by which the umpire (if an umpire shall have been appointed) shall deliver his final award, in the event of the arbitrators not completing their award by the expiration of such further time.—*Sec.* VII.—*Ibid.*

When a final award in a cause shall be made, either by the arbitrators or the umpire, it is to be submitted to the Court, under the seal and signature of the person or persons by whom it may be made ; together with all the proceedings, depositions, and exhibits in the cause. The Court is to pass a decree conformably to the award ; and the decree is to be carried into execution, in the same manner as other decrees of the Court.—*Sec.* VIII.—*Ibid.*

The award of an arbitrator or arbitrators is not to be set aside, except it be fully proved, to the satisfaction of the Court, by the oaths, or *solemn affirmations* of two credible witnesses, that the arbitrator or arbitrators has, or have been guilty of gross corruption or partiality in the cause, in which the award may be made.—*Sec.* IX.—*Ibid.*

Sec. VI, Reg. XXI, 1802.—" *To administer*," i. e., the Court is to administer—" *may grant commission*" this can be done under Act VII of 1841.

Sec. IX, Reg. XXI, 1802.—The Judge *must* draw a decree in conformity with the award, except corruption be alleged and proved : and by Sec. XXVIII, Reg. IV of 1802, which see under appeals—appeals against such decrees *must* be dismissed with costs unless such corruption can be shown to the appellate Court.

CHAPTER III.

INTEREST AND LOANS.

The Courts of Udalut shall not decree interest on money lent, or on debts, above the rate of twelve per cent per annum.—*Sec.* II, *Reg.* XXXIV, 1802.

Where a lower rate of interest may have been stipulated between parties than twelve per cent per annum, the rate so stipulated, and no other, shall be paid.—*Sec.* III.—*Ibid.*

Where the interest on debts, or on money lent, may have accumulated so as to exceed the principal money; the Courts of Udalut shall not decree a greater sum for interest than the amount of such principal money.—*Sec.* IV.—*Ibid.*

The Courts of Udalut shall not decree to creditors compound interest, arising from intermediate adjustments of accounts; but this rule shall not extend to cases where, accounts between the parties having been adjusted, the former bonds or agreements may have been cancelled, and new bonds or agreements taken for the aggregate amount of the principal, and the legal interest remaining due upon the adjustment consolidated into principal money.—*Sec.* V.—*Ibid.*

Upon all debts, or sums certain, payable at a certain time or otherwise, the Court before which such debts or sums may be recovered, may, if it shall think fit, allow interest to the creditor at a rate not exceeding the current rate of interest from the time when such debts, or sums certain, were payable, if such debts or

----

Sec. II, Reg. XXXIV, 1802.—Interest should be levied on whole sum decreed, costs inclusive, from date of decree to that of execution.—Cir. Ext. S. U. 28th September, 1846.
But not upon interest adjudged.—Cir. Ext. S. U. 26th April, 1847.
These orders not to have retrospective effect.—Cir. Ext. S. U. 26th May, 1847.
A similar prohibition as to rate of interest was made by 13 Geo. III, Cap. 63, Section XXX, which prevents its recovery in Her Majesty's Courts; and not only so but all contracts stipulating for a higher rate are declared to be *there* utterly void: while by evasion of the law in any manner, a forfeiture of thrice the value of the loan is incurred.
Sec. V, Reg. XXXIV, 1802.—A similar restraint is imposed on Officers in charge of Police, and on military puachayets, by Sec. XXXII, Reg. VII, 1832, which see at page 107—and on Courts of Requests, by Sec. IX, Act XI of 1841, which see at page 93.

sums be payable by virtue of some written instrument at a certain time, or if payable otherwise, then from the time when demand of payment shall have been made in writing, so as such demand shall give notice to the debtor that interest will be claimed from the date of such demand until the term of payment; provided that interest shall be payable in all cases in which it is now payable by law.—*Act* XXXII, 1839.

Bonds or other instruments shall from the date of the promulgation of this Regulation be recoverable in the Courts, notwithstanding their stipulating for the payment of a higher rate of interest than that which is at present, or may be hereafter declared to be the legal rate ; provided however, that the Courts shall not allow a higher rate of interest than that prescribed by law on such instruments.—*Sec*. VII, *Reg*. II, 1825.

Where suits may be prosecuted on bonds or instruments given prior to the issue of this Regulation, the Courts of Udalut shall not decree the adjustment of such debts at a higher rate of interest than twelve per centum per annum.—*Sec*. VII, *Reg*. XXXIV, 1802.

In cases of mortgages of real property, in which the mortgagee may have had the usufruct of the mortgaged property, whether he shall have held it in his own possession, or not; the usufruct shall be allowed to the mortgagee in lieu of interest, agreeably to the former custom of the country ; provided it shall have been so stipulated between the parties, and provided such agreement may have been made prior to the issue of this Regulation: in cases of such agreements bearing date subsequently to the issue of this Regulation, the same interest only shall be allowed on such mortgage bonds, as is allowed on other bonds granted on, or subsequently to, such date ; and all such mortgages shall be considered to be virtually, and in effect, cancelled and redeemed, whenever the principal sum of money, with the simple interest due upon it, may have been recovered from the usufruct of the mortgaged property, or otherwise liquidated by the mortgager.—*Sec*. VIII.— *Ibid.*

For the adjustment of accounts in the cases of mortgages above specified, where the mortgagee may have had the usufruct of the mortgaged property, he shall deliver into Court the accounts of his gross receipts from the property mortgaged, and also of his

---

Sec. VII, Reg. II, 1825.—By Sec. V, Reg. XXXIV of 1802, which is superseded by this enactment, bonds given subsequent to 12th July, 1806, bearing higher interest than 12 per cent were declared not recoverable in the Courts.

expenditure for the management or preservation of it; the mortgagee shall swear, or *make solemn affirmation*, that the accounts delivered are true and authentic; the mortgager shall have power to question the accounts, and to state objections on evidence; the Courts of Udalut shall then adjust the accounts accordingly.—*Sec.* IX, *Reg.* XXXIV, 1802.

Nothing in this Regulation shall be construed to extend to respondentia loans, or policies of insurance; the interest on which shall be regulated by the terms of the deeds, and the laws and usages which prevail respecting such transactions.—*Sec.* X.—*Ibid.*

The Magistrates, the Judges of the Zillah Courts, or other Officers, being covenanted servants of the Company, and the Collectors of the revenue and their assistants, are prohibited lending money, directly or indirectly, to any proprietor or farmer of land, dependent talookdar, or under-farmer or ryot, or their sureties; and all such loans as have been made, in opposition to the repeated prohibitions of Government, or which may be hereafter made, and declared not recoverable in any Court of Judicature.—*Sec.* II, *Reg.* XIX, 1802.

Arrears of revenue shall bear an interest of one per cent a month.—*Sec.* VIII, *Reg.* XXVII, 1802.

Sec. X, Reg. XXXIV, 1802.—A " respondentia" loan is one contracted by the owner or commander of a vessel, to enable him to carry on the voyage, and pledging as security the goods and merchandize it contains—as a loan on " Bottomry" is one in which the keel or ' bottom,' meaning the whole ship,—is pledged for the like purpose.

Sec. II, Reg. XIX, 1802.—This prohibits loans by the covenanted servants of the company to landholders or tenants of any description. *All* British subjects are prohibited by 37 Geo. III, Cap. 142, Sec. XXVIII, from lending money, or being concerned in transactions for borrowing money for, or lending money to, the Native Princes in India—under pain of being held guilty of a misdemeanor, and may be proceeded against in the Supreme Court—all bonds, &c., contrary to the said law are null and void to all intents and purposes.

CHAPTER IV.

REGISTRY OF DEEDS.

An office for the registry of deeds shall be established in each Zillah.—*Sec.* II, *Reg.* XVII, 1802.

Subordinate Judges are hereby authorized and required to perform the prescribed duties of *Register of Deeds.—Sec.* IV, *Reg.* XI, 1831.

Principal Sudder Ameens are hereby authorized and required to perform the duties of register of deeds, as prescribed in Regulation XVII, 1802.—*Sec.* V.—*Ibid.*

The register is authorized and required to register memorials of the following deeds.— *Cl.* 1, *Sec.* III, *Reg.* XVII, 1802.

Deeds of sale, or gift, of lands, houses, and other real property. —*Cl.* 2.—*Ibid.*

Deeds of mortgage on land, houses, and other real property; as well as certificates of the discharge of such incumbrances.— *Cl.* 3. —*Ibid.*

Leases and limited assignments of land, houses, and other real property; including, generally, all conveyances used for the temporary transfer of real property.—*Cl.* 4.—*Ibid.*

Wusseatnamahs or Wills.— *Cl.* 5.— *Ibid.*

Written authorities from husbands to their wives to adopt sons, after their (the husbands) demise.— *Cl.* 6.—*Ibid.*

Registry of Deeds.—In regard to registry of alienations and transfers of malguzary and lakaraj lands, in the office of the Collector, consult the following Revenue Regulations.

Sec.	VIII,	Reg. XXV,	1802.
Secs.	II & III,	„ XXVI,	„
„	XIV to XX,	„ XXXI,	„
„	XXIII & XXIV,	„ II,	1803.

Registers of Deeds shall intimate to the Collector of the district, all transfers of property made in their offices, where they have reason to suppose that the property affected by such transfer consists of emoluments attached to hereditary village or other offices in the Revenue and Police departments, as generally of property the alienation or missappropriation of which is illegal under Reg. VI, 1831.—Cir. Ext. S. U, 21st June, 1849.

It shall be left to the option of all persons to register, or not, as they may think proper, any of the descriptions of deeds specified in the preceding Section, that have been executed, or which may be executed, prior to *the 1st January*, 1805. The not registering such deeds shall in no wise operate to the prejudice of the rights of the parties thereto ; which shall remain the same as if this Regulation had never been enacted.— *Sec. IV, Reg.* XVII, 1802.

It shall also be left to the option of all persons to register, or not, as they may think proper, the several description of deeds specified in Clauses Fourth, Fifth, and Sixth, of Section III ; whether executed previous, or subsequent, to the *1st January*, 1805. The not registering of the deeds specified in those three Clauses, shall in no wise operate to the prejudice of the rights of the parties thereto ; which shall remain the same as if this Regulation had never been enacted.—*Sec.* V.—*Ibid.*

Every deed of sale, or gift, of the description specified in Clause Second, Section III, that may be executed on, or after *the 1st January*, 1805, and a memorial of which shall be duly registered according to this Regulation, shall, provided its authenticity be established to the satisfaction of the Court, invalidate any other deed of sale or gift for the same property, executed subsequent to the said date, which may not have been registered ; and whether such second or other deed shall have been executed prior, or subsequent, to the registered deed.— *Cl.* 1, *Sec.* VI.—*Ibid.*

Every deed of mortgage of the description specified in Clause Third, Section III, that may be executed on, or after *the 1st January*, 1805, and a memorial of which shall be duly registered according to this Regulation, provided its authenticity be established to the satisfaction of the Court, shall be satisfied in preference to any other mortgage on the same property, executed subsequent to the said date, which may not have been registered ; and whether such second or other mortgage shall have been executed prior, or subsequent, to the registered mortgage.— *Cl.* 2.—*Ibid.*

Sec. IV & V, Reg. XI, 1831.—" Register of Deeds." By Sec. II, Reg. XVII, 1802. This office was conferred on the Registers of the Zillah Courts, who were specially sworn in ; but the office of Register of the Zillah Court having been abolished, these provisions of Reg. XI of 1831, originally intended to be in force in the absence of the Register, are now the authority under which Sub Judges and Principal Sudder Ameens are, in all Zillahs, Registers of Deeds, as declared by S. U. Cir. Ext. 9th October, 1843, para 6.

Wherever therefore the term ' Register' is employed in this Regulation—it must be understood to mean Subordinate Judge or Principal Sudder Ameen.

Secs. IV, VI, Reg. XVII, 1802.—No penalty or disadvantage was to attend non-registration of any instrument executed prior to 1st January 1805 ; after that, registered deeds of sale, or mortgage, of real property, were privileged as in Sec. VI.

From the 1st day of May 1843, every deed of sale, or gift of lands, houses, or other real property, a memorial of which has been or shall be duly registered according to law, shall, provided its authenticity be established to the satisfaction of the Court, invalidate any other deed of sale, or gift for the same property, which may not have been registered, and whether such second or other deed shall have been executed prior, or subsequent to the registered deed : and from the said day, every deed of mortgage on land, houses, and other real property, as well as certificates of the discharge of such incumbrances, a memorial of which has been or shall be duly registered according to law, and provided its authenticity be established to the satisfaction of the Court, shall be satisfied in preference to any other mortgage on the same property, which may not have been registered, and whether such second or other mortgage shall have been executed prior, or subsequent to the registered mortgage, any knowledge or notice of any such unregistered deed, or certificate, alleged to be had by any party to such registered deed or certificate notwithstanding. Provided always that nothing in this Section contained shall be construed to extend to any deed or certificate made before the said 1st day of May 1843.—*Sec.* II, *Act* XIX, 1843.

No conveyance or other instrument affecting title to land, or any interest in the same, whether made before or after the said 1st day of May 1843, other than such deeds or certificates as aforesaid, are or shall be in any respect void for want of registration, any Act, Regulation or Law, to the contrary notwithstanding.—*Sec.* III.—*Ibid.*

The registry of all deeds shall be made in the register office of the Zillah in which the property affected by them may be situated ; and if the property be situated in the jurisdictions of two or more of the Courts of Udalut, the deeds affecting it shall be registered in the office of each jurisdiction.—*Sec.* VII, *Reg.* XVII, 1802.

Each species of deed shall be registered in a separate book ; each leaf of which shall be paged, and be attested, by the *Suberdinate Judge or Principal Sudder Ameen,* who shall note, in his own hand-writing, on the last page of each book, the number of pages contained in each book, and attest the note with his official signature. No register shall be deemed authentic, excepting such as shall be so paged and attested.—*Cl.* 1, *Sec.* VIII.—*Ibid.*

Sec. II, Act XIX, 1843.—This Section re-enacts Sec. VI, Reg. XVII, 1802, declaring in addition thereto, that a knowledge by the *registering* purchaser or granter of a previous *unregistered* deed in favor of another party, shall not operate to the disadvantage of such purchaser, or prevent his gaining a preference, by registration, for his instrument.

Every deed entered in a register book shall be numbered, and the date of the month and the year, as well as the time of the day, when every deed may be registered, shall be noted in the margin of the register books, which shall be deposited amongst the records of the Courts of Udalut.—*Cl.* 2, *Sec.* VIII, *Reg.* XVII, 1802.

The following forms shall be observed in the registry of deeds. —*Cl.* 1, *Sec.* IX.—*Ibid.*

The person, or persons, executing the deed, or his or their authorized representative, with one or more of the witnesses to the execution of it, shall attend at the register office, and prove by oath, *or solemn affirmation* before the register, the due execution of the deed; upon which, the register shall cause an exact copy of the deed to be entered in the proper register book; and, after having caused it to be carefully compared with the original, shall attest the copy with his signature; and shall also cause the parties, or their authorized representatives in attendance, to subscribe their signatures to the copy, in the presence of two creditable witnesses (whose names shall also be subscribed thereto); and shall then return the original, with a certificate under his signature endorsed thereon, specifying the date, and the time of the day on which such deed shall have been so registered; with references to the book containing the registry thereof, and the page and number, under which the same shall have been entered therein.—*Cl.* 2.— *Ibid.*

The certificate of the register, endorsed agreeably to the forms described in Clause second of the preceding Section, shall be considered in all Courts of Justice to be sufficient evidence of the registry.—*Sec.* X.—*Ibid.*

The register shall, on application being made to him, allow all persons to inspect the register books; as well as grant copies of all deeds registered by him, to persons whom they may concern; and such copies, in the event of the originals being lost, destroyed, or not forthcoming, shall be received as sufficient evidence of such deeds in all Courts of Justice whatever; proof being made, by the subscribing witnesses to the original deed, that the original was duly executed.—*Sec.* XI.—*Ibid.*

If any person or persons shall at any time be suspected, on sufficient grounds for commitment, of counterfeiting or falsifying any entry in any of the register books ordered to be kept, or any certificate such as is directed to be granted, by this Regulation; he or they shall be prosecuted, on the part of Government, in the criminal Court of Judicature; and the several registers shall, as agents for the prosecution, adopt every legal measure in their power for the proof of the crime, and the due execution of the laws against the offender.—*Sec.* XII, *Reg.* XVII, 1802.

Every register shall attend at his office for the dispatch of all business belonging thereto, during certain specified hours each day, between sunrise and sunset (Sundays and holidays excepted); and, after determining the particular hours of such attendance, he shall affix a written notice thereof, in some conspicuous part of his office for general information.—*Sec.* XIII.—*Ibid.*

The register shall be allowed a fee of two rupees for every deed registered by him, to be paid by the party causing the same to be registered, and no more : a fee of one rupee for every copy furnished of a deed registered by him, to be paid by the party applying for such copy, and no more ; and a fee of half a rupee for every search made on an inspection of the register, to be paid by the party inspecting the same, and no more. The register is authorized to refuse the official acts required from him until the fees be paid ; and from such fees he shall provide the necessary native officers to make the entries and copies directed, as well as the requisite stationary.—*Sec.* XIV.— *bid.*

Whenever the Subordinate Judge or Principal Sudder Ameen shall perform the duty of Register of Deeds, the net amount of such fees, after defraying the necessary expense of the establishment, shall be carried to the credit of Government.—*Sec.* VI, *Reg.* XI, 1831.

Sec. XII, Reg. XVII, 1802.—Such offences are punishable in the Criminal Courts under Sec. II, Reg. VIII, 1829.

Sec. XIII, Reg. XVII, 1802.—This is obsolete in practice—applications for Registry are attended to at any hour, whenever the Courts are open.

Sec. XIV, Reg. XVII, 1802.—Under Sec. VI, Reg. XI, 1831. The surplus of the fees is now carried to the credit of Government ; it is usual for the ' Register' to allot such portion thereof as he may consider an adequate remuneration, to the writer he employs to keep the book—and he uses stationary from his public store.

All contracts between Government and private individuals are to be registered free of the usual fee.—Cir. Lt. S. U. 16th May, 1846.

CHAPTER V.

RECORDS.

A native keeper of the records shall be appointed to keep the *Civil* records in each *Subordinate and Civil Court,* and in the Sudder Udalut.—*Sec.* II, *Reg.* XIII, 1802.

The keepers of the records are to keep a register in the language of the district in which the Court may be situated, of all the proceedings, documents, and other records belonging to the Courts to which they may respectively be attached, in a book each leaf of which shall be attested by the official signature of the *Judge, or Register in the case of the Sudder Udalut,* and on the last leaf of which they shall specify in their own hand-writing the number of pages contained in the book.—*Sec.* IV.—*Ibid.*

The keepers of the records are to endorse upon the back of every paper or document which they may enter in the register, the number of the page in which it may be registered, and the endorsement is to be attested with *their* official signature.—*Sec.* V. —*Ibid.*

It shall be the duty of the keepers of the records to see that the records of the Court are not destroyed by insects, damp, or otherwise, and that they are not removed without the orders of the Court.—*Sec.* VI.—*Ibid.*

If any records entered in the register shall be destroyed, in consequence of the neglect, or any omission of the keepers of the records, or if any such records shall not be forthcoming, and they

Records.—Parties stealing or injuring records are punishable by the criminal Courts under Regulation VIII of 1829.

The revenue records of each Zillah are kept by the Collectors, under Regulation XXIII of 1802,—which is, in its provisions, nearly identical with Regulation XVII of 1802. Collectors have also certain powers of punishing criminally, injuries to their records under Act XXXVI of 1837.

Sec. II, Reg. XIII, 1802.—The Civil Judge should exercise his discretion in transferring to the custody of the Subordinate Judge such portions only, of the records of the late Zillah Court as that officer may appear to require.—S. U. 6th November, 1843.

Record of appeal suit decided in Subordinate Court to remain there.—Cir. Ext. S. U. 5th March, 1844, para 2.

shall not be able to give a satisfactory account of them, they shall
be liable to dismission from their offices.—*Sec.* VII, *Reg.* XIII,
1802.

The keepers of the records are to be careful to attend to any
rules or orders, respecting the duties of their office, that may be
prescribed to them by any established Regulation, and also to any
directions that may be given to them by the Court to which they
may be attached, for the better keeping, preserving, or registering
the records.—*Sec.* VIII.—*Ibid.*

The Courts of Udalut established in the several Zillahs are to
keep a book in which the daily proceedings in each cause, and
every order or Act of the Court, are to be minuted in the language of the district in which the Court may be held ; and attested
with the signature of the Judge.   The plaint, answer, reply, and
rejoinder of the parties, and every deposition, exhibit, and paper
whatever, read, and filed in each cause, is to be minuted and referred to in this book, by marks or numbers, corresponding to
marks or numbers to be endorsed on each document when it may
be read in the cause.—*Sec.* IX.—*Ibid.*

The Sudder Udalut is to keep a book of daily proceedings, and
a separate record of the appeals or causes which may be decided
by them, in the same manner as is prescribed to the *Zillah Courts
in Sec. IX, with this difference that the entries in the book are to
be attested by the Register instead of the Judges of the Court.*—*Sec.*
XV.—*Ibid.*

Sec. IX, Reg. XIII, 1802.—This is called the " Diary"—and by Section XII, which
under the new system merges in this, the Provincial Courts were directed to keep similar
diaries.
   1st.   Each page of the Court Diary is to be numbered and signed with the initials of
the Judge.
   2nd.   Every interpolation, erasure or correction in the diaries, pleadings, exhibits, depositions, or other papers filed of record, shall be placed between brackets and signed as
above.
   3rd.   The total number of such corrections, &c., shall be noted at the foot of every
paper received or filed, and similarly verified.—Cir. Ext. S. U. 2nd February, 1850.

CHAPTER VI.

TREASURE TROVE.

Whenever any hidden treasure, consisting of gold or silver coin, or bullion, or of precious stones, or other valuable property, may be found buried in the earth, or otherwise concealed, within any part of the territories subject to this Presidency ; and, after due notification, the owner thereof may not be discoverable ; such hidden treasure shall become the property of the person or persons who may have found the same ; provided it shall not exceed in amount or value, tHe sum of one lac of rupees; and provided the finder or finders shall have conformed to the rules prescribed in this Regulation.—*Sec.* II, *Reg.* XI, 1832.

Whenever any person may find hidden treasure, of the description stated in the foregoing Section, he shall give immediate notice thereof to the Subordinate Judge or *Principal Sudder Ameen*, within whose jurisdiction the treasure may have been found ; and shall, at the same time, deposit the treasure in the Court, with an exact inventory thereof.—*Sec.* III.—*Ibid.*

The Subordinate Judge or Principal Sudder Ameen, receiving a deposit as above directed, shall return a receipt for the treasure deposited, after causing the same to be carefully compared with the inventory ; and shall issue a public notification, in the current languages of the country, to be published and affixed in his own Court House, and in the Cutcherry of the Collector of the district, requiring all persons who may have any claim of right to the treasure in deposit, to attend in person, or by vakeel, and prove their title thereto, within six months from the date of the notice. —*Sec.* IV.—*Ibid.*

It shall be the duty of the Collectors of land revenue, acting under the instructions of the Board of Revenue, to bring forward and to support, in conformity with the foregoing provision, any

---

Sec. II, Reg. XI, 1832.—" *Principal Sudder Ameen,*" the provisions of this Reg. wcre extended to Principal Sudder Ameens by Act XII of 1838, which see under Principal Sudder Ameen, at page 117.

claim of right which Government may appear to possess to such treasure. In the event of any claim of right being preferred, either on the part of individuals or of Government, pursuant to the prescribed notification, the Judge shall institute a summary inquiry into the claim preferred ; and if the title of Government, or other person, so claiming the treasure in deposit, or any part thereof, be clearly established, he shall adjudge the same accordingly ; subject to reimbursement of all expense incurred by the finder of the treasure, as well as to such compensation for the discovery of it as may, in each case appear just and reasonable.—*Sec.* V, *Reg.* XI, 1832.

If no claim of right be preferred, either by Government, or by any individuals, within the period limited by the notification directed in Section IV of this Regulation, or if the claim or claims so preferred shall not, on a summary inquiry, appear to be well founded ; and the amount or value of the hidden treasure found at the same time, or in the same place, shall not exceed one lac of rupees ; the Subordinate Judge or Principal Sudder Ameen shall adjudge the same to the person or persons who may have discovered the treasure, and deposited it in the Court, as required by Section II, subject only to the actual expense which may have been incurred in adopting the measures prescribed by this Regulation.—*Sec.* VI.—*Ibid.*

If the amount or value of any hidden treasure found at the same time or in the same place, shall exceed one lac of rupees, and no claim of right thereto be established, judgment shall be given according to the preceding Section in favor of the person or persons who may have discovered and deposited the treasure, to the amount of one lac of rupees ; and the excess above that sum shall be declared at the disposal of Government.—*Sec.* VII.—*Ibid.*

If any person discovering hidden treasure of the description specified in Section II of this Regulation, shall not, within one month after finding the same, give notice to the Subordinate Judge or Principal Sudder Ameen, in conformity with Section III, and make the deposit thereby required, he shall be considered to have forfeited all right and title to the treasure ; as well as all claim to a reimbursement of expense, compensation or reward, under the provisions of this Regulation, and the treasure so clandestinely withheld from public investigation, shall, on a summary suit, by any subsequent claimant of right, and proof of a just title thereto, be adjudged to the legal owner, with interest and costs ; or if no private claim be established, shall, on the application of the vakeel of Government, under instructions from the Board of Revenue, be liable to confiscation to Government.—*Sec.* VIII, *Reg.* XI, 1832.

The summary decisions of the Subordinate Judges or Principal Sudder Ameens, which may be passed under this Regulation, shall be open to a summary appeal to the Civil Courts, under the general rules in force relative to summary appeals.—*Sec.* IX.— *Ibid.*

The decision of the Judges of the *Civil Courts* on such appeals, shall be final; unless the Court of Sudder Udalut should, on the face of the decree, or on inspection of any documents exhibited with it, see just and sufficient ground for admitting a second summary appeal to that Court; in which case only, such further appeal may be admitted, and proceeded upon, under the general rules in force for summary appeals.—*Sec.* X.—*Ibid.*

CHAPTER VII.

STAMPS.

In modification of such part of Section II, Regulation XIII of 1816, as rescinds Regulation VIII of 1808, and Regulation II of 1813, it is hereby enacted that the provisions of those Regulations, shall still be applied to all deeds and instruments executed between the 1st of January 1809 and the 12th of July 1817.—*Sec.* III, *Reg.* VI, 1817.

Every bond, promissory note, bill of exchange, letter of credit, or other obligation for the payment of money, every receipt, or acquittance, whereby any sum of money or demand shall be acknowledged to have been paid, received, liquidated, discharged, accounted for, or in any manner satisfied, every deed of gift, sale, or other transfer of property, real or personal, *save a Will*—*Sec.* IV, *Reg.* II, 1825—every lease, deed of mortgage, or other limited assignment of land, every deed of contract, marriage settlement, partnership, agreement, security, or engagement for a sum of money, or for property exceeding the value of *sixty-four* rupees—*Sec.* IV, *Reg.* II, 1825—which may be executed within the provinces subject to the Presidency of Fort St. George, shall be written on paper (or some other material) impressed with the Government stamp, the value of which stamp shall be regulated as follows:

TABLE.

1. If the bond or other instrument shall be for a sum exceeding *sixty-four* rupees, or if the value of the property transferred, or otherwise affected by it shall exceed *sixty-four* rupees and not

---

Sec. III, Reg. VI, 1817.—Prior to the enactment of Regulation XIII, 1816. Stamp duty on instruments was levied under the provisions of Regulations VIII of 1808, and II of 1813; the operation of Regulation XIII of 1816, was deferred by Regulation VI of 1817, to the 12th July, 1817, when therefore an instrument bearing date between 1st January, 1809, and 12th July, 1817, is produced, reference must be had to them to determine the value of the stamp, they are not inserted at length here as being seldom required, and at hand in every office.

Prior to the passing of Regulation II of 1825, unstamped instruments, executed subsequent to 12th July, 1817, were absolutely inadmissible in a Court of Justice, under Section IX, Regulation XIII of 1816, which was then rescinded—Instruments executed prior to 12th July, 1817, were never so barred, they were especially declared not to be so by Section II, Regulation VI, 1817.

exceed 125 rupees, the deed shall be executed on stamped, paper of the value of four annas.

2. If above 125 rupees and not exceeding 250 rupees—eight annas.

3. If above 250 rupees and not exceeding 500 rupees—one rupee.

4. If above 500 rupees and not exceeding 1,000 rupees—two rupees.

5. If above 1,000 rupees and not exceeding 2,000 rupees—four rupees.

6. If above 2,000 rupees and not exceeding 5,000 rupees—eight rupees.

7. If above 5,000 rupees and not exceeding 10,000 rupees—sixteen rupees.

8. If above 10,000 rupees and not exceeding 20,000 rupees—thirty-two rupees.

9. If above 20,000 rupees and not exceeding 50,000 rupees—fifty rupees.

10. If above 50,000 rupees and not exceeding 100,000 rupees—one hundred rupees.

11. If above 100,000 rupees—one hundred and fifty rupees.—*Sec.* XI, *Reg.* XIII, 1816.

Sec. XI, Reg. XIII, 1816.—The preceding Sections of this Regulation constitute the office of superintendent of stamps, and prescribe rules for his guidance, in their preparation and sale, through the agency of the Collectors; which it does not appear necessary to insert here—it may suffice to note that by Clause 2, Section V, he is required to prepare stamped paper of *European* manufacture, to be used for the copies of the proceedings and judgments of the Court of Sudder Udalut, as also for all copies of decrees in regular or summary suits granted to the parties, by Sudder Ameens, Principal Sudder Ameens, Subordinate, or Civil Judges, or Sudder Udalut—and to affix the required stamp at the instance of an individual on Parchment, Vellum, or other material on which he may desire to prepare an instrument; which is then to be received in evidence by the Courts as if executed on common paper according to the ordinary practice of the stamp office ; and by Clause 3, Section X, Collectors, their assistants, or other European Officers authorized to dispose of stamped paper, are required, previously to issuing such paper to their native agent for sale, or to disposing of it themselves, to endorse their official signatures in writing upon each paper; and the Courts are directed not to admit or file any stamped paper unless so authenticated.

Prior to the modification of this Section by Section IV, Regulation II of 1825, all instruments above 16 Rs. were required by it to be on stamp, as also Wills : and C. O. S. U., 28th January, 1828, declared the modification not to have retrospective effect in regard to Wills, or to Documents between 16 and 64 Rupees, executed between 1st January, 1809, and 15th April, 1825.

Instruments specified in Section XI, Regulation XIII of 1816, must invariably be produced on the prescribed stamp in the Courts of the district moonsiffs.—Cir. Lr. S. U. 15th June, 1849.

Bill of sale for property sold in execution of decree should be on stamp according to value of property.—Cir. Ext. S. U. 16th April, 1850.

Any bond, or instrument, of the nature specified in Sec. XI, *Reg.*
XIII *of* 1816, which may not have been written on paper, or
other material, bearing the prescribed stamp, shall not be admitted in evidence, or otherwise received, or filed in any Court of
Judicature, until the party presenting the same, shall have paid a
penalty equal to ten times the amount of the stamp duty, which
would have been payable on such bond or other instrument, in
the first instance, if it had been prepared on paper, or other material, bearing the prescribed stamp.—*Cl.* 1, *Sec.* III, *Reg.* II, 1825.

When instruments may be admitted, on payment of the penalty
prescribed in Clause first of this Section, in any Court of Judicature, the payment of the penalty shall be certified upon the instrument by the Court; and such certificate shall render the instrument ever after admissible, in the same manner as if it had been
duly stamped.— *Cl.* 2.—*Ibid.*

The certificate mentioned in Clause second of this Section, shall
specify the date and place of the payment of the penalty, the
amount, and the name of the party by whom it may be paid: and
a corresponding entry of such payments shall be made by the Court
in a book to be kept for that purpose.— *Cl.* 3.—*Ibid.*

In cases where the penalty prescribed in Clause first of this Section, may be levied by a village, or district punchayet, the amount
shall be remitted to the district moonsiff, with a memorandum of
the date and place of payment and the name of the party by
whom it may be made.— *Cl.* 4.—*Ibid.*

District moonsiffs shall remit the sums received by them under
the provisions of Clause fourth, and also the amount of penalties
levied by themselves under the provisions of Clause first of this
Section, to the Zillah *Civil* Judge, accompanied by a memorandum of the date and place of payment, and the name of the party
by whom it may be made; corresponding entries of which payment shall be made by the Judge in a book specially kept for that
purpose.—*Cl.* 5.—*Ibid.*

If on the presentation of any instrument bearing the prescribed
certificate of payment of the penalty, the Court see reason to believe the certificate to be forged, a reference shall be made to the

---

Cl. 1, Sec. III, Reg. II, 1825.—This applies to instruments executed prior to the date
of the Regulation—C. O. S. U. 24th January, 1828.

An instrument written on a stamp below the prescribed amount is to be held as unstamped and pay the full penalty.—C. O. S. U. 17th January, 1832.

If higher than necessary, admissible.—C. O. S. U. 24th January, 1828.

register of payments kept by the *Subordinate or Civil* Court, for the purpose of ascertaining whether the penalty was paid according to the tenor of the certificate.—*Cl.* 6, *Sec.* III, *Reg.* II, 1825.

To prevent misconstruction, it is hereby declared, that every lease and its counterpart (pottah and caboolyet) or other engagement contracted between landlord and tenant, and every receipt or other acknowledgment for the payment of rent, exceeding *sixty-four* rupees, is required to be written on paper or other material bearing the prescribed stamp, supposing that such lease, receipt, or other instrument, relate to lands held exempt from the payment of revenue to Government, but that instruments of the correspondent descriptions, which have relation to lands subject to the payment of revenue to Government, need not be written on stamps.—*Cl.* 1, *Sec.* XII, *Reg.* XIII, 1816.

All authenticated copies of the documents specified in the preceding Section which may be prepared as legal vouchers by a cazee, mooftee, or other authorized person, shall be written on stamped paper, or cadjan, according to the rates prescribed for the originals of such deeds.—*Cl.* 2.—*Ibid.*

Security bonds for appearance (hazer zaminee), security bonds for the payment of eventual costs of suit, as well as all other security bonds not being for a specific amount, and all deeds of contract, partnership, or agreement, and engagements of whatever nature, which may not relate to a specific sum of money or to a specific value, so as to make it practicable to apply to them the table of rates stated in the preceding Section, are required to be written on stamped paper or stamped cadjan of the value of one rupee.—*Cl.* 3.—*Ibid.*

Engagements to subrent abkarry privileges and farms, as well as receipts and acknowledgments between renters and subrenters, are not required to be written on stamped paper; but shall be exempt from stamp duty in the same manner as instruments of correspondent descriptions which have relation to lands subject to the payment of revenue to Government are exempt therefrom under, Cl. 1, Sec. XII, Reg. XIII of 1816.—*Cl.* 2, *Sec.* IX, *Reg.* I, 1820.

Cl. 2, Sec. XII, Reg. XIII, 1816.—For " *legal vouchers*" but if for use or reference may be given on eight annas stamp, and when an original document is no longer required it may be returned to the party who filed it; a copy being retained, if requisite, on unstamped paper.—*See C. O. S. U. 8th January*, 1829. District moonsiffs cannot grant authenticated copies.—*C. O. S. U. 30th May*, 1829.

Cl. 3, Sec. XII, Reg. XIII, 1816.—The S. U. have ruled that security bonds executed by the sureties of paupers need not be on stamp.

On the institution of civil actions, on summonses, and on exhibits, the following stamp duties shall be levied.

TABLE.

1. In original regular suits instituted in any Court of Judicature, and in appeals regular or special, preferred from the judgments of any such Court to a superior Court—*unless by Paupers, Sec. VII, Reg. VII, 1818*—if the amount or value of the property claimed shall not exceed sixteen rupees, the plaint or petition shall be written on paper of one rupee.

2. If above 16 rupees and not exceeding 32 rupees—two rupees.

3. If above 32 rupees and not exceeding 64 rupees—four rupees.

4. If above 64 rupees and not exceeding 150 rupees—eight rupees.

5. If above 150 rupees and not exceeding 300 rupees—sixteen rupees.

6. If above 300 rupees and not exceeding 800 rupees—thirty-two rupees.

7. If above 800 rupees and not exceeding 1,600 rupees—fifty rupees.

8. If above 1,600 rupees and not exceeding 3,000 rupees—one hundred rupees.

9. If above 3,000 rupees and not exceeding 5,000 rupees—one hundred and fifty rupees.

10. If above 5,000 rupees and not exceeding 10,000 rupees—two hundred and fifty rupees.

11. If above 10,000 rupees and not exceeding 15,000 rupees—three hundred and fifty rupees.

12. If above 15,000 rupees and not exceeding 25,000 rupees—five hundred rupees.

13. If above 25,000 rupees and not exceeding 50,000 rupees—seven hundred and fifty rupees.

14. If above 50,000 rupees and not exceeding 100,000 rupees—one thousand rupees.

15. If above 100,000 rupees—two thousand rupees.—*Sec. XIII, Reg. XIII, 1816.*

Sec. XIII, Reg. XIII, 1816.—" Appeal" costs of suit not to be included in valuing appeal—C. O. S. U. 15th February, 1828, and in respect of appeal stamps.—See C. O. S. U. 5th November, 1829. B.

In suits for land paying revenue to Government, the value of the property shall be assumed at the amount of the annual produce of the land, to be estimated according to the rule prescribed in Section III, Regulation III, 1802.—*Cl.* 1, *Sec.* XIV, *Reg.* XIII, 1816.

In suits for land held exempt from the payment of the public revenue to Government, the value of the property shall be assumed at ten times the amount of the annual produce of the land, to be estimated as directed in Section III, Regulation III, 1802.— *Cl.* 2.—*Ibid.*

· In suits for houses, gardens, tanks, or other property, real or personal, excepting the two descriptions of lands mentioned in the two preceding Clauses, and in actions for the recovery of damages in matters relating to marriage, caste, or any personal injury, the value shall be estimated according to the rule contained in Section III, Regulation III, 1802.—*Cl.* 3.—*Ibid.*

No exhibit in any original regular suit, or in any appeal regular or special, shall be filed in any Court of Judicature, without an application praying the admission of the exhibit, which application shall be written on stamped paper, as follows:

In the Court of Sudder Ameen, on paper of the value of four annas.

In the *Subordinate* Courts, on paper of the value of one rupee.

In the *Civil* Courts, and in the Sudder Udalut, on paper of the value of two rupees.—*Cl.* 1, *Sec.* XVI.—*Ibid.*

Vakalutnamahs and mokhtarnamahs, arbitration bonds, security bonds for appearance, as well as security bonds for the eventual payment of costs, or for the performance of a decree, or for staying or enforcing the execution of a decree which may be executed in any original suit or appeal, shall not be liable to the stamp duty on exhibits.—*Cl.* 2.—*Ibid.*

In like manner no summons shall be issued for the attendance of any witness in any original regular suit, or in any appeal regu-

---

Sec. XIV, Reg. XIII, 1816.—" *Rule in Sec. III, Reg. III,* 1802."—See it at p. 167.
Sec. XVI, Reg. XIII, 1816.—" *In the Civil Courts.*"—The stamped papers used in the Zillah Civil Courts must be the same as were required by Regulation XIII of 1816, to be used in the late Provincial Courts—excepting in cases where the Judges of the newly constituted Zillah Courts may exercise the jurisdiction of a Subordinate Court as contemplated in Sec. XLV, Act VII, 1843, when of course the value of the stamps will be regulated by the nature of the functions they may be called on to discharge.—Cir. Ext. S. U. 25th September, 1843.

lar or special, without an application praying the attendance of such person, which application shall be written on stamped paper of the value specified in the preceding Section, according to the Court in which it may be delivered and recorded.—*Sec.* XVII, *Reg.* XIII, 1816.

In lieu of filing a separate application for the admission of each exhibit, and the attendance of each witness, it shall be sufficient to file one or more applications or lists, including any number of exhibits desired to be filed, and the names of any number of witnesses desired to be summoned; provided that such applications or lists be written on one, two, or more sheets or rolls of stamped paper, the total value of which shall correspond in amount with that of the stamped paper which would have been requisite had the application for each exhibit or witness been written on separate stamped paper, under the rules contained in Sections XVI and XVII of this Regulation.—*Sec.* XVIII.—*Ibid.*

Every answer, reply and rejoinder, every supplement, razeena-mah, or petition which shall hereafter be filed in any original regular suit, or in any appeal regular or special, shall be written on stamped paper, as follows:

In the Court of the Sudder Ameen, on paper of the value of four annas.

In the *Subordinate* Courts, on paper of the value of one rupee.

In the *Civil* Courts and in the Sudder Udalut, on paper of the value of four rupees.—*Sec.* XIX.—*Ibid.*

In all suits which in respect to value are cognizable by a Sudder Ameen, the same stamps shall be sufficient in any other Court, as would have been sufficient in the Court of a Sudder Ameen.—*Sec.* V, *Act* IX, 1844.

In all original summary suits and summary appeals authorized by the Regulations, the plaint, petition or application, the answer and other pleadings; all miscellaneous petitions and applications which may be presented to the different authorities in the judicial

---

Sec. XIX, Reg. XIII, 1816.—" In the Civil Courts."—See note on Sec. XVI. According to Government notification 23d January 1846, *Fort St. George Gazette, p.* 111, the " *answer*" in appeal suits filed in the Civil, but referred to the Subordinate Courts, should be on one rupee paper.

Sec. V, Act IX, 1844.—Parties instituting in a Superior Court suits within the competency of a Sudder Ameen may use the reduced stamps which might have been used in the Court of the Sudder Ameen.—Cir. Ext. S. U. 8th July, 1844.

department, and all mokhtarnamahs and vakalutnamahs, shall be
written on stamped paper as follows :

If preferred to a Sudder Ameen, on paper of four annas.

If preferred to a *Subordinate Court*, on paper of eight annas.

If preferred to a *Civil* Court, on paper of one rupee.

If preferred to the Court of Sudder Udalut on paper of two rupees.—*Sec.* XX, *Reg.* XIII, 1816.

All applications made by the Collectors, or the assistant Collectors, or by the Board of Revenue, to the Courts of Judicature, for
the apprehension or confinement of defaulters, or on any other subject relating to the public revenue, may be written upon common
paper without a stamp. This rule, however, shall not be considered applicable to any regular suit in which the Board of Revenue,
a Collector, or an assistant Collector, may be a party, either on
their own account as individuals, or on the part of Government.—
Sec. XXI.—*Ibid.*

No copy of any paper shall be authenticated by any public officer, or received as evidence in any Court of Judicature, unless
transcribed on stamped paper, according to the following rates, viz.

Copies of decrees passed by the Sudder Ameens, shall be written
on paper of the value of eight annas.

Copies of decrees passed by *Subordinate Judges,* and by Principal Sudder Ameens, shall be written on paper of the value of one
rupee.

Copies of decrees passed by the *Civil* Courts, shall be written
on paper of the value of two rupees.

Copies of decrees passed by the Court of Sudder Udalut, shall
be written on paper of the value of four rupees.

Authenticated copies of revenue and judicial proceedings, authenticated copies of accounts, statements, reports, or other documents which individuals may require for use or reference, shall be
written on paper of the value of eight annas.—*Cl.* 1, *Sec.* XXII.
—*Ibid.*

Copies of decrees which may be prepared by the Courts abovementioned, to remain with their own records, shall be written on
unstamped paper of European manufacture, of the same size and
description as that which may be stamped for the copies of decrees
to be delivered to the parties.—*Cl.* 2.—*Ibid.*

Copies of proceedings and orders, accounts, statements or other papers made for records of Court, or for transmission to other Courts or public offices, may be written as heretofore on unstamped paper, except in cases in which it may be otherwise specifically provided for by the Regulations.—*Cl.* 3, *Sec.* XXII, *Reg.* XIII, 1816.

All pleadings, petitions and applications, all deeds, documents and other papers, whether originals or copies, which are required by the Regulations to be written on stamped paper, are to be written in a fair, legible manner, and as they have been hitherto usually prepared, as well with regard to the size of the writing, the space between the words, and the number of lines in each page, as to all other matters regarding their engrossment.—*Cl.* 1, *Sec.* XXIII.—*Ibid.*

If the subject matter of any plaint, or petition of appeal cannot, under the rule contained in the preceding Clause, be conveniently comprised in a single sheet or roll of the stamped paper prescribed for such plaint, or petition of appeal, any additional sheets or rolls which may be required for that purpose, shall be of the description of stamped paper specified in Section XIX, of this Regulation. In like manner, if the subject matter of any answer, reply, rejoinder, or other pleading, cannot be comprised in a single sheet or roll of the stamped paper prescribed for such pleading, any additional sheets or rolls which may be required for that purpose, shall be of the description of the stamped paper specified in Section XIX of this Regulation.—*Cl.* 2.—*Ibid.*

If any party or vakeel, or other person shall hereafter file in *any Subordinate or Civil Court*, or in the Sudder Udalut, any plaint or pleading required to be written on stamped paper, which may not have been prepared in conformity with the foregoing provisions of this Section, the Court is authorized to impose on such party, vakeel, or other person, any fine which they may deem proper, provided that such fine shall in no instance exceed three times the amount or value of the additional stamped paper, which would have been required had the plaint or pleading been drawn up in conformity with the foregoing provisions.—*Cl.* 3.—*Ibid.*

If the subject matter of any miscellaneous petition or application, or of other papers specified in Section XX of this Regulation cannot, under the rule contained in Clause first of this Section, be conveniently comprised in a single sheet or roll of the prescribed stamped paper, any additional sheets or rolls which may be re-

Sec. XXIII, Reg. XIII, 1816.—For particular instructions in these respects, See C. O.'s S. U. 8th August, 1809, 28th June, 1828, A. and 15th February, 1830, B.

quired for that purpose, shall be of the value and description specified in the said Section of the Regulation in question; and if any such petition or paper which may not have been prepared in conformity with the foregoing rule, and with the rules contained in Clause first of this Section, shall be hereafter presented to any of the Courts or officers specified in Section XX of this Regulation, such Court or officer is hereby authorized to impose a fine on the party or person presenting it, under the same limitations as are prescribed in the preceding Clause.—*Cl.* 4, *Sec.* XXIII, *Reg.* XIII, 1816.

If during the trial of any regular suit, it shall appear that the plaint has been written on stamped paper of a less value than that which ought to have been used under the provisions of Section XIII of this Regulation, and the Court shall be of opinion that the error or omission did not arise from any fraudulent motive, or from any design on the part of the plaintiff to evade the provisions of the Regulations, it shall be competent to the Court, either to permit or to direct the plaintiff or appellant in the suit, to file a duplicate of the plaint on stamped paper, of such a value as may be sufficient to complete the full amount of the stamp duty prescribed by the Section above mentioned.—*Cl.* 1, *Sec.* XXIV.—*Ibid.*

In addition to the provisions of Section IV, Regulation XII of 1809, it is hereby declared that if, on the trial of any summary appeal preferred under that Section, the *Civil* Court shall be of opinion, that the original suit was not from its amount, regularly cognizable in the *Subordinate* Court, but that the irregularity in the institution of such suit did not arise from any fraudulent motive on the part of the plaintiff, it shall be competent to the *Civil* Court to direct the—Judge *of such Court* to refund to the plaintiff the amount of the fee or stamp duty paid by him on instituting the suit in *such* Court, and the plaintiff shall be permitted to institute his suit de novo in the *Civil* Court.—*Cl.* 2.—*Ibid.*

If on the suit of a pauper plaintiff a judgment be passed in favor of the plaintiff, and the defendant appealing from such judgment shall obtain a reversal of it with costs, so that the final judgment may be in favor of the defendant and the original claim shall be declared groundless, the amount of stamp duty, substituted for the institution fee, which such defendant may have paid upon his appeal, shall be returned to him or to his legal representative, by the Court into which the same may have been paid; and the amount shall be recovered from the pauper against whom the final judgment may be passed, in the event of his being found to possess property sufficient to make good the same, as provided in

Clause 1, Section IX, Regulation VII of 1816.—*Cl.* 1, *Sec.* XXV, *Reg.* XIII, 1816.

In all other cases, the Court of Sudder Udalut are authorized to direct a return of the whole or a portion of the amount of stamp duty, substituted for the institution fee, as on due consideration of the circumstances of the case, whether brought before them in appeal, or referred to them by a *Civil or Subordinate* Court, may appear to them just and proper.—*Cl. 2.—Ibid.*

Board of Revenue to publish rates—to take measures for prosecuting offenders against stamp law. Collector, or other public officer appointed by Government, to have charge of stamp office in each Zillah.—Secs. XXVI, XXVIII.—*Ibid.*

Any ministerial officer who may hereafter file in any Court of Justice, or in the office of any Collector, or other public officer, without the written order of such officer, any petition, pleading, or other document required to be written on stamped paper, which may not have been written on the prescribed stamped paper, or who shall furnish a copy of any paper or proceeding required to be written upon stamped paper, on any other paper than the required stamped paper, shall be liable to dismission from office, and to the payment of a fine to Government equal to ten times the amount of the stamp duty which would have been payable, if the prescribed stamped paper had been used for such petition, pleading or other document.—*Cl.* 1, *Sec.* XXIX.—*Ibid.*

Whenever a petition, pleading or other document, which may not have been written on the prescribed stamp, shall be filed in any Court of Justice, or in the office of any Collector or other public officer, or whenever it shall appear that a copy of any paper or proceeding shall have been furnished on paper not bearing the prescribed stamp, the Judge or Judges of the Court, the Collector or other public officer, shall call upon the ministerial officer by whom such petition or other document was filed, or by whom such copy shall have been furnished, to show cause why the prescribed fine should not be imposed upon him; and, on his failure to show good cause, shall forthwith proceed, in the ordinary manner, to levy from him the penalty prescribed; provided, however, that the levy of such penalty by the Sudder Ameens shall be subject to the restrictions contained in the latter part of Section XIV, Regulation VIII, 1816.—*Cl.* 2, *Sec.* VII, *Reg.* V, 1831.

Sec. XXV, Reg. XIII, 1816.—See rule for cases in which suits are remanded for trial de novo in C. O. S. U. 15th February, 1830.

The provisions of this Regulation are not intended to preclude
individuals from making for their private use, and at their own
expense, copies of the judicial or revenue papers, with the permission of the Court, Collector, or other public officer having charge
thereof, on any paper which they may prefer ; but if such copies
be not made on stamped paper of the prescribed rate, they shall
not be authenticated by the seal or signature of any Court, Collector, or other public officer, and shall not be received as evidence
in any Court of Justice, or in any public office whatever.—*Sec.*
XXX, *Reg.* XIII, 1816.

Nothing in this Regulation shall be construed to affect suits instituted before the native tribunals established under the provisions
of Regulations IV, V, VI and VII of 1816, or suits preferred to
Collectors under Regulation XII of 1816. Provided however,
that in appeals from·the decisions of district moonsiffs under Section LIII, Regulation VI, 1816, the petition shall, agreeably to
the amount or value of the property claimed, be written on stamped
paper of the rate prescribed in Section XIII of this Regulation ;
and provided also, that in all other cases which may be brought
before the different authorities in the judicial department under
the Regulations referred to in this Section, the petition shall be
written on stamped paper of the rates specified in Section XX of
this Regulation.—*Sec.* XXXI.—*Ibid.*

Whenever a suit pending in any Civil Court within the territories subject to the Presidency of Madras shall be dismissed on application of the parties, the plaintiff shall be entitled to claim from
the Court a certificate, stating the amount of stamp duty paid on
the plaint with specification of the number and endorsement of
the paper filed, and whether the suit was dismissed before or after
the completion of the pleadings.—*Sec.* III, *Act* XVII, 1848.

On presenting any such certificate to the Collector of the district within three calendar months after the dismissal of the suit,
the plaintiff shall be entitled to receive back half of the stamp
duty, if the certificate purports that the suit was dismissed after
the completion of the pleadings ; and if before, the whole of the
said stamp duty ; provided always, there be no exception taken to
the paper or endorsement thereon.—*Sec.* IV.—*Ibid.*

Sec. XXX, Reg. XIII, 1816.—See C. O. S. U. 8th July, 1836, No. 32, and 8th June,
1838, No. 53.

Sec. XXXI, Reg. XIII, 1816.—" Sec. VI, Reg. VI, 1816, &c."—But now by Section II, Act XVII of 1848, which see at page 30, Stamp duty as prescribed in this Act
is payable in the Courts of the district moonsiffs instead of Institution fee.

CHAPTER VIII.

VAKEELS OR PLEADERS.

The office of pleader in the Courts of the East India Company shall be open to all persons of whatever nation, or religion, provided that no person shall be admitted a pleader in any of those Courts unless he have obtained a certificate, in such manner as shall be directed by the Sudder Courts, that he is of good character and duly qualified for the office, any Law or Regulation to the contrary notwithstanding.—*Sec.* IV, *Act* I, 1846.

Provided nevertheless, that every Barrister of any of Her Majesty's Courts of Justice in India, shall be entitled as such, to plead in any of the Sudder Courts of the East India Company, subject however to all the rules in force in the said Sudder Courts applicable to pleaders, whether relating to the language in which the Court is to be addressed, or to any other matter.—*Sec.* V.—*Ibid.*

Section XXV, Regulation XIV, 1816, of the Madras Code, shall cease to be enforced, excepting for the purpose specified in Section VII of this Act.—*Sec.* VI.—*Ibid.*

Parties employing authorized pleaders in the said Courts, shall be at liberty to settle with them by private agreement the remuneration to be paid for their professional services; and it shall not be necessary to specify such agreement in the vakalutnamah, provided that when costs are awarded to a party in a regular suit, original or appeal, decided on the merits, against another party, the amount to be paid on account of fees of pleaders, shall be calculated according to rules contained in Section XXV, Regulation XIV, 1816—and that when costs are awarded in other cases

---

Vakeels or Pleaders.—The provisions of law in this chapter concern only vakeels in the European Courts, and those in the Courts of the Principal Sudder Ameens, Sudder Ameens, and district moonsiffs. The rules for the guidance of vakeels before village moonsiffs and punchayets, and before district punchayets, and Collectors, will be found under those heads.

Sec. VI, Act I, 1846.—" Section XXV, *Regulation* XIV, 1816." This prescribes the rate of fees, and prior to the passing of this Act it was obligatory on vakeels to take neither more or less.

the amount to be paid on account of such fees shall be one-fourth of what it would have been in a regular suit decided on its merits. —*Sec.* VII, *Act* I, 1846.

Private agreements between parties and their pleaders respecting the remuneration to be paid for professional services shall not be enforced otherwise than by a regular suit.—*Sec.* VIII.—*Ibid.*

Persons taking legal opinions from authorized pleaders *as provided for in Sec.* XX, *Reg.* XIV *of* 1816, shall be at liberty to settle with them by private agreement the remuneration to be paid for such opinions.—*Sec.* IX.—*Ibid.*

Whenever a pleader has rendered himself liable to a fine in the Court of a Principal Sudder Ameen, or Sudder Ameen, it shall be competent to such Principal Sudder Ameen, or Sudder Ameen to impose such fine; provided that an appeal from all orders imposing such fines shall lie to the Zillah Judge whose decisions thereon shall be final.—*Sec.* X.—*Ibid.*

Nothing in this Act contained shall apply to vakeels who may be employed in the Courts of the village moonsiffs; or before the village or district punchayets; or before the Collectors of Zillahs, under the provisions of Regulations IV, V, VII and XII, 1816 of the Madras Code.—*Sec.* XIII.—*Ibid.*

The provisions of Act I of 1846, shall not be deemed to apply to private agreements between parties and their pleaders made before the passing of the said Act.—*Sec.* I, *Act* XXX, 1850.

The Sudder Udalut and the several *Zillah Courts* are empowered to appoint to the office of vakeel in their respective Courts, such a number of persons duly qualified for the situation, as may from time to time appear to them to be necessary.—*Cl.* 1, *Sec.* III, *Reg.* XIV, 1816.

Persons who may hereafter be appointed to the office of vakeel in the Zillah Courts, or the Sudder Udalut, shall receive a sunnud of appointment duly authenticated by the Court to which they may be respectively attached. This sunnud, which is not required to be written on stamped paper, shall be drawn up according to the form No. I, in the Appendix to this Regulation.—*Cl.* 1, *Sec.* IV.—*Ibid.*

Whenever a vakeel may be dismissed from his office, or may die, or may resign his situation, his sunnud of appointment shall be re-

---

Sec. IV, Reg. XIV, 1816.—" Form No. 1." This and the other forms mentioned in this Regulation are omitted as at hand in every Court.

called and cancelled by the Court, to which such vakeel may have been attached.—*Cl. 2, Sec. IV, Reg.* XIV, 1816.

Every vakeel, previously to being allowed to practice, shall *make and subscribe* before the Court to which he may be appointed, *a solemn affirmation*, drawn up according to the form No. 2, of the Appendix to this Regulation.—*Sec. V.—Ibid.*

Pleaders employed in the several Courts of Civil Judicature shall be liable to dismission from their office, whenever they may be guilty of encouraging or promoting litigious suits, of wilfully delaying the suits of their clients for their own advantage, or refusing or omitting, without sufficient cause to be shewn to the Court, to carry on the suits of their clients, after having accepted a vakalutnamah; or of fraudulent practices, neglect, or other misconduct, in the discharge of their professional duty; or of gross profligacy or misbehaviour in their private conduct.—*Sec.* VI.—*Ibid.*

The vakeels are required to use due precautions to ascertain the real names and the identity of persons who may propose to employ them as pleaders; and any authorized vakeel, who shall hereafter receive and file a vakalutnamah from any person under a fictitious name, shall be liable to be dismissed from his office; provided, however, that * * upon full enquiry into the circumstances of the case, the *Zillah Civil Court*, shall deem him to be deserving of such punishment.—*Sec.* VIII.—*Ibid.*

The vakeels are hereby enjoined not to file any plaint, answer, or other pleading, without previously ascertaining that such pleading has been duly prepared in conformity with the Regulations; that it contains no unnecessary repetitions of former pleadings, no terms of personal abuse, or reproach against the opposite party, his vakeels, witnesses, or other persons; and no groundless imputations on any Court of Justice, or public officer, but that it contains such matter only as is apparently material and relevant to the suit. Every pleading filed by an authorized vakeel, shall be signed by him, in testimony of his having considered and approved its contents.—*Cl. 1, Sec.* IX.—*Ibid.*

Sec. VIII, Reg. XIV, 1816.—In the original the *Zillah Judge* was directed to report the circumstance to the *Provincial Court.* The *same* vakeels now practice in the Civil and Subordinate Courts, but they are considered vakeels of the Civil Court, and if a Subordinate Judge or Principal Sudder Ameen consider a vakeel to be liable to dismissal under this Section or under Section X, he must proceed as directed in Section XI of this Regulation.

Cl. 1, Sec. IX, Reg. XIV, 1816.—Vakeels may be called on to explain pleadings filed by them under Clause 2, Section X, Regulation XV of 1816, which see at page 169.

In order that the expense, trouble and inconvenience, frequently experienced by filing irrelevant exhibits, and by summoning useless witnesses, may be avoided, the vakeels are hereby further required to examine the documents which their constituents may propose to exhibit in proof of their claims, previously to their being filed in Court; and to ascertain from their constituents, previously to summoning any witnesses, the specific points which such witnesses are expected to prove by their testimony.—*Cl. 2, Sec.* IX, *Reg.* XIV, 1816.

The Courts will carefully point out to the notice of the vakeels such parts of the pleadings as are irregular, irrelevant, or otherwise objectionable, and shall record their censure of any vakeel whose conduct, in opposition to the preceding rules, may in any particular instance demand such animadversion. If notwithstanding such recorded censure, a vakeel shall again be guilty of similar misconduct, he shall be liable in each instance to such fine to Government, not exceeding twenty rupees, as the Court may deem it proper to impose.—*Cl.* 3.—*Ibid.*

The Sudder Udalut, and the several Zillah Civil Courts, will at all times exercise their discretion in removing from office any pleader of their respective Courts, who may be guilty of any of the acts abovementioned, or who may be otherwise deemed unfit for the situation.—*Cl.* 1, *Sec.* X.—*Ibid.*

Whenever a *Subordinate* Judge *or Principal Sudder Ameen* shall be of opinion that a vakeel, attached to his Court, is unfit for the situation, in consequence of his having been guilty of any of the acts mentioned in the preceding Sections, or that he is otherwise disqualified for the office of pleader, *he* shall report the circumstances of the case, together with his own opinion upon it, to the *Zillah Civil* Court, who will pass such orders on the case as may appear to be proper, or will call for any additional information, or direct any further enquiry that the nature and circumstances of each case may appear to demand.—*Cl.* 2.—*Ibid.*

The *Subordinate* Judges *and Principal Sudder Ameens* are em-

---

Cl. 3, Sec. IX, Reg. XIV, 1816.—" *Liable, &c.* " In the original to *forfeit his fee, &c.*, or such fine, &c., as the fees are not now deposited, this punishment must necessarily always be in the shape of a fine.

Principal Sudder Ameens, and Sudder Ameens by Section X, and district moonsiffs by Section XII, Act I of 1846, which see at page 23, are authorized to fine vakeels in all cases in which a Civil or Subordinate Judge can do so—an appeal however lies to the Civil Judges : the orders of Subordinate Judges imposing fines on vakeels are final under Clause 2, Section XV, Regulation XIV, 1816, which see at page 316.

powered, without the previous sanction of the *Zillah Civil* Court, to suspend from his office any pleader attached to their Courts, who may be guilty of any gross act of fraud or misconduct; but in such instances it shall be *their* duty to report the circumstances of the case, with as little delay as possible, for the information and orders of the Zillah Civil Court.—*Sec.* XI, *Reg.* XIV, 1816.

The parties in a cause are authorized to prosecute their respective pleaders in the Civil Courts of Judicature, for any damages or injury which they may have sustained from any breach of the Regulations on the part of their pleaders, or from any fraudulent conduct, or malpractices, committed by their pleaders regarding the suit.—*Cl.* 1, *Sec.* XII.—*Ibid.*

Any party in a suit, who may be dissatisfied with the conduct of his pleader, shall be at liberty at any stage of the trial previously to the decision, to withdraw the power delegated to his pleader, and to appoint another vakeel to plead the cause. In such cases the party is to present a petition to the Court, notifying that he has withdrawn the management of the suit from such pleader, and is to file a new vakalutnamah in the name of the pleader whom he may appoint to carry on the suit: all acts, however, which may have been done by the first pleader on the part of his client, previously to his having been dismissed, are to be held valid * * * *. —*Cl.* 2.—*Ibid.*

If a pleader should be unable to attend the Court in consequence of indisposition, or other sufficient reason, he is to notify the same in writing to the Court, on unstamped paper; and the hearing of any cause in which such pleader may be employed, is to be postponed to a future day, unless the party or his authorized agent shall commit the management of the cause to any other pleader of the Court, or unless the party himself shall be present and willing to plead the cause in person. If the management of the cause shall be entrusted to any other pleader of the Court, instead of filing a new vakalutnamah, it shall be sufficient for the party or his agent duly authorized, to endorse on the back of the original vakalutnamah, a written declaration that he has appointed some other vakeel of the Court to conduct the cause, either permanently or during the absence of the pleader first appointed * * * *.—*Sec.* XIII.—*Ibid.*

Cl. 2, Sec. XII & Sec. XIII, Reg. XIV, 1816.—In the original the duty of allotting the fee between the two vakeels was thrown upon the Courts, but under Act I of 1846, this is a matter for settlement between the vakeels and the parties.

If a pleader shall fail to attend in Court on any day fixed for the transaction of Civil business, and shall omit to notify in writing to the Court his inability to attend in consequence of indisposition or other sufficient cause, the Court is authorized to impose on such pleader, a fine for the first offence, not exceeding the sum of fifty rupees; and for the second offence, not exceeding one hundred rupees. If such pleader shall be guilty of a similar offence a third time, he shall be liable to dismission from his office.—*Cl.* 1, *Sec.* XIV, *Reg.* XIV, 1816.

If any pleader shall be guilty of disrespect to the Court, in open Court, the Court is empowered to impose a fine upon him, not exceeding the sum of one hundred rupees.—*Cl. 2.—Ibid.*

All orders imposing fines on pleaders, which may be passed by the Judges of the Zillah *Civil or Subordinate* Courts, in conformity with this Regulation, shall be final, and the amount of the fines shall be levied * * * by the process which is prescribed for the execution of decrees.—*Cl. 2, Sec.* X V.—*Ibid.*

Whenever a pleader has rendered himself liable to a fine in the Court of a Principal Sudder Ameen, or Sudder Ameen, it shall be competent to such Principal Sudder Ameen, or Sudder Ameen to impose such fine; provided that an appeal from all orders imposing such fines shall lie to the Zillah Judge, whose decisions thereon shall be final.—*Sec.* X, *Act* I, 1846.

The vakeels attached to one Court are not to be allowed to plead in any other Court; but this rule is not intended to preclude the Zillah Judges from making such an allotment and distribution of the pleaders attached to their Courts, as may from time to time appear convenient, on a consideration of the Civil business in their own Courts, and in those of the Sudder Ameens. —*Sec.* XVI, *Reg.* XIV, 1816.

The authorized pleaders of the *Zillah Civil* Courts are hereby prohibited, without obtaining the previous sanction of the Judges of those Courts, from officiating as agents in any prosecution, trial, or proceeding, before the Magistrates or their assistants. This prohibition, however, is not intended to apply to the cases of

---

Cl. 2, Sec. XV, Reg. XIV, 1816.—See note on Cl. 3, Sec. IX of this Regulation.

Sec. XVI, Reg. XIV, 1816.—The *same* vakeels now practice in the Civil and Subordinate Courts—Separate vakeels are attached to the Courts of Sudder Ameens. The vakeels in a Sudder Ameen's Court having requested permission to practice in the Civil and Subordinate Court so far as to carry on in those Courts appeal suits, in cases in which they have conducted the original in their own Court—the Sudder Udalut decided that it could not be allowed.

pleaders, who may be employed on the part of Government in conducting the prosecution of persons charged with criminal offences, or in the execution of any other duties in the criminal department, which such pleaders may be directed or authorized to perform on the part of Government, under the Regulations which are now, or may hereafter be, in force.—*Sec.* XVII, *Reg.* XIV, 1816.

Whenever a vakeel attached to a Zillah *Civil, or Subordinate* Court may die, or may be removed from his office, or may voluntarily resign his situation, the Judge of such Court shall notify the same in a publication, to be affixed in his own Court, and in the Courts of the Sudder Ameens, and *in the office of the* Collector of the district; the publication shall contain a statement of the several depending cases in which such vakeel may have been employed, and a requisition to the parties who have retained such vakeel to attend in person, or to substitute another vakeel in room of the pleader, formerly appointed by them, within a reasonable period, to be fixed by the Court, not being less than six weeks. In such instances, instead of filing a new vakalutnamah, it shall be sufficient for the party, or his agent duly authorized, to endorse on the original vakalutnamah a written declaration, that he has appointed some other vakeel of the Court, in lieu of the pleader, who may have died, or resigned his office, or have been removed from his situation.—*Cl.* 1, *Sec.* XVIII.—*Ibid.*

A publication issued in conformity with the preceding rules shall be held and considered to be a good and sufficient notice; and if any party shall not attend or appoint another vakeel, within the period limited in the publication, he shall be required to shew cause for the omission; and if sufficient cause be not assigned, the Court shall proceed as in case of default, in conformity with the provisions in force.—*Cl.* 2.—*Ibid.*

A similar notification shall be issued on the death, resignation, or removal, of any pleader attached to the Sudder Udalut; the publication shall be affixed in that Court, and in such of the *Zillah Civil, or Subordinate* Courts, in which it may appear necessary to publish the same, with reference to the depending causes in which the vakeel may have been employed; and the period to be allowed to parties to appear and substitute another vakeel, shall not be less than three months.—*Cl.* 3.—*Ibid.*

The Courts are authorized to apply the principle of the preceding rules to cases, in which the decision of suits may be materially delayed by the protracted indisposition of a pleader, or by his continued inability to attend the Court from any other cause, which may be expected to be permanent or of considerable duration.—*Cl.* 4, *Sec.* XVIII, *Reg.* XIV, 1816.

The Courts of Civil Judicature are hereby empowered to permit any of the authorized vakeels of their respective Courts, to be arbitrators in depending suits, subject to the several rules and provisions in force for referring suits to arbitration.—*Sec.* XIX.—*Ibid.*

The authorized vakeels of the Sudder Udalut, of the *Zillah Civil, and Subordinate* Courts, are hereby empowered to receive fees for legal opinions, under the provisions contained in the following Clauses of this Section.—*Cl.* 1, *Sec.* XX.—*Ibid.*

Any person who may be desirous of obtaining the opinion of an authorized pleader, regarding the legal validity and sufficiency of any claim, right, or title, which he may suppose himself to possess, and on the consequent expediency of prosecuting or defending, either originally or in appeal, such supposed claim, right, or title, in the Courts of Civil Judicature, may submit a written statement of his claim under his seal, signature, or mark, to the pleader, whose opinion he may wish to obtain.—*Cl.* 2.—*Ibid.*

The pleader, to whom such statement may be submitted, after an attentive consideration of the laws, regulations, usages, or precedents, which may be applicable to the case, and of the arguments and proofs which may be adduced in support of the claim, shall furnish to the party under his signature, a written declaration of his opinion, and of the grounds upon which that opinion may be formed.—*Cl.* 3.—*Ibid.*

Any pleader who, under the preceding rules, may knowingly furnish an opinion of a nature evidently calculated to promote the institution of unfounded or litigious suits, or to discourage the amicable adjustment of dubious claims, shall be liable to be dismissed from his office * * *.—*Cl.* 6.—*Ibid.*

When a party in a cause may be desirous of retaining a vakeel for the prosecution or defence of any Civil suit, he shall execute

---

Cl. 1, Sec. XX, Reg. XIV, 1816.—Fees for legal opinions. The rate to be settled between the parties. Such opinions are also required from vakeels conducting pauper suits under Clause 2, Section V, Regulation VII, 1818, and also from vakeels preferring special appeals under Clause 3, Section IV, Regulation XV of 1816, which will be found under " pauper suit," and " special appeal."

Cl. 6, Sec. XX, Reg. XIV, 1816.—This Clause in the original provided for the forfeiture of his fee in case of his being employed in the suit—but the Court does not now hold the fees in deposit—the party whom he may dishonestly mislead would have his remedy under Clause 1, Section XII, Regulation XIV of 1816.

to him a vakalutnamah, constituting him pleader in the cause, and authorizing him to prosecute or defend the suit, and further binding himself to abide by, and to confirm, all acts which such pleader may do or undertake in his behalf in the cause, in the same manner as if such party had been personally present and consenting ; the party is to attest the instrument with his seal, or signature, or with his mark if he cannot write, in the presence of two credible witnesses, who are likewise to attest it in the same manner ; and who are to attend the Court and prove the vakalutnamah in all cases in which it may be judged requisite.—*Cl.* 1, *Sec.* XXI, *Reg.* XIV, 1816.

Such vakalutnamahs are to be written on the stamped paper prescribed in Section XX, Regulation XIII of 1816, but shall not be liable to the stamp duty on exhibits under Section XVI of that Regulation.—*Cl.* 2.—*Ibid.*

When a vakeel, to whom a vakalutnamah may have been executed under the preceding Section, shall consent to undertake the prosecution or defence of the suit, he shall affix his signature to the back of the vakalutnamah, together with the date on which such signature may be affixed ; and shall thenceforward be precluded from being employed in the same cause against the party who may have so retained him.—*Sec.* XXII.—*Ibid.*

In all regular suits which may be instituted, either originally or in appeal, in any of the Zillah Civil, and Subordinate Courts, or the Sudder Udalut, the vakeels employed by the respective parties are to be allowed for pleading the causes of their clients, the rates of fees calculated as follows :

In suits for money, effects, or for other personal property, or for land, or other immovable property of any description, if the amount or value of the claim, estimated according to the provisions of Section XIV, Regulation XIII of 1816, shall not exceed 5,000 rupees—five per cent.

If the amount or value shall exceed 5,000 rupees and shall not exceed 20,000 rupees ; on 5,000 as above, and on the remainder two per cent.

If the amount or value shall exceed 20,000 rupees and shall not exceed 50,000 rupees ; on 20,000 as above, and on the remainder one per cent.

Cl. 2, Sec. XXI, Reg. XIV, 1816.—They are specially exempted also by Clause 2, Section XVI, Regulation XIII of 1816, which see under stamps, at page 304.

If the amount or value shall exceed 50,000 rupees, and shall not exceed 80,000 rupees ; on 50,000 as above, and on the remainder eight annas per cent.

If the amount or value shall exceed 80,000 rupees, the fee to the vakeel shall be one thousand rupees ; and shall in no instance exceed that sum, however great may be the value or amount of the suit in which such vakeel may be employed.—*Cl.* 1, *Sec.* XXV, *Reg.* XIV, 1816.

In all the preceding calculations, where the amount or value may be in fractions of rupees, such fractions are to be rejected in calculating the fees thereupon.—*Cl.* 2.—*Ibid.*

For every sum which may be paid to a vakeel by a Civil Court, on account of his fees, such vakeel shall give a receipt written on the stamped paper prescribed in Section XI, Regulation XIII, 1816.—*Cl.* 3.—*Ibid.*

The parties in a suit are respectively permitted to entertain two or more pleaders.—*Cl.* 1, *Sec.* XXX.—*Ibid.*

It shall be sufficient in such cases for the party employing two or more vakeels in the same suit, to file a single vakalutnamah.—*Cl.* 2.—*Ibid.*

If the party shall agree to pay to each of the vakeels employed by him the full amount of the authorized fee, the opposite party in the suit shall in no case be required to make good re than the fee of one of those pleaders, or such part of that fee as may be adjudged against him by the Court. The fees of the other pleader are to be considered as a separate expense to be defrayed exclusively by the party entertaining him, and for which he is not to be reimbursed in any case whatever.—*Cl.* 3.—*Ibid.*

If a suit shall be withdrawn or dismissed on default without a determination upon the merits of the case before all the requisite pleadings shall have been filed in Court, *the plaintiff, or appellant, withdrawing the suit, or suffering it to be dismissed on default, shall be charged, with one-fourth or if after, all the requisite pleadings shall have been filed, with one half of the established fee, on account to the yakeel of the defendant or respondent,* which he would have received had judgment been given in the cause, together with all

---

Sec. XXV, Reg. XIV, 1816.—This Section is now of use for the purposes specified in Section VII, Act I of 1846—Sections XXVI and XXVII, of this Regulation have reference to the mode of entering the fees and other costs in preparing decrees, and will be found under " Preparation of Decrees" at page 192.

the admitted costs incurred by the defendant or respondent.—*Sec.* XXXI, *Reg.* XIV, 1816.

The same rules shall be considered applicable to cases adjusted by razeenamah, except that the fees of the pleaders and all other costs of the suit, shall be paid by the parties in such manner and proportions as may have been agreed upon, and inserted in the razeenamah.—*Cl. 2.—Ibid.*

Pleaders are to give written receipts on unstamped paper, for all accounts, writings, or documents, which may be delivered to them by their clients in the course of any suit or process; and if a pleader shall refuse to return such accounts, documents, or writings, the Court, upon a petition being presented to them for that purpose by the owners of the papers so withheld, shall cause them to be restored.—*Sec.* XXXVI.—*Ibid.*

One or more of the authorized pleaders of the Sudder Udalut, of the *Zillah Civil, and Subordinate* Courts, shall be appointed for the purpose of conducting the prosecution or defence of any suits in those Courts respectively, which may be directed to be carried on at the public expense by any Regulation, or by a special order from the Governor in Council, or other authority competent to pass such order. Those pleaders shall be furnished with a sunnud, or written authority to that purport, in the English and Persian languages, under the signature of the Secretary to Government in the judicial department, and the sunnud shall be drawn up according to the form No. 5, of the Appendix to this Regulation.—*Cl.* 1, *Sec.* XXXVII.—*Ibid.*

The *Sudder Udalut, and Zillah Civil Courts* shall report to the Secretary to Government in the judicial department, the death, resignation, or removal, of any of the vakeels of Government attached to their respective Courts; and shall at the same time nominate, for the approbation of Government, a proper person, being one of the authorized vakeels of the Court, to succeed to the vacant office. The Courts shall in all instances select from amongst the established pleaders, such individual as may appear best qualified for the situation, by his character and capacity.—*Cl. 2.—Ibid.*

Sec. XXXI. Reg. XIV, 1816.—This Section has been altered to suit the present law under Act I of 1846—it originally provided for fees, at the rates mentioned, to vakeels on both sides—as it now stands it might operate very hardly in the case of a defendant who shall engage a vakeel and pay him in advance a large fee—the plaintiff might withdraw his plaint before pleadings were completed and under Act XVII of 1848, would receive back all the stamp duty; he could only be made to pay ¼ of the established fee to the defendant, who might have some difficulty in recovering any part of what he had paid to his vakeel.

The pleaders for Government are to undertake all causes, which they may be directed to plead by orders from Government, or which may be directed by any Regulation to be carried on at the public expense, upon receiving an order for that purpose either from Government, or from any officer or officers, empowered by any Regulation to superintend and to furnish instructions for conducting such suits. The order of Government, or of such officer or officers, is to be filed in Court as the authority of the pleader to plead the cause, and is to form part of the record of the proceedings.—*Cl.* 3, *Sec.* XXXVII, *Reg.* XIV, 1816.

The pleaders of Government are prohibited from giving any advice to the parties opposed to Government in any Civil suit or proceeding, and from being concerned, directly or indirectly, on their behalf, in suits which are directed to be carried on at the public expense ; but in all other suits the pleaders of Government are to be at liberty to plead for either of the parties, in the same manner as the other authorized pleaders of the Courts.—*Cl.* 4.—*Ibid.*

The pleaders for Government are to be paid the same fees in causes directed to be pleaded at the public expense, as pleaders employed in causes between individuals, and under the same rules and restrictions.—*Cl.* 5.—*Ibid.*

In pleading suits directed to be carried on at the public expense, the pleaders for Government are to be subject to all the rules prescribed for their guidance when pleading on behalf of individuals, except in matters or cases, in which it may be otherwise specially directed by any Regulation.—*Cl.* 6.—*Ibid.*

The Board of Revenue, or any other authorities, entrusted with the management of suits on the part of Government, are empowered to associate with the established vakeel of Government, any other authorized pleader, in cases in which such aid may, from the importance of the suit, or any other reason, be judged necessary or advisable ; such additional pleader shall be furnished with a vakalutnamah, duly authenticated by the officer or authority employing him, and shall be entitled to receive the same fees, and under the same rules and restrictions, as if he were employed on the part of an individual.—*Cl.* 7.—*Ibid.*

Cl. 3, Sec. XXXVII, Reg. XIV, 1816.—Government Vakeel. This functionary is instructed to move for time to answer in public suits by Clause 2, Section II, Regulation I of 1823, which see at page 214. He has also certain duties to perform at the instance of the Collector in moving the Courts for confinement of defaulters under Section XIII, Regulation XXVII of 1802, which see at page 205—the manner in which papers, &c., are transmitted between himself and the Collectors is prescribed in Section XXVII, Regulation XXVII of 1802, which see at page 212.

No part of this Regulation is to be construed to prohibit, or to prevent, any individual from appearing and pleading his own cause in person, in any of the Courts of Civil Judicature, without employing an authorized pleader.—*Sec.* XXXVIII, *Reg.* XIV, 1816.

The provisions of this Regulation are not intended to apply to vakeels, who may be employed in the Courts of the village moonsiffs, or before the village or district punchayets, or before the Collectors of Zillahs, under the provisions of Regulations IV, V, VI, VII and XII of 1816.—*Sec.* XXXIX.—*Ibid.*

That the pleaders in the several Courts, as well as all other persons, may have it in their power to render themselves acquainted with the Regulations enacted by the British Government, there shall be kept, for public inspection, in the several Courts of Judicature, printed copies of all such Regulations, and of the translations in the native languages, bound up with the annual indexes; until the Regulations, which may be passed in each year, are so bound up, the separate copies of each Regulation, with the translation which may be printed and circulated to the Courts, are to be exposed as above directed; the Regulations are to be deposited upon a table, expressly allotted for that purpose, in some part of the Court-room, and to lie for public inspection every day, Sunday excepted, during the ordinary hours of business, when the pleaders of the Courts and all other persons are to be at liberty to refer to the Regulations, or to take copies or extracts from them in the Court-room: on receipt of the translations of the Regulations in the country languages, the several Courts of Civil Justice shall cause the same to be publicly read in their *Courts*, and shall require the native pleaders of their respective Courts, to take copies of any of those translations, which relate, directly or indirectly, to the administration of Civil Justice.—*Sec.* XL.—*Ibid.*

CHAPTER IX.

LAW OFFICERS, AND CAUZEES.

The Governor in Council of Fort St. George, shall direct what law officers shall be appointed to the Zillah Courts established under this Act, and shall order the manner of their appointment, and such officers shall be subject to the same·rules as the law officers of the Provincial Courts of Appeal.—*Sec.* LI, *Act* VII, 1843.

The Court of Sudder Udalut shall continue, as at present, empowered to confirm the appointment, removal, and resignation of the law officers of the *Zillah Courts.*—*Cl.* 2, *Sec.* III, *Reg.* VII, 1822.

The law officers of the Sudder Udalut are to be appointed by the Governor in Council ; and shall not be removable but for incapacity, or misconduct, in the performance of their public duty, or for any act of flagrant profligacy in their private conduct, proved to his satisfaction.—*Sec.* II, *Reg.* XI, 1802.

The law offices in the several Courts are to be conferred on persons well versed in the laws, and of unblemished moral characters. —*Sec.* III.—*Ibid.*

The qualifications of candidates for the situation of law officers shall be ascertained by examination before the law officers of the Sudder Udalut with reference to the provisions of Section III, Regulation XI, 1802, and Clause 2, Section III, Regulation VII, 1822.—*Sec.* II, *Act* XXVII, 1836.

The Mahomedan law officers of the Courts of Civil Judicature, previous to entering upon the execution of the duties of their offices, are to make and ·subscribe a *solemn affirmation* before the

---

Sec. LI, Act VII, 1843.—None have been appointed, but the Mahomedan law officer was *retained* by Section XXXI, Act VII, 1843. See note on Section XVI, Regulation III, 1802, at page 155.

Sec. II, Reg. XI, 1802.—The law officers of the Sudder Udalut being appointed and removed by the Government, charges of misconduct against them are to be prosecuted under Act XXXVII, 1850.—All law officers are forbidden to engage in trading speculations.—See Cir. Lr. S. U. 28th December, 1843.

Court to which they may be respectively attached.—*Cl.* 1, *Sec.* V, *Reg.* XI, 1802.

At the expiration of every six months that is, on the 1st of January and the 1st of July in each year, the Mahomedan law officers of the Courts of Civil Judicature are to make and subscribe the following solemn affirmation before their respective Courts.— *Cl.* 2.—*Ibid.*

The pundits to the Court of Sudder Udalut previous to entering upon the execution of the duties of their offices, are to make and subscribe the following declaration before that Court.—*Sec.* VII.—*Ibid.*

The rules prescribed in Section XII, Regulation XII, 1802, respecting charges of corruption or extortion lodged against the native ministerial officers of the Civil and Criminal Courts, are to be held applicable to charges of a similar nature, that may be preferred against the Hindoo or Mahomedan law officers of the several Courts, with the following qualifications.—*Cl.* 1, *Sec.* VIII, *Reg.* XI, 1802.

An appeal shall lie to the Sudder Udalut from all decisions which may be passed by the *Zillah Civil* Courts, whereby a charge of corruption or extortion against any law officer may be decreed not proved, or by which any such charge may be adjudged to be proved, whatever may be the amount decreed to be paid; notwithstanding any thing that may appear to the contrary in any other Regulation.—*Cl.* 2.—*Ibid.*

No decrees passed by any *Zillah Civil* Court adjudging a Hindoo or Mahomedan law officer guilty of corruption or extortion, shall be carried into execution in the event of the law officer against whom such decree may be passed, appealing from the decree, and giving the securities required by Section XII, Regulation IV, 1802, and Section X, Regulation V, 1802, in cases of ap-

---

Cl. 1 & 2, Sec. V, Reg. XI, 1802.—Forms of affirmation omitted as at hand in all Courts—that prescribed by Clause 2, is I believe, never now required.

Sec. VII, Reg. XI, 1802.—" *Pundits to Sudder Udalut*"—originally to " Courts of Civil Judicature," but the Sudder Udalut alone has Pundits now attached to it.—See note on Section XVI, Regulation III, 1802, at page 155—Form omitted.

Sec. VIII, Reg. XI, 1802.—" Law officers of the several Courts." This Section continues applicable to the law officers who remain attached to the new Zillah Courts, or may be appointed thereto under Section LI, Act VII, 1843 : Clauses 6 and 7 of this Section provided for transmission of decrees affecting law officers to the Governor in Council with whom their appointment, removal, &c. then rested, but as by Clause 2, Section III, Regulation VII, 1822, that control has been transferred to the Sudder Udalut—their provisions are virtually obsolete.

peals from decisions for sums of money passed by those Courts respectively, and the execution of which they are empowered to suspend upon such securities being given.— *Cl. 3, Sec.* VIII, *Reg.* XI, 1802.

The *Zillah Civil* Courts are to enforce by the usual process all decrees which they may pass adjudging their law officers guilty of corruption or extortion, that may not be appealed against within the limited period; and transmit copies of the decrees to the *Sudder Udalut.— Cl. 5.—Ibid.*

When a *Zillah Civil* Court, shall adjudge a charge of corruption or extortion, that may have been preferred against any law officer, not to be proved; and the prosecutor shall not appeal from the decree, within the time limited; the Court is to transmit a copy of it to the *Sudder Udalut.— Cl. 8.—Ibid.*

Upon a vacancy occurring in any law office in a Court of Judicature, by death or resignation, the Court is to report the vacancy to the *Sudder Udalut;* and recommend a person duly qualified to fill it.—*Sec.* IX, *Reg.* XI, 1802.

The Cauzee-ool-Coozzat, or head Cauzee of the Sudder Court of Fort St. George, shall be head Cauzee of the Provinces, and shall not be removeable from his office, but for incapacity, or misconduct in the discharge of his public duty, or acts of profligacy in his private conduct, proved to the satisfaction of the Governor in Council.— *Cl. 1, Sec.* II, *Reg.* III, 1808.

The head Cauzee is to use a circular seal, two inches in diameter, on which shall be inscribed the designation of his office, and his name, in the Persian language, as follows—" The seal of the Cauzee-ool-Coozzat of the Provinces subject to the Presidency of Fort St. George." (Name of the head Cauzee.)— *Cl. 2.—Ibid.*

The Cauzees stationed in the Cities, Towns, or Purgunnahs, in the Provinces, shall not be removable from their offices, excepting for incapacity or misconduct in the discharge of their public duty, or acts of profligacy in their private conduct. The Cauzees so stationed are to use a circular seal, one inch and a half in diameter,

---

Sec. II, Reg. III, 1808.—The office of Cauzee was declared by the preamble of this Regulation to be requisite at the Cities, and principal Towns, and in the Provinces, for the purposes of preparing and attesting deeds of transfer and other law papers, celebrating marriages, and performing such religious duties or ceremonies prescribed by the Mahomedan law, as have been hitherto discharged by them under the Native Government, and the following rules for its Regulation were therefore enacted.

on which shall be inserted the designation of their office, and their name, in the Persian language, as follows. " The seal of the Cauzee of the City (Town, Purgunnah or Purgunnahs) of (Name of the Cauzee.)—*Cl.* 1, *Sec.* III, *Reg.* III, 1808.

The rule contained in the preceding Clause is not to be construed to preclude the Governor in Council from abolishing the office of Cauzee, at any place where, from the number of Cauzees stationed in the district, or other cause, the continuance of such an officer may appear to him unnecessary.—*Cl.* 2.—*Ibid.*

The office of Cauzee is declared not to be hereditary.—*Sec.* V. —*Ibid.*

The Zillah *Civil, and Subordinate* Courts, are to report to the Sudder Court, every instance in which it may appear to them, that the Cauzee of any Purgunnah, City, or Town, within their respective jurisdictions, is incapable, or in which it may be proved to their satisfaction that he has been guilty of negligence, or misconduct, in the discharge of his public duty, or of acts of profligacy in his private conduct.—*Sec.* VI.—*Ibid.*

It shall likewise be the duty of the head Cauzee to report to the Sudder Court, in writing, every instance in which it may appear to him, that the Cauzee of any City, Town, or Purgunnah, is incapable, or in which any such Cauzee may have been guilty of misconduct in the discharge of his public duty, or acts of profligacy in his private conduct.—*Sec.* VII.—*Ibid.*

The head Cauzee, and the Cauzees stationed in the Cities, Purgunnahs, and Towns, are to keep copies of all deeds, and law, or other papers, which they may draw up, or attest, and are to affix thereto their seals and signatures. They are likewise to keep a list of all such papers ; and in the event of their death, resignation, or removal, the list and papers are to be delivered complete to their successors.—*Sec.* VIII.—*Ibid.*

The Judges are to furnish the Cauzees stationed in their respective jurisdictions, with copies of the Persian translates of all Regulations, printed and published in the manner directed in Regulation I, A. D. 1802.—*Sec.* IX.—*Ibid.*

The Cauzees stationed in the several Zillahs are to be liable to be sued in the Court of Udalut, for any undue practices in the discharge of the duties which shall be prescribed to them by any Regulation, printed and published in the manner directed in Regulation I, 1802.—*Sec.* X.—*Ibid.*

CHAPTER X.

NATIVE MINISTERIAL OFFICERS.

The appointment and removal of the ministerial officers of the Courts of Judicature, shall be subject to such rules and orders as the Governor in Council in his discretion may from time to time see fit to issue.—*Cl.* 1, *Sec.* III, *Reg.* VII, 1822.

The seristadars, or other head native officers, moonshees, mohurrers, and nazirs, of the Civil and Criminal Courts, previous to entering upon the execution of the duties of their offices, shall *make* and subscribe the following *solemn affirmation*, in open Court, before the Judge, or Judges, of the Court to which they may be attached.—*Sec.* IV, *Reg.* XII, 1802.

The Subordinate officers and vakeels who shall be appointed to the Zillah Courts established under this Act, shall be subject to the same rules as are applicable to the Subordinate officers and vakeels of the Provincial Courts of appeal.—*Sec.* L, *Act* VII, 1843.

The *Judges of the several Courts*, are to procure all acts of the Courts to be executed. The native officers attached to the Courts, are to assist, in performing the abovementioned duties, and in translating and transcribing papers, and in arranging and keeping the records of the Courts. The native officers, are to perform the duties specified in this Section, in the manner, and conformably to the rules, which the Judges of the Courts to which they may be respectively attached may think it proper to prescribe. The native officers of each Court are not to interfere in any other manner than as above directed, publicly or privately, in any cause or matter depending before the Court; or which may have been, or shall be intended to be, brought before it.—*Sec.* XI, *Reg.* XII, 1802.

Cl. 1, Sec. III, Reg. VII, 1822.—The nature and particulars of the misconduct of any native officer who may have been dismissed or suspended should be briefly stated in the appropriate column of the quarterly report on that subject.—Cir. Lr. S. and F. U. 9th February, 1844.

Sec. IV, Reg. XII, 1802.—Form omitted—and the practice greatly disused.

Sec. XI, Reg. XII, 1802.—The principal native officers may also be employed in taking depositions of witnesses under Section XXII, Regulation VII, 1809, and Section VIII, Regulation XII, 1809, which see at page 177.

Heads of offices may grant leave of absence to the ministerial officers of their establishment without reference to higher authority.—Cir. Lr. S. U. 15th December, 1846.

The ministerial officers of the Civil and Criminal Courts (under which designation are comprehended, all native officers attached to the Courts,) are declared amenable to the Courts to which they may be respectively attached, for acts of corruption or extortion; and the Courts are empowered to receive any such charges that may be preferred against them. Previous however to receiving the charge, the Courts are to require the complainant to make oath *or solemn affirmation* to the truth of it, and give security in what-ever sum they may judge proper, to prosecute the charge without delay. Unless the complainant shall previously take the oath, or subscribe the abovementioned *affirmation*, and give the required security, the Courts are not to receive the charge.—*Cl.* 1, *Sec.* XII, *Reg.* XII, 1802.

The Sudder Udalut, and the Foujdaree Udalut, are empowered to receive any charge of corruption or extortion, not relating to any suit or matter depending before them, or decided by them, that may be preferred to them against any ministerial officer of a Zillah Civil or Session Court; and to refer it to the Court to which the accused may be attached, by a precept under the seal of the Court, and attested by the register: provided the complainant shall prove, to their satisfaction, that he preferred the charge, in the first instance, to such Court; and offered to make the required oath or *affirmation*, and to give the security prescribed in Clause first; and that the Court notwithstanding, omitted or refused to receive the charge; and shall moreover make the required oath or *affirmation*, and enter into the security prescribed in the above-mentioned Clause. But if any person shall prefer a charge of corruption or extortion, against any ministerial officer of a *Zillah Civil or Session* Court, to the Sudder Udalut, or Foujdaree Uda-lut, in any appeal or matter which may be depending, or has been decided in the two last mentioned Courts, the Courts may receive the charge, and refer it to the *Zillah Civil or Session* Court, to which the accused may be attached, without further enquiry: provided the complainant shall previously make the oath or *affirmation*, and give the security required in Clause first.—*Cl.* 2.—*Ibid.*

The Sudder Udalut is empowered to receive charges of corrup-

---

tion or extortion, not relating to any matter depending before them, or decided by them, that may be preferred to them against any ministerial officer of a *Subordinate* Zillah Court; and to order the Court to which the accused may be attached, by a precept under their seal, and attested by their register, to receive the charge: provided the complainant shall prove to their satisfaction, that he preferred the charge in the first instance to such Court; and offered to make the required oath or *affirmation*, and give the security prescribed in Clause first; and that the Court notwithstanding, omitted, or refused to receive the charge: and provided also, that the complainant shall further prove, to the satisfaction of the Court, that in consequence of such refusal, he preferred the charge to the *Civil* Court of the *Zillah*, and offered to make the required oath or *affirmation*, and give the security prescribed in Clause first; and that the *Civil* Court nevertheless omitted, or refused to receive the charge; and shall moreover make the required oath or *affirmation*, and enter into the security prescribed in the abovementioned Clause. The Sudder Udalut is likewise empowered to receive charges of corruption, or extortion, which may be preferred against a ministerial officer of a *Subordinate* Zillah Court, that may have been preferred in the first instance to the *Civil* Court, in any appeal or matter depending before it, or which may have been decided by it, and to refer it to such *Civil* Court, or to the *Subordinate* Court to which the accused may be attached: provided the complainant shall prove, to the satisfaction of the Court, that he preferred the charge to the *Civil* Court, and offered to make the required oath, or *affirmation* and give the security prescribed in Clause first; and shall moreover make the required oath or *affirmation*, and enter into the security prescribed in the abovementioned Clause. But if any person shall charge a ministerial officer of any *Subordinate* Zillah Court, before the Sudder Udalut, with corruption, or extortion, in any suit or matter, that may be depending before it, or which may have been decided by it, the Court may receive the charge, and refer it for trial to the Court to which the offender may be attached, without further enquiry: provided the complainant shall previously make the prescribed oath or *affirmation* to the truth of the charge, and give the security required in Clause first.—*Cl. 3, Sec.* XII, *Reg.* XII, 1802.

The *Zillah Civil* Courts are empowered to receive any charge of corruption, not relating to any suit, or matter depending before them, or decided by them, that may be preferred to them against any of the ministerial officers of the *Subordinate* Zillah Courts, within their respective jurisdictions; and to refer the charge to the Court to which the accused may be attached: provided it be proved, to their satisfaction, that the accuser preferred the charge, in the first instance, to such *Subordinate* Court; and offered to make the oath or *affirmation*, and give the security required in Clause first; and that the Court, notwithstanding, omitted or refused to receive the charge. But if any person shall charge a ministerial officer of any *Subordinate* Zillah Court, with corruption, or extortion in any appeal, or matter which may be depending, or has been decided in the *Civil* Court, such Court may receive the charge, and refer it to the *Subordinate* Zillah Court to which the accused may be attached, without further enquiry: provided the complainant shall previously make the prescribed oath or *affirmation*, and give the security required in Clause first.—*Cl.* 4, *Sec.* XII, *Reg.* XII, 1802.

If the Foujdaree Udalut shall receive a charge of corruption, or extortion, against any ministerial officer of a *Session* Court, or, if the Sudder Udalut shall receive any such charge against a ministerial officer of a *Zillah Civil* Court, or a *Subordinate* Zillah Court; and there shall appear to those superior Courts respectively, upon a consideration of the circumstances of the case, any objections to referring the charge to the Court, to which the accused may be attached; they are empowered, according as they may judge expedient, either to cause the charge to be tried by the Sudder Udalut; or, if the charge be against any ministerial officer of a *Subordinate* Zillah Court, to cause it to be tried by the *Civil* Court of the Zillah in which such Court may be situated.—*Cl.* 5. —*Ibid.*

If a *Zillah Civil* Court shall receive a charge of corruption, or extortion, against any ministerial officer of a *Subordinate* Court, and there shall appear to the Court, upon a consideration of the circumstances of the case, any objections to referring the charge to the Court to which the accused may be attached; they are to report the grounds of their objections to the Sudder Udalut, which Court are empowered to cause the charge to be tried by such Zillah *Civil or Subordinate* Court, according as they may deem expedient.—*Cl.* 6.—*Ibid.*

Charges of corruption, or extortion, that may be preferred against the ministerial officers of any Civil or Criminal Court of Judicature, under this Section, are to be considered as civil actions; and, accordingly, are to be prosecuted in the Civil Courts. Conformably to this rule, whenever the Sudder Udalut, or the Foujdaree Udalut, may receive any such charge against their own officers, or exercise the powers vested in them by Clause fifth, they are to direct the complainant to prosecute the charge in the Sudder Udalut; and whenever the *Zillah Civil or Session* Courts, may

receive any such charge against any of their own ministerial officers, or the ministerial officers of any *Subordinate* Zillah Court;
or in the event of any such charge being referred to them, they
are to direct the complainant to prosecute the charge before the
Zillah Civil Court; and whenever any *Subordinate* Zillah Court
may receive any such charge, against their ministerial officers, or
any such charge may be referred to them by the Sudder Udalut,
or the *Zillah Civil* Court, they are to direct the complainant to
prosecute the charge in the *Subordinate* Court of the Zillah.—*Cl.*
7, *Sec.* XII, *Reg.* XII, 1802.

If a native ministerial officer of any Civil or Criminal Court,
who may be prosecuted for corruption or extortion under this Section, shall be proved to have received, or taken, the whole, or any
part of the money, or property, which he may be charged with
having received or taken; the Court is to adjudge him to refund
the amount or value of the money or property, which he may be
proved to have so received, or taken; and to pay a fine of three
times the amount of it to Government. In enforcing the decision,
the Court is to observe the rules prescribed for enforcing other
decisions of the Court. The Court may suspend a native officer,
against whom a charge of corruption, or extortion, may be preferred, until the final decision may be passed, if they shall see
cause for so doing.—*Cl.* 8.—*Ibid.*

If any person shall prefer a charge of corruption or extortion,
against a ministerial officer, of any Civil or Criminal Court of Judicature, under this Section, and the charge shall not be proved;
the accused is to have the option of suing the accuser for damages,
in any Court of Civil Judicature, to which he may be amenable.
—*Cl.* 12.—*Ibid.*

If a native servant, or dependent, of any Judge of a Civil or
Criminal Court of Judicature, not being a public officer attached
to the Court, shall extort, or receive directly or indirectly, any
money, or other valuable consideration, under any pretence whatever, from any party or person, on account of any suit, to be instituted, or that may be depending, or has been decided, in the
Court, he shall be committed as for a contempt of Court, and be
punished, by a fine equal to treble the sum of money extorted or
received, or by imprisonment, or corporal punishment, at the discretion of the Court; and the Judge is required to discharge such
servant or dependent, and never to employ him, directly or indirectly, in his public, or private capacity. If the offender shall not
appeal against the decree within the limited time, or if an appeal
shall not lie from the decision, or if the decision shall be confirm-

ed in appeal, the Court by which the final decree may be passed shall transmit a copy of it to the Governor in Council; and the offender, in addition to the penalties or punishments specified in the decree, shall be further liable to be declared by the Governor in Council incapable of serving Government in any capacity whatever.—*Sec.* XIV, *Reg.* XII, 1802.

CHAPTER XI.

MISCELLANEOUS REGULATIONS AND ACTS.

I.

COURT OF WARDS.

Regulation V, 1804.

Regulation V of 1804, constitutes the Board of Revenue a Court of Wards, and " declares the powers vested in the said Court, de- " fining the rules under which those powers are to be exercised."

II.

TENURE OF LANDS BY EUROPEANS.

Regulation XIX, 1802. *Act IV*, 1837, *&c.*

No European, of whatever nation or description shall purchase, rent, or occupy, directly or indirectly, any land out of the limits of the town of Madras, and the Supreme Court of Judicature, without the sanction of the Governor in Council; and all persons now so holding land, beyond the said limits, without having obtained such permission, in opposition to the repeated prohibitions of Govern-ment, or who may hereafter so purchase, rent, or occupy land,

---

Chap. XI.—The subjects which will be found treated of in this Chapter, and under this head, are such as could not be left unnoticed in this work, but which present themselves so rarely in the ordinary business of the Courts, that to insert the Acts, &c., relating to them at length would have unnecessarily swelled the size of the volume. I have con-sidered it sufficient therefore merely to give the titles, and in some cases portions of the enactments, with such explanatory notes as seemed necessary.

Reg. V, 1804.—Court of Wards.—This Court moves in the matters within its sphere, upon the *reports* of the Collectors ; who by Section VI, are liable to prosecution for mak-ing such negligently, or for malicious purposes. If parties reported by Collector to be in-capacitated as being females, minors, lunatics, or idiots, desire to dispute the grounds of the report, Section VII, provides for the ultimate decision of the question by the Sudder Udalut, after examination and enquiries, held at their direction, by the inferior Courts.

Section XX, refers to certain cases in which the Zillah Judge is to be called on to no-minate a Guardian for an incapacitated heir.

Section XXIII, provides that Guardians be included in all actions against Wards, and allows Wards to impeach Collector, Guardians or Manager before the Court of Wards. In case of fraud on the part of the Guardian, the Court of Wards is authorized by Sec-tion XXIV, to try the case, and pass judgment thereon ; subject to a regular appeal to the Sudder Udalut. The provisions of Regulation V, 1804, are in certain cases extended and modified by Regulation X of 1831.

shall be liable to be dispossessed of the land at the discretion of the Governor in Council; nor shall they be entitled to any indemnification for buildings which they may have erected, or other account.—*Sec.* III, *Reg.* XIX, 1802.

Europeans who are not prohibited from lending money to proprietors, or farmers of land, dependant Talookdars, under farmers or ryots, and who may make loans to them on the security or mortgage of their lands or leases, shall not be allowed, directly or indirectly, to hold possession of lands, the proprietory right in which, or lease whereof, may be mortgaged to them as security for the loan; or to make or appropriate the collections; or to have any concern or interference whatever, in the management or collection of the rents or revenue of the lands.—*Sec.* IV.—*Ibid.*

It shall not be competent for Europeans to purchase lands on their own account at public sale; and lands actually purchased for Europeans, shall be absolutely forfeited unless such lands may have been purchased by the consent of the Governor in Council had and obtained in writing for that purpose previously to the sale.—*Sec.* XIX, *Reg.* XXVI, 1802.

The Board of Revenue shall not farm lands to Europeans, directly or indirectly, without the authority of Government; or accept the security of Europeans for renters, farmers, or land holders.—*Sec.* XLI, *Reg.* I, 1803.

Collectors shall not grant lands in farm to Europeans either directly, or indirectly. Collectors shall not accept the security of Europeans for proprietors or renters of land, or for farmers of the public revenue.—*Sec.* LXII, *Reg.* II, 1803.

Secs. III, IV, Reg. XIX, 1802.—These Sections, as well as Section XIX, Regulation XXVI, 1802, which follows, prohibit *all* Europeans from acquiring interest in land without permission of Governor in Council. This prohibition was rescinded as to " *natural born subjects*" of the British Crown by 3 and 4, Wm. IV, Cap. 85, Section 86, *which see below,* and which also gave permission to the Government of India to extend the same indulgence to *any* subjects. Under which permission Act IV, 1837, was passed, making it lawful for *any* subject of Her Majesty to hold land in perpetuity or for a term of years ; so that all Europeans, save *Her Majesty's subjects,* are still under the prohibition—a French or Austrian subject, though a European, cannot hold land within the British territories in India, unless with the sanction of Government. Nothing is said of Americans, but I presume all would be excluded, save such as are subjects of Her Majesty, who would be embraced by Act IV of 1837, though not Europeans.

Sec. XLI, Reg. I, 1803, and Sec. LXII, Reg. II, 1803.—These prohibitions originally extended to " descendants of Europeans"—but the inability was removed as regards them by Sections VI and VII, Regulation IV of 1832.

The prohibition as to the farming of lands to Europeans, must be taken as qualified by subsequent enactments, as explained in note on Sections III and IV, Regulation III, 1802.

It shall be lawful for any natural-born subject of *Her* Majesty authorized to reside in the territories *of the East India Company*, to acquire and hold lands, or any right, interest or profit, in or out of lands, for any term of years, in such part or parts of the said territories, as he shall be so authorized to reside in : provided always that nothing herein contained shall be taken to prevent the said Governor General in Council from enabling, by any laws or regulations, or otherwise, any subjects of *her* Majesty to acquire or hold any lands, or rights, interests, or profits in or out of lands, in any part of the said territories, and for any estates or terms whatever.   *3d & 4th Wm.* IV. *Cap.* 85.—*Sec.* LXXXVI.

It shall be lawful for any subject of Her Majesty to acquire and hold, and hold in perpetuity or for any term of years, property in land, or in any emoluments issuing out of land, in any part of the territories of the East India Company.—*Sec.* I, *Act* IV, 1837.

All rules which prescribe the manner in which such property as is aforesaid may now be acquired and held by natives of the said territories, shall extend to all persons who shall, under the authority of this Act, acquire or hold such property.—*Sec.* II.— *Ibid.*

III.

COPYRIGHT.

Act XX. 1847.

An Act for the encouragement of learning in the territories subject to the Government of the East India Company, by defining and providing for the enforcement of the right called copyright therein.

" Section IV *to* VI, *treat of its Duration, Registry, &c."*

In the event of any person without the jurisdiction of the Supreme Courts offending against the Act in any other part of the territories subject to the jurisdiction of the East India Company, he shall be liable to a suit in the Zillah Court within the jurisdiction of which he shall have so offended, which shall and may be prosecuted in the same manner in which any other action of damages may be brought and prosecuted there ; and if he shall have so offended in any such last-mentioned part of the territories subject to the Government of the East India Company, in which there is no Zillah Court, to a suit in the highest local Court exer-

cising original civil jurisdiction in such part of the territories.—
Sec. VII.

After the passing of this Act, in any such suit or action as last
aforesaid, brought in any Zillah Court, or other local Court, as
aforesaid, the defendant shall state in his answer all such matters
as he means to rely on, and which, by the last preceding Section,
the defendant in any suit or action brought in any of the Courts
of Judicature established by Her Majesty's Charter is required to
give notice of in writing : otherwise such defendant shall be subject to the same consequences for any omission in his answer, as
a defendant is made subject to by the last preceding Section for
any omission in his notice.—*Sec.* IX.

IV.

WAGERS.

Act XXI. 1848.

All agreements, whether made in speaking, writing or otherwise, by way of gaining or wagering, shall be null and void : and
no suit shall be allowed in any Court of Law or Equity for recovering any sum of money or valuable thing alleged to be won
on any wager, or entrusted to any person to abide the event of
any game, or on which any wager is made.—*Sec.* I.

V.

APPRENTICES.

Act XIX. 1850.

An Act " Concerning the binding of Apprentices."

Any child, above the age of ten and under the age of eighteen
years, may be bound apprentice by his or her father or guardian,
to learn any fit trade, craft or employment, for such term as is set
forth in the Contract of apprenticeship, not exceeding Seven years,
so that it be not prolonged beyond the time when such child shall
be of the full age of twenty-one years, or in the case of a female,
beyond the time of her marriage.—*Sec.* I.

Sec. IX, Act XX, 1847.—" *Last receding Section,*" Section VIII, to which reference
is here made, prescribes the course to be followed in the Supreme Court, and directs that
defendant give plaintiff notice in writing of the nature of the defence he intends to set
up ; in the Mofussil Court the same particulars are to be mentioned in the answer, which
may not afterwards be amended or added to.

Act XXI, 1848.—Perhaps this might more properly have been inserted at page 155—
but it escaped notice.

Act XIX, 1850.—The Act prescribes the manner of binding, registering, &c., and vests
all Magistrates or Justices of the Peace with certain powers in respect of complaints
made by apprentices against masters, or masters against apprentices.

VI.

IMPROVEMENT IN TOWNS.

Act XXVI. 1850.

An Act to enable improvements to be made in Towns.

If it shall appear to the Governor or Governor in Council, or Lieutenant Governor of any Presidency or Place within the territories under the Government of the East India Company, that the inhabitants of any Town or Suburb, not within the Town of Calcutta, Madras, or Bombay, are desirous of making better provision for making, repairing, cleaning, lighting or watching·any public streets, roads, drains, or tanks, or for the prevention of nuisances, or for improving the said Town or Suburb in any other manner, the said Governor or Governor in Council, or Lieutenant Governor, may order this Act to be put in force within such Town or Suburb. —*Sec*. II.

VII.

CHARGES AGAINST PUBLIC SERVANTS.

Act XXXVII. 1850.

An Act for regulating enquiries into the conduct of public servants not removable without the sanction of Government.

The Act in Sections I to XXIV, *provides for the constitution by Government of a commission, and prescribes rules for the conduct of the enquiry thereby in all its stages.*

Nothing in this Act shall be construed to affect the authority of Government, for suspending or removing any public servant for any cause, without an enquiry under this Act.—*Sec*. XXV.

VIII.

REGISTERED COMPANIES.

Act XLIII. 1850.

An Act for the Regulation of Registered Joint Stock Companies.

Every unincorporated company of partners, associated under a deed containing a provision, that the shares in the stock or busi-

---

Act XXVI, 1850.—Upon the Government being satisfied that the inhabitants desire it, the Act is to be declared in operation, and a commission nominated for putting it in force.

The commission is authorized to levy assessments for the purposes of the Act, to frame municipal regulations, and impose fines for the breach of them.

Act XXXVII, 1850.—" Not removable, &c." this includes Principal Sudder Ameens, and the law officers of the Sudder and Foujdaree Udalut.

Act XLIII, 1850.—The Act says nothing as to proceedings by or against such a company in the Mofussil Courts ; but it is here noticed because it is presumed such company may sue or be sued there in its corporate capacity.

ness of the said company are transferable without the consent of all the partners and also every company established for some literary, scientific, or charitable purpose, which does not carry on any business for the pecuniary benefit of any of the proprietors or shareholders, shall be entitled to registration under this Act. —*Sec.* I.

IX.

DOWER.

Act XXIX. of 1839.

An Act for the Amendment of the Law relating to Dower.

This Act, in fifteen Sections, extends to the Territories of the East India Company, the amendments made in the English Law of Dower by 3rd and 4th William IV, Chap. cv. *Cases requiring its application must necessarily be of such rare occurrence in the Mofussil Courts, that it seems sufficient to refer to it without inserting it at length.*

X.

INHERITANCE.

Act XXX. of 1839.

An Act for the Amendment of the Law of Inheritance.

This Act, in thirteen Sections, extends to the Territories of the East India Company, the amendments made in the English Law of Inheritance by 3rd and 4th William IV, Chap. cvi. *Reference only is made to it for the reasons assigned above under the head of Dower.*

INDEX

TO THE REGULATIONS AND ACTS QUOTED IN THIS VOLUME.

ERRATA.

CPSIA information can be obtained
at www.ICGtesting.com
Printed in the USA
BVHW061447020519
547209BV00009B/253/P